THE

HISTORY

AND

CONFESSIONS OF A MAN,

AS PUT FORTH BY HIMSELF,

Showing how he became a Methodist and a Methodist preacher, and how, as he grew older, he gave up part of the Methodist belief, and was expelled, and giving a true view of Methodism on both sides, the fair as well as the foul, the bright as well as the dark, together with a long and wonderful account of many other matters worthy to be read and thought upon.

WORTLEY:

PRINTED AND SOLD BY J. BARKER, AND BY ALL HIS AGENTS.

CHAPMAN BROTHERS, LONDON.

1846.

THE HISTORY AND CONFESSIONS OF A MAN, AS PUT FORTH BY HIMSELF.

INTRODUCTION.

I promised some time ago to publish the history and confessions of a man,—and I now proceed to do so. I hope my readers will be profited by the work. I am sure that the man himself, whose history I am about to give, had no other object in allowing it to appear, but the welfare of his fellow-men, and the glory of God; and I cannot but think myself, that a candid and careful perusal of the story is adapted to answer those great ends. However, whether the work be calculated to promote our improvement or not, there is no reason why we should not improve. We *have* many means of improvement, whether this history should prove one or not. If this history therefore should *not* prove a means of promoting our improvement in knowledge and goodness, let us make so much the better use of those other means of improvement with which we are so richly favoured. Whatever this history may teach, one thing is certain, that a constant endeavour to grow wiser and better is both our duty and our interest, and the man that neglects to grow wiser and better will be left without excuse.

I wish to observe, that tho' the name of the person whose history we are about to give is withheld, yet the history may be relied upon as perfectly true and genuine. It is no fiction. It is not only *like* truth; but truth itself. It is not something *founded* upon fact; but fact itself. The man who speaks in the history did himself really live in our world, and did, and suffered, and thought, and experienced, all that is here recorded, as truly as you now live and read these lines. I do not say but that there may be some slight *mistakes* in the record; it is perhaps impossible for a person to write the history of a long life without such mistakes. But there are no fictions or fables in it: nothing feigned or forged for the occasion: every thing that is given is transcribed from a good and faithful memory, or from records which were written from time to time by the person himself, as his life was passing along.

But to the story. And whether the plan be objected to or not, the subject of the story will speak in his own person,—the *first* person. When a man writes an account of his own life, he is obliged to do so, or else put himself to a good deal of trouble. And I see no reason why a man should put himself about for any such purpose. It is true that when a lengthy story is given in the first person singular, it requires a great many capital I's; but that is the printer's concern, and if *he* does not complain, there is no necessity for any one else to do so. As for the charge of *Egotism*, I reckon little of that. Things are not always faulty because they happen to be egotistical. In other words; a person may speak in the first person, he may say, *I* did this, and *I* thought that, and *I* did the other, without being egotistical at all in the offensive sense of the word. *Egotism* is the Latin word for *I-ism*; and what I mean is, that *I-ism* is not always wrong; it is sometimes better than *He-ism*. It is when a man boasts, or sets himself forward as more than he is, that his *I-ism* becomes offensive. However, if the use of the first person be a fault, it is no great one. And I have this for my excuse; the manuscript from which I print, was supplied to me in that form, and I saw no reason for altering it.

REASONS FOR WRITING THE HISTORY.

My reasons for writing the history of my life are various.

1. I want to remember it myself. There are many things in the history of my life that, when I think of them, make me feel thankful to God, and strengthen my faith in God's providence, and make me feel comfortable and safe. There are many things which, when I remember them, make me see more clearly the evil of sin and the worth of religion, and so strengthen and encourage me to shun the evil and pursue the good. And I find that I cannot well remember a many weighty things in my history, unless I make haste and write them down.

2. I also want my children to know my history. There are many things in my history which I think will do them good,—which will tend to make them studious, fond of knowledge, industrious, chaste, sober, religious, lovers of God and lovers of men.

3. Besides, my children wish to know my history, and this is an additional reason for writing it.

4. And many of my friends wish to know my history, and have often requested and pressed me to publish it; and I being wishful to please my friends, and believing that the history of my life will be of use to them, comply with their requests.

5. Again; if *I* do not write and publish the history of my life, somebody else will. Whether I be a good man or a bad man, a wise man or a fool, a Christian or an infidel, people have made so much to do about me,—I have so many friends and so many foes,—and my friends are so kind, and my foes are so fierce and cruel,—and I have been mixed up with so many stirring affairs, that there is sure to be a life of me. If I do not give a true account of my life, some one else will give a false one. If I, who am acqainted with my history, do not write it, some one will write it that is not acquainted with it. And this is another reason for writing it.

6. Besides, if some one else should after all choose to write my history, it will be as well for him to have my own account to help him. Whether I write it as I ought or not, I shall at least supply others with some materials for their account of me.

7. But again; I wish to give to the world a true and full account of the character and workings of Methodism. Methodism is a very important thing: it has proved a great blessing and a great curse; it is proving a blessing still in some of its workings, and in others it is doing fearful mischief. It is one of the most interesting and terrible things of our day. It is one of the most wonderful mixtures of good and evil, of light and darkness, of freedom and slavery, of clericism and laicism, of Jesuitry and Christianity, of Popery and Protestantism, of Calvinism and pelagianism, of superstition and religion, of weakness and power, of fanaticism and piety, of priest-craft and charity, of villany and virtue, that the world has seen for nearly three hundred, if not for fifteen or sixteen hundred years. It is desirable therefore that the world should become acquainted with it. It is desirable that people should know what to hope or to fear from it. It is only by knowing what it is, that they can tell how to labour for its reformation,—that

they can be prepared for opposing its errors, and upholding its truths,—for checking its evil workings, and helping its good ones. A knowledge of what Methodism is, of what Methodism is doing, and of what Methodism is likely to do, cannot fail to do great good in the world. Throw light on the system, and its power to do mischief is lessened at once. Throw light on the system, and it must either be reformed or destroyed. In the dark the evil is almighty: in the light the good alone is strong. In the dark the errors of Methodism spread rapidly and take fast hold; in the light the truths alone that are mixed up with the system can spread and take hold of the minds of the people. I am wishful to give the needed light. As yet, Methodism has not been fairly set forth before the public. The works that have been published on the subject, are all, so far as I have been able to learn, partial and false. This is true not only of the works published by Methodists themselves, but also of the works published by their opponents. One gives false praise; the other withholds praise really deserved. One hides faults; the other magnifies them. Some have written in ignorance of Methodism, and others have written under the influence of strong passions. I am wishful to present a true and faithful account of the system, without either concealing its blemishes, or over-looking its excellencies. Having been a Methodist nearly twenty years,—having passed through all its stages, from a private member on trial, to a superintendant travelling preacher,—having taken part in all its meetings, from the prayer-meeting and class-meeting, to the district-meetings and conferences,—having experienced all kinds of treatment in the body, from favour and promotion, to censure and expulsion,—having heard all kinds of Methodist preachers, both local and travelling, both learned and unlearned, and having conversed with them in private, and corresponded with them by letters,—having passed through all a preacher's stages myself, and having had the freest intercourse with all classes of members both in their religious and their social meetings, and having had, during the whole of this long period, an inquiring and observant mind, I am certainly likely to have the necessary information for my task. A doubt may rest on the minds of some, as to whether the way in which I have been treated by the Methodists may not lead me to do the system injustice; but I trust that a perusal of my remarks will remove this doubt. My desire, then, to give to the world a true and full account of the character and workings of Methodism, is my seventh reason for writing and publishing my life.

8. And lastly; there has been that in my history which I think may be useful to all. I have had a rather large and varied experience. I have been very ill, and very well; very weakly, and very strong; I have been very poor, and then again well enough off; much despised, and much respected; much praised, and much abused; much feared and hated, much beloved and trusted; I have had great trials, and great comforts; great sorrows, and great joys; great conflicts, great fears, great hardships, great anxieties, great temptations, and yet great helps and great deliverances. I have had to do with many kinds of men, and seen strange revelations of human character. I have also travelled far in the spiritual world. I began my course in the land of darkness and superstition, and have travelled the whole distance between that and the land of heresy or light, where I now am walking. I have also had much to do with the temperance and peace reformations, and have seen much in connexion with both of them of great concernment. I have also had experience in trade, both as a workman and an employer. I have travelled also both at home and abroad, and have had intercourse with people of different countries and of various ranks, especially with the most numerous rank of all, the poor and working part of mankind. And I have read a great deal, and written a great deal, and I have thought and felt, and suffered and enjoyed a great deal. I have tried the power and the worth of religion in almost all conditions, and can speak with some confidence respecting it. Both my character and my views have undergone great changes, and those changes have affected others as well as myself. It is impossible that a man should have lived as long as I have lived, and gone through as much as I have gone through, without learning much that may be useful to his brethren. I am wishful to tell what I have gone through, and to teach what I have learned, and as far as I can give others the benefit of all.

CHAPTER I.

BIRTH, ANCESTRY, PARENTAGE, ETC.

I was born in 1806, at Bramley, an old Country Town in the West Riding of Yorkshire, on a hill about four miles north west of Leeds, and near to the Leeds and Bradford road. My parents forgot my birth-day, but I am inclined to believe it was the eleventh of May. But that is of little moment. I *was* born; and if the eleventh of May, 1806, was not the time, it was *near* the time. My father before me was a native of Bramley, and so were my grandfather and great grandfather I understand : but I don't know much of my fore-elders, except my parents. Some of them were rich, I suppose, and others of them poor; some of them good, and others of them bad; some of them wise and clever, and others of them thoughtless and foolish. Whether there were any among them that were renowned in their times for great services rendered to their fellow-men, I cannot tell. Perhaps there were; or perhaps there were not. There was a person of my name about two hundred years ago, that was a printer, and printer to the king, and I have often seen his name on a black letter Bible printed in those days. I have also seen books printed about the same time, from which I learned that some persons of my name had laboured as authors; but whether they were ancestors of mine or not is quite uncertain. My ancestry is wrapt in darkness : the history of the line from which I sprang is lost,—lost to me at least for the present. Whether it will ever be revealed to me, I cannot tell. Perhaps it will. I should think such things *will* be revealed to us in heaven. It would be a curious thing to be able to trace the history of one's family to its beginning : to learn all its joys and sorrows, its toils and travels, its ups and downs, its virtues and its vices; to see in what strange states of society it had lived, what various forms it had born, what mighty changes it had witnessed in the religions and sciences, in the politics and trades of the world, and how it had acted in those dfferent states, and how it had been influenced by those different changes. It would be a curious thing, I say, to learn all this; and it would be a pleasant thing too. I often feel very curious when I think of this subject; when I wander in thought through the long dark ages that have rolled over one's family, from the time when it first was placed on the earth, to the present hour. I should like to know whether any of my forefathers were prophets or martyrs, reformers or heretics, or whether they were the foes to reform, or not. I should like to know, whether they took the lead in finding out and teaching the great truths of religion; or whether they hung behind, and hindered and kept back the improvement of the world. If any of them *were* reformers, I should like to know their history. I should like to know what errors they detected and opposed; what truths they discovered and spread abroad; what corruptions they sought to reform, and what institutions they sought to establish. I should like to know what enemies they had, and what friends and helpers they met with. I should also like to know what were their hopes and disappointments, and what were their fears and their deliverances. But these are things which we cannot know at present. Well; God's will be done. That darkness which God throws over things, is as good as light. It is better, perhaps, that the history of the past *should* be so generally lost. Perhaps the improvement of the world is promoted by so great a forgetfulness of the past. Perhaps our ignorance of the events of the past, prepares us better for a knowledge of those truths which are eternal. A knowledge of the history of particular men from the beginning of our race to the present times, might unfit us for better knowledge, and indispose us for our proper work. Some one observes, that if the old were not to die, they would prevent the progress of science, and the improvement of our race. The old are generally opposed to change, and their years naturally give them great influence; so that if God were not to take them away, they would hold fast the world in its errors and follies for ever. Even as it is, reform is no very easy work: but if the old were to live for ever, and to increase in numbers and power without bounds, it would be next to impossible, if not impossible altogether. And as it is with *men*, so it is, to some extent, with the *history* of men. If the history of each family and tribe were handed down from the beginning, it would tend to fix the families of the earth in one state; to stereotype the race; to perpetuate errors and follies; to make the childishness of our race eternal. The history of our forefathers could hardly fail to make us tremble at innovation. Either innovation would destroy old history, or old history would prevent innovation. We cannot both multiply new things, and retain our knowledge of all the old. The tendency of old history to perpetuate old errors and vices, and prevent the improvement of our race, is manifest in the influence of the Scriptures. What multitudes are kept from that perfection of virtue for which God has designed them, by their reverence for the sentiments and customs of the fathers and founders of the Jewish nation. There are multitudes that have no idea that there are any better rules of life, or any more certain principles of religious knowledge, than those contained in the Old Testament. The ten commandments are still, by multitudes, supposed to be the most perfect law in existence. Even Christianity itself is made void to the majority of men, by their reverence for the more ancient but less perfect system of Moses. Reverence for ancient men, produces reverence for their imperfections. Americans justify slavery, and Englishmen justify war, and Turks justify the practice of having more than one wife, and Jews justify circumcision, by their reverence for Moses and Abraham. This reverence for ancient men and ancient things has had similar bad effects in connexion with Christianity. Some of the earliest Christians used water baptism, anointed the sick with oil, laid hands on people when they appointed them to certain tasks, exchanged the friendly kiss on meeting, broke bread, and washed each others feet, and hence, as if all these things were the highest and most important forms of heavenly excellence, they are practised and contended for by many as essential to Christianity, and as necessary to salvation. Some have stood out against the doctrine that the sun stands still and that the earth rolls round it, while others oppose the plain teachings of geology and zoology, and others again believe in witchcraft, astrology, necromancy, and demoniacal possessions on the same principle. They find that certain notions were held in ancient times,—they find that those notions were held by the good of ancient times, and their reverence for antiquity, makes them cherish its errors. And if people are so influenced by the histories of people to whom they can claim no peculiar relationship,—if Gentiles are so influenced by the history of ancient Jews, how would they have been influenced by the history of their own particular ancestors? See how the Jews are influenced by their reverence for their ancestors. See how the nations of the East are influenced by their reverence for their early fathers. The Jews were so wedded to antiquity, that they could see no beauty even in Christianity itself. Their reverence for the institutions of Moses was like a veil, which prevented them from seeing the truth and excellence of Christianity. And this veil remains upon the hearts of many of them to this hour.

And if the Scriptures have this unhappy influence to some extent, what would be the influence of particular histories of all the various families of the earth? It would ruin the world. It would frustrate all God's purposes respecting us. It would split the world into sects without end, and make each sect an image, a resemblance of ancient ignorance and ancient vice. The Scriptures give us the history of the *best* of men; they give us the history of the best of institutions. The principal persons presented to our view in Scripture were reformers; discoverers of great truths; detectors of old errors; opponents of corruption; teachers of righteousness; examples of temperance, of justice, and of charity; lovers of truth, lovers of God, lovers of goodness, lovers of men. This was especially the case with Abraham and Moses, with Job and the prophets. It was still more the case with John, and Jesus, and Paul. There is, in consequence, an influence exerted by Scripture history, of a most healthy and heavenly kind. We never hesitate to place the Bible by itself, as worthy of a place above all ancient books in existence. Still, its better influence is checked or enfeebled by those other influences of which we have spoken. Nay more: those other influences of which we have spoken are so powerful in many cases, as to prevent people from feeling those higher and more heavenly influences which the faithfulness of Abraham, the perseverance of Moses, the patience, the purity, the charity of Job, and the still more perfect life and teachings of Jesus and Paul, were designed to exert on mankind. It is well, therefore, that we have no more of antiquity than we have. It is well that we have what we have; but it is better perhaps that we have no more. It is well that the fathers are dead; and it is well that their history is forgotten. It is well that the history of the *greatest*, the *wisest* and the *best* of them has remained; but it is well that the history of the rest has perished. Though the remnants of antiquity which we have, have a tendency to hold the human race back in some things; they have a tendency to help us forward in others. This is true both of our Jewish and Christian antiquities, especially of the Christian. Even the tendency of Pagan antiquities is not wholly bad. The remnants of Grecian and Roman antiquities have their uses; though their evil influences are both great and numerous. But all things have been ordered well. If we had been God, we should doubtless have ordered things as he has done. If we were as wise and good as God is; if we could see the way in which he has done things, and know the reasons of all he has done, we should be filled with thankfulness and wonder, and should cry out with all our souls, He hath done all things well. And as all things have been well and wisely done in the past, so will all things be well and wisely done in ages to come. All is well. The Lord reigneth, and men should rejoice and be glad.

Well then; I leave my forefathers. If they did well, they are blest; if they did ill, their sins have found them out. If they did *well*, *I* will do well too. If they did ill, I will try to make amends for it, by doing the best I can. If they were reformers, *I* will be a reformer; if they were persecutors of reformers, I will try to make up for their folly and sin, by being as liberal as possible. If any of my forefathers did good, I will try to make it more; if any of them did ill, I will try to make it less. If the family has lived six thousand years to no purpose, it is time it began to mend; and let us hope it will mend: and if it *has* lived to some purpose, let us hope it will never grow worse. If the history of our family which God has written in heaven be a *black* book up to the present, let us see to it that the following part of the book be fair and bright. Let it be written there, whether it be written and acknowledged on earth or not, that in the eighteenth or nineteenth century the family took a happy turn,—that several of them became eager for the discovery and the spread of truth, for the detection and overthrow of error, for the promotion of temperance and peace, for the practice of justice and charity,—that some of them got rich, and instead of hoarding or wasting their money like most people, spent it in cheapening books, and building schools, and helping the poor, the fatherless, and the widow,—that some of them were poor, but still honest and truthful, and examples of purity and temperance, of peace and gentleness and love,—that some of them were tradesmen, but refused to live by businesses that were hurtful to their fellow-men, and gave up the offer of wealth, for the good of their race, and in obedience to the will of God. In short, let it be written, that from the eighteenth or nineteenth century, the family formed a league, both of male and female, both of rich and poor, both of weak and strong, both of old and young, for the instruction and improvement of their race, and that they joined and used all their talents, whether money or learning, whether powers of speech, or might of mind, whether pen or press, for the spread of truth, for the overthrow of error, a league for teaching, and freeing, and mending, and blessing the whole of their fellow-men.

This we can do. As for the past, if we could get to know what it was, we could make no better of it. It *is* past, and Almightiness itself cannot call it back. The coming *is* in our power. We can make it as bright as we please. If we cannot have the pleasure of learning what our fathers have done, let us please ourselves with the thoughts of good deeds to be done by ourselves and our children. If we must not read the history of the past, let us get something ready for a new history. Let us do things which will never need to die. Let us do something that neither God nor men will willingly let die: something that both God and men shall take delight in keeping alive for ever. Let us go as far forward in truth as we can. If we go beyond our age, all the better. Even if men kill us for it, it will still be well. All great reformers went beyond their age; some a hundred years, some two hundred, some only twenty or fifty. Jesus went nearly two thousand years before his age. Luther went two hundred and fifty; but he turned back again. John Wesley went forty in some things. William Dell, George Fox, and William Penn went two hundred before their age in many things. These all served their fellow-men,—these all pleased God and helped forward the cause of truth and righteousness in the world, in proportion as they gave themselves with single-mindedness to truth and duty, and passed beyond the many of their age. And though by outrunning their brethren they caused great alarm, and even brought upon themselves many hard thoughts, many hard speeches, and much unjust and cruel usage,—though the wisest and best of them got stoned or crucified as well as slandered, yet now they have a name above every name, a fame above all fame, and a greatness and blessedness almost like to the greatness and blessedness of God himself. I say then, let us take courage. Let us be just to the truth, and welcome it whenever we meet with it, however unlike to the thoughts of our fathers it may appear. And let us be bold enough to make known the truth among our neighbours, though men should say all sorts of evil of us for so doing. And let us be brave enough to do right, though by doing it we should leave ourselves without a friend in the world. All will be right in the end. All *is* right, so far as we are concerned, when *we are* right; and all will be *seen* and *felt* and *acknowledged* to be right in the end. Good bye, then, to the past. We give it up. We leave it to God. The passing and the coming are for us, and to them we will give our care. We will look to that which *is*, and to that which is to *come*, and try to have *them* right; and will trust all else to God.

I was saying that I knew but little of my fore-elders, except my own parents. Of their history I know a good deal. My father was the son of a Clothier in Bramley, and was one of a large family. My grandfather and grandmother were married very young: my grandfather was not sixteen, I believe, and my grandmother was younger still. I have heard my father say, that when they had two children, the ages of both father and mother and children did not amount, when all put together, to more than thirty-two. My grandmother died when she was rather young, and left her husband, I am told, with twelve or fourteen children. My grandfather did not make the best of his lot. He began to drink more freely, and became a drunkard, and neglected his business and his children. From what I have heard, he must have drunk a great deal, and quite disabled himself to look after his trade and his household. His children had therefore to look out for themselves and for each other, or to be taken under the charge of the Town-overseers. Some of the girls got places as servants, and some of the lads got places as apprentices, and the rest did I know not how. One of the daughters was married to a Church-of-England minister at Abberford, in Yorkshire; but though she got plenty of what money can buy, she had not the most happy of husbands. The priest was a drunkard and a cock-fighter, unless he be belied, and you may judge whether a man of that sort could be a good and comfortable husband. My father went apprentice to a clothier, and for ought I know, stopped in his place till he was twenty-one. But I cannot be certain. But I know this, that either soon after he was loose or else a while before, he hired into the militia, and was drilled, and marched up and down the country for a number of years, till he had a wife and one or two children. I have heard him tell many sad tales about this part of his life, which might be of some use if they were written down and printed. From what he said, the militia must have been used more harshly and cruelly than the regulars. Some were flogged to death, or died soon after flogging; and some were flogged and drummed out of the regiment, and then left in the hands of a press-gang to be carried on board a man-of-war. The officers seem to have crossed and tormented the men on purpose to make them enlist into the regulars, and many of the men did so. Among the rest two brothers of my father went into the regulars, and were engaged in the wars both in Europe and Asia for a number of years. They both lived to come home again, and one is living still, though neither of them was ever good for much after, either in body or soul, poor things. My father stuck to the militia, and though he had nothing of an easy or a pleasant life of it, yet in two respects it was overruled for good. In the first place my father got a good and clever wife, and in the second place, he got brought under the power of religion. In the first place he got a good and clever wife. She was poor, like himself, and had been born and brought up in the midst of hardships and sorrow; but she was a lively and spirited woman, and very strong and lasting in her love. And she could read and write, and sing and spin, and live on homely fare, and make old clothes look almost as well as new, and make a house with but little furniture and little fire, look nearly as comfortable as richer dwellings. She was clean both in her soul and body, and she was cleanly in her ways and manners. She was very fond of her husband, though a little inclined to be masterful; and she was unutterably fond of her children. Her soul was full of love, and it flowed forth most freely towards her family, and towards mankind at large. My father met with her in Devonshire. She was a native of Chumleigh in that County. When she was married she was about eighteen years of age, and my father was about twenty-two or three. While my father remained a soldier, my mother lived chiefly at home with her mother and sister. She had no father; or if she had, he was on the sea, engaged in the cruel wars. My father went at times to see her, walking as much as fifty miles a day sometimes for that purpose. At length she brought forth her first-born, a son, and some time after joined my father in the camp. How long she stayed with him I cannot tell, but at length she removed into Yorkshire, and lived with my grandfather and two of my father's sisters at Bramley. My grandfather had by this become a steadier man, and was mending his shattered business. While my mother was at Bramley, my father got among the Methodists in Kent, and began to be religious. This was the beginning of a new life to my father, and he rejoiced in the change very much. Religion brought him into fresh company, gave him new friends, led him into new ways of life, gave him new thoughts and new feelings, new loves and new pleasures, new hopes and new work. It was, in truth, like a new creation or new birth to him. He now felt more strongly for his wife than ever, as well as for his little infant child. He wanted to write her a letter, but, alas, he could not write. He could not even read. He did not even know a single letter in the *A. B. C.* He knew the *names* of the letters off the book, but he did not know the *forms* of the letters. He could *say* his *A, B, C*, without book, but he did not know which letters were a, b, c, and so forth. He could not tell the name of a single letter when he saw it in the book. But he would try to learn. So he got a Reading Made Easy, and began. He found the Alphabet, and looked at the first letter, and he knew they called it *a*. So he looked what it was like, and tried to make another like it with a piece of chalk or something. He then looked at the second letter, which he knew was called *b*, and learned what that was like; and so he went on to the end. He then went to the small letters, and learned them. It was well my poor father met with a Reading Made Easy with the A, B, C, in right order; for if he had happened to meet with one with letters out of order, like some that I have seen, he would have been quite fast. As it was he went on cleverly. By a little help he learned to put the letters into words, and spell; and in a month or little more, if I remember right, he could both read and write. He now sent word to my mother about all that had taken place. My mother, poor woman, was quite overpowered, and went out into a lonely place to weep. She was resolved to be religious too. And she was resolved to see her husband as well. And either she set off to go to my father, or sent for my father to come and see her, and before long they were living in their own little house together, as happy as love and religion could make them. They were poor; but what of that? They had but few wants; they had both of them been used to hard work and poor fare, so that hardships were no strange thing to them. They had no concern about appearances. A supply of wholesome food, a clean whole gown for my mother, and a whole plain coat for my father, with clogs or shoes to keep them from the ground, and a good flock bed on which to rest their well-tired limbs at night, with loving and religious souls, and a Bible and a Hymn Book, were all the world to them. They hardly thought of more. They sang and prayed; they talked and read together. They went together to the class, the preaching, and the prayer-meeting. My mother hugged her child, and my father walked alone, and both sent forth their souls in prayer to God for his blessing, and their prayers were heard and answered. They looked on the preacher as God's trumpet, and every word was welcomed as the word of God. Every feeling of love or joy was regarded as the working of God's holy spirit, and they looked upon themselves as dwellings of the Holy One. And they were right; for so they were. They knew nothing of theology, nothing of controversy. Their simple creed was that there was one God, one Christ, one hope, one religion, one heaven. To love God and all mankind, to shun evil and do good, to go through life with clean hands and pure hearts, rejoicing in hopes of everlasting blessedness, was all they cared about. This was their religion, their theology, their all. The world was as wide in those days as it is in ours; but it was very little that *they* knew of it. And there were worthless professors, no doubt, and hypocritical priests; but these were things my parents never dreamed about. They were truthful themselves, and they fancied no deceit in others. They looked on all who professed religion,—all who professed to have been awakened and converted after the Methodistical fashion, as really saints. They listened to their prayers, and to the statement of their experiences, with the most reverent and humble state of mind, regarding all as the utterings of the holy spirit. Those who could pray well; who were ready with their words, and warm or earnest in their manner, they regarded as specially gifted, specially favoured, specially inspired by God. On those who professed to be wholly sanctified, and who, in agreement with their profession, spoke always in a solemn, religious tone, talking only on religious subjects, my parents looked as on angels of God. The reverence they felt for them was almost unbounded; the awe with which they looked up to them was unutterable. At least, this was the impression made on my mind by the way in which my parents talked of those persons in my hearing, and by the way in which they acted towards them in my sight. There were three persons whom they looked upon as the best, the most holy of all. Their names were William Field, John King, and James Hobson. William Field I never knew. John King and James Hobson I did know. James Hobson was a very old man when I knew him, not less than eighty or ninety years of age. I was too young to know much of his character for myself; but he used very frequently to give out this verse of one of Wesley's Hymns, I suppose;

> 'What! never speak one evil word,
> Or rash, or idle, or unkind!
> Oh how shall I, most gracious Lord,
> This mark of true perfection find?'

And I suppose he used to act on this principle, namely, to speak as seldom as possible about earthly things, and to say what he did say as gravely and solemnly as possible, and always to add a few words about religion to those with whom he had to do. John King I knew a little better. He was a schoolmaster part of his life, and when I was a child I was sent to his school. In his manner of talk and constant solemnity, and in his endeavour to act in agreement with his notions of perfect sanctification, so that all he said and did should be but the work of that direct and special influence of which he believed himself the organ or the instrument, he excelled James Hobson. And my recollections of John King's conduct and character are all, or almost all, of a favourable kind. For instance; I have no recollection of his using severity with his scholars. I do not recollect that he ever flogged either me or the other scholars. Unless I am much mistaken, he trusted much to the power of gentleness and love. Yet he used to keep his school in good order; he kept us tolerably quiet, and got us tolerably well on in our learning. And I fancy he could judge pretty correctly of the character of his scholars. One day my mother had a great deal to do to get me to school. I turned stupid, in fact, and refused to go. My mother, poor woman, when she had done what she could in the way of beating, took and dragged me or drove me to school. When she got me there, she told her sad tale to the master, and complained greatly. 'Betty, Betty,' replied the master, 'Joseph is not to be driven; he is to be led.' Never mortal uttered a truer word than that; and my mother, poor body, felt it to be true. And she acted agreeably. She gave up the driving plan at once with me, and tried the leading plan ever after, and it answered well. I say nothing could be nearer to truth than this remark of John King's, and this I regard as a proof that he had some good sound sense. Many have tried to drive me since then, but they could never make any thing out at it. They might *carry* me perhaps, but not *drive* me. But let them attempt to lead; let them deal gently and kindly with me, and they would melt and overpower me with ease. I never could resist love,—but I could always resist violence or threats. A gentle and loving word has always been mightier with me than force or threats. And so it is still. They might break me by force, but not bend me. They might bend me by words of truth and gentleness, but not by force or terror. So easily have I been moved by gentleness and kindness, so hard has it been for me to stand out against those lovely powers, that I have thought myself deficient at this point, and felt myself obliged to harden myself a little to protect myself from evil.

My parents had many trials, especially my mother, and being a stranger at Bramley, she felt her trials all the more keenly. Still she bore them with a great deal of patience, and at times went through them with a heart full of joy and triumph. From the accounts which I have heard from her at times, I may give you the following. She was sometimes placed among very unreasonable and disagreeable neighbours. Their next door neighbours in one place must have been very dreadful characters. At times they would quarrel almost all the night through, and frequently did my mother hear the husband threatening to cut his wife's throat. My mother's second child was then about three years old, and could hardly be able to do much mischief; but when folk are ill disposed, they are not often fast for an excuse for quarrelling. This woman came in a rage to tell my mother that my poor little brother had done something wrong; and, in addition to other hard words, she threatened to stab my mother. Unable to do any good with talking to the woman, my mother fell down on her knees, and began to pray with all her soul. This confounded the woman, and after standing and staring awhile, she went back about her business, while my mother praised God in an ecstacy of delight.

It was the custom at Bramley, and all the country round, to give nick-names to almost every one, especially to strangers. My parents and their children came in for an extra share of such names. Even this was a trial to my tender hearted mother, especially as she found that it grieved her children. But she always advised us never to give nick-names to others, —never to quarrel with any one,—never to fight though we should be struck first, but always to run home : and when she saw that her children were put upon, she had always, instead of going to scold, recourse to prayer, and always found comfort and relief.

My mother had also much to suffer from poverty at times. Yet she still found consolation in religion. When I was born my poor mother had to work very hard, and though she had children rather rapidly, yet she never had had the luxury of a nurse. She would be working in pain till twelve o'clock at night to get all straight and clean against the important moment : she would become the mother of an additional child before two o'clock, and next day be attempting to do something at her household work. This was th case when I myself was born. And worse than that. Her attempts to wash up within a day of her confinement, had given her such a dreadful cold, that for a fortnight she could neither taste nor smell. Yet all that time she had no kind friend or household servant to attend her. She had no young chicken; no sago, arrow-root, or tapioca; no nicely buttered cake; no richly flavoured drink; but the homeliest and the scantiest fare. Her richest breakfast, poor tender-hearted mother, was bread and water. At the end of the fortnight or soon after, she rose and dressed herself, and prepared her meagre meal. Afraid lest some one should come in and find her with water only for her drink, she coloured it with a little treacle. Just then she passed the looking-glass as it hung on the wall, and saw her pale thin face, and was sadly struck with her wan and melancholy appearance. 'Dear me,' she thought, as she looked first at her reduced and sickly form, and then at her morsel of dry bread and her coloured water, 'this is but poor fare for a person in my state. But then,' thought she again, 'God can make this as nourishing as the richest food in the world.' And her sorrow was turned into joy; her lowness of spirits gave way to hope and gratitude, and she ate her scanty meal with gladness and thanksgiving.

I have said how happy my two parents were in the early part of their religious life. But their lot was not all happiness; nor had they always so much enjoyment as they had at first. All who have great raptures, have also deep depressions. All who rise high in ecstacies, sink low in grief and despondency. It was so with my parents. My mother was a woman of tender feelings and strong affections, full of life and spirits. Her spiritual enjoyments were therefore of the highest and richest kind. And they lasted too a good long length of time. But they could not last for ever. At times she was very low and comfortless, and as she advanced in life, her seasons of delightful ecstacy were fewer and farther between. This was a serious matter for my poor mother. She had been taught to regard those pleasant excitements as the evidence of her acceptance with God,—as the direct witness of the spirit that she was an adopted child of God and an heir of heaven,—as a proof both that she loved God, and that God loved her. She had been taught that when she lost those pleasant feelings or ecstacies, the spirit was withdrawing itself,—that God was hiding his face from her,—that the devil was gaining some advantage over her,—that her state was dangerous,—that she must have grieved God by some unknown sin,—that she must have done something that she should not have done, or left undone something that she should have done,—that she had harboured some wrong thought, or given way to some unbelieving doubt or carnal reasoning, which had caused God to leave her to herself for a time, or to hide his face from her. This made her very unhappy. To recover the lost blessing, she would humble herself in prayer, confess her great unworthiness, lament her short-comings, beseech God to show her the hidden evil lurking in her soul, or the unknown sin she had committed that had provoked his wrath. She would wrestle and plead with God with all her soul, and at times shed many tears. If her feelings happened to be pleasantly excited again, she regarded it as a recovery of the lost blessing, as a restoration of her soul to favour, as the voice of God whispering within and saying, 'Daughter, go in peace, thy faith hath made thee whole.' If she could not succeed in obtaining pleasant feelings, her sorrow continued, and her fears grew greater. And thus she suffered. If she had been aware that God loves all who love him,—that he is pleased with all who try to please him,—that he requires nothing of any one but faithfulness to the light he gives,—that *love*, love to the brethren, is the true proof or evidence that we are approved by God and in a state of safety,—that pleasant feelings are not a proof of our acceptance with God, and that low or melancholy feelings are no proof that God has forsaken us, or is angry with us;—had she understood that to seek for truth and do right,—that to labour daily to grow wiser and better was the whole of true religion, the only thing that can secure the favour of God, she might have rejoiced evermore. At least she might have always been at peace, and gone on comfortably with her work, and have frequently enjoyed much pleasing and rapturous excitement as well. But as it was, her sorrows were often greater and more frequent than her joys; she was oftener in the darkness than the light. And even her pleasures themselves were embittered. When her mind was full of delight and joy, she would be suddenly troubled with dread at the thought of losing her blessedness. She felt that her delightful feelings was something that she could not command,—that it came like the wind, she knew not how, and went, like the wind, she knew not whither,—that often when she sought for it, she could not find it, and that it often came when she was neither seeking for it nor looking for it. Still she thought she ought to have it always,—that she was never safe a moment if she was without it,—that she might any moment die and fall into everlasting torments unless she had it. And these foolish notions caused my poor mother a vast amount of misery. And what is true of my mother, was true of my father also. He was just about as liable to his ups and downs as she was, only his feelings were less lively than hers, so that when he was up he did not rise so high as my mother, and when he was down he did not always sink so low. But they both lived this up and down, this shuttle-cock sort of a life for a great many years.

But this was not the only drawback on the happiness of my parents. They both believed in the Methodist doctrine of instantaneous and full sanctification. They believed that it was possible, by a single act of some kind of faith in the blood of Christ, to obtain, in a single moment, in the twinkling of an eye, a full deliverance from all sin, from all that which they call the carnal mind, the sinful nature,—that something in the soul that makes duty at times feel hard, and sin feel tempting,—they believed that it was possible to reach a state in which they should be completely delivered from that source of temptation which is in man's own nature, so that they should have no temptations but from *without*, from the world and the devil,—a state in which pure enjoyment should reign, in which the soul should be free from all doubt, all fear, all darkness, and live in something like perpetual esctacy,—a state in which they should have done with their ups and downs, and live the life of heaven on earth. This was the doctrine which was preached by the travelling preachers, and my parents never appear to have dreamed till long after, that the travelling preachers could preach error. This was the doctrine taught by John Wesley himself. And multitudes professed to have got this second blessing; this full sanctification. There were some who professed entire sanctification, or Christian perfection, in almost every society. There were such at Bramley. They stood up in the love-feasts, and declared that God had made them quite clean,—that there was neither spot nor stain remaining on them,—that they were entirely emptied of sin, and filled with God,—that they could tell the moment and point to the spot where the glorious work had taken place,—that now they were free from all doubt, free from the fear of man, free from all conflict *with themselves*,—that they were sanctified throughout body, soul, and spirit,—that their souls were full of light and joy,—that they had sensible communion with the Father, the Son, and the Holy Spirit. They would also frequently repeat such verses of hymns as the following:

'O Love, thou bottomless abyss!
  My sins are swallow'd up in thee;
Cover'd is my unrighteousness,
  Nor spot of guilt remains on me,
While Jesu's blood, through earth and skies,
Mercy, free, boundless mercy cries!'—*H.* 189, *v.* 3.

'No condemnation now I dread;
  Jesus, and all in him, is mine!
Alive in him, my living Head,
  And clothed in righteousness divine,
Bold I approach the' eternal throne,   [*v.* 5.
And claim the crown, through Christ my own.'—*H.* 201,

Then again they would add;

'In a rapture of joy My life I employ,
The God of my life to proclaim.'

'Not a cloud doth arise, to darken the skies,
Or hide for a momemt my Lord from my eyes.'

Then another would give out:

Lord, I believe a rest remains,
  To all thy people known,
A rest where pure enjoyment reigns,
  And thou art loved alone:

A rest, where all our soul's desire
  Is fix'd on things above;
Where fear, and sin, and grief expire,
  Cast out by perfect love.

O that I now the rest might know,
  Believe and enter in!
Now, Saviour, now the power bestow,
  And let me cease from sin.'—*H.* 403, *v.* 1—3.

Then the meeting would sing it with all their soul and strength. Then another would give out;

> 'Refining fire, go through my heart,
>   Illuminate my soul;
> Scatter thy life through every part,
>   And sanctify the whole.
>
> No longer then my heart shall mourn,
>   While, purified by grace,
> I only for his glory burn,
>   And always see his face.
>
> My steadfast soul, from falling free,
>   Shall then no longer move;
> But Christ be all the world to me,
>   And all my heart be love.'—*H*. 961, *v.* 9—11.

Then the preacher would add:

> 'Faith, mighty faith, the promise sees,
>   And looks to that alone;
> Laughs at impossibilities,
>   And cries, "It shall be done!"'—*H*. 360, *v.* 9.

My parents must therefore seek this second blessing: they must labour to enter this rest: they must be perfect. They believed it to be both their duty and their privilege to be thus sanctified wholly; to be,

> 'Saved to the utmost, saved below,
>   Till they could sin no more.'

They believed it to be their privilege to experience this salvation *now*:

> 'This moment end their legal years,
>   *Sorrows*, and *sins*, and *doubts*, and *fears*.'

They sought for the blessing; they tried to believe for it; but they sought and tried to believe in vain. Then they began to think hardly of themselves, and to imagine that none had such hard and unbelieving hearts as theirs. Then they sought again more diligently than ever. They went to the early meetings; ran after the most powerful preachers; wept and prayed in secret; read the Scriptures with closer application, and sometimes added fasting also; still the great blessing did not come.

W. Bramwell was the favourite preacher with the people generally, and with my parents among the rest. Bramwell professed to live in a state of perfect sanctification continually; and he constantly urged the blessing on others. He was considered to be the most successful preacher in the Connexion, both in awakening sinners, and helping them into liberty, and bringing them forward into full sanctification. He appears to have been a very powerful man, both in preaching and in praying, both in public meetings and private meetings, both in prayer meetings, class meetings, and love feasts. And unless report be much more generous towards him than just, he was a really good man. He is said to have been very liberal to the poor, giving them both food and clothing when they needed it, and even parting with what was almost necessary to himself to relieve them. He is also said to have been very faithful in reproving and warning the rich, denouncing sin without respect of persons. Many believed him to have the power of working miracles, and instances are given in his life by James Sigston, of miracles that were wrought by him. He was also believed to have the power of reading people's hearts, of telling who were hypocrites and who were sincere, who were backsliders, and who were not; and I have heard my parents relate instances in which he singled persons out by means of this supposed gift before the public congregation or the private meeting, and charged them with hypocrisy to their face. To this wonderful preacher the people flocked in hopes of obtaining under his preaching or prayers either the first blessing of justification, or the second blessing of full and instantaneous sanctification. My parents went among the rest, longing and sighing for the second blessing. Some who went, being greatly excited, believed they had got the blessing, and shouted for joy. Others, whose souls were not worked up to the proper pitch, or who were unable to believe that their strong or pleasant feelings were the sought-for blessing, returned sorrowful and sad. Of this class my parents appear to have been. Either they never fairly believed themselves in possession of the blessing, or if they did, they soon believed themselves to have lost it, and fallen back into their former state of simple justification. Many of those who fancied that they had got the blessing on Sunday, believed that they had lost it again on Monday. Some got the blessing one moment, and lost it next; got it while they were praying, and lost it before they got up from their knees. I heard of one person lately in Newcastle-on-Tyne, who lost the blessing as he was walking along, by unguardedly allowing his eye to wander to the other side of the street. And multitudes have lost the blessing as suddenly, and by means as marvellous and unaccountable. My parents, being either unable to get the blessing, or else unable to keep it, went on mourning and struggling as before. Sometimes they prayed and wrestled on their knees; at other times they sang their prayers while at their work; while at other times they mourned their short comings at the class. The hymns they used to sing were such as the ones already quoted on pages 24, 25. One of my father's favourite hymns was the following, which I have heard him sing while spinning at his jenny many a time.

'My God! I know, I feel thee mine,
 And will not quit my claim,
Till all I have is lost in thine,
 And all renew'd I am.

I hold thee with a trembling hand,
 But will not let thee go,
Till steadfastly by faith I stand,
 And all thy goodness know.

When shall I see the welcome hour,
 That plants my God in me!
Spirit of health, and life, and power,
 And perfect liberty!

Love only can the conquest win,
 The strength of sin subdue,
(Mine own unconquerable sin,)
 And form my soul anew.

Love can bow down the stubborn neck,
 The stone to flesh convert,
Soften, and melt, and pierce, and break,
 An adamantine heart.

O that in me the sacred fire
 Might now begin to glow,
Burn up the dross of base desire,
 And make the mountains flow!

O that it now from heaven might fall,
 And all my sins consume!
Come, Holy Ghost, for thee I call,
 Spirit of burning, come!

Refining fire, go through my heart,
 Illuminate my soul;
Scatter thy life through every part,
 And sanctify the whole.

No longer then my heart shall mourn,
  While, purified by grace,
I only for his glory burn,
  And always see his face,'—*H*. 361, *v*. 1, 2, 3, 5—10.

My mother's favourite hymn was the following.

'Give me the enlarged desire,
  And open, Lord, my soul,
Thy own fulness to require,
  And comprehend the whole:
Stretch my faith's capacity
  Wider, and yet wider still;
Then with all that is in thee
  My soul for ever fill!'—*H*. 372.

This she used to utter in her prayers, rather than sing it at her work. Then they would read or sing such words as the following:

'In hope, against all human hope,
  Self-desperate, I believe;
Thy quickening word shall raise me up,
  Thou shalt thy Spirit give.

The thing surpasses all my thought;
  But faithful is my Lord;
Through unbelief I stagger not,
  For God hath spoke the word.

Faith, mighty faith, the promise sees,
  And looks to that alone;
Laughs at impossibilities,
  And cries, "It shall be done!"'—*H*. 360, *v*. 7, 8, 9.

'Come, O my God, the promise seal,
  This mountain, sin, remove:
Now in my gasping soul reveal
  The virtue of thy love.

I want thy life, thy purity,
  Thy righteousness, brought in;
I ask, desire, and trust in thee,
  To be redeem'd from sin.

For this, as taught by thee, I pray,
  And can no longer doubt;
Remove from hence! to sin I say;
  Be cast this moment out!

Anger and sloth, desire and pride,
  This moment be subdued;
Be cast into the crimson tide
  Of my Redeemer's blood.'—*H*. 417, *v*. 1—4.

Then would follow another mystical hymn, of a tender and touching kind, like the following:

Thou Shepherd of Israel, and mine,
  The joy and desire of my heart;

For closer communion I pine,
   I long to reside where thou art:
The pasture I languish to find,
   Where all, who their Shepherd obey,
Are fed, on thy bosom reclined,
   And screen'd from the heat of the day.

Ah! show me that happiest place,
   The place of thy people's abode,
Where saints in an ecstacy gaze,
   And hang on a crucified God:
Thy love for a sinner declare,
   Thy passion and death on the tree;
My spirit to Calvary bear,
   To suffer and triumph with thee.

'Tis there, with the lambs of thy flock,
   There only, I covet to rest,
To lie at the foot of the rock,
   Or rise to be hid in thy breast:
'Tis there I would always abide,
   And never a moment depart;
Conceal'd in the cleft of thy side,
   Eternally held in thy heart.'—*H.* 228.

In this way did my father and mother spend a great part of their life, troubled, alarmed, perplexed, bewildered, writing bitter things against themselves, charging themselves with unbelief; suspecting themselves of secret, unimaginable sins; finding fault with their own hearts, charging them with being hard, deceitful, and desperately wicked; blaming the devil, and at times (though I believe they were too good to do it often or seriously,) entertaining hard thoughts even of God himself. Thus did they toil, and pray, and wrestle, and wait for sanctification, when all the while they *were* sanctified in the true and Scripture sense of the word. Thus did they weary themselves in pursuit of shadows; thus were they troubled and tormented because they could not find an imaginary blessing.

This notion of instantaneous sanctification is one of the most troublesome and mischievous of all. Thousands have been troubled and afflicted with it almost all their life long. Even some of the preachers have been thus troubled and tormented. This was the case with David Stoner, one of the best and most useful preachers in the Body. It appears from his life, written by John Hannah and W. Dawson, that *he* found it as difficult to find or keep the imaginary blessing, as my father and mother did. Many of the preachers now-a-days do not believe in the doctrine as taught by Wesley, and of course never trouble themselves in seeking for the second instantaneous blessing. A few of the preachers do believe in the doctrine, and trouble themselves accordingly. And *all* the preachers *profess* to believe the doctrine, and solemnly promise to preach it as laid down in John Wesley's sermons and notes A man cannot be admitted either as a preacher in full connexion, or as a preacher on trial, without professing to believe this doctrine as taught by Wesley, and promising to preach it. The preachers therefore that do not believe and preach the doctrine, profess a lie, and are promise breakers. Nor have they, in fact, any legal right to preach in Methodist pulpits at all, unless they believe and teach this doctrine. But curious enough, while few of the preachers believe the doctrine as taught by Wesley, and while not one out of fifty profess to enjoy the second blessing,—nay, while the doctrine is so far out of date with most of the preachers, that they would ridicule a brother that might seriously profess the second blessing; yet they all still preach the doctrine. They all of them speak of regeneration as one blessing, and of sanctification as a second blessing: and even those that will acknowledge, in private, that the doctrine of Wesley respecting sanctification was very erroneous or ill expressed, never contradict any of his statements, never expose any of his errors, never correct any of his unscriptural representations. They still leave the people under the impression that Wesley's words and Wesley's notions were all right, and that they themselves hold the same opinions that Wesley held. It is a principle with the preachers in fact, never to *seem* to differ from Wesley on any of these points; and if any *should seem* to differ from Wesley,—if any one should speak out and tell the people that John Wesley's opinions on this subject were erroneous, unscriptural, inconsistent, contradictory and mischievous, he would be required to retract his statements, or to promise not to speak in such a way again. And if he did not retract or promise to mend, he would be expelled. Yet the very men that expelled him, would, in private, with confidential friends, and among each other, acknowledge that the person was right, and that Wesley's views were unscriptural and false. The principle of never *seeming* to differ from Wesley is not only acted upon by the preachers, but expressly avowed occasionally. It was avowed by one of the principal preachers in the Connexion in the controversy respecting Joseph Cooke, the travelling preacher at Rochdale, who was expelled by the Leeds Conference many years ago. Many of the preachers seem to think it necessary to keep up among the people their blind reverence for John Wesley, as a means of securing their submission to rule and authority, and their steadfast adherence to the Connexion.

I may also observe, that what I have said on this subject in reference to the preachers of the Old Connexion, is true of the preachers of the New Connexion also. Formerly the preachers in the New Connexion had greater liberty; and were allowed both to differ on many subjects, and to express their differences. But since the great trouble which that Connexion has had with some of its preachers, the Conference has decided, that each one is to believe and teach the doctrines of Methodism as laid down by John Wesley. How far the preachers *do* believe the doctrines of Methodism, is another matter. To me it seems that no man can believe them as laid down in Wesley's works; for they are taught contrary ways. However, such is the decision of Conference, and to that decision the preachers must submit. It is however a fact, that sanctification as a separate work from regeneration, or a second instantaneous blessing, is neither taught nor believed in the New Connexion, except in very few instances. I never myself met with more than two or three preachers in the New Connexion that professed to believe it, that I remember. W. Trotter was one, and Andrew Lynn was another. W. Trotter professed to have obtained the blessing instantaneously, by a simple act of reliance on the blood of Christ, while conversing on the subject with Sophia Bairstow. See his own account of the matter in Christian No. 5. Since then W. Trotter has joined the Plymouth brethren, and become very Calvinistic in his views. Whether Andrew Lynn ever professed to have got the blessing or not, I cannot tell; but he used to preach about it and pray about it a great deal. These were the only two preachers in the New Connexion that I remember to have heard talk much of sanctification as a second and instantaneous blessing, and one of them is now no more in the Connexion, and the other I think is not much thought off. Still, so far as the influence of Conference goes, the old Wesleyan errors continue to be upheld, and the people to be misled.

I say the old Methodistical notions about sanctification are exceedingly mischievous. They not only cause people endless uneasiness and perplexity, but hurt them grievously in other ways. They tend to prevent people from making progress in holiness, from obtaining true Christian perfection or excellence. If my parents had understood that their whole business was to do their duty so far as they understood it, and to labour to grow wiser and better every day,—if they had understood that their great business was to try to please God, by doing good to man, they would have gone on comfortably, becoming more like Christ and more like God every day. If they had been taught to mortify or put to death all remains of evil within them, by denying themselves of all ungodliness and sinful pleasures, devoting themselves to the study of truth and the practice of charity, they might both have enjoyed much more comfort, and made much better out in religion than they did. They might have mastered their tempers more perfectly, and gained much knowledge, and proved a greater blessing both to their children and their fellow-men. As it was, their principal concern was to keep up their fancied evidence of the *first* blessing of justification, and to realize the mysterious or imaginary *second* blessing of full and instantaneous sanctification, while other things of real worth and moment were in a great measure overlooked or neglected. Neither my father nor my mother ever thoroughly mastered their own tempers. They did a great deal, but not all that they might or would have done, if their notions had been rational or Scriptural. As it was, they were taught that it was impossible for them to improve their tempers by curbing or controlling them,—that no man can make himself pure,—that to expect to be perfect in holiness by degrees, or to seek after Christian perfection by trying to improve our own tempers and dispositions, or by increasing our knowledge of God and of his works, is to seek salvation by *works* instead of by *faith*, and to prepare for ourselves disappointment and ruin. Take the following representations of this subject from John Wesley himself. He first teaches that men are sanctified by faith, and by faith alone.

'I have continually testified in private and public, That we are sanctified as well as justified by faith. And indeed the one of these great truths does exceedingly illustrate the other. Exactly as we are justified by faith, so are we sanctified by faith. Faith is the condition, and the only condition of sanctification, exactly as it is of justification. It is the condition; none is sanctified but he that believes: without faith no man is sanctified. And it is the *only* condition: this alone is *sufficient* for sanctification. Every one that believes is sanctified, whatever else he has or has not. In other words, no man is sanctified till he believes: every man when he believes is sanctified.'—*Wesley's Works, vol.* vii. *p.* 312, 313.

He then proceeds to state that the faith by which men are sanctified or made perfect, is 'a divine evidence or conviction, 1. That God hath promised it. 2. That what he hath promised he is *able* to perform. 3. That he is able and willing to do it *now*, and 4. That he *doeth* it now. In that hour,' he adds, 'it is *done*.' He then states that the work is instantaneous, and adds the following:

'Look for it then every day, every hour, every moment. Why not this hour, this moment? Certainly you may look for it *now*, if you believe it is by faith. And by this token you may surely know whether you seek it by faith or works. If by works, you want something to be done *first, before* you are sanctified. You think, 'I must first *be* or *do* thus or thus.' Then you are seeking it by *works* unto this day. If you seek it by faith, you may expect it as *you are:* then expect it *now*. It is of importance to observe, that there is an inseparable connection between these three points, expect it *by faith,* expect it *as you are,* and expect it *now!* To deny one of them is to deny them all. To allow one, is to allow them all. Do *you* believe we are sanctified by faith? Be true then to your principle; and look for this blessing just as you are, neither better nor worse; as a poor sinner that has nothing to pay, nothing to plead, but Christ *died*. And if you look for it as you are, then expect it *now*. Stay for nothing: why should you? Christ is ready; and he is all you want. He is waiting for you: he is at the door! Let your inmost soul cry out,

> 'Come in, come in, thou heavenly Guest!
> Nor hence again remove;
> But sup with me, and let the feast
> Be everlasting love.'—*Wesley's Works, vol.* vii. *p.* 318.

Under the influence of such doctrines as this, people neglect the proper work of life, the cultivation and improvement of their own souls and character, and wait anxiously for God to do it for them. Instead of growing in knowledge, and abounding in works of usefulness, and *thus* perfecting holiness, they labour to work themselves up into the belief that God *doth* NOW, THIS VERY MOMENT, sanctify them wholly. This is their great and continual endeavour. They readily enough believe that God has *promised* to cleanse them,—that he is *able* and *willing* to fulfil his promise, and even that he is able and willing to do it *now:* the difficulty is to believe that he *does* do it now, or that the work is *done*. In order to be able to believe that God *does* NOW sanctify them wholly, they must, in general, be greatly excited; be worked into raptures. In hopes of getting thus excited, of being worked into those raptures, they read exciting stories of other people's glorious experiences, run after powerful and moving preachers, go up and down to love-feasts, attend prayer-meetings and fellowship-meetings, and pray and wrestle with all their souls in secret, while the quiet, the every-day duties of life, and the regular, the rational, the Scripture way of religious improvement, are almost wholly neglected or forgotten. Hence multitudes fall away from their religious profession altogether, and become miserable backsliders.. Some begin to suspect that religion is a delusion,—that its professors are hypocrites and liars,—and many become downright infidels. A vast number of the infidels in the lower ranks of society have been Methodists in their time. So with the advocates of infidelity. Many of them are persons that once were members of the Methodist societies. It is the natural consequence of the doctrine before us, and of other similar doctrines of the system.

Some seek the second blessing as it is called, and think they find it. They get greatly excited, or in a reckless and resolute sort of a way, persuade themselves that God has sanctified them, and for a time they are at rest. But even these are not happy long. If it was excitement or rapture that enabled them to believe themselves wholly sanctified, they soon begin to doubt again, and fall into their old condition. They cannot live in raptures long. Their souls cannot bear it. And when once the raptures are gone, their high opinion of their state goes too. And those who persuade themselves that they are fully sanctified without raptures, cannot believe as firmly and as constantly as they could like. They are obliged to think a little, sooner or later; and they cannot think without doubting their high attainments. They may struggle against thought and doubting, and try hard to believe that they believe when they do not believe; but it is hard work fighting against one's own soul,—against plain matter of fact and common sense. Some, there is reason enough to believe, become hypocrites after their raptures or first strong efforts at believing give way, and profess what they know to be a lie. Some come to think it right to say they believe themselves sanctified, or blessed with the direct witness of God's spirit, when they really do not so believe. They appear to think that believing, and venturing to say they believe, are the same thing,—that to say they believe, or to resolve to speak as if they believed, when in reality their minds are full of doubt, is conquering the devil, is believing in hope against hope, and walking by faith and not by sight. In this way their souls get into a state of complete disorder, in which they can neither grow in knowledge nor make progress in religion. Their souls and their lives are quite unnatural. Many are quite alarmed at the idea of thinking. They could no more entertain the idea of beginning freely and thoroughly to examine their own notions, in order to see whether they agree with scripture or with common sense, than they dare leap into eternal torments. If any one oblige them to think by any means, they are quite miserable, and oftentimes dreadfully enraged. Their intolerance, their zeal against reformers or thinkers, their eager desire to have them expelled, and their prayers to God to have them plagued with his judgments that they may be forced to repent, or taken away from the world that they may be unable to do any more mischief, are truly horrible. Hatred, ill-will,—hatred of the bitterest and deadliest kind, is thus generated towards all that would bring them from their unnatural state. These evil effects are also produced by the erroneous notions of Methodism about conversion, justification, and the witness of the spirit, as well as by its errors about sanctification. Hence few are in so hopeless a state with respect to true spiritual improvement as this class of Methodists.

It was thus, to some extent, with my poor dear parents. They first suffered great anxiety and restlessness because they could not obtain the fancied second blessing. They were then hindered from setting heartily to work to master and correct their own tempers, and improve their own characters, under an impression that it was impossible for them to do any thing effectually till they were wholly sanctified, and under the notion that they must be sanctified or perfected, not by their own endeavours, not by degrees, not through the increase of their knowledge and the exercise and culture of their better affections, but in a moment, in the twinkling of an eye, by some strange single act of faith. Then at times they were tempted to think hardly of God, or even to doubt the truth of religion. Thus they were led to spend their lives to but little purpose. They did little in the way of reading or seeking for knowledge, and but little for the improvement of their fellow-men. They would teach people to read; but not supply them with the means of information. They would try to bring people to be religious after the Methodist fashion; but their explanations of religion were such as to make people dread it rather than love and revere it. Besides, being under the impression that so long as they lived without the second imaginary blessing, they were living below their privilege, and falling short of their duty, and that they were in consequence unprepared for heaven, they were not in a state to enter cheerfully and heartily on efforts either for the enlargement or improvement of their own minds, or for the instruction and improvement of their neighbours. What was knowledge to them, compared with the eternal salvation of their souls? What heart could they have to attend to smaller or secondary things, so long as the great thing was yet unaccomplished? And what propriety could there be in troubling themselves to teach others to read or think, while they themselves had not obtained their necessary fitness for heaven? And thus my poor parents went on.

Another disadvantage that my parents laboured under in consequence of their erroneous notions about sanctification was this: they could not recommend religion to their children so effectually. The following story will partly explain this point. One night my mother was talking to me seriously about my soul, and asking me how I dare lie down to sleep without being ready for heaven. I knew that the Methodist doctrine was that none were ready for heaven till they were fully sanctified, and I also knew that my mother did not profess to have got this peculiar blessing, so I answered; "But are *you* ready for heaven, Mother?" This was a question which my mother had plainly never looked for, and for which she was quite unprepared. She said, No, she was *not* quite ready. I replied, 'Then I am as safe as you are.' My mother could hardly acknowledge so much as that, but she felt this, that her warning had not produced the full effect it was meant to produce. It is my belief now that my mother *was* ready for heaven at the time I refer to; but neither I nor my mother believed so then.

My parents had other draw-backs on their happiness in Methodism. They believed in eternal life in torments. They believed that all who were not converted and sanctified in the Methodistical fashion, would not only be shut out of heaven, but confined for ever in a lake of fire and brimstone, and kept alive in unutterable torments for ever. They believed that all who were not converted and sanctified after the Methodist fashion, were really in the arms of the devil, and would be dragged by him as soon as life should end, to their eternal doom. Hence they were unable to think of their children or their neighbours without horror. They fancied them 'hanging over the burning pit by the brittle and untwisting thread of life,' and each moment liable to sink into endless and unutterable woe. The idea of their children growing up to manhood, and thus becoming liable to such a doom, would at times fill them with the greatest dread. They were tempted to wish that their children might die in their childhood, before there was any danger of their eternal damnation. Whether my parents ever really wished that their children might die in their childhood, I cannot tell; but I very well remember a horrible saying of my eldest brother on this subject. My eldest brother was about nineteen or twenty years old at the time, and was a young man of very serious thought, and great warmth and energy of spirit. And it was too soon for him to have children of his own; so that the workings of his religious notions in reference to children had but little to check them. He was standing with his back against the fireplace, and I and my mother were in the room just by, when he said, 'Mother, if God would allow me, I would take a sword and kill every child in the world.' His reason was this. If the children were to grow up, they would all, according to Methodist opinions, run the risk of eternal and horrible torments both of soul and body; but if they died in infancy, they would all be sure of eternal life in unspeakable blessedness. It was a horrible wish: yet it was perfectly rational, and even benevolent and Christian, on the principles of Methodism. I have felt the same principles producing similar effects in myself in my life time. And such, in some degree or other, are their effects in people generally.

The notions of many Calvinists on this subject are more

horrible still. Methodists, though they believe that children are born naturally corrupt, totally depraved, under the wrath and curse of God, and *liable* to eternal damnation ; yet believe that children never *are* damned in reality. They allow reason, on this subject, a place in their creed. They believe that it would be unjust in God to allow children to be eternally tormented for the sins of Adam. They believe, therefore, that though children are depraved and cursed by Adam, they are in some mysterious way purified and blessed by Christ. They have, therefore, the comfort of believing that all little children go safe to heaven. But not so with the Calvinists. Some of them, I suppose, have begun to believe in the salvation of all children ; but others still believe that there are millions of little children in hell at this moment, suffering the tortures of eternal fire. Some of them even believe that all children go to hell who die before they come of age to believe in Jesus, and experience a saving change of heart. The Scotch Calvinists are worse than the English in this respect. A friend of mine, in Glasgow, told me several dreadful stories on this subject. One was a man that he knew, whose son John died without showing the necessary signs that he was ' a subject of Divine grace.' The man prayed for his son very earnestly, but saw not the signs of conversion that he looked for. He was praying for him in his closet at the time that he died, and when he received the sad intelligence, he said, ' Well ; John is damned, and God is glorified, and I am satisfied.' Other stories he told me of a similar character, tending to show, not only that the Scotch Calvinists generally hold the horrible doctrine of infant damnation, but that the tendency of this doctrine is to harden people's hearts, and to make them utterly unnatural. In this respect, Methodism has the advantage over Calvinism. And the advantage is no trifling one. And it is owing to Methodism in some measure that many Calvinists have been led to lay aside the horrible doctrine of infant damnation. Still, after all, the Methodist notions in reference to children are very far from truth, and in many ways tend to prevent such as hold them from enjoying the full pleasures, or reaping the full advantages, of the religion of Christ.

Whether my parents ever troubled themselves much about the doctrines of the Trinity and Satisfaction to Justice or not, I am unable to state. I am inclined to think they did not. I never recollect hearing them talk about those subjects. I do not recollect either my father or mother ever using the word trinity; nor do I remember ever hearing them use such words as three persons in one God; God the Father, God the Son, and God the Holy Ghost; nor do I remember ever hearing them pray to Jesus, or to the Holy Spirit. I believe they were, so far as the trinity was concerned, simple Christians. They did not *deny* the trinity; but they had never heard of it, or had never thought of it. John Wesley observes, in his Sermon on the Trinity, that not one Christian believer in twenty ever thinks of the trinity, or adverts to it at first. And this, no doubt, was the case with the early Methodists: the subject never entered their minds. So it was with my parents, I imagine. They believed in just one God, and they prayed only to one. One God was sufficient for them. They needed nothing but what the one Great God could give: they knew of nothing to be done for them, but what the one great God could do. Hence their prayers and conversation were as free from trinitarian phraseology, so far as I can remember, as my own. I do not even remember hearing either my father or my mother sing the trinitarian hymns. They *may* have sung them; but I do not remember them doing so. My parents appear not only not to have troubled themselves about things which they could not understand, but even to have purposely avoided them. They were practical people, and little but what was practical seems to have engaged their thoughts. Some would have it that there is no great warmth of piety apart from a belief in the trinity. Yet none need be more warm, more earnest, more full of life and feeling, than my parents; yet *they*, I imagine, no more believed in the trinity, in the earlier years of their Methodism, than I do now.

What their thoughts were about the person of Christ, I cannot tell. I never heard them speak of him as God; I never heard them pray to him, except when singing hymns addressed to him. They appear to me not to have troubled themselves with thoughts about his person, but to have contented themselves with looking on him as a person employed by God for the instruction and salvation of mankind. They believed in Christ as their teacher, their example, their guide, their Saviour, their judge; they loved him; they trusted in his words; but as for believing him to be God, I have no recollection that they ever did any thing of the kind.

I may add, that the Methodist preachers themselves did not talk much about the Trinity or the Godhead of Christ till about twenty or thirty years ago. The *earlier* Methodist preachers were more of practical exhorters, than controversial lecturers. The object of the better sort of them was to bring people to be religious,—or to bring them to give up their sins and to live a new life, and not to bewilder them with the mysteries of priestly theology. Others of the Methodist preachers appear to have cared little about any thing but living on the people, and bringing people under their sway. These latter were the persons that first began to deal much in priestly theology; but even they did not trouble themselves or the people with the mysteries of the trinity. They talked a deal of Adam's sin, and natural depravity, and Christ's atoning blood, and trust in Christ's merits, and recumbency on Christ's righteousness; yet they seldom, if ever, disputed about the trinity. The first time I ever heard much talk among the Methodists about the trinity, was about twenty or twenty three years ago. This talk was brought over from America, I believe, and began to be heard among the Methodist preachers, about the time that Timothy Dwight's works began to find their way among the Methodist preachers. And even then such talk was confined to a few. It was only a few of the *leading* preachers that used to preach sermons about the trinity, the divinity of Christ, the personality of the spirit, and the doctrine of satisfaction. And even those did not preach often on those subjects, but only on extra occasions, such as chapel openings, anniversaries, and the like. The first that I recollect throwing out hints against anti-trinitarians was Billy Dawson, and David Stoner. The next was a man of the name of Wilson, a very zealous, one might almost say a raving person, who, as I was told, was degraded shortly after for drunkenness. The next was a local preacher at Bramley. I had been hearing David Stoner preach a sermon partly on the Godhead of Christ, and he wished me to give him the substance of the sermon, as he said he was thinking of preparing a sermon on that subject himself. I gave him as much of the sermon as I could recollect, which was not very much to his purpose. No matter; he found better help elsewhere, and shortly after, he delivered his sermon, which was very much spoken of by some. About this time it became quite fashionable for Methodist preachers to preach about the trinity and the Godhead of Christ; and almost every preacher that wanted to seem big, or get a great name, would be trying to get up a sermon on those subjects. Sermons on those subjects soon came to be called *great* sermons by many, and those preachers who could preach such sermons were often called *great preachers*. I fancy there must have been some case of *heresy* among the travelling preachers about this time, that caused this new way of preaching to become so common. Perhaps the case of Joseph Cooke, at Rochdale, and his friends, had something to do with it. For though Joseph Cooke himself did not become a public opponent of the trinity, several of his followers did. However, so it was, that till about twenty or twenty three years ago, the trinity and the Godhead of Christ were subjects rarely preached about by Methodist preachers, and very little talked about or thought about by the members.

And so with the doctrine of Satisfaction to God's Justice by Christ's death. The Methodists taught and believed that Christ died to redeem or to save men in *some* way, but what way that was, they were not so particular to enquire. They believed that Christ had done something which no one else had ever done, but they had not agreed as to what it was; they had never so much as discussed the question. They believed that, in some way, God loved people, and forgave their sins, and heard their prayers, and would take them at last to heaven, *for Christ's sake;* but they had never pretended to understand the *particulars* of Christ's work, or the way in which God was influenced or worked upon by Christ. If the people had any particular ideas at all on this subject, they would be that Christ moved God, and caused him to be merciful, by the greatness of his sufferings, and by the earnestness of his prayers for people. God was regarded as a great and awful Being, who had been grievously offended by his creatures, and was hardly willing to have any thing to do with them again. Christ was regarded as exceedingly kind; as full of compassion and love; as bearing all the punishment which sinners had deserved in their stead, in order to rescue them from hell, and bring God to have mercy on sinners; as going to heaven to present himself and all his bleeding wounds before God, and, as adding to the influence of his bleeding wounds, his earnest and ceaseless prayers; and as succeeding, by this joint influence, in reconciling or inducing God to forgive the sinner's sins, and receive him again to favour. These were the ideas that I myself received early of Christ's work; and they are the ideas that prevailed most generally among such of the Methodists as had any ideas at all. And the character of the hymns that were most commonly sung by the Methodists of those times, and that were sung with most relish and energy, especially in love-feasts, class-meetings, prayer-meetings, and at their daily labours, answered to those notions. Those hymns,—their *favourite* hymns, all gave those views of the subject which I have just laid down. One of the greatest favourites was the following:—

'Arise, my soul, arise,
  Shake off thy guilty fears;
The bleeding sacrifice
  In my behalf appears;
Before the throne my Surety stands;
My name is written on his hands.

He ever lives above,
  For me to intercede,
His all-redeeming love,
  His precious blood, to plead;
His blood atoned for all our race,
And sprinkles now the throne of grace.

Five bleeding wounds he bears,
  Received on Calvary;
They pour effectual prayers,
  They strongly speak for me;
'Forgive him, O forgive,' they cry,
'Nor let that ransom'd sinner die!'

The Father hears him pray,
  His dear Anointed One;
He *cannot* turn away
  The presence of his Son:
His Spirit answers to the blood,
And tells me I am born of God.

My God is reconciled,
  His pardoning voice I hear,
He owns me for his child,
  I can no longer fear;
With confidence I now draw nigh,
And, Father, Abba, Father, cry!'—*H.* 202.

Here Christ is set forth exactly as I have stated, as the sinner's surety; and the sinner is therefore called to shake off his fears. He is represented as standing bleeding, and pleading with God in the sinner's behalf. He pleads his love, his precious blood, and holds forth his five bleeding wounds, which plead with still greater power for the sinner. The Father is unable to resist the prayers and the bleeding wounds of his son; he is conquered by the pleading and sorrows of his Son, and reconciled to the sinner, and constrained to acknowledge him as his child. The same sentiments are expressed in other hymns. In some Christ is represented as *purchasing* God's favour,—as dying to buy for men pardon, and peace, and heaven, from God,—as paying man's debts, and doing man's work; and all these views or notions of Christ's work prevailed among the Methodists, both members and preachers. Still, they had no particular theory on the subject; no clearly explained system; no carefully defined notions. The subject had never been discussed among them, so that they just talked at random,—talked just as their forerunners had talked before them, without any regular theory at all. And this is, in truth, the case with them still to a great extent. True, some of them have got *theologised* within the last twenty or thirty years, and since the efforts of J. Barker and his friends began to rouse the attention of the public, several others have been led to *theologise* a little. Still the opinions of the multitudes, both of preachers and people, are of that confused, unscriptural and unworthy description which we have just laid down.

What influence these doctrines had upon the minds of my parents, it is hard to tell. Their thoughts of what Christ had done for them had certainly a tendency to produce strong feeling, and work the soul to ecstacies. Their notions had also a tendency to make them feel uncomfortably towards God, as exceedingly severe and unmerciful. Those notions had also a tendency to make people less regardful of duty, less fearful of sin, and they produced this effect on many. If God is well pleased with the sinner for the sake of Christ's righteousness,—if Christ has paid our debt and done our work, —if Christ has borne our punishment, and fulfilled in our stead all righteousness,—if sinners may be forgiven by relying on Christ's merits, and claiming forgiveness in his name as bought for them by him, what follows? This follows, that sin is not so terrible a matter,—that sinners are not in so perilous a condition,—that righteousness in us is not so very requisite. And many, as I have said, were led by this doctrine to live loosely, carelessly, profligately. They first began with little things, then went on to greater, till at last they became workers of almost all iniquity. They would lie, cheat, steal, commit fornication and adultery, or give themselves up to the selfish pursuit of money and to a worldly life, and yet, relying for acceptance on the merits of Christ, claiming pardon or acceptance in the name of Jesus who paid their debt, and asking for heaven on the ground that Christ had done their work or fulfilled all righteousness for them, they still went on singing, shouting, praying and exulting as if they were the first and boldest of God's true people.

There were others however who were not thus influenced by the doctrine. They were happily inconsistent enough to believe, that though Christ had fulfilled all righteousness for them, they were still required to fulfil all righteousness themselves,—that though Christ had in some way paid their debt, they would still have to suffer if they did wrong,—that though Christ had done their work, it was necessary for them to work also if they would be accepted of God,—that though they were to be accepted and blessed on account of the merits of Christ, they would still have to be judged and rewarded according to their own doings,—that whatsoever a man sowed, that should he also reap. This was the case with my parents. Either they understood and believed nothing at all about what the hymns said about Christ doing our work, and God accepting and saving people on account of Christ's sufferings and prayers, or else they were happy and inconsistent enough to believe flat contradictions. For this is certain, they always believed that goodness alone could secure God's approbation and blessing, and that sin must always provoke God's displeasure, and shut men out from happiness and heaven. And on this principle they acted. They seem to have had a notion that all Christ did and suffered was necessary to make God willing to accept men's return to righteousness, to love the good, to reward the *obedience* of his children. But it is difficult to say how they were influenced by their belief. The truth appears to be this. They thought they must believe or sing what they found in the hymn book, and practise what was written in their own hearts. Theology was to be *said* or *sung*, but common sense and religion were to be practised. My parents, like many others, had too much natural goodness and sound plain sense to be seriously corrupted by theology. Still, they did not escape its bad influence altogether, and there is reason to believe that they would have been both better, and happier, and more useful people, if they had been left to the simple teachings of Jesus, and their own unperverted common sense.

My parents were both believers in witchcraft and fairies, as well as in some other superstitions. They believed that some persons, especially certain women, had the power of causing diseases in men and cattle, and of harassing and injuring people in various other ways, by an evil wish, or by diabolical influence. I remember my father telling a curious story about some mischief that was done to the beer of R. A., a friend of his, by witchcraft. He said that while working in the tub it became green, and so stringy, that instead of falling in drops when poured, it would hang like treacle. Who it was that they supposed had bewitched the beer, I cannot tell; but both my father and R. A. believed that it *was* bewitched, sure enough, and so did we all, so far as I can remember. Poor R. A. believed himself hurt by witchcraft in other things besides his home-brewed beer. A female class-leader also once fancied herself bewitched, and at one time, not thirty years ago, a great part of the town was thrown into alarm and uproar by witchcraft tales. Some said they had found *witch cakes* hid behind their fire places, and others said they had found them in their chimnies, and others in other places. These witch cakes were masses of dough, I suppose, stuck full of crooked pins, old nails, and the like. Those cakes were to be placed somewhere about the house or premises of the parties to be bewitched. The injury to be done to the party who was to be bewitched, would, I suppose, depend on the will of the witch herself. But sometimes, according to the common talk, the parties would be taken ill, not of a fever, or consumption, or any known or common kind of complaint, but of some other complaint which no one could perhaps describe, but which was more terrible perhaps than any common complaint. Or perhaps a child would be struck dumb, or seized with sudden weakness and waste away. Or perhaps the cattle would die, or the cows would suddenly refuse to give their milk, or the milk would all be bad, or all things would go cross in the house, the field, or the shop. Then nothing could be done, by common remedies, for the cure of witchcraft. Nothing could be done but by charms, or some dreadful and cruel arts. One person, a Methodist, who professed to be able to cure witchcraft, told me, that the way to cure a person bewitched in his own body, was by bleeding the person, and letting the blood run into a very hot fire. By this means, he said, the witch herself might be burned to death. When the blood ran into the fire, the witch, wherever she might live, and whatever she might be doing, was, he said, thrown into the fire at the same time, and if the fire was hot enough to consume the blood, it would inevitably consume the witch as well. I once went with this man to see a poorly old man, who, in my opinion, was suffering under dropsy. After we came away, he asked me privately what I thought was the matter with the man. I answered; but he said he was bewitched; and so far as I know he believed what he said.

Some fancy that those foolish and horrible notions have now past away,—that people no longer believe them. This, however, is a great mistake. There are thousands on thousands of people in the Methodist society that still believe them. In some places there are but few, I fear, who disbelieve them. They no more doubt the existence and power of witches, than they doubt the existence of God or the devil. Many would consider a person an infidel if he did not believe in witches and witchcraft.

My mother's belief in *fairies*, or *pixies* as they are called in Devonshire, was as strong as her belief in witchcraft. She really believed that there was a race of beings, resembling men in shape, but eight or ten times less, that lived in our world, and meddled in men's affairs, hurting or helping people, making them rich or making them poor, taking away their children and bringing others in their place, and stirring up and down unseen except by particular people. She never saw any of those powerful little beings herself, but I have heard her tell tales about her mother or her mother's acquaintances seeing them regularly. One of her mother's acquaintances used to tell her, that they came regularly to her house every night, and span at her wheel,—that if she left the house nice and clean when she went to bed, and left a little fire on the hearth, and a mug full of fresh clean water, they never failed to come and spin up all her *slivers*, or flax. She said she had looked through a nick in the boards, and seen them many a time busy at their work. Such were the tales Joan Rew, and my grandmother too perhaps, used to tell my mother, and she believed them as firmly as she believed in religion. Whether my father believed in such things I do not know; but I know he believed in ghosts, or *boggards*, as we call them in Yorkshire.

What particular influence these notions had on my parents, I can hardly tell; but they had certainly no favourable influence on their children. They tended to make me feel as if the world was ruled by wild and lawless powers,—as if there was no security in the world,—as if our life and interests were in the hands of a terrible and mysterious order of beings, in which we could place no confidence or trust. Such notions shut out the idea of a ruling God, and turned providence into chance. They reduced, in fact, the influence of religion to a trifle, to nothing, and made me feel as an atheist in the world. And I fancy they had the same effect on my parents to *some* extent. Still, in *them*, the belief in God rose above their belief in witches and fairies, so that though they were foolish enough to cling to the superstitions of their childhood, their religious belief was, in general, the great ruling principle of their lives.

One thing I may observe, that though I sat under Methodist preachers from my childhood till I was twenty years of age, yet I have no recollection of ever hearing any of them speak against those foolish and miserable notions. If the people were in the dark, they might remain in the dark, for any thing the preachers choose to do to enlighten them. The people might believe all the horrible superstitions of old Paganism almost, for any thing the preachers ever taught them on such subjects.

As a sample of my mother's credulity on those subjects,

and of the credulity of the people generally in those parts of the country, I may mention the following. When I was a child, about four or five years of age, the notorious Mary Bateman was going up and down the country, pretending to cure diseases partly by the power of charms, or witchcraft, and partly by drugs or drinks. She poisoned a woman at Bramley, a relation of my father's, and had nearly poisoned her husband too. This woman, after a lengthy and horrible career, was tried and hung for the murder of my father's relation, and the attempted murder of her husband. My mother told me that while this woman was in her cell, previous to her execution, the gaoler went once to see her, and could find nothing but a great black toad. My mother had heard the tale, and she believed it. It was a general belief that this Mary Bateman had the power of assuming almost any form she pleased, in virtue of an agreement she had made with the devil, when she sold him her soul.

And this is but a sample of the notions that prevailed among the people amongst whom we were brought up. The idea that men could raise the devil, and sell themselves to him, receiving in return for their souls a certain length of life, and unlimited supplies of money, was as common as a belief in God. A book by John Bunyan, called the history of Mr. Badman, abounded in such stories; and both my parents and the Methodists believed them to be as true as truth. They never had a doubt of their truth, that ever I learned. But I must bid you farewell, and rest awhile. Only let me add, that it is plain we are living in better days. Let us be thankful to God. And let us be hopeful too. If we are living in better times than the times of our fathers, let us hope that our children will live in times still better than ours. Let us hope that the world will go on improving without end. Let us hope, that as a belief in witchcraft, and fairies, and infernal bargainings, have partly passed away, so the belief in the horrors, and blasphemies, and follies of orthodoxy will pass away in like manner. And let us work as well as hope. Do not let us be like the priests, who stand idly by, and leave error to live on or be killed by others. Let us labour with all our might; let us fight against error and wickedness of every shape; and let us see if we cannot hasten the illumination and salvation of our race.

CHAPTER II.

INFANCY AND CHILDHOOD.

As I have said before, I was born at Bramley, in 1806. What happened to me for the first two years I do not remember, but my mother tells me that I was never very well, and that in consequence I was very cross, and very troublesome. I was, in truth, the most cross and troublesome child she had. From what I have been told, I must have cried a great part of my time, when I was not asleep. I must have been a great and terrible trial to my poor dear mother. It was with difficulty she could contrive either to get into bed at night, or to rise in the morning, or to get on with her work through the day for me. Frequently after she had got me to sleep with a great deal of trouble, I should awake and begin my crying again, just as she was carefully laying me down in the cradle or in bed, and thus force her to begin the task of getting me to sleep again. She was frequently obliged to dress or undress herself with me upon her knee or at her breast, and lie down at night, or begin her work in the morning, without daring to move me. She had frequently to begin her work before she was quite dressed, and to prepare the breakfast, or sit working at the bobbin wheel, with her troublesome child hanging at the breast, or sleeping on her knee. My poor mother could not bear to hear a child cry, if it was possible in any way to quiet it, hence the trouble and sorrow I caused her was immense. Her neighbours advised her to give me some *Godfrey*,* assuring her that it would do me good; and she did so. But she observed after awhile that it rather stupified me than got me soundly to sleep, so she took the alarm and gave it up again. She tried the doctor to see if *he* could do any thing for me; but without success. She was obliged to bear her affliction as well as she could. But she offered many fervent prayers for me, and hoped that the time would come, when I should not only be better, but make up for the trouble that I caused her.

* An opiate or anodyne of that name.

One of the first things I recollect was falling into the town well. I was playing on the upper side of the well with a number of other children, when some one pushed me over, and I fell into the water on my back. I have no recollection of having had any fear at the time, though I recollect very well being stripped of my clothes after I was taken out of the water. I suppose I was too young to have fears of being drowned.

One of the next things I recollect was the escape of a sheep from a butcher's shop, just as they were about to kill it, I suppose. When I saw the people running after it to take it, I felt the greatest excitement. This trifling affair was to me at that time as serious and as stirring an affair, as the wars of the French Revolution could be to the upgrown man. I recollect distinctly that the escape of the sheep and the stir that followed, seemed a matter of unutterable importance.

The next thing I remember was being put into a dark cellar, and told that the *boggard* should have me. This was the most terrible affair of all. I was dreadfully frightened. I really believed that there was a boggard in the cellar, and for any thing I knew to the contrary, I saw it plainly, at the bottom of the cellar steps. The image of the boggard remains with me to this day. How it was that I was not frightened out of my wits, I cannot tell. Little did my mother imagine the horrible effect that fright had on my mind. I would not myself frighten a child in such a manner knowingly for all the world. Parents should avoid the frightening system altogether. It is a dreadful system. I never can think of it without horror.

All those things took place when I was from two to three years of age. I remember a number of other things which took place about the same time, but there is no necessity to mention them.

When I was three or four years of age, my parents removed to another house, where we lived till I became a man. It was here that I properly began to live; and it is from this period that I am able to remember distinctly the principal events of my life.

On looking back on the earlier periods of my life, I first see proofs that the orthodox doctrine of original sin, or of natural, total depravity, is a falsehood. I was *not* born totally depraved. I never recollect the time, since I began to think and feel at all, when I had not good thoughts and good feelings. I never recollect the time since I began to think and feel at all, when I had not many good thoughts and strong inclinations to goodness. So far was my heart from being utterly depraved or hardened, that I sympathized, even in my childhood, with the humblest of God's creatures, and was filled to overflowing with sorrow at the sight of distress. I recollect one Sunday, while I was searching about for something in one of the windows up stairs, I found a butterfly that had been starved to death, as I supposed. When I laid hold of it, it crumbled to pieces. My feelings were such at the thought of the poor butterfly's sufferings, that I wept. And for all that day I could scarcely open my lips to say a word to any one, without bursting into tears.

I was also a ready believer in the great doctrines of religion. I believed in God, in Christ, in the evil of sin, in the rewards of righteousness, in the punishment of the wicked, and in the everlasting life of the good. And my faith was unmingled with doubt. And I feared and loved God; and I loved Jesus; and I looked on sin with horror; and on goodness with satisfaction and delight. And I loved my parents, my brothers, and my sisters, and I hated no one upon earth. And I loved God's world; I was pleased with the flowers with which he covered the fields, and with the birds and beasts with which he had peopled the earth. Was this total depravity?

And I recollect well what a struggle I had when I first told a lie. A school in the neighbourhood had a feast, ours had not, so I played the truant, after a serious struggle, to have an opportunity of seeing the scholars walk. I had a miserable afternoon, for I felt I was doing wrong, and I was afraid lest my mother should find me out. My sister found me out and told my mother, but my mother was loth to believe her till she had asked me myself. When I went home my mother asked me if I had been to school, and I said, yes, and my mother, as she had never found me out in a lie before, believed me. But I was sadly distressed after, when I thought of what I had done. That lie caused me days of remorse, and my sufferings were all the severer in consequence of my mother having so readily believed what I said.

When I was about six or seven years of age, I had many serious thoughts and many strong desires to be good; and so had my next elder brother. One morning as we were going together to school we were so thoroughly taken up with talking about being good, that we forgot to turn up the yard where the school was held, and did not find out our mistake or oversight till we had got a good way beyond the place. But already our minds had got darkened by false notions of religion. We had been taught, young as we were, that to be religious was something different from being good, and doing right. We had been taught that we were born corrupt, depraved, that we were sinners by birth, in consequence of our descent from Adam, and that before we could be pleasing to God we must undergo some great mysterious change. Our parents had taught us the doctrines of Methodism on this subject, and we were perplexed and bewildered by them. We knew not what to do. We were quite at a loss. We were willing to shun bad ways, and bad company; to attend school, learn our lessons, speak the truth, obey our parents, and do what else we believed to be right, but this, according to Methodism, was not enough.

Our parents talked about a change from nature to grace, about conviction, conversion, and sanctification; about some kind of strange mysterious faith, and we were thus set fast. If we had known, that to be religious was simply to be good,—that in order to be pleasing to God we had only to do right so far as we knew,—that to act according to our knowledge and to seek for still further knowledge, was all that God could require of us, we might have gone on our way rejoicing, young as we were. But as it was, we were troubled very much; and after struggling after some kind of imaginary goodness to no purpose, our religious anxieties died away, and left us perhaps farther from goodness than before.

Some time after this, I recollect reading Bunyan's Pilgrim's Progress. I took the book to be a true history of some man, that had found a way to heaven of his own, and often did I wish that *I* could find such a way. I cared nothing about the difficulties and dangers of the road; all I cared for was to *find* a road. My great grief was this, that I could find no way at all; or that the way of which I heard people talk was a way that I could not see, which I could not understand, and in consequence, no way at all to me. Young as I was,

I felt as if I would have given any thing, done any thing, risked any thing, suffered any thing to have had the way placed plain before me. The Slough of Despond, the Hill Difficulty, the lions, Apollyon, the Valley of the shadow of death, the dangers of Vanity Fair, the perils of Jordan, were but little to me; I was prepared for all if I could but find the way. But that I could not do. I inquired of my mother after this new way of the Pilgrim, but received no satisfactory answer; so I was obliged to go forward in the dark, or to stand wretchedly and hopelessly still.

My parents had eleven children in all, four older, and six younger than myself. The oldest, called Samuel, died when nearly twenty-one years of age. He was a good, an excellent young man, and of more than common abilities. He was exceedingly kind to his mother from his earliest childhood. He was very ready at his learning, and had read the Bible through at a very early period of his life. When he was about eleven years old he began to go to class, and became a member of the Methodist society. He threw away his childish play things, and resolved to live like a man. He was only about fourteen years of age when he began to preach, and he had not preached long before he began to be a favourite preacher with many. At one place to which he went to preach, the people would hardly allow him to go into the pulpit at first. His appearance was so youthful and laddish, that they could not believe he was the preacher. But they were astonished when they had heard him, at the soundness and truth of his remarks. They were then desirous of having him to come again as soon as possible.

He was very fond of hearing Billy Dawson. He would travel ten or twenty miles on a Sunday to hear him, though he had to work hard all the week through. His relish for clear, and rational, and energetic preaching, was intense. A good, a truthful sermon gave him the greatest delight. But he could not bear a careless, or trifling preacher. He once told one of the travelling preachers who *could* preach well, but who was too idle to do so, that he deserved whipping home with a horse whip. He had an excellent memory, and he cultivated it carefully. He could tell the travelling preachers every text they had preached from at Bramley for two whole years together, though they were preaching there every Sunday. One of them, who thought it hardly possible, tried him, and found that he remembered them all, and could repeat them in the order in which they had been preached, giving chapter and verse for them all. This was before he began to preach himself, I believe. When W. Atherton was stationed at Bramley, he was unable to go to his circuit for a month or so; and my brother was chosen to supply his place during that time. And this he did to the satisfaction of the people, though he had to work through the week at his loom all the time.

And my brother had something of the reformer about him too. He would not only think for himself, but when he *had thought*, he would tell his thoughts, and abide by them too, so long as he believed them to be true. He was once called to an account for some opinion which he had uttered, and his judges decided that the opinion was wrong, and Samuel was called upon to retract: but Samuel refused to retract, unless they could show him that his opinion was not true. The preacher, the travelling preacher, filled with the spirit of the priest, told him that he ought to submit to his superiors. Samuel did not know who were his superiors, and still stood out, refusing to give way in the least, unless proofs were brought forward to convince him that he was wrong. The preacher charged him with obstinacy, but Samuel still kept his ground. Something had been said about my brother going out as a travelling preacher, and no one questioned his piety or abilities; but this proof that he gave of a free and independent spirit appears to have stopped up his way. No one is fit for a tyrant, who cannot be first a slave. The tyrants are fully aware of this; hence they never like to take a man into their number, till they are satisfied that he will sacrifice his conscience to the interests of their party. A determination to think for oneself, and to make every thing bend to the authority of conscience, is the unpardonable sin in the eyes of a tyrant or a priest. My brother had proved himself guilty of this sin, and the doors of the priesthood were accordingly closed against him.

My brother was very fond of books, but he had not the means of procuring many, poor lad. He had very little money at his command, and books were exceedingly dear. Books which the conference could have afforded to sell for sixpence or eightpence, they sold for six or eight shillings. Thus the selfishness of the conference kept my brother in spiritual want, and continues to keep thousands in want to this hour. Kind friends among the *members* sometimes bought him or gave him a book or two, and he remembered their kindness to the last. Mr. Burton bought him Wood's Dictionary of the Bible, and Simeon Musgrave gave him bishop Beveridge's Private Thoughts on Religion. If books had been as cheap as they ought to have been, those friends might have purchased him more; but they were not. Wood's dictionary of the Bible cost twenty-seven shillings, but ought not to have cost more than four.

When my brother once got a book, he never could rest till he had gone quite through it. Whether in bed or up, he would still go on with his reading till his books were done. He has worked at the loom fourteen or sixteen hours through the day, and then, after going to the class meeting or preaching in the evening, spent a great part of the night reading in bed. My parents would not let him sit up to read; so he used to sit reading in bed.

He was very fond of Baxter's Saints' Rest. He read it again and again. He carried it in his bosom by day, and took it with him to bed at night. He read as long as he could read, and then placed it under his pillow and fell asleep.

My brother was a youth of great determination. If he thought he ought to do a thing, he would do it, and no one could hinder him. But I cannot say that his determinations were always right; they were sometimes rather singular. For instance, he had a very nice head of hair, which curled very beautifully, and at times drew forth expressions of admiration from people. One time, when he was about to preach at Bramley, he cut off all his curls to the very root. Some person that he expected to be one of his hearers, had expressed great admiration of his fine curls, and he was resolved to check what he regarded as their foolish admiration. Again; he never would preach before his father. I recollect hearing him tell my father once, when he was going to preach at Bramley, that he would not preach if he went to the chapel. And I have no doubt but he would have given up his sermon in the middle, if he had seen my father go in. But he had no objection to my mother's hearing him: he could preach before her without difficulty. He gave other proofs of his resoluteness in his management of his younger brothers and sisters. If ever he thought we ought to do any thing, he would make us do it, if possible. He could master us better than my father could; though there was one that even *he* could not fairly subdue. I never could bear to be mastered myself. And though I might seem to be subdued for awhile, I always revolted in heart, and embraced the first opportunity of asserting my freedom. God never made me to be in subjection to man.

My brother was very fond of singing and music. When he was once leading me by the hand in Leeds, a martial band of music struck up at a short distance, when off he ran, as if carried away by a whirlwind, and returned no more till the music had ceased to play.

He delighted to get his brothers and sisters together to sing

'Before Jehovah's awful throne,
Ye nations bow with sacred joy,' &c.

And often did we join to sing it for him.

Through a great part of my brother's short life my parents were poor, and my brother had hard to suffer both from hard work and insufficient food. We seldom used to taste wheat bread, except once or twice a week, and butter was out of the question. We thought a bit of wheat bread a great luxury without any butter. Sometimes my poor brother would steal a piece of wheat bread, and hide it in some wool at the end of his loom. If he was not found out he would eat of it when he was hungry till it was done, and then partially starve till he could steal a bit more. I recollect once he had stolen a whole small cake, but he was found out, and it was taken away from him. Whether it was during his life-time or not, I cannot exactly tell; but once I remember we were thirteen weeks and never had a piece of wheat bread in the house, and at times we were without even a bit of oat cake.

Yet my brother was a very hard worker. He had a great spring of life and strength in his soul, and he spent it most freely in his labours. He rose early, and worked late, and never lost any time either in rest or recreation. And he used to weave very fast. He would always keep up to the quickest around him, and generally leave them behind. My mother would at times go up stairs and beg him to take his time; but it was not in his nature to take time. What he did, he must do with his might. 'Samuel, Samuel, why art thou working so hard?' said my mother one day. 'I want to get you out of debt, mother, and earn you some money to make you better off,' replied Samuel. He often lamented the hardships which my mother had to bear, and said how he longed and hoped to see her more comfortably provided for.

Hard work, long hours, close thought, and hard fare at length undermined my poor brother's constitution, and destroyed his health. Instead of being able to relieve my poor mother, he was doomed to add greatly to her afflictions. A swelling came under his arms, and then in his back, and though he submitted to painful operations, he never recovered his health. A cough came on at length, and soon it became plain that my brother was in a consumption. He went to Ilkley, and was somewhat better, and returned to his work with fresh spirit; but it was not for long. In five or six weeks he was dead. He suffered patiently, and he died in peace. Though unutterably fond of life, he was resigned to the will of his heavenly Father, and prepared to die. But his death was a terrible trial to my poor mother. Her love to all her children was great; but Samuel was her first-born, and her best; and her love for him was unbounded. She hung over his bed as long as he lived, with great anxiety, and shed many tears, and offered many fervent prayers. And when he was gone, though she believed that all things would work for her good, she mourned him long with tears, and she mourns and weeps for him yet. She never murmurs against God, yet she seldom can speak of her departed son without tears, though it is now more than thirty years since his death.

My brother had fallen in love with an own cousin, but her parents refused to allow her to be married to him; and this might tend to shorten his life. In love, as in other things, he did nothing by halves. He loved most devotedly, and his disappointment was a very severe trial. His cousin died about six months after himself.

My brother left his books for the one who should be fondest of reading, and that, in my mother's judgment, was myself. They were accordingly given to me, and the chief of them are still in my possession. I often wish he were living now, and could share my lot of books. He little thought, poor youth, that I should be so well supplied with books; much less did he think that I should ever take part in making books more plentiful and cheap to others.

My mother sometimes thought that God had taken away my brother because she was not worthy of such a son: she thought it was too great an honour for a person so unworthy to have a son a preacher. This led me to resolve that I would try to be good and endeavour to become a preacher, that I might take my brother's place, and comfort my mother, and show her that her thoughts on this subject were not correct. And though I often forgot my resolution, yet it often came back to my mind, and at length it was realized. And more than that; my mother has lived to see several of her sons preachers, and one of them a writer and printer as well.

But I must now come more directly to the History of my own Life. And here let me observe, that instead of dividing my history into *years* or *periods*, according to the usual plan, I shall divide it into *subjects*. I shall follow a similar plan to that which Henry follows in his history of Great Britain. He divides his history into chapters as other historians do; but each chapter is confined to one *subject*. In one chapter he gives the history of the *Laws* of the empire for a certain period, in another a history of its religion, in another of its commerce, in another of its literature, and so on all through. And this is the plan which *I* shall follow. I shall divide my history into chapters, but the chapters will mostly treat on different *subjects*. One chapter will be a chapter of *Sorrows*, another of *Joys*. One chapter will give my history as a *Reader*, another will give my history as a *Writer*. One will contain an account of my opinions;—of the opinions with which I began life,—the changes which my opinions have undergone,—the opinions which I hold at present, with a statement of the value which I set on them. Another chapter will contain an account of what I have done with a view to promote the improvement and welfare of my fellow-men,—of what I should have liked to have done,—of what I intend to do if I should ever be able, and of what I should wish my friends and other people to do, and what I think they might do if they would try. In one chapter I may give a history of my connection with the Old Connexion of Methodists, in another the history of my connection with the New Connexion, and in another a history of what I have had to do with Quakers, Unitarians, &c. In one chapter I may give an account of myself as a preacher, a sermon-maker, a lecturer, &c., in another I may give an account of my experience as a teetotaler, and of my labours as a teetotal advocate. In one chapter I may give an account of what I have had to do with unbelievers, and in another of what I have had to do with religious revivalists, and professors of full sanctification. One chapter will be given to early recollections, to remarkable dreams, to curious temptations, and other remarkable things. In one chapter I may give a number of revelations with respect to things future, or a number of prophecies some of which I *know* will be fulfilled, and others of which I have reason to *believe* will come to pass. In one chapter I shall speak of myself as a Printer, a Publisher, and a Bookseller, and give a history of what I have had to do with other printers, publishers, and booksellers. Some chapters will have to be added of a mixed character, embracing several subjects, and containing anecdotes, corrections of errors, accounts of things omitted in former chapters, together with a full list of all the false, and foolish, and wicked, and impossible stories which have been forged or fabricated and circulated respecting me from the time I began to be a preacher and reformer to the present time. And first, I shall begin with a Chapter of Sorrows.

CHAP. III.

A CHAPTER OF SORROWS.

There are several things connected with this part of my history which I cannot relate without some degree of reluctance. I refer to the sufferings and humiliations through which I had to pass at one period of my life in consequence of extreme poverty. I have many friends now who are rich, and who have never been any thing else but rich. I have some friends who occupy high places in society, and who mingle with those who occupy the highest. And some of those friends may feel uncomfortable when they learn, that the person whom they have acknowledged as their friend, whom they have welcomed to their houses, and treated as a brother and an equal, had the humblest origin, and has passed through the depths of poverty and want. Still, as a knowledge of those things is necessary, to enable people properly to understand other parts of my history, and as this history would fail to accomplish one great object for which it is written if those tales of poverty and hardship were left out, I shall give them at full length. And if there be any who cannot bear to have such things known respecting one whom they have been accustomed to receive as a brother and whom they reckon as their friend, they must give me up.

But perhaps my wealthy friends will not be troubled at those revelations. Perhaps they will remember that poverty is not a crime, and that when it is not the result of crime it is, in reality, no disgrace. Perhaps they will remember that the best and wisest one of our race was poor,—that at one time he was a working carpenter, and that at another he lived on what was given him by his friends, and had not where to lay his head. Perhaps they may remember that poverty was the lot of Luther in his early days, and of George Fox and Wesley, and that some even of the reigning monarchs of our times have been poor and pennyless in their day.

But whether they remember these things or not, I must tell my story. The poor will bear with me, and reap comfort from the tale of my sorrows. The poor, especially the *young* that are poor, will learn from my story that however great their poverty, and however severe their trials, they have still a right to hope, and may still become as happy as they would wish to be. The poor young man, who is almost famishing for want of food, and who is fancying in his troubles that the way to knowledge, to usefulness and happiness is shut against him, may find out his comfortless notion to be a mistake by reading this story, and take heart again. He may learn not only that there is a way to knowledge, to usefulness, and to happiness from the midst of want and sorrow, but that want and sorrow are themselves great teachers and benefactors of youth,—that there are lessons to be learned from them that can be learned from no other teachers, and blessings to be derived from them that can be derived from no other source. I shall, therefore, as I have said, tell the tale of my sorrows without reserve, and leave the results with God. To begin then;—

I was born with a weak and delicate constitution. My mother had more trouble with me during my childhood, than with any other of her children. From the first that I can recollect, I do not remember that ever I enjoyed for any great length of time very good health. My stomach was always disordered, and my food never seemed to agree well with me. From the age of eight to twelve or fourteen, I recollect being so very weak in my knees, that I could scarcely ever go an errand of any length without having to sit down on the road to rest myself; and frequently I was so feeble, that when I had once sat down, it was with very great difficulty I could get up again. Going up and down steps was especially a very great trial to me. I could contrive to get *up* a few steps without falling, but I could hardly contrive to get down again without falling, unless I had something to hold by. And even then I could not get down without great pain. This was especially the case during the winter season. During the summer season I was better and stronger. This I attribute in a great measure, to bathing in cold water during the summer, a practice of which I was exceedingly fond, and in which I used to indulge very freely. This weakness and pain in my knees led to other sufferings. I used to fetch milk from the Back Lane, perhaps nearly half-a-mile from where we lived. This was a greater distance than I could walk at once, and at times I had to sit down on the snow or the cold flags to rest myself. This gave me serious colds, and injured my health still more, as well as increased my sufferings. I was seldom free from soreness in my chest, and I had frequently painful and violent coughs. Many a time did I cough almost the whole day long, and at night I was often deprived of my sleep by my coughs for hours and hours together.

During one part of my early life, my father was in better circumstances for awhile. He received some property from his father's estate, and became a manufacturer of cloth. But about the close of the French wars, there was a very great fall in the price of wool, and consequently in the price of cloth. This, with other unfavourable events, caused a great and general panic amongst the cloth manufacturers, and perhaps amongst tradesmen generally. My father could not sell his cloth at times for much more than the wool had cost him. He was unable to go on any farther without involving himself and his family in ruin; so he gave up. He was in some debt at the time; but he paid every person his own in full. After that we were very poorly off at times indeed. We had to begin to earn our bread by labouring for other people at a time when work was exceedingly scarce, and for several years we were in very great difficulties, and had to suffer grievous hardships. Sometimes we had no work, and when we had work, wages were very low, while provisions were very high. I believe that for a year together, the whole family, consisting of nine or ten persons, did not earn more than twenty shillings per week. Out of that sum from four to five would go for rent, and something would have to go for coals and taxes. And at that time flour was seven shillings and sixpence per stone, and oatmeal was dear in proportion. We, of course, were unable to obtain sufficient to supply our daily wants. I recollect being for years together during that period of my life without ever having sufficient to satisfy the cravings of hunger, except on rare occasions. When I look back upon that period of my life, it seems to me at present as if I had spent it in one long continued state of famine. We were of course unable to spend much in clothing. I recollect going up and down at times without shoes and stockings; and often were my shoes unable to protect my feet from the cold and wet. My other garments were often in as bad a state of repair as my shoes and stockings. We were often both ragged and hungry. Of course, my parents could do but little for what is called the education of their children in these circumstances. Almost the only opportunity I had of learning any thing, except what I might learn at home, was by attending the Sunday School. When we had work we had no time to go to school; and when we had not work we had nothing with which to pay school wages: so that a Sunday School was our only resource. What little learning, therefore, I did get, I got it at home from my brothers and sisters, and at the Sunday School. I recollect my eldest sister and my elder brothers teaching me my letters from a large family Bible that we had, and I also recollect teaching my younger brothers their letters afterwards from the same great book.

I am not certain whether the want of sufficient clothing, and the want of a sufficient supply of suitable food, did not tend to make me worse in health than I otherwise might have been; but I recollect that I was far from either enjoying good health or much bodily vigour during this part of my life. I also recollect being very much troubled with dreadful and indescribably awful dreams, and for several months during certain parts of the year I was accustomed to rise during my sleep, and walk about the house in a state of sleep for hours together.— I say in a state of sleep: but I cannot exactly describe the state in which I was. It was not *perfect* sleep, and yet I was not properly awake. My eyes were open, and I saw, as far as I can remember, the things around me, and I could hear what was said to me. But neither what I saw nor what I heard seemed to have power to penetrate far enough into my soul to awake me properly. During those occasions, I was frequently very unhappy, dreadfully unhappy, most horribly miserable. Sometimes I fancied I had been doing something wrong, and my fancied offence seemed horrible beyond all expression, and alarmed and overwhelmed me with unutterable terrors and distresses. On one occasion I fancied that both I and my father had been doing something wrong, and this seemed most horrible and distressing of all; and as I wandered about in my mysterious state, I howled most piteously, and cried and wept as if my heart would break. I never recollect being roused from that dismal state while I was walking about the house, except twice. Once was when I struck my shins violently against the edge of a large earthenware bowl and hurt myself sadly; and another was when I was attempting to go up the chimney: I put my foot upon the fire and burnt myself, and that awoke me.

I suffered in this way for several years. After I went to bed at night I soon fell asleep, and slept perhaps an hour or nearly two. I should then begin to cry, or moan, or howl, and at times to sing. One night I sang a whole hymn of eight verses through; the hymn in Wesley's Hymn Book, beginning

> With glorious clouds encompassed round,
>   Whom angels dimly see,
> Will the unsearchable be found
>   Or God appear to me?

It is a foolish and melancholy hymn, but at that time I thought it very good and solemn, and I sang it in a melancholy tune. After crying or singing for a time, I rose from my bed and began to walk about the house, going from one room to another, sometimes howling or crying in the most pitiable manner, sometimes shrieking with terror, sometimes silent and sad, and sometimes comparatively calm and even playful. Sometimes I fancied myself looking after birds' nests; and then again, fancying that some one had taken a nest away, I should go up and down crying, 'They've ta'en it; they've ta'en it.' Sometimes I fancied Bonaparte had come, and taken possession of the country; and then I cried out at the stretch of my voice, 'The Sickener's come; the Sickener's come!' Once I fancied that my father had stolen some water from a neighbour's pump, and even this seemed a horrible offence at the time. At another time I fancied that he had stolen a neighbour's cows, and that the cows had flown back over the houses and fields to their pastures again. That night the burden of my cry was, 'John Waite's cows: John Waite's cows!' I should generally walk up and down in this melancholy way, three or four, or even five or six hours each night. I sometimes got up before my parents and some others of the family had gone to bed. Then they would talk to me and call, Joseph, Joseph, and try to awake or arouse me. I heard all they said, I saw their faces, and saw the light, and the fire, and all other things: but nothing that they said or did had power properly to awake me. I still went on with my crying or my melancholy work, till the time for my awaking of myself arrived. At other times I did not rise from my bed to begin my nightly walks till my parents and the rest of the family were all asleep, and all the lights put out. Then I walked the house alone and in the dark, and did, I hardly know what, and suffered at times what words are unable to describe. When left thus in the dark and alone, I frequently fancied that I had people around me, my play-fellows and the like; and at times I fancied that I was playing with them at our usual games. When I hurt my shins against the large bowl I fancied that I was playing at *cat*, as we called it, a game resembling crickets a little; and having struck the *cat*, I was running with all my might to *get one*, when I struck against the hard sharp edge of the bowl, and awoke shortly after. In general, perhaps in all cases except two, I walked till nature was almost exhausted, and then went back to bed without waking, and slept till I was called to my daily work.

This affliction of mine was very distressing and perplexing to my poor parents, especially to my mother; and had my parents had any idea of the horror and bitterness of soul which I endured, they would have been more perplexed and troubled still on my account. My sufferings were enough to have melted the hardest heart in the world to tears, if they could only have felt or understood them. Yet my parents never consulted any physician respecting me at this period of my life. I suppose their limited means would not allow them to go to the expense of consulting a physician; and then again they thought I should get better of myself as I grew stronger, and got older. I was left therefore to suffer without help, and without any means being employed for my recovery. I believe that God has caused all things to work for my good, and that the bitterness and sorrows of this bygone period of my life have been made to contribute to my present happiness. Still, I cannot call to mind how long and grievously I was left thus to suffer without medical advice or help, without thinking and feeling that there was something wrong somewhere, and that all was not done for me that kindness or justice required to be done. Yet I cannot throw the blame on my parents, though I think they would have acted rather differently if they had been differently trained, and been placed under better religious instructions. My mother was as kind as a mother could be, but she had never had the opportunity of learning anything about health and disease. And the preachers whom she helped to support neither helped her to books, nor gave her verbal instructions on such subjects. And she had never been ill herself, except of the headache perhaps, and was not therefore able to understand what I suffered. And as for my father, he never was ill scarce a day in his life, not even of the headache, and his knowledge of the laws of health and disease was still less than my mother's if possible. In truth, they nether of them knew anything about any such matters, and those who ought to have enlightened them, rather added to their darkness.

My father was, in many respects, an exemplary man. He was a very conscientious, truthful, honest, and indeed a kind-hearted man as well. As a professor of religion he did honour to the gospel. He never would go into debt if he could help it, and when he did go into debt, he would always pay what he owed as soon as he was able. And he would pay a debt twice rather than not pay it at all, and has done so when there happened to be a doubt on his mind with respect to its payment. But his fault or failing was, that his kind-heartedness was not always joined with wisdom or prudence. He would often help others when we needed help ourselves; and especially would he contribute to the chapel he attended, and to the support of the hired preachers, when he had not even the means of procuring for his children sufficient either to eat or to wear, much less to procure for them the help or advice of a doctor, or needful assistance in the pursuit of knowledge.

My mother was more thoughtful of her children than my father, and more afflicted when unable to obtain for us what we needed. I recollect frequently when, in running along, I had struck my bare feet against the edge of the flags and gone in crying with my toes all bleeding, my mother would weep and say, 'But the children shall have shoes, if I have less to eat myself.' And she had little enough to eat already, poor woman, and even far too little. But my father still was wishful for us to do with as little as possible for ourselves, rather than curtail his contributions to the chapel and to the preachers; and to their shame and disgrace be it spoken, the preachers encouraged him in this. And they do so still. Like the Scribes and Pharisees of old, they make void the law of God by their selfish traditions. The Scribes and Pharisees of old told children, that if they would give what money they had to spare to *them*, they would not be under any obligation to support their needy or helpless parents, though the law of God required them to honour or support their parents. The Scribes and Pharisees of the present day do the same, and a little more. They tell people that God and his cause have the *first* claim on their income, whether it be small or great, and they are very careful to impress people with the idea that God and his cause means *them* (the priests,) and the cause *they* have in hand. Having brought people thoroughly to believe that to support them and their cause is to give to God and to support *his* cause, they tell them to honour the Lord with their substance, and with the *first-fruits* of all their increase; and assure them that if they do this, their barns will be filled with plenty, and their presses will burst out with new wine. They teach he poor people that God has not only a right to the *first* part of their income, but to a *liberal* part,—that in ancient times the people were required to offer to God the *best* of their flocks and the *best* of the produce of their fields and gardens; and they tell them that God requires of his people the best things still. They not only exhort children to give them their spare money, while their sick and aged parents are in need of it; but they exhort poor parents to give them a portion of their scanty earnings, while their children can neither get food nor clothing convenient for them. There are persons at this present time who are giving money to the preachers, while their parents are in the union work-house. There are persons who are contributing to the support or the enrichment of the preachers, while their parents are nearly starving for want. And the preachers *know* it. They know that some of the parties whom they exhort to give money to them, have children without shoes and stockings, without decent clothes or necessary schooling, and that others of them have parents in a state of want, and almost bordering on starvation. Nay more; they even urge people whom they know to be in debt to give. And when men mention their debts as a reason for not subscribing to their funds, the preachers will say to them, 'God is your first creditor; you owe him your *all* : and you ought to let him have the first instalment. Pay your debts; but pay God first.' And worse than this: I myself have even heard a preacher exhort people, if they had *robbed* any one of money in trade, by mixing water with their milk, or by any other kind of fraud, to give the money to them by way of restitution. And when those persons are remonstrated with for their conduct in this respect, they will tell us; that however money be got, or however filthy it be, only let it be given to the cause of God, that is, to *them*, and it will be clean at once. By such exhortations and fraudulent representations, were my poor father and mother induced to contribute to the preachers, while their own poor children were in want of bread. At one time while my parents, from a false idea of duty, were contributing to the support of the preachers, we were thirteen weeks and never had a piece of wheat bread in the house; and it was not always that we had even a piece of oat-cake. At times we had neither oat-cake nor wheat-bread, nor oat-meal, nor flour to make porridge or hasty-pudding. I have seen the time when I have come home so hungry, that I scarce could bear, and yet could find neither bread nor potatoes in the house. I once found an onion, and sought all over the house to find a piece of bread to eat to it; but I could not find any; so I ate the onion by itself at last. Yet the preachers were receiving money from my parents at that very time.

On one occasion my father contrived to manufacture one or two pieces of cloth, and took them over to the Isle of Man, in hopes of selling them there to better advantage. He was absent from home between six and seven weeks. During that period we had nothing on which to subsist, except what my mother could obtain on credit, or what the children could obtain by gathering sticks or begging. During that seven weeks *I* supported myself chiefly by begging. I went along with another young lad that had been somewhat practised in the art of begging, and we succeeded very well. We generally chose to visit out-of-the way places, at a considerable distance from home, for fear of being seen or found out by our friends: for though the business was honest, we were still rather ashamed of it. We should have blushed terribly, and have been sadly confounded, if we had been seen at our calling by our neighbours.

On one occasion, before I had been able fairly to submit to beg, I recollect leaving home about three o'clock in the morning without breakfast, and travelling till between three and four o'clock in the afternoon, without having any thing to eat except a little wild fruit, such as here and there a nut, and now and then a few black-berries, which we collected on our way, and a very few raw mushrooms which we gathered in the fields. At that time one of my brothers was with me, and I very well recollect quarrelling with my poor brother, and almost striking him, because he had thrown away the stalk of a mushroom before it was eaten sufficiently near to the root. I think I never felt the pangs of hunger more than I did that day. About four o'clock in the afternoon, before I had got any food, I was so afflicted with hunger, that I wished I could see a soldier, and that I might prove old enough and tall enough for a soldier myself, that I might enlist and get a shilling, and so be able to procure a little food. If I had met with a soldier, I believe I should have offered to sell myself for a shilling, simply for the sake of getting something with which to purchase bread. We found a field at length, in which something was growing, which we took to be some kind of turnips, though they were so different from any other kind of turnips that we had ever seen, that we could not be certain whether they were fit to eat or not. We could not even tell whether they were poisonous or not, for we had none of us ever seen any thing like them before. Notwithstanding this, our hunger was such that we took a few roots, and began to eat them, and we relished them very much. It was a warm day, and the roots were so juicy and rich, that they served both for food and for drink. Though doubtful whether the roots were wholesome or poisonous, I eat till I could eat no more; till I was sickly, in fact. The root of which we ate so heartily was Mangold Wurzel. At length we went to a house by the way-side, and asked for something to eat. They gave us a quantity of rice boiled in milk, which we eat with the greatest greediness; and oh what a luxury it was to me! No one who has not felt something like the same degree of hunger, can imagine with what relish and delight we ate up that apron full of rice. I never tasted any thing more delicious in my life, though I have since tasted luxuries of almost every kind.

We then called at another house, and got some cold fruit pudding; and that was as pleasant as the rice had been, and perhaps more welcome, because more solid and substantial. After that day's trials I was not so delicate about begging as I had been before, but went out almost daily, and either called at houses, or asked relief from persons whom we met on our way, and that without much ceremony. And after we began to beg freely, we were always able to obtain what supplied our wants, and often something over besides. And we could have obtained much more than we did, if we had chosen to make the most of our calling. But we never did. Still, we always obtained bread enough and to spare, and we frequently obtained tolerable supplies of money as well. Sometimes we met with harsh and unkind refusals, and sometimes with cruel jeers and taunts, and even with threats; but generally speaking we met with kind consideration and relief. I still remember many of the houses where we used to be most kindly treated, and where we used to get the best supplied, and I have often felt a wish, since I was placed in different circumstances, to visit them again, and pay them, at least with thanks, for the kindness I received at their hands. We always got well supplied with bread, and often with richer kinds of meat, at the Earl of Harewood's, and if ever we met with any members of the family, we were sure to receive money as well. And we always received money from the old clergyman also at Harewood; the same old man that is preacher there still. Though a thorough-going Calvinist, he was still always gentle and kind in his conduct towards us. He never refused us food, and I don't recollect that he ever sent us away with less than sixpence in money. He little knew what kind of a person he was feeding, when he was feeding me. He little knew what thoughts would pass through my mind in after life. He little thought how great a heretic I should become, and what a lot of heterodox tracts I should write and send abroad. How little we know of the future life of the child that asks our aid! How little we know what events may hang on the life we are asked to sustain! It is true, the hungry ragged child who solicits our help may become a thief, a profligate, an unbeliever; but he may become something far different; he may become something far better. He may become, if preserved by your charity, a man of worth and greatness. He may become a monarch of a mighty empire. He may become a man of learning and philosophy. He may become a teacher of the ignorant, a helper of the poor, a benefactor of his race. It may be a youthful Luther that stands begging before you barefoot; for Luther was once a poor barefoot beggar boy. It may be a youthful Milton or Cowper that asks you for bread, or a youthful Jesus or Paul.

On one occasion we ventured to beg rather nearer home than usual, though it was still several miles away. Alas, how dreadfully was I confounded when the servant came to the door of one of the houses at which we called, to find that it was a daughter of a near neighbour of ours, that knew me very well. However it was too late to conceal our business; our object was manifest to the servant, so we made the best of it we could. And she, poor girl, was very kind and pitiful, and relieved us very liberally.

On another occasion I was as sadly put about in a somewhat different way. We had got a quantity of provisions, and had got within a mile or two of home. We were busily at work dividing our receipts on the side of the road, when quite unexpectedly a neighbour came riding by on horseback. He knew us, and he soon discovered our business. We were sadly confounded, and he saw our confusion, but he did not insult or reproach us. He simply exclaimed, ah, ah, I have found you out, and smiled, and rode rapidly on. And I never heard that he exposed us to any one, or made any talk about the matter.

We generally travelled about twenty miles a day, and if we had chosen to take advantage of every opportunity of getting money or provisions that came in our way, we could easily have obtained several shillings a day, besides plenty of almost every thing else. But we were not very greedy. We begged from necessity, and were satisfied when our wants were supplied. We never entertained the thought of making begging a regular trade ; at least *I* did not. I followed it only for want of better employment, and was ready to change it for other employment as soon as other employment could be got. I should have been glad to work for a shilling a day at the hardest kind of work I ever had. We therefore pursued our occupation rather carelessly. Still, easily as we took things, we always got plenty of food and frequently a shilling or more each in addition.

We almost always went one round. I never felt any inclination to make fresh acquaintances after the first or second round. On one occasion however we deviated from that plan, and took another route ; but we had a weary and unprofitable day. We started about four o'clock in the morning, with a half-penny between us in our pocket. We passed through Leeds on the way to Tadcaster and York, and made only two attempts to beg all the day. It was a new road, and every thing was strange, so we were very timid, and scarce dare enter a house at all. We called at one house and got a few cold potatoes ; and near the end of the village we went into another, but there appeared to be some one very ill in the house, for the family seemed all in confusion and anxious excitement. They could not therefore attend to us, so we had to go away unserved. The few cold potatoes therefore was all that we got in that village, and we were too discouraged to call elsewhere. We took a turnip or two from a field as we went along, and that was all we had to eat until late in the evening. It was our purpose when we started that morning, to go as far as York, and there to spend the night. I had heard that the *tide* came up in the river Ouse at York, and I was very desirous to see it. The ebbing and flowing of the tide seemed to me a most wonderful and mysterious thing. It seemed to me at that time the sublimest and most interesting of all miracles. I had often therefore longed to see the sea, or at least a tidal river, that I might see this miracle for myself, and it was partly to gratify my eager desires in this respect, that we had left our customary round, and ventured on another. Then again it was March, and the spring assizes had just taken place at York, and we had heard that a noted thief from Stanningley, a neighbouring village to our own, was to be hung, and, shocking as it may seem, a wish to see the execution of this thief was an additional motive in inducing us to visit York. But our poor success in begging shook our resolution, and when we got within a few miles of York, more than twenty miles from home, we both began to feel uncomfortable, and secretly to wish ourselves at home. We had no money but the solitary half-penny already mentioned. And we had no friends or relations about York: we were perfect strangers there. And though the weather was fine, yet the season was cold, and the nights were very frosty, so that we could hardly think of sleeping out of doors. What should we do? We first betrayed to each other our reluctance to go forward by moving slowly along, and looking queerly and significantly in each others face. But neither of us was disposed to give in first. We were unwilling to appear cowardly to each other. At length we agreed to decide the matter, if I remember rightly, by tossing up our halfpenny, and thus we were led to turn our faces homewards again. It was four o'clock in the afternoon or after when we set off back. And we had more than twenty miles to go to Bramley. And we were tired already, snd hungry and dis-spirited besides. Still, we had no sooner decided to return, than we set off running at a rapid rate. To enable me to walk or run still faster, I took off my shoes and stockings, and for several miles went barefoot. At Tadcaster we spent our solitary halfpenny, and then moved onwards towards Bramley, poor and hungry enough. Tadcaster would be about nineteen miles from

Bramley, and we had already walked about twenty-eight miles. This nineteen miles we must walk chiefly in the dark, and so far as we could see, with no supply of food. But things turned out better than we looked for. We had not got many miles out of Tadcaster, when we overtook a decent looking man, who entered into conversation with us. We told him what we were, where we had been, what we had been about, and how we were circumstanced, and without being asked, he called at the first public-house we came to, and bought us each a penny cake, and a little small beer. The cakes were soon gone, and the beer too, and off we set again, cheerful and lively enough. Indeed, such was the effect of the small beer upon me, that it half intoxicated me, and weary as I was, I began to run after the rabbits that were feeding on Brammam moor, as we passed along. The name of the person who thus kindly relieved us was Haddock. He was a master chimney sweeper, residing in Marsh Lane, Leeds. We walked with him all the way to Leeds. He talked very kindly to us, and advised us, before he left us, not to venture on such an excursion again.

When we got between Leeds and Bramley I was so worn out with fatigue and want of sleep, that it was with the greatest possible difficulty that I could keep myself from lying down on the road, and falling asleep on the cold wet ground. I felt as if I could have lain down comfortably even in a ditch, and slept without difficulty, half covered with water or mud, cold and frosty as it was. I am not certain whether I did not sleep as I walked along. I believe I did occasionally. I was thoroughly exhausted. Though I had now got so near home, yet it seemed as if it would be impossible for me to reach it. Yet we still moved on, and with great effort I succeeded at last, and got to my father's house about twelve o'clock at night. But I never shall forget that day. I never ventured so far from home again during that period of my life, and I never again ventured out of my usual track in pursuit of my melancholy occupation.

I sometimes tried to get food by fishing, but here my success was exceedingly small. I recollect starting one morning early without breakfast. Instead of my breakfast I plucked and rubbed some ears of wheat as I went along, and I plucked a few more and put in my pocket to eat on the water-side. I caught several small fishes, but nothing that would have bee likely to sell for any thing. At length dinner time came, and I was very hungry. I had no bread, nor had I any thing with which to buy bread. So I had to content myself with eating my few ears of corn. But my hunger was not appeased. I took therefore and eat the few small fishes which I had caught. They were raw, to be sure, but they had got partly dried and baked in the sun, so that they were not quite so disagreeable as one might think. Still, the next day I was very unwell. My bowels were terribly disordered, and I suffered great and long continued pain. Next day I was better, but still my lot was one of want and sorrow.

It was a very great trial to me to be unable to obtain sufficient clothing to cover me properly. I felt it a great humiliation when I had to mingle with a crowd of others, to see so many that were well and comfortably drest, while I had scarce raiment sufficient to cover my nakedness. I recollect feeling this part of my affliction very keenly one day when I was going to Woodhouse Moor, where there was to be a large meeting of persons to witness a *Gelstick* match between two young men that were neighbours of ours. At that time my trowsers, besides being sadly out of repair in other respects, had got torn from the bottom quite up to the thigh. I fastened the severed parts together as well as I could with some thorns from the hedges, and in that plight trudged along to make one of the mighty company. But I was far from comfortable. I was afraid to go near any one that was decently clothed, for fear they should feel my presence as a disgrace, and scold me or force me away. While they therefore walked on the causeway, I took the cart road; and when the crowd was assembled on the moor, I stood alone and solitary.

One winter I recollect I had no hat nor cap, so I used as a substitute the top of an old stocking, which I stretched and pulled over my ears, and it kept them very warm.

I said that work was very scarce, and that when we had work we had to work very hard. That was the case when I was from nine to twelve years of age. I recollect very well being called up in the morning before it was light, and having to work at winding bobbins till eight or nine, and sometimes ten o'clock at night. I used to work till the skin of my fingers was quite worn through, and I had to use many expedients to prevent the thread from cutting to the bone. It frequently pierced to the quick, and caused me grievous pain. And I worked for weeks and months together with my fingers and hands cut through in this way, and often bleeding in several places at once. Then, to make this hard labour more painful still, I had very poor health at that time of my life. I had a very distressing head-ache about two full days every week. I awoke with it in the morning, I carried it through the day, and I had to go to bed with it at night. At times I used to run away from my work, especially in summer, in hopes of obtaining a little relief from the violence of my head-ache, by exposing my forehead to the cool air as it blew; but I often made bad worse by this means. Before I had been away from my work above an hour perhaps, my father would be after me, and instead of obtaining relief from my wearisome and sickening head-ache, I should get a good flogging for my pains. I frequently complained of my head-ache to my father and mother, but I got but little sympathy I fear. My father I fancy did not believe my complaints. He never had suffered much from any kind of ache himself, and perhaps he was unable in consequence to feel for those that did so suffer. My mother would believe me, perhaps, but she was not master in those matters. Hence I never obtained a day's rest from my work on account of my head-ache all my youthful life through.

Again, I used every morning, whether my head ached or not, after I had eaten my breakfast, which almost always consisted of oat-meal porridge and a little milk, to turn sick, and to go into some private place and throw up again what I had eaten. So that besides being so grievously afflicted with the head-ache, I was weakly and poorly generally.

Then again, even when things were rather better with us than usual, we had but very indifferent supplies of food. For a long time my mother used to have to measure out to us the milk which we had to our oat-meal porridge, in a tea cup, and we used to think we were pretty well served if we got the tea cup filled up to the *blue*.

Some may wonder why my parents did not seek for parish relief in their poverty. The reason, I suppose, was an unwillingness to be dependent on others for help, and perhaps the idea that relief could not be obtained without difficulty, and some kind of humiliation.

During my father's absence in the Isle of Man, however, my mother was *obliged* to seek relief from the Town Authorities, and she succeeded, though not without some difficulty, in obtaining a single four shillings and sixpence. The parties who had the disposal of the poor rates seemed to think, that those who never *had* applied for relief, never *ought* to apply, while those who had received town pay for years, were relieved as a matter of course. My mother was greatly distressed at the thought of being beholden to the town for anything, and as soon as she was able, she carried back the sum she had received, and so made all things straight. The truth is, that so far from the Town Authorities willingly helping us in our poverty, they compelled us to *pay* poor rates. Instead of granting us assistance, the Town Authorities made our burdens heavier by their exactions.

And here I may say a few words respecting the old poor law and its administration. Whatever advantages *others* might derive from the old poor law, *we* never derived many from it. Nor can I think that the old poor law, as it was administered at Bramley, was ever a friend to the honest, industrious, and truly deserving part of the poor. The chief part of the poor rates of Bramley were spent on illegitimate children and their mothers, on old worn out thieves, poachers, gamblers, cock-fighters, dog-breeders, and drunken, profligate, idle folks, that would not support themselves and their families by honest labour when they might, but who could succeed, either by importunities or by threats, in extorting money from the Town Authorities. I believe that the old poor law at Bramley did little else but mischief. In nineteen cases out of twenty it was an instrument of oppression to the honest, industrious, deserving poor, and an encouragement to vice to the other part of the poor. Such is my judgment.

One way by which we used to endeavour to obtain supplies of food in our difficulties was by gleaning during harvest, and by gathering sticks in the woods during other portions of the year, and selling them for so much a bundle. I spent many weeks and months, I should think, in nothing else but gathering sticks, and carrying them, sometimes one, and sometimes two miles, in great bundles, and selling them for two-pence, three-pence, or four-pence a bundle. My father too used to join us in those labours, and many a day my father and several of us children have laboured from morning till night for one, or two, or at most three shillings a day. Sometimes I should get a job in gathering potatoes, getting in coals, or assisting in weeding a garden, or collecting stones from a neighbour's field, and by these means help to obtain a little bread for the family. At other times we gathered manure from the streets or from the highways and sold it for bread. But we seldom got much. We were often on the verge of starvation. One year I recollect there was a general failure in the crops of corn: the wheat was out in the fields about Bramley as late as November and December, and never got ripened at all. A cousin of my father's had some very extensive fields of wheat thus belated, and he gave us, along with others of his neighbours, permission to go and take a quantity of it after it had stood in the field till it had sprouted and become unfit for bread. I recollect that much of the bread which we got that year was of a very disagreeable character. We never could bake the cakes hard quite through. A thin crust on the outside could be hardened, but the rest remained like bird-lime or paste. It was very unpleasant to eat, and unwholesome too; but we must either eat that or starve outright.

I may observe that the distress which we suffered was general in our neighbourhood. I have gone through the whole of Bramley, where there ought to have been some hundreds of looms going, and have not heard more than one, or two, or three, in the whole length of the town. There were scores and hundreds of persons entirely out of work. Many of them went off in groups and begged their bread, as I did. Some few, after they got into the way of begging, never returned to regular habits of industry after. Their characters were ruined. But nearly all were glad to return to work as soon as they were able to obtain it.

I believe that my eldest Brother Samuel died in consequence of hard work and hard fare. He was very fond of his mother, as I have said before, and sympathized very much with her in her distresses. It was a great pain to him that his parents should be in debt, and he was wishful to do his utmost to get them out. Hence at the time when he was growing, and ought to have been well fed and lightly worked, he toiled from morning till night, from Monday morning till Saturday night, and by this means I believe, along with hard study and an insufficient supply of wholesome food, he brought on the consumption which ended in his premature removal to another world. But he died very peacefully. He had no doubt of his acceptance with God, or of his future blessedness. But his death was a great affliction to my mother: it weighed down her spirits most fearfully: and that for a very long time. The loss of her affectionate and godly child was the heaviest affliction she ever had, and she weeps at the thought of it to this day.

Our other accommodations were poor in proportion. We had no bedrooms, properly speaking. My parents' bed was in the kitchen, another was in a narrow damp parlour, and the rest were in the work-chambers with the looms and jennies. The air, of course, was impure, and dirt and dust and loathsome smells were so familiar to us, that we seldom if ever felt ourselves annoyed by them. But there were some things that I *did* feel as annoyances. The windows were generally very much broken, and the cold winds blew upon our beds, and in winter often made us very cold. And the roofs were bad, and let in both the wind and rain and snow. I have laid in bed all night too tired and sleepy to keep properly awake, and yet unable to fall properly asleep in consequence of the cold rain continually falling drop, drop, drop upon my head and face. The walls next our bed were not only always damp, but often soaked and even washed with wet. And the boards underneath were soaked as well. And even the snow drifted through upon the bed as well as the rain. I one time, when I awoke in the morning, found a drift of snow on the bed an inch or two thick.

Another calamity was a scarcity of books. I had always a thirst for knowledge, and an eager longing for books; and yet the only books we had in the house were the Bible, Wood's Bible Dictionary, some of Bunyan's works and a few other religious books that had belonged to my eldest brother. And there were no public libraries then; and the preachers neither offered to give or lend us any books, nor tried to make them cheap that people might buy them for themselves or one another. And the richer people generally were as bad as the preachers. Many of them cared little or nothing about books themselves, and as for giving or lending books to their poorer neighbours, they had never been taught such lessons. They were, in those respects, almost as thoughtless or selfish as the preachers. Neither the preachers nor the leading members among the Methodists appear to have had the least desire to spread knowledge, or to make people intelligent and wise. The idea of furnishing the means of improvement in every kind of useful knowledge to their members and to people at large,—the idea of raising the people from ignorance and superstition, and bringing them to be a clever, knowing, free, and godlike race of beings, appears never to have entered into their souls. Either they were too ignorant and brutish ever to think of such a thing, or else they were too selfish to cherish the noble thought and carry it out into action.

One of the greatest, or at least one of the most painful calamities resulting from our long continued poverty, and the general badness and great and continual unsettledness of trade was this: We got the idea that all things on earth were utterly uncertain,—that the world, or at least that part of the world where we were living, was rolling on at random,—that chance, or a dark and malignant fatality, ruled over all,—that the best days of the world had all gone by, and that risks and ruin were now to be our common and unchanging lot. I felt, and others felt as well, as if prosperity was fled for ever from our own part of the world. We had an idea that things were better in America; but as for Europe, its light seemed to have entirely gone out, and its glory and the welfare of its people seemed to have perished for ever. Hence we were always afflicted with the fear of want. Even when we had plenty for the present, we had no good comfortable hope that we should have plenty long. For myself, and I believe it was so with most others at that time, I lived continually in the fear of starvation, in dread of literally dying for want of food. There was one way, it is true, in which it seemed possible to secure a regular supply of food, and only one, and that was by becoming a soldier. But soldiering in those days was a fearful thing; it looked more like the way to speedy death, than to plenty and an easy life.

I say that others, I believe, felt the same afflicting and tormenting fears of want with myself. I know that this was the case with my brothers, and I believe it was the case with my parents and their companions too, to some extent. I recollect them sitting and talking on those subjects in the most melancholy way imaginable. Emigration to America was their only hope. And this was the way of their talk. 'It is over with cloth-making,' said one of my father's friends, 'it will never look up again.' 'It is here,' my father would reply, 'I look on it that *we* MIGHT get through, for our time; but it's the children I look at.' And thus the doleful, melancholy sounds of fear fell on our ears perpetually. Oh, those were mournful, miserable times.

How was it that my parents did not trust in God, and cast their care on him? How was it that they did not take the advice of Jesus, to look at the fowls of the air, and to consider the lilies of the field, and, making the best of their lot, rest assured, either that God would give plenty, or make want to work for their good? How was it that they did not look up to God as their father, and feel at rest in him? Why did they not teach their children to look on God as their Father and to rest at Peace in him? I cannot tell. But for one thing they were never taught to regard God so much as a tender and affectionate Parent, as a stern and terrible Law-giver and Judge. Their ideas of God were orthodox; they were dark and repulsive, rather than cheerful and attractive. They *called* God Father in name, but their *idea* of God did not answer to that dear delightful word. Then my parents had human imperfections and weaknesses. Their thoughts and belief were better than their life perhaps in this respect; their trust in God might not be so strong as their notions of his goodness might require. Then their trials were very severe, and they were long continued, and it requires great virtue indeed to bear up under such long continued distresses, and to keep alive hope under so many and grievous disappointments. Or perhaps my parents did trust in God in general, and only spoke despairingly on rare occasions; while I, perhaps, more fearful and melancholy than they, remembered only their words of distrust and fear, while I forgot their expressions of hope and confidence. But my belief is that they never were taught properly to trust in God, either by sermons or examples, and that in this respect their religion was defective. But however it was, those days were terrible days. Some people talk of the days of their childhood as their happiest days, and one man asks,

'Who would not wish once more to be a boy?'

But the days of *my* childhood were days of gloom and sorrow, and there is one at least who would *not* wish once more to be a boy. My childhood's pleasures were very few indeed; while my trials and griefs were both great and almost ceaseless, and I almost wonder at times that I am still alive.

Besides the sorrows I have already mentioned, there were others, which, though little to look upon now, were painful enough at the time. My brothers and I used to be more nick-named than others, more frequently beaten, and wronged, and insulted than others, and worse teazed and tormented in general. We were differently trained from most others also, and were less bold and more sensitive in consequence. Our parents used to warn us against fighting, though others should strike or insult us first. And this, with other advices and influences, tended to make us feel cowardly and timid, and allow others to usurp a sort of lordship over us, and to practise their little tyranny over us. Then this made us shun the company of other boys to a great extent, and lead a more solitary and unsocial life than they. Then we generally felt our inferiority to others in other respects. My father would not allow us to play as other parents allowed their children to play. He looked upon play of all kinds as utterly irreligious, as utterly inconsistent with being good. For a child to be good or religious, according to his opinion, was to give up all play or recreation of every description, and not even to go to listen to a band of music that might chance to pass the door. And as he wished us to be religious, he always discouraged in us all love for play or recreations. Hence he never bought us a top, a whip, a marble, a ball, or any other kind of toy from the day of our birth to this hour. And he never made us a *gelstick*, a *nur*, a *spell*, a *kite*, a cricket stick, or *swing*, nor did he ever, that I recollect, either give us a half-penny towards buying a toy, or assist or direct us in making a play-thing for ourselves. The whole system of play and recreation in his estimation was an 'abomination, and he was consistent enough to keep himself unspotted from it in all respects. My eldest brother had had the same kind of notions when he first became a Methodist, and accordingly flung all his play-things away. But *he* changed his views as he grew elder, and would have ventured, in a field by himself, or with us, to have looked at a kite, or assisted in flying it, and have ventured even to have a *rise* with a *nur*. I recollect my father reproving him once for taking such a liberty as this. But my brother did not regard it as a sin. And, considering the notions of the Methodists of those days on such subjects, this was no slight proof that my brother was a free and independent inquirer, and had made some progress in disenthralling himself from Methodistical errors and superstitions. But I'm rather digressing. I was wishing to say that my father's notions on those subjects, and his conduct flowing from those notions, was an additional source of misery to us in our youthful days. We scarce ever had a play-thing worth looking at, till we got to be something like young men. The other boys were always before us in this respect. They had nice round *nurs;* we had only rough and ill-formed ones, or none. They had nice *gelsticks*, and sometimes *spring-spells;* while we had neither *gelstick* nor *spell* at all, or only poor and unsightly ones which we made for ourselves. And so with most other things. I recollect crying nearly one whole day for a half-penny to buy a top, before I could get it. And no one can imagine, who has not felt the like, how miserable I was that day, till I got what I craved; though I grant I was happy enough when I had succeeded. It was my mother that gave me the half-penny; my father would never have thought of giving me any thing.

But this was not all. My father's ideas about the evil of play carried him farther, and made him very unjust. If we chose to work very hard, we could sometimes get through a day's work in nine or ten hours, and so have a few hours to ourselves for play. At times therefore I used to ask my father in a morning, to *set me my work;* to tell me how much I must do, how many bobbins, or how much yarn, I must wind for the day; and at times he would tell me. But he always took care to tell me enough, and at times even set me more than he thought I could do. He knew that I wanted to have a little time to go out to play, and he set me more to do on purpose to keep me from what he thought danger. But that was not the worst. It was bad, but not half nor a tenth as bad as what frequently followed. I was vexed enough to have to ask and pray so long to have my work set,—I was more vexed still to have my reasonable request so frequently denied,—and I was vexed again, when my work was set me, to have such unreasonable tasks required,—but what was my grief and my rage when my father, after my enormous task was done, refused to let me at liberty. Yet this he did over and over again. Sometimes he would set me fresh jobs, and at other times he would question whether I had really got through my work so soon. This provoked me and enraged me to the utmost. It made me miserable beyond all expression. Sometimes I abused my father, and reproached him for his injustice to his face. Then came a threat, or a flogging with a sharp heavy rope. Then I reproached him again, while I cursed him in my heart. Then flogging or threatening again. But flog me as often and severely as he would, I never submitted in soul; I felt it was cruel and unjust, and in my soul I resolved on revenge. At times I should run out of the house, and take off to the fields. Sometimes my father would run after me and bring me back, while at others he would allow me to escape, but prepare me a flogging against I returned at night. At times I was so enraged at my father's injustice and cruelty, that I did serious mischief to the work or the things in the house. Once while my father was flogging me in this way, I broke loose from him, and, grasping hold of as many threads of my father's web as I could hold in my hand, I tore them all out, and thus made him a day or two's work, besides making a blemish in the cloth. Then catching immediately hold of the scales in which they weighed the yarn, I snapped the ropes asunder in a moment, and ran off, howling and threatning with all my might. I declared, as I ran past my mother, that I would drown myself, that I would, and off I flew. This was the most terrible vengeance I ever took. My mother was sadly distressed, for she knew I was treated unjustly; and she was terribly alarmed as well, for she feared I should really be destroying myself. And my father was partly tamed after that. I think he began to see into the folly of his proceedings, for I don't recollect that he flogged me when I returned at night, nor do I recollect that he was ever so unreasonable or cruel to me after.

My mother often used to remonstrate with my father about his flogging me so severely, and so did my eldest brother. My eldest brother used to speak very strongly and severely at times. I recollect him telling my father at one time that he never was fit to have children, that he knew no more how to manage them than the door post, adding, that even I had more sense in one of my little fingers than he had in all his body together. This was far from being true, but I fancy my father must have felt that it was partly deserved.

In another place I have spoken of my father as kind-hearted, and he was so. He was kind-hearted even towards me. Nor do I lack proofs of what I say. He would have toiled all night to get us bread, and no one could have grieved him worse than for any one to hurt or annoy us. He has toiled like a horse in his day, and has carried loads too heavy for two men. He has walked fifty miles a day, and carried a pack of forty or fifty pounds weight, to procure for us the means of support. And if he heard that any one was ill using us, he could not contain himself. Though, in general he was so mild and meek that he got the nick name of quiet Jonathan, yet when some one went and told him once that a man was ill using me, he ran off to my help immediately, though he was partly undressed and in the act of washing himself, and prepared to chastise my oppressor. And I have known him do the like for one of my elder brothers. My father is at this time suffering almost total blindness, brought on chiefly, I believe, by hard work for his children. And the joy that he has had to see us all do well, and especially to see me do well, has been almost too great for his heart to hold. He has wept scores of times for joy at our welfare. Then why did he treat me so harshly and cruelly? I answer, he was cruel because he was kind; he used me so ill because he loved me so well; he was concerned for the welfare of my soul. It was not for lack of kindness that he was unjust and cruel towards me, but because his kindness was joined with orthodox Methodistical superstition. I lay the blame of my father's unreasonableness and of his oppressions of his children, on the infernal delusions which have been blended with religion. If a man thinks that his child's soul will be doomed to eternal and unutterable torments if it be not weaned from childish play, and brought to experience some strange, mysterious or fanatical sort of transformation, he must, to be consistent, if he loves his child, do as my father did.—

Love for his child itself will prompt him to do so. What my father needed was, not more kindness, but, as I have said before, more prudence, more sense ; more rational, more enlightened, more true and worthy views of religion, of God, and of human nature. It was ignorance, or his false and superstitious notions about religion then that were to blame for his cruel, unjust, and unreasonable conduct towards his children, and not a lack of natural kindness.

There was one thing happened during the days of our poverty which was regarded at first as an additional calamity, but which afterwards proved to be a great blessing. It was this : the person from whom we obtained some work was unable to pay us our wages in *money*, and so paid my father with flour instead. We had, in consequence, more flour than we wanted, and were obliged to dispose of a portion to others, in order that we might have money to purchase other things which we needed. This unexpectedly led us into shop-keeping. When people had once had flour at our house, they came for it again; and when they had got into the way of coming for flour, they wanted other things along with it. This led us to purchase a supply of different articles for sale. Then other articles were wanted by customers, and we procured them also, and sold them, and thus became at length regular shopkeepers in a little way. This assisted us in obtaining what was necessary for the support of the family. My mother also got some draperies, and visited one or two neighbouring towns or villages that she might dispose of them more rapidly, and wonderfully well she succeeded. We were all glad to make the best we could of this new means of obtaining a living and of getting out of debt, and I, as well as others of the family, took part in the work. When I had no other employment, I sometimes went up and down in hawking cotton and other similar things about the neighbourhood. Our circumstances improved from that time. I do not recollect after this that I ever suffered much for want of bread. We never neglected our old work of weaving and spinning, &c., to attend to the new work of shop-keeping which had come thus unlooked for into our hands. We never depended upon the shop for a living, but went on with our usual employments diligently, whenever work was to be obtained. After this also the cloth trade itself began to improve, and work became more regular. Wages also rose a little, and flour and the like got cheaper. But here was another evil: we were so anxious to be straight with all the world,—we were so wishful to be completely out of debt, that we worked beyond our strength. I many a time rose in summer by three or four o'clock in the morning, and kept at my work with scarcely any intermission till eight or nine in the evening; and that too at a time when I was growing rapidly. One consequence of this in my case was a partial deformity in my frame, and another was increased affliction from indigestion and general weakness. At this period of my life one shoulder rose considerably above the other, in consequence of such constant and laborious application to the Spinning Jenny. This deformity disappeared afterwards, when I was favoured with a somewhat easier life, and change of employment, &c.

My afflictions in other respects were overruled for my good. They tended to promote in me a serious thoughtfulness about religion, God, and duty, and to bring me to the ways of godliness. I never was happy in the neglect of religion, and at times I was exceedingly miserable. On some occasions, when at my work spinning, I had such solemn and terrible thoughts of God, of duty, of my accountability, and of eternity, that I started suddenly from the floor, as if raised by some violent shock; and when I indulged in the common sports and pastimes of my age, I never found any thing in them to satisfy my mind, and seldom sufficient even to divert it for any considerable length of time. I had cravings which no pastimes nor pleasures within my reach could satisfy. I had besides a consciousness that I was made for something higher than to seek for satisfaction in such things as those: yet I was unwilling to deny myself and give up my will to the will of God, or to my sense of duty. At an earlier period of my life it was knowledge chiefly that I wanted, a knowledge of what was right and wrong, of what constituted true goodness or religion; but at *this* period of my life it was my *will* that stood most in my way. I saw the right, to some extent, and I approved it too; but had not the heart at once to begin and practise it. I saw what was wrong too in many particulars, and even shrank from it or trembled at it; I could not help regarding it with dread: but still my inclinations towards it were very powerful. I found it difficult even to *attempt* to break lose from my evil ways; difficult even to form a resolution to enter on another and better course of life. This struggle lasted for a length of time. Sometimes it was feebler, and at other times more violent ; but at all times it was a source of pain and torment to me. At times, the struggle between conscience and inclination became so violent, and my unhappiness in consequence became so great, that I wished I had never been born. At times I was exceedingly melancholy. I was vexed at everything and pleased with nothing. I was vexed at my parents that had been the instruments in bringing me into the world, and I was vexed at that great and awful Being who had been the *author* of my existence. My soul raged terribly both against the earthly instruments, and the heavenly author of my life. In this melancholy state of mind I frequently left my companions, and wandered alone in the woods, and by the side of the river, or amongst the ruins of a large old abbey about a mile from my father's house.* Sometimes I would wander alone by day, and at other times I would wander or sit solitary by night, thinking, crying, struggling, and yet unwilling to give myself to what I believed to be the will of God. This was the most miserable period of my existence. Bodily toils and bodily wants had been a great affliction, but they were slight and trifling compared with the sufferings which I now endured of a spiritual description.

And then again, to make the matter worse, I was still at a loss to understand what true religion was. I was still ignorant of what was called 'the plan of redemption, and the way of salvation,' and this, I have no doubt, made it the more difficult for me to form the resolution at once to become religious. I still had the impression that there was some great mystery about religion that I should never perhaps be able to understand. I still supposed that it would not be enough to give up all I believed to be evil, and to do what I believed to be my duty. I had still the impression, that denying myself of ungodliness and worldly pleasures, and living soberly, righteously, and godly in this present world, were but a very small part of religion,—that these things were in fact but an *introduction* to religion,—that religion was something different from these,—something far above them ; but what it was, seemed still a mystery. And then again I was afraid that if I did cease to do evil, and begin to do well, I should not be able

* Kirkstall abbey.

to proceed. The erroneous notions that I had been taught about God's grace, made both the beginning and the continuance of a religious life appear a matter over which men themselves had but little or no control. At first I was told that I could do nothing without something called the special or converting grace of God; and then again I was taught that I could not command God's grace, or obtain it whenever I might wish to have it. Religion was represented to me more as something done *for* man by *another*, than as something to be done *by* man *himself*. It was represented rather as a supernatural miracle and mystery, than as obedience to the light of truth, and to the laws enjoined on us by Christ, and written on our hearts or constitutions. It was represented as consisting rather in forms, and beliefs of particular opinions, and in wonderful excitements of feeling, rather than in the regular and orderly cultivation of our own souls, the improvement of our own divine affections and god-like faculties or powers. Instead of being presented to my mind in a rational form, as the most natural and lovely of all things, it was presented to my mind as a dark and mysterious terror, stern beyond measure in its authority, and infinitely terrible in its threats; but dreadfully dark and incomprehensible in its teachings and requirements. I was, in consequence, often at a loss both what to think and what to do. Sometimes I blamed old father Adam, under the impression that *he* had put all things wrong; and at other times I silently blamed the Almighty, for placing Adam in too responsible a situation, and allowing too much to depend on him. I was sorry that God had not placed every one's happiness in his own hands, instead of trusting the interests of all into the hands of Adam, as I had been taught he had done; and at other times I thought God should at least have made it possible for men to fall back again out of existence, if they should happen not to succeed in becoming truly religious, and not keep them on in eternal torments when the object or end of their existence had been unhappily frustrated. And thus I was harrassed and bewildered in my thoughts. The mixture of orthodox delusions with religious truths; the mixture of the doctrines of natural depravity, or birth pollution, and of our accountability for Adam's sin, and of all the foolish notions about the effects of Adam's sin both on us and on the world we live in,—the doctrine of special grace, and trusting in

Christ's merits, and wrong notions about the witness of the spirit, conversion, and sanctification,—the doctrine of God's eternal, universal, and absolute foreknowledge, coupled with the doctrine of eternal life in torments and the like; these doctrines, and others of a similar description respecting the character of God, the trinity, justification by faith alone, and satisfaction to God's justice thro' the death of Christ,—I say these doctrines, all of which I then supposed to be true, so far as I knew any thing about them, being mixed with the simple revelations of religious truth and duty by Jesus Christ, perplexed and bewildered me beyond measure, and increased the apparent difficulty of being religious, a hundred fold. Under the influence of those delusive and perplexing notions, I was for a while set fast. I had a fear that I should never be able to get religion,—that I should never be able to obtain those feelings of delight, that impression of God's favour which they called the witness of the spirit, or to realize that instantaneous regeneration, and that instantaneous second work called sanctification; and yet I was given to understand that without these, all belief in Christ, all love to God and to the truth, all renunciation of sin, all hearty and faithful devotedness to God's will, all love to man, and all efforts for man's good, would be nothing, or worse than nothing; works partaking of the nature of sin, increasing one's guilt and condemnation, and adding to the severities of my eternal damnation. The thought of these difficulties drove me at times to such fearful extremities, that I almost wonder that I did not altogether lose my senses. If God had not kindly watched over me, and led me in the right way even when I saw it not, I should have been driven into madness, or led to put an end to my existence.

CHAPTER IV.

A LITTLE OF MY RELIGIOUS EXPERIENCE.

At this time I gave my parents, especially my mother, very great trouble, and caused them many hours of intense anxiety and grievous fears, both for my present and future safety. My mother often looked at me in sorrow, and sometimes thought and even said that I seemed born to break her heart, and to bring down her grey hairs with sorrow to the grave. What tried her worse perhaps than any thing else, was that I tried to defend myself against her admonitions by asking puzzling questions about religion, and speaking as if I entertained doubts with respect to some of its doctrines. And then again I caused her grief in other ways. My mind sought relief from its anxieties and torment by rushing into various crimes and follies. I never was a drunkard, but I did, at this period of my life, begin to keep company with drunkards; and my parents were as much troubled perhaps on that account as if I had been a drunkard myself. I was also rather fond of boxing or fighting, and often tried my strength in battles with young persons like myself. And this was a source of great terror and grief to my parents.

The last time I had any thing to do with boxing was in a regular set battle with a near neighbour, a little older than myself. I bore the young man no ill-will, and I am not aware that he bore me any; yet somehow or other our respective companions made arrangements for a trial of strength and skill in fighting between us. The meeting took place one Sunday evening. I was then turned sixteen years of age. My father and mother had gone to the chapel, and so had my elder brothers and sisters, all except myself and my next elder brother. To prepare myself for the battle, I got at that time a quantity of home-brewed beer, foolishly fancying that it would make me stronger for the encounter; but this turned out to be a great mistake: it caused me to be sooner exhausted. The battle continued for a length of time, perhaps an hour or nearly so. I was seriously injured in my face, and one of my eyes was swollen up, so that I could scarcely see, while one of my companion's thumbs or wrists was out of joint. Yet neither would yield, and the conclusion of the battle was put off to a future time. But the time never came; the battle was never fought out. While I was engaged in my melancholy work, some one had got my mother news at the chapel of what I was doing, and she came out at once, full of distress and terror, to seek for me. Some one told me she was coming, and I escaped. She still pursued me,—weeping, crying, full of anguish, and out of breath to overtake me. I eluded her search, but made my way home, and got there before her, and placed myself down in a corner near the fire. At length she came, and threw herself over me, weeping, and scarce able to speak. I was overpowered, and cried out, You shall never have to do this again, mother. And she never had. Not long after I gave up my old companions, and my old ways, resolved to give myself to the service of God.

My mind was never at rest while I was living in sin. I was almost always haunted with fears of eternal ruin, as well as troubled with strange longings after something which nothing of an earthly kind had power to bestow. Then my eldest brother Jonathan lost his wife about this time. He was much afflicted with his loss, and I could not help but sympathise with him in his sorrows. He had been always kind to me, and from the first that he began to be religious, had manifested a deal of brotherly, affectionate anxiety to have me brought under the influence of religion also: and his efforts were not without effect. The loss of his wife made him more zealous in his affectionate endeavours to reclaim me from evil, and my affection for him, and my sympathy with him in his sorrows, prepared me for benefitting the more from his endeavours. After we came from the funeral we walked together along the fields not far from where we lived, and he talked to me very seriously. I said little in return, but I felt a great deal. I made no promises, but I felt serious purposes begin to spring up in my mind to begin to lead a religious life. There were difficulties in the way, and the thought of those difficulties created a struggle. I had my companions, and it seemed hard to give them up. I was also exceedingly fond of liberty; the thought of restraint was always painful to me: it seemed a tremendous thing to place myself under restraints which were to exert an influence over all my thoughts, my passions, my conversation, my behaviour, and which were, in fact, entirely to remodel my character, my tastes, my pursuits, and thoroughly transform and create the whole anew. And the difficulty was heightened by the still remaining mists and clouds of darkness that hung over the subject of religion. Still conscience and a regard to my eternal interests called for submission, and I felt inclined to yield to the call. Still my determination to yield was not quite full. I had gone up the street one evening in expectation of meeting with a favourite companion. I waited at the usual place beyond the usual time, and my companion did not appear. I then moved on till I came opposite the Methodist Chapel, and hearing singing in the Vestry, I went to the door, and stood a short time to listen. While standing there, a person that was going to the meeting came up, and observing me listening and thoughtful, invited me to go into the meeting, and I went in. I felt rather strange, so I got into a corner behind the door, and there remained till the close of the meeting. I do not recollect well what were my thoughts and feelings while in the meeting, but I recollect well what took place *after* the meeting. My brother had been at the meeting and had seen me come in, and regarded it as a proof that I was fully resolved to begin a religious life. As soon as the meeting was over and I had got out, he came up to me, full of delight and affection, and of kind solicitude for my welfare, and began to talk to me in a very encouraging way. On the following Sunday morning my brother called on me to go with him to the fellowship-meeting, a meeting at which the members of the Methodist Society are accustomed to tell their experience, as they do in love-feasts. It is, in fact, a love-feast on a small scale, without the bread and the water, the tickets and the collection, and is all the more free and edifying perhaps in consequence of there seldom or *never* being any hired-preacher there. That meeting was a means of good to me. What I heard and what I felt, strengthened my determination to live for God. During the Sabbath and the following week my brother still continued his kind attention to me, and seemed full of desire and anxiety that I should not go back to the world. Both he and others were wishful that I should go forward in the right way. On Thursday night some one called on me to invite me to go with him to a class-meeting, and I went. I do not recollect anything particular that took place at the first-meeting. I sat and listened to what was said, and as I heard it was the custom for the leader not to ask persons any questions the first time they went, much less to expect from them any answers, I felt little anxiety or fear, and my resolution to be religious was confirmed, I believe, by going to that meeting. I went to the class again the Thursday following. That night I expected to be questioned, and to have to give answers to the questions that might be proposed. The consequence was, I was full of fear and anxiety. I could pay but little attention to what was said, either by the leader or by the members, my mind was so perplexed and troubled with the thought that it would soon be my turn to say something. My chief recollection of that meeting is that it was a miserable meeting. The leader proposed his questions and I said something in answer to them; but my mind was so confused and bewildered at the time, that I do not remember now what I said, and I am not certain that I knew exactly what I said even at the time that I was speaking. I continued to go to class regularly from that time; and never missed more than once or twice for a number of years. The burden of the leader's observations and exhortations to me was the necessity of some kind of mysterious faith, and some mysterious change of heart, and some kind of incomprehensible and indescribable witness of the spirit, but I did not understand him, so that I could not, of course, tell how to make any good use of his exhortations and observations.

As I have stated in the Tract on *Saving Faith*, my mind was very much bewildered and perplexed. I tried to believe in the Methodistical way, in some way different from the way in which I *did* believe, and I prayed for some extra change of heart, and for some kind of sudden, direct, irresistible, and indubitable testimony to my soul that I was converted, forgiven, accepted, and saved. And they used to pray with me very laboriously, in order to induce God to give me those mysterious blessings; but prayers never seemed to have any great effect. They were like my own, they could not bring blessings which were not to be had. I had all the faith I needed, and God had no other faith to give. And my heart *was* changed from evil to good, and God required no other change. And I had the witness of the spirit too, testifying, in the sacred Scriptures, to the acceptance and forgiveness of all who believe and obey the Gospel, and I had an inward consciousness both that I believed in God and Christ in the common rational way, and that I had surrendered my soul and consecrated my life and all my powers to God. But this I was taught was not enough. How I continued to seek for those fancied blessings and imaginary changes, and how I sought in vain,—how I was sometimes comforted and sometimes afflicted,—how I was sometimes lifted to heaven in brief but delightful extacies, and how I was soon cast down as into the depths of the pit,—how I wept at times for joy, and then again for sorrow, and how, at other times, I stood gazing and motionless, and cold and chilled, all full of fears, and troubled with dark thoughts and mournful musings, and afflicted with fearful misgivings and fears, you may see related in my tracts on 'Saving Faith.' I cannot relate them at full here. That period of my life was a fearful time to me, and if it had not been that God by his unseen hand led me, and gave me, in my consciousness of right intentions, partial and occasional consolations, gradually inspiring me with confidence towards himself, I must have perished,—I must have been driven to distraction by the false, the unscriptural, the irrational theology that my leader and the preachers used to press upon my mind. I never got fairly converted according to the Methodistical notion or description of conversion. I never fairly or fully got saving faith, according to *their* unscriptural notion and definition of saving faith. And I never had the witness of the spirit, according to *their* accounts of the witness of the spirit. I never was truly religious according to their notions of religion. I never had any other conversion than a turning of my soul and of my life to God. I never found any other faith than a simple belief in the religion of Christ as true and divine, nor any other witness of the spirit than the general testimony of God, that all believers in Christ that give themselves up to God's service, are adopted, accepted, forgiven, and saved, and that gradual confidence which sprang up in my mind that *I* was a converted man, and that God therefore did accept, forgive, and love me.

I was very much tempted after I gave myself to God, and joined the Methodist society, and that in different ways. A very short time after I joined the society, there was a great boxing match between the principal boxer of my native place, and some other boxer from another part of the country. I had always been fond of seeing a fight so that this of course was a strong temptation indeed. I felt my old love of witnessing that brutal and dangerous sport come upon me with great power. The impulse, was terrible: it seemed as if it would almost have compelled me to go and witness the meeting. At the same time, I felt that it would be wrong to go. I believed it to be my duty to avoid all such scenes. Then came the struggle between conscience and inclination, between duty and temptation, and no one that has not felt a similar struggle, can conceive its violence. I was spinning at the time the battle was about to take place, The people were flocking to the scene of action. A great part of the people in the neighbourhood had left their work to go, and I seemed to be left almost alone. The struggle was so violent, that I forgot myself at times, and I forgot my work for a season, and stood still as if entranced and motionless, unconscious of what was around me. But I mastered, and I never was tempted, that I recollect, in such a way again.

I said I began to go to class, but some of my readers will need to be told what class-meetings are, and how they are generally conducted.

The class-meetings are held weekly. The classes ought, according to rule, to consist of ten or twelve members; but they sometimes contain as many as thirty, forty, or fifty, and at other times not more than three or four. Each member kneels down as soon as he enters, to pray a little to himself. The leader then begins the meeting by giving out a hymn, and the members stand up to sing. Then the leader prays, gives out another hymn, and then tells his experience. Sometimes he tells what trials he has met with, and what deliverances he has experienced through the week,—what joys and sorrows he has had,—how he felt at the lovefeast, the prayer-meeting, or the fellowship-meeting,—what liberty he had in secret prayer,—how he felt while reading the Scriptures, or hearing sermons, or while busy at his work,—what passages have come to his mind, or what promises have been applied to his soul. At other times he simply tells how he feels at that moment; while at other times he says nothing about his experience or feelings, but just gives thanks to God for what he has done for him, in a general way, or offers a few words of exhortation or preaching to the members. He then asks each member in turn the state of his mind. A very common form of the question is, Well, brother, or well sister, how do you feel the state of your mind to night? At other times it will be, Well brother, will you tell us what the Lord is doing for you? Different leaders have different ways of proposing the question, and the same leader varies his question at times. When the question is put, the member answers. Some of the members tell a long and flaming story; others say little or next to nothing. Some speak loud and even shout: others speak so low that they cannot be heard, either by the leaders or the rest of the members. Some are always happy, according to their story; others are always doubtful and fearful, and can never say much either about their feelings or performances. One tells you he has been on the sunny side of the hill all week; another says he has been on the mount of transfiguration, and that he could say with one of old, Master, it is good to be here. Another has been with Moses on the Top of Pisgah, and got a view of the promised land. Another felt that he was like the beloved disciple in the Isle of Patmos, in the spirit on the Lord's day, and that he had not lost the blessing he received under the Sunday morning sermon's all the week through. It frequently happens that when the first has told a good experience, that the rest follow the example; while when the first tells of troubles and trials, the rest generally speak of having had the same kind of trials, or something similar. If the first is on a high key, they are almost all on a high key; but if the first be on a low key, the rest are on a low key too. There will generally be one or two in a large meeting that *will* tell a fine bright tale, let the rest tell what kind of tale they please: and there will generally be one or two in a large meeting that will tell a low desponding story, let the rest tell what story they will. Still it commonly happens that the first person who speaks gives the turn or the tone to the meeting generally.

I may observe that in most class-meetings, indeed in almost all class-meetings, as well as in love-feasts, fellowship-meetings, and band-meetings, a happy experience is accounted creditable, while a low and desponding experience is counted rather discreditable. As it is generally accounted a honour in the world to be rich and well-dressed, insomuch that the rich and well-dressed are, in the language of the world, called *respectable;* so it is generally accounted respectable or creditable in the Methodist world to be rich in religious consolations or experience. And as it commonly happens in the world that the *appearance* of wealth secures the same respect as wealth itself, so does it commonly happen in the Methodist world, that the appearance of religious wealth, the profession of rich consolations and plentiful supplies of spiritual blessings, secures the same respect and reverence that real religious excellence alone deserves. For as it is often impossible to tell whether people in the world are rich or poor; so it is frequently impossible to tell whether people in the religious world are as happy or comfortable as they profess to be. As some people in the world are taken to be rich when in truth they are sinking in debt, or quite beggared and ruined; so some people in the religious world often profess great attainments and talk of great consolations and rapturous enjoyments, and are taken for something extra, when in truth they are cheerless and miserable, worthless and self-condemned. And as it frequently happens in the world at large that the richest people care least about appearances, and will sometimes dress so plainly and talk so freely and familiarly with their neighbours that you would take them for most homely and unimportant people, while those who are very poor or on the point of beggary, are most extravagant in their dress and living, and most affected and particular in their talk and manners, as if on purpose to prevent their poverty from being seen or suspected; so it is in the religious world. Those who are truly good, who most excel in goodness, are frequently most modest and retiring, saying little or nothing about their feelings or attainments; while those who are worthless and base make the greatest and loudest professions, as a cloak for their hypocrisy and villainy. And as in the world at large it is hard for people to suspect persons of poverty who have on them and around them all the signs and appearances of wealth; so in the world of Methodism, it is hard for many people to believe that persons who profess to enjoy such abundant consolations in their souls are selfish, deceitful and vile. Hence in almost all religious societies, not excepting even the Quakers and the Baptists, profession is respected, and a *high* profession, joined with some appearances of great feeling and solemnity, secures respect proportionately high. There is in consequence, a great and a constant temptation to people to profess what they do not feel; to say they enjoy what they do not enjoy; to say they have a confidence or an assurance which they have not. And multitudes are overcome by this temptation. They wish to be believed to be something,—or they are carried away by the force of example and prevailing custom, and use words which they do not understand, or profess enjoyments which they never felt. R. G., a leader and circuit steward in the G——— circuit, once declared in my hearing, that at a certain meeting, I think it was the first love-feast that he attended, he told a wilful lie. He said he told the people he was very happy, when in truth he was not happy at all, but miserable. Several others had said they were very happy, and he fancied that he must say the same; and thus he told them a great, a wilful lie. He made this acknowledgement in a meeting; I was present and heard it myself.

And there are thousands, I am persuaded, that have been led to do the same thing, and that are doing the same thing still every week. Nothing is more common in love-feasts and class-meetings than this false and formal way of talking. In many cases you see at those meetings, as clearly as you can see the darkness or the light, that the persons to whom you are listening are talking at random, talking by rote, talking by imitation. You see it from the very words they use, and from the way in which they speak them. You cannot help but believe, when you hear them, that their words are one thing and their feelings another; that their words and their feelings have no agreement with each other; that they either say they know not what, or say what they know to be false. A cousin of mine once told me that he once preached nearly half-an-hour and did not even know what he *said*, much less know what the words he used should mean. And people do the same in praying, in singing, and in telling experiences. They frequently do all, not in sincerity, but from emulation, for show, or for fear of shame, or merely through the force of custom or example. Some tell fine flaming stories *to keep up their reputation*. They told a fine story one week, and it would look so bad if they were not to have as good a one for this. They really were happy perhaps when they first told such a delightful experience; they were happy perhaps for a number of weeks, and said no more than they believed and felt. But their happiness gave place to conflict and to sorrow; their joy was turned to sadness; perhaps their spirits were exhausted with excitement, or perhaps they had yielded to temptation and done wrong. What shall they do now? Shall they stay away from the class? That would be a neglect of duty, they think, and an adding of sin to sin. And what good reason could they assign for their absence when questioned on the subject? No; it would not do to miss their class. But what shall they say at the class? Shall they confess their sin? But that is not the custom; and it would be too great a humiliation. Shall they tell how sad and comfortless they are? That would still excite curiosity, and the leaders and members would wish to know what they had been doing, and perhaps suspect them to be worse than they are. And how discouraging it would be to others, who have looked up to them with so much confidence and admiration, to tell them a doleful and melancholy story! What shall they do then? They will go, and trust God for the result. They will take no thought what or how they shall speak; for the Holy Spirit itself shall give them in that hour what they shall say: for it is not they that speak, but the Spirit that dwelleth in them. They go, hoping to be happy and joyful before their time for speaking comes; but alas, they are not. They have to speak before they expected. They are taken by surprize, and are confused, fluttered, and speak in a great measure as usual: their customary phrases come off as a matter of course. They are now very near being wretched and miserable hypocrites. They have broken down the hedge, and will be in the hypocrite's wilderness next week. And numbers are ruined in this way.

I said you might know, if you heard some people talking in their classes, that they were speaking insincerely, hypocritically,—that they either did not know or did not care what they said. The leaders and some of the members *do* know that this kind of hypocrisy prevails. The leader can hardly help but know in many cases, even while the person is speaking to him, that he is speaking at random, that he does not know what he is saying, or that he does not care what he is saying. I have myself felt in scores or hundreds of cases, that the persons addressing me in the class, or speaking before me in love-feasts, or praying in prayer-meetings, were thus violating the great law of truth.

In many cases this false way of speaking is the result of mere thoughtlessness perhaps, or of ignorance joined with the notion that it is their duty to pray or to say something in public. The parties have no *intention* to deceive: but being called on to speak, or invited to pray, they begin, and catch hold of such words as they can find, whether right or wrong, whether true or false. And their words are oftener foolish or false, than wise or true. Their talk is at times most foolish and ridiculous. I will give an example or two. It is customary for people when praying for preachers, to say, 'Lord, bless thy servants when they stand up to declare thy word: be thou *mouth, matter*, and *wisdom* to them.' This has some meaning in it when offered in reference to a preacher, especially a preacher about to preach. In other cases it would be most foolish and ridiculous. Yet I once heard a person in a prayer-meeting at Chester use this same form of expression in behalf of the sick and the dying. 'O Lord,' said he, 'bless the sick and the afflicted, and those that are in the article of death; be thou mouth, matter and wisdom to them.' At another prayer-meeting at Chester on a *Friday* Evening, one of the leaders gave out the following lines:

'Another six days' work is done;
Another SABBATH *is begun,' &c.*

I once heard a woman say in class, 'I do thank God that he ever gave me a desire to seek that death that never, never dies.' And the rest of her speech was of a similar character. There was a man that was once appointed with me as a prayer leader, that would pray a length of time, and scarce ever utter a sentence that had any sense in it. He would pray for God to bless our iniquities, and to fill our transgressions with his holy spirit, that they might run like oil from vessel to vessel, refreshed with new wine. And though this latter can hardly be called a sample of Methodistical praying and talking, it is a sample of what prevails on a smaller or less palpable scale in almost every Methodistical society that I have come in contact wtth. Unmeaning, foolish, ridiculous, random, false and hypocritical talking is to be heard in abundance in almost every prayer-meeting, class-meeting, or love-feast in the Methodistical world. Such talking is in truth the common kind of talk; and true, and rational, and hearty talk, talk answering to the thoughts and feelings of the soul, and in harmony with the teachings of Jesus, is very uncommon. You hear it at times, but very seldom.

There are many phrases which have been common among the Methodist Societies for a long time, which I myself could never understand. For instance, one man prays that God would cause his grace to go from heart to heart, *as oil from vessel to vessel;* while another prays that there may be a shout of a king in their camp; and a third prays that God would bless the preachers, and that they may *hear the sound of their Master's feet behind them.* There are others of a similar description. Some of their old stereotyped phrases are not unintelligible. For instance, when they pray that the sick or the absent may have Benjamin's mess,—that God would bless the ram's horns,—that they may have their lamps always trimmed and burning,—that while the minister draws his bow at a venture, God may direct the arrow, all these phrases have a meaning which *some* can understand. Still most use those phrases, and others of a similar kind, simply because they have heard others use them, without having any idea at all of their meaning.

It is the same with a multitude of other phrases of a different kind. They talk of coming to Christ, of following Christ, of sitting at Christ's feet, of leaning on his arm, of dwelling within his wounds, of sinking into the purple flood and rising into the life of God, without the least idea of the meaning of the words they use. Some of the people that use those words have good thoughts and feelings which they *put into* those words, so that the words come to have a meaning to *them;* but most employ them at random, and neither mean anything by them themselves, nor understand what others mean by them.

When a member in the class has told his experience, the leader addresses him in return, giving him instruction, counsel, or encouragement, as the case may appear to require, or as the leader may be able to impart. In most cases the leaders are ignorant men, and talk as foolishly and as much at random as the majority of their members, and their addresses to their members are foolish or formal accordingly. Some have a certain round of expressions or little speeches which they use as some of the preachers use their sermons, over and over again without end. Others speak off hand, and adapt their remarks to the experience of their members pretty well; while others aim constantly at raising and keeping up excitement in the minds of the people. It seldom happens that a class-leader is truly intelligent, and gives sound and rational instruction in Christian truth and duty. And even if a leader *is* intelligent, and *does* give good and useful instruction, he is often disliked by many. They say he is *dry*. Many of the people that go to class do not go for instruction; they go for excitement, or pleasure. They do not want to be taught anything; they want a lift towards heaven, as they call it; they want to be helped to feel comfortable, and self-satisfied, without being put to the trouble of learning, thinking, or self-improvement. The leader therefore that is most clever at raising people to a high state of pleasant feeling is considered by most the best class-leader, and he will have the largest and most prosperous class. If a person were to say anything in class calculated to correct the people's errors, or to enlarge their views of Christian truth, he would, in general, be considered out of order. Thinking, reasoning, judging, seeking to draw forth truth, and to help each other to clear, correct and comprehensive views of gospel principles, are not the business of class-meetings. Suppose a person, in the middle of a large class-meeting led by an exciting leader of the more powerful or clever kind, to begin in a calm and rational way to state his views on any religious subject, and to quote the Scriptures to show that his statements were correct, he would throw a damp on the meeting at once,—the leader would be almost paralysed,—the people would feel almost chilled and frozen. The feeling produced by ranting, is quite a different feeling from that which is necessary to sober and rational conversation. There is as much difference between the common kind of class-meeting, Methodistical excitement, and that calm and comfortable state of mind resulting from the discovery of the truth and obedience to God's will, as there is between the wild, the fitful, and unnatural ecstacies of drunkenness or madness, and the delightful, stable pleasures of the healthy and rational man. The man who seeks for amusement is vexed if you offer him a lesson in logic instead; and the person who seeks for excitement is vexed if you offer him a lesson in religious truth or duty. People go to theatres to get pleased with things profane or common, and people go to class-meetings, &c., to get pleased with religious or spiritual things. The love of pleasure is frequently the ruling passion in the professor and profane alike; though they seek for pleasure in different objects and in different ways. And both are disappointed, chilled, enraged when instead of helping them to pleasure, you put them to the task of serious thought, or zealous, self-denying, Christ-like labours. Hence even those class-leaders who are intelligent and well-informed seldom venture to offer instruction to their members in the class-meeting. They seldom or never correct their errors, or reprove their faults, or even give them particular advice during the class-meeting. If they instruct them or reprove them at all, it is privately after the meeting is over. Nothing must interfere with the religious or unnatural excitement of the meeeting. Men that are as sensible as yourselves in conversation, will talk week after week in their class-meetings, and never teach one truth, never expose one error, never reprove one prevailing sin.

When the leader has gone round, and spoken to all present, he gives out a verse or two of a hymn, and concludes with prayer. Sometimes he prays himself; at other times he calls on one or two of the members to pray. Then all sit down while he calls over the list of names in his class-book, and puts opposite each name a mark. Those who are absent he marks A, those who are present and do not pay anything he marks P, those who pay a penny, two-pence, six-pence, or a shilling, he marks 1d., 2d., 6d., or 1s. accordingly. The sick will have the mark S, those kept away from class by business or distance from home will sometimes have the mark B or D.

The rules for classes, as published in John Wesley's works are the following:

'There are about twelve persons in every class, one of whom is styled the leader: it is his business,

1. To see each person in his class, once a week at least, in order,
2. To inquire how their souls prosper;
3. To advise, reprove, comfort, or exhort, as occasion may require;
4. To receive what they are willing to give, towards the support of the *gospel*.

5. To meet the ministers and the stewards of the society once a week, in order,

6. To inform the minister of any that are sick, or of any that walk disorderly, and will not be reproved:

7. To pay to the stewards what they have received of their several classes in the week preceding; and,

8. To shew their account of what each person has contributed.

4. There is one only condition previously required of those who desire admission into these societies, viz. 'a desire to flee from the wrath to come, and be saved from their sins:' but wherever this is really fixed in the soul, it will be shewn by its fruits. It is therefore expected of all who continue therein, that they should continue to evidence their desire of salvation;

First, By doing no harm, by avoiding evil in every kind; especially that which is most practised. Such as,

The taking of the name of God in vain:

The profaning the day of the Lord, either by doing ordinary work thereon, or by buying or selling.

Drunkenness; *buying* or *selling spirituous liquors;* or *drinking them*, unless in cases of extreme necessity:

Fighting, quarrelling, brawling; brother *going to law* with brother; returning *evil for evil*, or *railing for railing;* the *using many words* in buying or selling:

The *buying* or *selling uncustomed* [smuggled] *goods:*

The *giving* or *taking things on usury*, i. e. unlawful interest:

Uncharitable or *unprofitable* conversation; particularly speaking evil of magistrates or of ministers.

Doing to others as we would not they should do unto us:

Doing what we know is not for the glory of God; as,

The *putting on of gold or costly apparel:*

The *taking such diversions* as cannot be used in the name of the Lord Jesus:

The *singing* those *songs*, or *reading* those *books*, that do not tend to the knowledge or love of God:

Softness, and needless self-indulgence:

Laying up treasure on earth:

Borrowing without the probability of paying; or, taking up goods without a probability of paying for them.

5. It is expected of all, who continue in these societies, that they should continue to evidence their desire of salvation,

Secondly, By doing good, by being in every kind merciful after their power, as they have opportunity: doing good of every possible sort, and as far as possible to all men;

To their bodies, of the ability that God giveth, by giving food to the hungry, by clothing the naked, by visiting or helping them that are sick or in prison:

To their souls, by instructing, reproving, or exhorting all we have any intercourse with: trampling under foot that enthusiastic doctrine of devils, that, 'We are not to do good unless our hearts be free to it:'

By doing good, especially to them that are of the household of faith, or groaning so to be; employing them preferably to others;

buying one of another; helping each other in business: and so much the more, because the world will love its own, and them *only:*

By all possible *diligence* and *frugality*, that the gospel be not blamed:

By running with patience the race that is set before them, *denying themselves, and taking up their cross daily;* submitting to bear the reproach of Christ; to be as the filth and off-scouring of the world; and looking that men should *say all manner of evil of them for the Lord's sake.*

6. It is expected of all who desire to continue in these societies, that they should continue to evidence their desire of salvation:

Thirdly, By attending on all the ordinances of God: such are,

The public worship of God:

The ministry of the word, either read or expounded:

The Supper of the Lord:

Family and private prayer:

Searching the Scriptures: and,

Fasting or abstinence.

7. These are the general rules of our societies; all which we are taught of God to observe, even in his written word, the only rule, and the sufficient rule both of our faith and practice. And all these we know his Spirit writes on every truly awakened heart. If there be any among us who observe them not, who habitually break any of them, let it be made known unto them, who watch over that soul, as they must give an account. We will admonish him of the error of his ways: we will bear with him for a season. But then, if he repent not, he hath no more place among us. We have delivered our own souls.

May 1, 1743.   J. and C. WESLEY.'

There is reason to believe that Rule 4, respecting the duty of the leader, has been altered by the editors of John Wesley's works. In John Wesley's plain account of the Methodists the rule stands thus:

To receive what they are willing to give towards the support of the *Poor.*—Vol. vi. 292.

And in the same work, vol. vi. 296., it is expressly said that the weekly contributions were to be distributed *as every one had need.* It seems plain therefore to me that the unfaithful editors have corrupted John Wesley's works in this particular, as they have done in many other cases. They have, it appears, put *Gospel* instead of *Poor*, to justify their taking the money designed for the relief of the poor members and keeping it themselves.

It will be seen that in the rules as given above there is nothing said about giving a penny a week, or a shilling a quarter. All that is said about contributions is simply this, that the leaders should receive *what the members were willing to give.* On this point also the preachers have altered the rules, inserting a rule to the effect that all must give a penny a week, and a shilling a quarter at least, if they be able, and more according to their ability; yet they still continue to put at the end of them the names of John and Charles Wesley, as if they had made and sanctioned the whole.

It is the custom, after a person has met a few weeks, to give him a copy of the rules, but it is not expected now that he will pay any regard to many of them. On the contrary, it is generally expected that he will break many of them every day of his life. It is *known* both by the preachers and leaders, and by the members too, that the person to whom they give those rules, will break them the next day. Nor is it expected that the leader will observe all the rules which relate to him. On the contrary, it is confidently expected that he will break even the very first of them. That rule requires that he ' shall see each person in his class *once a week at least:* ' but it is known that he does no such thing, and that he never thinks of doing it. Nor is the law on this point ever enforced, or the transgression ever punished. The law which has been added by the preachers, requiring each member, if able, to pay a penny a week or more, and a shilling or more a quarter, is enforced and expected to be observed, and so are a few others; but as for others of them, both preachers and leaders would feel quite offended at you, or laugh you to scorn, if you were to say anything about them. For instance; the rules require you *not to buy or sell spirituous liquors,* and not to *drink* them, except in cases of extreme necessity. But many even of the leaders both buy and sell spirituous liquors. Many of them are distillers, spirit merchants, licensed victuallers and publicans. The preachers *buy* spirituous liquors, if they do not sell them; and they drink far more than they buy. There is scarce a class of persons in the country perhaps in which you will find fewer abstainers from spirituous liquors than the Methodist travelling preachers. And it is a curious fact, that though they expressly declare at the end of the rules, that they know God's Spirit writes this rule against buying, selling and drinking spirituous liquors on every truly awakened heart, and though they also declare that any one who habitually breaks it shall be expelled, yet they not only break it themselves, but at this time they are letting part of their Centenary Hall, as a shop for the sale of those same spirituous liquors.

It is the same with other rules. One forbids brother going to law with brother; yet the preachers themselves have repeatedly gone to law with each other, even about the chapels and school-houses, while Methodists going to law with Methodists on other subjects is far from being uncommon.

One rule says you shall not use many words in buying or selling: but how many preachers or members pay any regard to it? Another rule forbids the members to put on *gold* or *costly apparel*; yet many of the preachers preach in gold rings, and carry gold watches, and exhibit their gold watch guards and quizzing glasses, while their wives and children are adorned or dressed almost in the height of the fashion. As for the leaders and members, many of them put on gold and wear costly apparel every day of their lives without a blush.

Other rules forbid softness and needless self-indulgence, and laying up treasure on earth; yet few, either preachers or leaders, ever think of observing them. And so with others. Laws are printed, put into your hands, declared to be the laws of God, and said to be written on every awakened heart, and yet are trampled on or disobeyed without either remorse or shame.

One rule requires them to show their desire to flee from the wrath to come, ' By doing good, by being in every kind merciful after their power, as they have opportunity: doing good of every possible sort, and as far as possible to all men; to their bodies, of the ability that God giveth, by giving food to the hungry, by clothing the naked, by visiting or helping them that are sick or in prison: to their souls, by instructing, reproving, or exhorting all we have any intercourse with.' Now there is not one man in fifty, I believe, either among the travelling preachers, the class-leaders, or the private members that obeys this rule. If all the Methodist preachers, and all the members of the Methodist societies were to obey this rule,—if they were all to be merciful in every way, and to do good to the utmost of their power, good of every possible sort, and as far as possible to all men, both to their bodies and their souls, they would reform and revolutionize the world. But they do not obey it; they never have obeyed it; they never mean to obey it. *John Wesley* appears to have obeyed this rule; *he* appears to have acted on the principle of doing as much good as he could to all mankind; but his followers, as they are called, have not. They bear his name; they call themselves *Wesleyans*, but there is almost as much difference between John Wesley and the Methodist travelling preachers and the leading members of the Methodist societies, as between Jesus of Nazareth and the selfish and intolerant bishops of the third and fourth centuries after his death.

Let any one consider a few of the ways in which men may show mercy and do good to the bodies and souls of men, and then ask what the Methodist travelling preachers and the leading members of the Methodist societies are doing in such ways.

One of the simplest ways of doing good is that of feeding the hungry, clothing the naked or the ragged, and supplying the wants of the sick, the aged, and the weak. What do the Methodist preachers and their wealthy leading friends do in this way? What do they do in this way in Bramley, my native town? Joseph Sutcliffe was kind, and took pleasure in doing good to the poor; but where, among all the preachers that have travelled in the Bramley circuit, will you find another that has done so? I know not one. They have all been willing that the poor, the sick, the aged and the weak should contribute to *them*, and supply them not only with things necessary, but with the means of growing rich; but I know not one of them, with the exception of Joseph Sutcliffe, that has shown the least anxiety to supply the wants of the poor and helpless. Simeon Musgrave, a private member, once gave my poor brother Samuel, when he was ill and near death, a pound; and John Burton, I am told, offered, after my brother's death, to pay my father his debts; and twice James Hobson carried my mother one and sixpence or two shillings of the love-feast money; and old John Haley, another member, sometimes helped the widow and the helpless; but I never heard of the Methodist travelling preachers in Bramley, with the exception of Joseph Sutcliffe, helping any one. They do not even support their own members in age or helplessness. It is quite a common thing to leave them to the tender mercies of the poor-law officers, or to the melancholy and misery of the poor-house. In some cases they have been known even to demand from their members part of their poor-law allowance; and in many cases they allow the names of the old and friendless to drop off the class-books, and fare as they can, when they can no longer attend the class and contribute to their salaries. Friends of my own have met with cases of this description, when going on their errands of mercy. John Wesley instituted a sort of dispensary, to supply the sick poor with medicine and medical advice; but where is the dispensary instituted by the Methodist travelling preachers? John Wesley had an institution for the support of poor widows; but where is the travelling preacher's institution for the support of poor widows? John Wesley had a benevolent loan fund; but where is the benevolent loan fund of the travelling preachers or of their principal friends? Or where is the institution to supply its place?

And what are the Methodist travelling preachers and their principal friends doing for the instruction and improvement of men's minds? One of the principal means of instruction is schools: what do they do for the ignorant poor in the way of providing them with schools? They build and support Sunday schools, but what do they teach there? Reading? Yes. Writing? No. Arithmetic? No. Grammar? No. Geography, history, philosophy? No. Nothing but reading. The preachers have forbidden the teaching of writing in the Sunday schools: they profess, in the Minutes of Conference, to believe that the Sunday is too holy to be spent in teaching writing, and some of them perhaps do believe so; but others assign another reason for discountenancing instruction in writing on the Sunday. They say that if the children of the poor are taught to write, they will go farther, and be getting those situations and reaping those advantages which they wish to be reserved for their own children. But have they not schools for giving instruction to the poor in writing, gratis, on other days? No? But if they had, they could be of little use, for many of the poor have not the opportunity of going to day schools; nor have they, in many cases, the opportunity even of getting to a night school. But the preachers and their leading friends do not supply to the poor instruction in writing gratis, either by day schools or night schools. The travelling preachers ask the poor to support schools for the liberal instruction of their own children; they make collections among the poor for the support of Kingswood and Woodhouse Grove schools, but as for helping the poor to liberal instruction, they do nothing of the kind.

Another means of instructing the poor multitudes is cheap books. Teach people to read, and give them books, and they will do. They will instruct themselves in other matters. They will learn to write; they will learn Arithmetic, Mensuration, Algebra, Geography, Astronomy, Anatomy, Botany, History, Zoology, Religion, every thing: but deny them books, and they are lost. What do the Methodist travelling preachers do towards supplying the poor with cheap books? Their other transgressions may be forgiven if they are faithful here. If they supply plenty of cheap good books, they must be friends to knowledge, friends to the general improvement of the people. If they supply to the people plenty of good cheap books, we shall believe that they love mankind, that they wish them well,—that the tales about them wishing to keep them in ignorance, that they may rule them and enrich themselves from them, are false. But do they do this? Do they supply abundance of cheap good books for the people? They do not. They publish comparatively few books; and what they do publish are generally but very poor ones: and as for the prices, they are mostly unusually high, most shamefully high. Chambers publishes cheap books, and tolerably good ones too in general; and some of the London publishers publish cheap good books: but the Methodist preachers do not. The books which they sell for a shilling, they could afford to sell for a penny or twopence, and the books which they sell for ten shillings, they could afford to sell for a shilling or eightpence. But have the Methodist travelling preachers the means of printing and publishing cheap books? They have: they have the best opportunities imaginable for supplying cheap books. They have a Printing establishment and a Book room nearly a hundred years old. They can get paper and ink and type and labour as cheap as any one. They have agents for the sale of books almost all over the world, who sell them for about ten per cent. They have all good salaries, so that they are not dependant on their profits for a living. They could therefore afford to supply books cheaper than tradesmen generally. They could, if they would, publish all the best books in the country at eightpence or sixpence for a good sized volume, and not only lose nothing thereby, but gain twenty or thirty thousand pounds a year. Yet, with all these advantages, they are not publishing a single cheap book:

with all these advantages, they sell books dearer than even worldlings and infidels sell books. Yet they say, and say truly in this case, that the law which requires people to do all they can for the instruction and welfare of their brethren, is the law of God.

Another way of doing good to men is by promoting peace, and opposing war; by seeking the abolition of bad laws, and the overthrow of corrupt and oppressive institutions; by promoting the spread of temperance and free inquiry. I need not say how little the Methodist travelling preachers, or even their leading friends, are doing in these departments of charity.

Still, though the preachers and leaders and principal members do not keep the rules of the society, some of the members keep them, and many of them, when they are first taken into the society, *purpose* to keep them. I fully intended to keep the rules myself when I was received as a member, and I *did* keep them, so far as I knew, as long as I continued a member. I neither did what the rules forbade, nor did I neglect what the rules commanded. I neither took God's name in vain, nor profaned the sabbath as it is called. I never mentioned God's name except in prayer or singing, or in solemn, grave, religious talk. As for the sabbath, as Sunday is falsely called, I neither bought, nor sold, nor worked at my ordinary work on that day. I would not even buy bread when hungry on a journey on that day, nor buy drink when thirsty. And so far was I from doing my ordinary work on that day, that I would not even brush my shoes or shave myself on that day. If I forgot to brush my shoes on Saturday night, as I did once or twice, I went with them dirty: and if I forgot to shave myself on a Saturday night, as I once or twice did, I wore my beard till Monday, though it was a full week old. I gave up all diversions, sang no songs, read no novels. In short, so far as I understood the rules, I obeyed them most conscientiously. I attended most regularly on what are called the means of grace. Three times on a Sunday I went to chapel to hear the preachers, and once in the week besides. I attended the class every week for several years, missing only twice when I was ill. I went every Sunday morning to the fellowship-meeting or prayer-meeting at seven o'clock. At eight I got my breakfast; at half-past eight I went a long round to visit some sick and aged people, in company with Joseph Haley, and Joseph Hobson; after that we held our band meetings, or else went to the Sunday school; and after the evening preaching I went to a prayer meeting. I was equally attentive to private duties. I read the scriptures daily, and sometimes read a great part of the New Testament in a day. I committed all the most clear and practical passages to memory. I made it a rule to commit to memory some portions every day. I had my hours for secret prayer, which I observed with the greatest care. I took the Lord's supper, as it is called, whenever it was administered: and paid my penny a week at class with the greatest regularity. I contributed also to the missionary fund, and gave at all the collections. I had a high idea of the preachers, and even of the leaders and members generally. I read the Hymn book through, and got off nearly all the hymns. I believed the hymns in general were inspired of God, the pure outbreathing of the holy spirit. I sang the hymns at my work, and sang them with all my power. I kept a watch even over my looks, scarcely allowing myself either to laugh or to smile, and I struggled hard with my passions and inclinations, bringing all into subjection to my ideas of religion, or duty. I suppressed all lightness of spirit, and all inclination to humour or wit, as offensive to God, and injurious to the soul. I not only kept the rules on those points, but even went beyond the rules. I was conscientious in my Methodism, and I was a Methodist of the strictest order.

And I not only kept the rules myself, but laboured to bring others also to observe them. And I suppose I knew no other at that time, but that all who professed to be Methodists would be willing to obey the rules, if they were made to understand them. I therefore tried to help people to understand them, when I had any thing to do with them. I was not aware at that time that the preachers, and leaders, and principal members had united to set the best and the most important of them aside, and that they cared nothing about the rules except so far as they might answer the purposes of selfishness and ambition. I was sincere myself, and I was too young and inexperienced to suppose that others were otherwise minded.

It was the custom of our leader to read the rules over once a-quarter, instead of asking us the state of our minds. And it was also his custom before he began to read, to tell us that we were at liberty to speak on each rule, and to point out any thing that we might consider a transgression of any of the rules. One night when he read the rules I asked him, when he came to that against putting on of gold, if the seals which were hung to his watch were not gold? He was rather staggered and confounded at the question, and seemed to know not what to say. He did however mutter something out at last, but I cannot recollect what it was. It was nothing to the purpose, I know. He was convicted of breaking the rules, and his excuse was good for nothing. He could not deny the fact; and he could not condemn the rule. He was regularly taken by surprise. The truth is, he did not read the rules out of any love to piety or charity; but out of selfishness. He was a draper, and one of the rules said that we were to *buy one of another*. This was the rule that he was concerned about. He wished to press upon the members the duty of going to his shop in preference to other shops kept by persons who were not Methodists. Hence he regularly stopped to explain this rule, and he never, that I recollect, stopped to explain any other. I don't recollect that he ever read the rules any more in the class, so long as I remained. He might; but I do not remember that he did.

Many people when they first go to class, go with a full intention of being truly religious, truly good; and as they regard the Methodist rules as the rules of goodness, they go with the intention of obeying those rules. And they keep to their intention for awhile, doing carefully as the rules direct. But very few persevere. They find that others do not keep the rules,—that the preachers themselves do not keep them,—that though it is hard work to keep some of them, they yet get no credit for keeping them. They then begin to slacken, and at length become as careless and negligent of the rules as others.

Once a quarter the class is met by one of the travelling preachers. In addition to speaking to the members, he gives each a ticket, and receives their quarterly contributions. Once a year he asks each what he will give to the yearly collection. The new year's gift in the classes was not invented while I was a Methodist.

It is customary in many classes for the leader to ask one of the members occasionally to lead the class, or a part of the class, partly perhaps for the purpose of exercising the member's gifts and thus preparing him for after usefulness, and partly to encourage or please the member, and engage him more thoroughly in the cause. Most members like to be honoured, and it is generally considered an honour to be employed in any work, especially in the work of leading a class or preaching. It is astonishing how such honours are prized in the Methodist societies, and how much the careful or skilful distribution of such honours tends to perpetuate the strength and increase the resources of the body. Men that had not a word to say for Methodism or Methodist preachers yesterday, will talk for hours in their praise to day, because the preacher called upon him by name to pray in the class last night, or because the leader employed him in leading a portion of the class. Men that never thought of giving above a penny a week and a shilling a quarter till lately, will now give three-pence a week and half-a-crown a quarter, because they are appointed leaders or assistant leaders. Persons that never used to give more than copper at a collection, will give silver or gold now, because they were invited to sit on the platform lately at a Missionary meeting, or were appointed collectors at the late chapel anniversary. This love of honour appears to be universal in the Methodist society; it is felt all through the body, from the class and the prayer-leaders' meeting, to the district meeting and the conference.

As I have said, there is little instruction given in the classes. The talk, both of the members and the leaders, is generally formal and common-place; seldom or never such as is calculated to make people truly great and good.

It was to one of those classes I went. The leader was a draper of Bramley, called George Bolton. He was a ready talker, and a zealous Methodist. He was loud in his praying, rather bold in his manner, but very ignorant, and willing, for any thing I could ever see, to remain so. He was a great preacher's man, and fond of little honours, and would do any thing to be well thought of or favoured by the preachers. He knew too that to be on good terms with the preachers was the way to get customers to his shop; and he was very fond of gain. He had no scruples against laying up treasure on earth, though he read over Wesley's rules to us every quarter. He was a great respecter of persons, and though he seemed to have sense enough to know that it was wrong, he had not virtue or shame enough to keep him from practising it even in the face of the whole class. He had abundance of respect for the richer members of his class, or at least he was abundantly ready to *show* respect to them; but with the poorer members he could use as much freedom as you could like. He would tell the poorer members to speak up; but he never told the richer ones to do so, though the richer ones were generally most prone to speak very low. The rich members used generally to get into one corner by themselves, while the poor ones sat any where about the room. When he came to the rich members' corner, and found that scarce one of them could speak loud enough to be heard either by himself or us, he used to feel rather at a loss sometimes what to do, especially when he had just before been urging some of the poorer members to speak; but he durst not complain, not he. Then how did he do? He did just like himself. When he knew that some would be thinking, Why does he not ask them to speak up? he would exclaim, 'Glory be to God. They are as happy as queens here in the corner.' I wonder how we could bear with such a shallow worthless person for a leader; but we knew no better, I suppose, then. After I left, the leader grew worse, or else showed his badness more. Among other things he seduced his servant. He told her, I suppose,* that Abraham and Jacob had more wive's than one, and that what was right in them, could not be wrong in him. The girl was a Methodist herself, but yielded to his artful and wicked solicitations. The girl was pregnant; and the child was poisoned, I suppose. How often this occurred I don't know, but the crime came to light at length, and he was expelled. He is now separated from his wife, perhaps divorced, and is living with his partner in guilt in a neighbouring town.

---

* So the girl stated afterwards, I am told.

CHAPTER V.

BOOKS AND READING.

The first book I remember to have read was the Bible. I read it chiefly as a book of history, and was very greatly delighted with many of its stories. The effect which it had upon my mind at this early period, I can scarcely recollect, but one effect was to lead me to regard miracles as nothing improbable, and another was, to impress upon my mind the doctrine of one God, the creator, upholder, and governor of all things, the ruler, the judge, and the rewarder of mankind, and to strengthen in my mind the sense of right and duty.

The next book that I remember to have read, was Bunyan's Pilgrim's Progress. I regarded that book also as a history. I had no idea that it was a parable or an allegory. My impression was, that the whole was literal and true,—that there was, somewhere in the world, a real city of destruction and a new Jerusalem, and that from the one to the other there was a path through some part of the country, just such a path-way as that which Bunyan represents his pilgrim as treading. And, as I have said before, I often used to wish that I could find that way to heaven. The mystery that hung about religion made me very wishful to find some other way than that which was talked about among the Methodists, a way that I could *see* and trace with my eyes open, that would conduct me to a place of blessedness. One of the next books that I read, was a History of Joseph, a work written in a similar style to that of Klopstock's Messiah, or Milton's Paradise Lost, being partly fiction and partly truth. But I regarded that also as a true story. I had no idea at that time that people could write and print anything in the form of history, that was not real matter of fact. I was naturally a firm believer in all that was gravely spoken or printed. Another work that I early got hold of was, Richard Burdsall's Memoirs. Richard Burdsall was an early Methodist local preacher of York. My chief reason for wishing to see that book was, that I had heard there were some ghost stories in it. One of the stories was to the effect that he had been preaching at

Calverly, and slept at night at Calverly old hall,—and that through the night he was twice or thrice thrown out of his bed upon the floor in some mysterious way. I cared little about the rest of the book. I was impatient till I came to that story, and then I was satisfied. The other parts of the book I either did not understand or did not relish. But that story I did relish, and I regarded it as certain truth. As I have said already, I was a great believer in those days. I doubted nothing that I found in books. I doubted nothing that was told me by those that were older than myself. I had no idea that people could gravely either write or speak that which was not strictly true.

Another book that I read was Fawcett's advice to Youth. It was given to me by the teachers or superintendants of the Sunday School that I attended, as a reward for committing to memory and repeating some long pieces at one of the school anniversary festivals. There were some things in that book that I liked, some things that I could understand; but generally speaking it was tasteless and unintelligible, and in consequence, unprofitable. I have read it again since then, but found very little in it. It is a *made* book. I do not wonder that I took but very little interest in it when a child. It is, both in style and matter, quite of the common, milk-and-water, chaff-and-straw, good-for-nothing, orthodox kind of a theological book.

Some time after this I began to be fond of another kind of books. I read with great greediness all the fairy tales I could get hold of, and any kind of wild and foolish romances. I also read the tales of Baron Manchausen, a thousand notable things, The oddest of all oddities, and a number of similar productions. I read all, in fact, that came in my way, and that with great greediness. I then got hold of the Life and Adventures of Robin Hood, Blind Jack of Knaresbrough, Eugene Aram, Mary Bateman, and some other stories of remarkable persons or great thieves and highwaymen. A little earlier than this perhaps, I read Robinson Crusoe. But that also I regarded as a true story. I had no idea at the time I read Robinson Crusoe, that there were such things as novels, works of fiction, in existence. I liked Robinson Crusoe very much till I came towards the latter part, and then I began to be weary, and even to be disgusted with some things,— things which seemed to me to savour of profaneness. Some of the parties, if I remember right, use oaths, or oath-like expressions, and these shocked me.

I cannot, at this period, have had much discernment with respect to what was true or false, right and wrong, probable and improbable. I read accounts of the most wicked, and as they appear to me now, the most brutal and diabolical practices, without horror. Even with respect to Robinson Crusoe, though I felt shocked and disgusted at the use of what appeared to me profane expressions, yet I thought nothing amiss of his killing the poor Indians. Thus murder seemed a little thing, while a bad word seemed a great thing.

Still I was not in my *worst* state in this respect when I read Robinson Crusoe. While I was reading some of the works previously named, the life of an out-law seemed to me to be a fine way of life. To rob and kill, and live in a cave, on the banks of a river, under the shade of a wood, and set at defiance all law and authority, seemed one of the happiest or most enviable ways of life in the world, and many a time did I covet as the highest or happiest thing conceivable, to be a Robin Hood or little John. I should think that reading those books must have had a bad effect on my mind. At an earlier period of my life, I fancy I should have looked at many of those things with horror, at which I then looked with admiration. And my judgment is, that it would be well to keep such books, if it could be done, out of the hands of children, and supply their place with interesting books of another description. Children will have some kind of stirring books,—they will have some kind of stories full of life and wonder, if they can get them, and it is right that they should. But there are plenty of stirring and wonderful stories that are both true and of a worthy, elevating character, if people would make them cheap. We ought to use means to put such stories, as well as all other kinds of useful and interesting books into the hands of all the children in the world. We might thus both please and profit the young. We might both minister to the gratification and growth of their spiritual faculties, and to the cultivation of their moral or religious character. We have no more need of unnatural stimulants or excitements for children's souls than we have for their bodies. All that is wanted, both properly to satisfy their intellectual appetites, and to promote their spiritual growth and health, may be found in the storehouses of truth and goodness.

A little later on I began to read another kind of books. I met with a *Pleasing Instructor* and English Reader, which I read with a great deal of pleasure. I was very fond of some of the poetry, especially those pieces in which the rhymes were perfect, and in which the lines seemed to run on at a quick trot or gallop. But blank verse I did not like at all. I could not conceive at that time how it was that they could call any thing poetry that was not in rhyme. I could make nothing at all of blank verse. It was neither poetry nor prose in my estimation, unless it happened to be something very plain and lively indeed. And I was not over fond of those long, even lines, in such pieces as

'Pity the sorrows of a poor old man,' &c.

Or 'the Hermit,' by Parnell. After a while I met with the *Young Man's Companion*, and began to take a great deal of pleasure in reading it, especially the short pieces on natural philosophy, zoology &c. that I found there. That book gave me a taste for philosophical reading generally, and I began to be very wishful to find books that might explain to me the various departments of natural philosophy, and introduce me to a knowledge of the universe; but I could not get hold of many such books. I met with one book that *partly* gratified my taste and my wishes in this respect; it was a large, thick, old folio volume on anatomy and surgery, by Helkiah Crooke, physician to King Charles the first, I believe. I read that work through and through; yet I could hardly be more than fourteen or fifteen years of age at the time. I was wonderfully delighted with it, after I began to get fairly into it and understand it. It was a world of delight to me to have unfolded to my mind the countless and endlessly varied wonders and mysteries of the human form. But though I was greatly delighted with the work generally, I was still most delighted with certain parts of the work which treated on subjects which are generally wrapt in mystery by people, and which my parents would have been least disposed for me to think about or understand. But I soon got deprived of this book. The way in which I lost it was the same as that in which I have lost many other things since then. I could never keep my knowledge to myself. Whenever I met with any thing that delighted me, I wished to impart it to all my companions. I was as wishful to teach as I was to learn. I had not a particle of selfishness about me in this respect. I had not the least inclination to be wiser than other people; on the contrary, I felt great pleasure in making other people as knowing and clever as myself. When therefore I had learned something respecting the human frame, its wondrous structure, its various parts and their wondrous uses, I began to communicate this wonderful knowledge to others. The public street became a school of anatomy, and I knew no better than to teach its deepest mysteries to any that were willing to learn them. It was this that got me into difficulties. I used to call together my companions and others about the same age as myself, in the evening, and tell them in the streets all that I had read and learned on this marvellous subject. Some of them went home and told their mothers what I had been saying, who took the alarm at once, and caused a great outcry against me. Some of them threatened to kill me, while others complained of me to my parents, and the consequence was, I got severely reproved, and my book of wonders and of mysteries was taken away from me. That was a terrible loss to me, and bitterly did I deplore it. I contrived, however, after a while, to get the book back again, on condition that I would *paste up* two particular parts of it. But I soon took the liberty to break loose the sealed-up parts, and read them again. Still I made a more discreet use of the contents after this.

One of the next works that came into my hands was 'Wood's Bible Dictionary.' I read that also, not so much for the religious or the theological information that it gave, as for the small portions of historical, geographical, botanical, zoological, or philosophical information that it gave. I liked to read any book that contained accounts of natural history, botany, and even civil history. I cared very little for the religious portions of any of the works I met with, and I do not wonder at it now, for the theology was generally of the common place, orthodox, foolish description, neither profitable for man nor child. This was the case with the theology of the Bible dictionary.

I got hold of some other works of John Bunyan, sometime before this, that partly pleased me for awhile, such as his 'Heavenly Footman,' his 'Visions of Heaven and Hell,' his 'History of the town of Mansoul,' and what appeared to me then the most interesting of all his works, his 'History of Mr. BADMAN.' I liked his history of Mr. BADMAN best, on this account; it contained a great number of most wonderful and terrible stories about fearfully wicked persons, who had been punished by Providence in a most signal and horrible way. I was particularly excited with his stories about such as had sold themselves to the devil, and had been fetched and carried away by the devil in person, at the time specified in the written agreements which they had made with him when they sold themselves. The devil dragged some of those wretched parties, *according to the book*, from the midst of their pleasure parties, and flew up with them into the air in the presence of many witnesses, and then tore them limb from limb, and scattered their different members over the ground beneath. I read those stories over and over again while a child, and was greatly affected by them. I am not certain whether they had not something to do in causing that sleep-walking, and those terrible afflictions of soul connected with it, which I have described before. The excitement caused by such stories was certainly too great for a child, and the pictures presented were far too terrible, whether they caused those afflictions or not. And I regarded all these stories as true. I do not recollect that I suspected one of them, or any part of any one of them.

Man certainly is not born an infidel. The belief in God, in spiritual powers, in providence, in law, responsibility, rewards and punishments, is, without question, natural to man, and disbelief or unbelief is *un*natural, and acquired by unnatural causes. If I were to judge from my own experience, I should say that man is *made* to believe,—that he is especially made to believe in the great, the sublime, the terrible, the supernatural, the divine,—in short, that he is made for religion—made to be a religious being,—that religion is perfectly natural to man,—that infidelity or irreligion is *un*natural,—that superstition is a natural error into which man's religious nature runs, while man is ignorant, childish, or untutored,—that infidelity is an *un*natural error into which man runs, but not without great difficulty, sometimes in consequence of discovering that he has been so often and so much deceived by priests and theologians, and at other times in consequence of becoming the slave of evil habits, and yielding to base impulses which dislike the restraints which religion lays upon the soul.

Another work in which I found many things that I liked, was an old volume of the Methodist Magazine. The things which pleased me most were extracts from Dr. Gillies' historical collections, with respect especially to the persecutions and martyrdoms of several christians and reformers. The other things that pleased me were some wonderful stories of providential escapes, or accounts of remarkable appearances or events in the natural world. The theological department, as usual, was flat and unprofitable. It was either foolish and false, or else not adapted to my years; so that I seldom read long in the religious department before I was weary and lost.

After I began to be religious I began to read a new order of books altogether. I thought it my duty to read chiefly religious books, and I acted accordingly. Some of the religious books which I met with I read with pleasure, and others of them I read with difficulty. The first class I went through because they instructed or helped me in my duty; the others I plodded through because I now thought it my duty to read religious books. I read some religious books through a dozen times over, I should think, though I could not understand them at all. Many a time did I trudge from the beginning to the end of a great old book without obtaining one particle of clear religious light, one particle of Christ-like, practical instruction, one particle of any thing that was calculated to make me a wiser, a better, and a happier man.

Among the religious books that I liked best at this time were some of Baxter's works, such as his CALL TO THE UNCONVERTED, his SAINT'S REST, his TREATISE ON CONVERSION, &c. I was also partly pleased with 'Watts' world to come' I was better pleased still with 'Joseph Benson's Sermons.' They were not only tolerably plain, but were very full of rousing and terrible representations of the danger and misery of transgressors, as well as of tender and urgent exhortations, and I always liked any thing of that kind during the early years of my religious life. I read several of Wesley's Works, but either they were too high for me, or else they were foolish and unintelligible in many things. I know I did not feel the same pleasure in reading them in general, that I felt in reading several other religious works at that time. I fancy one reason was this. I used to read, not what I might have chosen myself, but what a *neighbour* chose. He had not time to read them himself, so he got me to come and read them to him while he was weaving. And he perhaps would wish me to read the controversial or doctrinal sermons, as they are called, such as those on the trinity, justification, perfection, regeneration, imputed righteousness, natural depravity. And these would be the very sermons least likely to satisfy me. I wanted something plain and true; something rational and practical. I always disliked confusion, inconsistency, and folly, especially religious folly. And it is a fact, that even on some practical subjects, Wesley's writings are confused, erroneous, inconsistent. This is especially the case with his remarks on love to God and charity. In most of his sermons there is something about charity and love to God, and yet in no case, that I recollect, does he speak on the subject long together without talking nonsense, without getting confused, without proving that he did not properly know what he was saying. I have since read several of Wesley's works with great pleasure and profit, especially those on the use of money, the danger of riches, the duty of self-denial, and some others of a similar character. I have also read with pleasure and profit some others of his writings. But his works generally are so full of confusion and error, that few of them are likely to have any long existence, or to be generally read by the masses of mankind.

I afterwards got some of Fletcher's works. Some of these I liked a great deal better than Wesley's works. The first of his works, his 'Appeal to matter of fact and common sense,' in which he labours hard, and at great length, to prove the common orthodox doctrine of natural, universal, hereditary depravity as the result of Adam's one transgression, I liked it exceedingly after I began to preach, and once I preached a great part of it over in one of my sermons. It seemed, as I thought then, to make the subject tolerably plain. And I was pleased with any thing that seemed to give me light,—that seemed to make the opinions that I had been taught look credible,—that gave me some intelligible foundation on which to rest my belief. I have, of course, since then changed my views on the subject of original sin, and total natural depravity. I do not believe in the orthodox doctrine now. I believe the doctrine to be unscriptural and false. I now regard Fletcher's reasonings on that subject as unsound. I believe that he frequently goes on a false foundation, and that he frequently builds with unsound materials. I consider the work to be exceedingly erroneous, and very mischievous in its tendency also. I also liked, at the time referred to, many parts of Fletcher's works in opposition to the great Calvinistic doctrines of eternal, universal, and absolute predestination; of partial, unconditional election and reprobation; of limited redemption and final perseverance, and justification by faith alone; but other parts of those works I did not like so well. Some of his arguments on those points did not appear quite clear and conclusive, and what he advocated as the truth, appeared to be only a part of the truth. There appeared to be something beyond what he laid before his readers as the truth, which was necessary to make his system complete,—something which was necessary to be brought out in order to make those subjects perfectly plain. Though I could not but see and feel that his arguments in opposition to Calvinism were unanswerable, yet I could not but feel the force of some of the Calvinistic objections grounded on Methodistical concessions. I did especially feel that some of the same arguments employed by Fletcher against the doctrine of eternal, universal predestination, were equally forcible against his doctrine of eternal, absolute, and universal fore-knowledge. Hence Fletcher seemed weaker than I liked him to seem, when treating on this subject. In grappling with the arguments of Calvinists grounded on the doctrine of fore-knowledge, neither Fletcher nor Wesley appeared to me to advantage. I never felt satisfied, that I can recollect, with the manner in which they met the Calvinists on that point. Indeed, never till I was led to give up the common doctrine of eternal, infinite, and absolute fore-knowledge, did the doctrines opposed to Calvinism appear to me to rest on their proper foundations, and to be secure against the assaults of their adversaries.

On the subject of salvation also there appeared to be something wanting, both in the sermons of Wesley and in the works of Fletcher, but especially in the sermons of Wesley. Both Wesley and Fletcher taught the doctrine of justification and salvation by works, to some extent, but neither of them appeared to go far enough on that subject. Indeed, Wesley appears to have said scarce any thing in favour of the doctrine, except in the 'large minutes.' Justification and salvation by works, or by obedience to that law, whatever it may be, under which God may have placed men, was so terribly unpopular, that both of them, but especially Wesley, appear to have been afraid to do it justice. The violent opposition, and the loud and terrible outcries which the Calvinistic theologians of the day raised against them, when they ventured to take a few steps towards the truth on this point, appears to have frightened them so much, that they never were able to muster courage to follow out their principles as they ought. I was pleased with those 'Minutes of Conference' in which the principle was laid down, that men are justified and saved both *on the condition* of obedience, and *because of*, or *for the sake of* their obedience, and in which it was laid down as a principle, that we are every moment pleasing or displeasing to God, according to the whole tenor of our dispositions and character; and I was pleased with many things that John Fletcher said in favour of these minutes: but I was not pleased at his attempts, as they appeared to me, to explain away or soften down those great, those truly Christian but offensive principles, nor could I see the reasonableness nor the propriety of many of Fletcher's distinctions on the subject of justification. He appeared to me to indulge his fancy, rather than to investigate Scripture doctrine on that subject. Nor could I feel satisfied with much that he wrote by way of reconciling, as he called it, the apostle Paul and the apostle James. He said enough to convince me, if I needed any convincing, that Calvinism was wrong, but not enough to make it plain to me that Methodism was altogether right. I had, even at that time, though very young, a feeling that there were mysteries and clouds hanging over religion and the way of salvation as taught by Methodism, which needed to be scattered, and I had also thoughts at times, and some slight hope, that I might be able at some future period to assist in scattering those clouds, and presenting those subjects to the minds of men in the clear full light of Scriptural truth. Still, though those works did not satisfy me, they did me a great deal of good. They gave me on many subjects a good deal of light; and where they did not give me light, they helped me to think,—

they exercised my spiritual faculties,—they presented subjects of thought and investigation to my mind,—they strengthened my feelings against the principal horrors and abominations of Calvinism,—they awakened or strengthened my desires to understand the truth, and they made me resolve, by the help of God, to go through the investigation of those subjects, as time and opportunity might permit, and never to rest until I had obtained that clear full view of truth that would perfectly satisfy my mind, and enable me to rest in religion as one harmonious revelation of the character and the will of God.

Another book which I read, perhaps before I read Fletcher's works, was 'Beveridge's private thoughts on Religion,' his 'Resolutions' and his 'Sermons.' At that time I thought favourably of the work, and saw nothing particular to object to in the writer's sentiments. And there was something in his style that rather pleased me. At present I neither like the style nor the sentiments of the former works; his 'Private Thoughts' and 'Resolutions.' The style is very affected, laboured, and unnatural; and the sentiments are exceedingly anti-scriptural, irrational, and Calvinistic. Some of his sermons are much better: they are tolerable both in style and sentiment: but they are far too vague and general. Though the matter is often true, perhaps generally so, yet the discourses are not sufficiently pointed and close to do much good.

It was somewhere about this time, or perhaps a little later, that I first read some works in favour of Infidelity, in opposition to Christianity. One of the first works of that description which I read was a part of 'Carlisle's Republican.' A volume of it was lent me by a neighbour who was an Infidel, a professed Atheist. Some friend of mine had been inviting this man to come and hear me preach, and he had offered to do so, provided I would preach from the first verse of the fourteenth Psalm, '*The fool hath said in his heart there is no God.*' I engaged to preach from that text. I preached. The object of the discourse was to prove that there *was* a God, such a God as the Scriptures set forth, and that the evidence in favour of the existence of such a God was such, that none but a fool, none but an ignorant or a bad man could say in his heart there was not a God. My sermon was a very long one, and it got much praised by several.

I gave most of the arguments to be found in writers on that subject. I examined Doddridge's lectures, Pearson on the creed, Dwight's system of theology, Watson's theological institutes, and some others, and took all the arguments I found in them, so far as they appeared to be sound, and arranged and modified as the case appeared to require. I also noticed some of the theories of Atheists respecting the origin and government of the world, as well as their chief objections to the doctrine that there is a God. I added various observations of my own to what I gathered from books, and especially on the origin of the world, and the necessity of a belief in God to human happiness. I may give the substance of the sermon in a future part of this memoir. It was a long discourse, and took me nearly one hour and a half in delivering it, though my utterance was very rapid. Several unbelievers came to hear me as well as the person at whose request or suggestion the discourse was preached. What effect the sermon had on them I cannot exactly say. I believe it led some of them to think less of the wisdom of Atheism than they had done. It also led the person at whose suggestion it was preached, frequently to seek my company after for the purpose of conversation. In addition to saying what he had to say, he lent me this book of Carlisle's. I was very much struck in reading some portions of the work, and agitated and shaken by its arguments on some points. The object of many of its articles was to prove Christianity irrational and false. The principal doctrines which it assailed were such as the trinity,—the common notion about the fall of man, and its effects upon the human race,—the Calvinistic notions of eternal, universal, and absoulte predestination, unconditional election and reprobation,—the Calvinistic notion of God's sovereignty or partiality,—the utter depravation of every human being born into the world, and yet the obligation of those utterly depraved beings to steer clear of all evil, and to do all that is right and good, on pain of eternal damnation. The doctrine of satisfaction to justice, also, was assailed, and the doctrine of the immateriality of the human soul, and the notion that because it is immaterial, it must, as a consequence, be immortal. I confess, that though I saw evident proofs that the writer of the work, R. Carlise, was not a lover of truth and of goodness,—though I saw, what appeared to me to be most evident proofs, that the object of the author, and the tendency of the work, was to throw down all hindrances to licentiousness, and to free men from all the restraints of virtue, and from all sense of moral obligation,—in short, though I saw plainly, as it appeared to me, that the author of the work was a bad man, and that his aims were any thing but pure and virtuous, yet I could not resist the force of many of the arguments which he brought forward on those subjects. The consequence was, that my mind was thrown into a state of doubt and suspense. I cannot say that I doubted the truth of the Christian religion exactly, but still I doubted the truth of certain doctrines which I had been taught to regard as parts of that religion. I can hardly describe the doubts I had. I neither saw clearly that those doctrines to which he objected were no part of the Christian religion, nor could I see any way by which those doctrines could be defended and proved to be rational and true. One thing began to seem almost certain, either that Christianity was not true, or that those doctrines, as generally laid down, were no parts of the Christian religion. This led to investigation. I was wishful to ascertain whether those doctrines which were assailed as irrational, were parts of Christianity or not. I began to converse on the subject with one of my religious companions, and I began to read on the subject as I had opportunity. My companion was rather troubled and alarmed at the doubts that I expressed with respect to the correctness of some of the common doctrines of what was considered orthodoxy; still, what I said had some influence on his mind, for he told me shortly after, that he wished he had never heard my doubts, for what I had said had spoiled some of his best sermons; he would never be able to preach them with comfort more. Whether he ever did preach them after that, I cannot say, but he is a preacher now in connection with the Independents. Perhaps he modified his opinions, or his way of stating them, so as both to satisfy his conscience, and to avoid offending the tickle ears of orthodoxy; or perhaps he sacrificed his conscience to the love of that easy sort of respectable life which hired preachers in general are permitted to live. This is certain, he always *meant* to be a hired preacher, either in one body or another. He tried the New Connexion; he tried the Association, formed at the time of Dr. Warren's expulsion; he hung himself for awhile on the temperance society and the order of Rechabites, and at last he got a place and a salary among the Independents. And no change looks more suspicious to me than a change from Methodism, and Methodism in its more enlightened forms, to Calvinism, the most horrid, the most revolting and unnatural system in the world. One thing however is certain, he never showed any signs of a belief in Calvinism so long as he had intercourse with me.

The book that I *chiefly* read at this time was the New Testament. I had not as yet met with any works on the corruptions of Christianity, or on the errors of what was called orthodoxy, so that I was obliged to go to the Scriptures, and search and judge for myself as to what the Scriptures taught on the points in question. Hence I was somewhat puzzled at first. There appeared to me to be many passages which, according to the common interpretation, favoured the doctrines of orthodoxy. And as I had never met with any other interpretation, those doctrines appeared to me to be Scripture doctrines. It appeared to me, for instance, that the Scriptures taught the doctrine of a trinity,—it appeared too that the Scriptures taught some kind of a doctrine of natural depravity,—it seemed as if some passages taught that Adam's sin had made all men really sinful, wicked,—morally, naturally, and, as a natural and unavoidable result, practically depraved,—it appeared from some passages that children were born into the world corrupt, under the wrath of God, and that none could be saved, not even little children, except on account and by means of the atonement made by Christ Jesus for original transgression. At the same time I found other passages, which appeared to me to contradict those passages already referred to. Some passages seemed to speak as if children were all right, made just as they should be, such as 'Suffer little children to come unto me and forbid them not, for of such is the kingdom of heaven,' and 'Except ye be converted and become as little children, ye shall in no wise enter into the kingdom of heaven;' 'In wickedness be ye children, but in understanding be ye men.' These and some similar passages seemed to contradict those other passages which appeared to teach the doctrine of infant guilt and natural depravity. So also many passages of Scripture appeared to teach that there was but one God, and that God was one,—that Christ was a man, God's son, God's messenger,—that God the *Father* was the only true God, and that Jesus Christ was that God's servant,—that God was *Christ's* God as well as *our* God, *Christ's* Father as well as *our* Father,—and that the apostles had been accustomed in their sermons, as was plain from those recorded in the Acts of the Apostles, to speak of Jesus, not as God, or as a person in the Godhead, but as a man approved or attested of God,— a man whom God raised from the dead, and made Lord and Christ. Nay more, it also appeared that though Jesus Christ was Lord for the present, and had all power given to him, both in heaven and in earth, yet he was still indebted to God for all, and that the day would come, when he should deliver up the kingdom to God, even the Father, and when God (even the Father) should be all in all.

On the doctrine of satisfaction to justice also there appeared to be contradictions in the Scripture. Some passages seemed plainly to speak as if all that God required in order that he might forgive and bless men was, that men should repent of their sins, turn away from the evil of their doings, return to obedience, do justly, love mercy, and walk humbly with their God; deny themselves of ungodliness and worldly lusts, and live soberly, righteously, and godly, in this present evil world. These, and a vast multitude of passages in fact, appeared to speak as if all that God concerned himself about was man's amendment or return to righteousness, and as if all that we had to concern ourselves about was to receive the truth as declared or revealed unto us by God, and to live according to the truth,—that if we did well we should be accepted, and that if we did ill we should have to answer for it,—that doing well was the simple reason why God blest and approved of some, and that doing ill was the simple reason why God was displeased and resolved to punish others. But there were other passages which spoke in such a way about reconciliation, redemption, atonement, propitiation, expiation, sacrifices, and the like, that according to the interpretation to which I had always been accustomed, the only interpretation that I had ever heard or read of, it seemed as if God had to be directly appeased by blood, as if the sufferings and death of Christ were a price paid to God to induce him to have any thing to do with man,—as if God, whatever change there might be in man, would still destroy him utterly and for ever, unless he was completely paid back, by some other party, all the honour of which man had robbed him,—unless he had complete compensation made him for all the loss of man's services which he had sustained. This was the interpretation which the hymn book and the preachers put upon great numbers of Scripture passages; this was the sense in which such words as redemption, propitiation, and reconciliation were used by all with whom I conversed, and at that period I had no suspicion that such interpretation was wrong. I was placed in a world of comparative darkness, surrounded with apparent inconsistencies, bewildered, perplexed, at a loss what to believe and what to reject, and at a loss how to proceed in my enquiries and investigations, so as to escape from this perplexity and bewilderment, and come to a clear, satisfactory knowledge of the truth. I had not a mortal to take me by the hand and guide me; not one by a single hint or suggestion to direct me, or by any little information to set my mind at rest. I had few with whom I could speak freely. I felt also unequal to the task of unravelling, by my own efforts, the multiplied mysteries with which I was wrapt round. I felt as if I were buried under ground, crushed and weighed down by a great mass of superincumbent darkness, and so completely held in, that I was scarcely able to move, and it seemed as if it would have to be a long long time before I should be able to scratch my way to the surface, and look out from the grave in which I felt myself buried, upon the light and the world above me. When I began to come near to the surface, and to see through the breaking sod above me, I caught a little glimmering of light; but I saw nothing clearly. Still I did not despair. I was determined, if possible, to clear away the darkness and the perplexity with which I was surrounded. I was resolved, if possible, to struggle from my grave, and clamber up to light, and I had some hopes that great and arduous as the task appeared, I should at last succeed. I felt a hope that I should still be able to understand religion, and to teach it to others sometime too. I resolved, among other things, that I would lay aside all such words and forms of expression on religious matters, as were not clearly and plainly warranted by the language of the New Testament. I was resolved to separate from all those notions that I had seen assailed in the '*Republican*,' and which I had been led partially to doubt, every thing that was not clearly, plainly, directly, and undoubtedly taught by Christ and his apostles, and thus reduce the doctrines, both as to substance and to words, to their purest form and to their original state. With these purposes I began to read the New Testament afresh. I soon found that in the New Testament there was no such word as *Trinity*, and I rejected the word, and never used it after. I found but one passage in which the word *person* was applied to God, and not one in which the word *persons* was applied to him; so I rejected the word persons in reference to God, and ceased to use it when speaking of God. On finding afterwards that the word *person* applied to God in one of the epistles was not a correct translation of the original, I gave up using the word *person* as well as the words persons and trinity, when speaking of the divine being. I also, on searching the Scriptures, discovered that it was nowhere said that Christ had paid our debts to God, or that he had become our substitute or surety, or that he had satisfied divine justice. I also discovered that the Scriptures said nothing about the merits of Christ, or the imputation of Christ's righteousness, or about trusting in Christ's blood, or relying upon his sacrifice for acceptance and salvation; so I laid aside all these forms of expressions. I proceeded in my investigation, still labouring to separate what was plain and manifestly Scriptural from that which was not Scriptural, reforming both my religious dialect and my religious sentiments, until at length I began to perceive clearly that some of the doctrines which Carlile had spoken of as Christian doctrines, were no such things, but were appendages of men, were human inventions or traditions. By this means, partly, I was preserved from infidelity. But in the estimation of professing Christians generally, I became *a heretic*. The doctrine of the trinity *as usually held*, I was led to lay aside almost altogether. The doctrine of satisfaction to justice also I was led to lay aside in like manner. With the trinity I laid aside the doctrine of the eternal sonship of Christ, or if I held it in any measure, I held it slightly, as a notion altogether doubtful or uncertain. The perusal of those infidel productions was thus overruled for my good. Though such works are dangerous, and though the perusal of them caused me much anxiety and fear, yet after awhile they were the means of conducting me to such perceptions of truth as I had never before had.

I was helped in searching after truth, a little after this time, by reading Adam Clarke's Commentary. I got a copy of it of one of the preachers, in parts, a part at a time, beginning with the New Testament, and I read it through as it came into my hands. Many an hour did I spend at night, after I had toiled hard at my work through the day, poring over Adam's Notes, and though I met with many things in the commentary which did not commend themselves to my mind as true and reasonable, I met with many other things that did. I also met with many things that, whether I liked them or not, had a tendency to make me think, and thus to prepare me to judge for myself between what was true and what was erroneous. I was very much struck with what Adam said in opposition to the eternal sonship, and though I cannot say that I adopted his notion that Christ was called the Son of God in reference to his miraculous conception, I rejected the opposite notion, the notion against which he argued, that Jesus was in some way eternally begotten according to his divine nature, and was called the Son of God in consequence of this supposed eternal generation. I was greatly assisted by Adam Clarke's commentary in getting entirely over some difficulties connected with the Calvinistic notions of election, unconditional reprobation, partial redemption, and the like. There were several passages of Scripture which I could not understand,—which I could not properly reconcile with the Methodistical doctrine, till I read Adam Clarke. I was convinced that the Calvinistic theory was false, that it must be false. I not only saw that it was contrary to multitudes of the plainest passages of Scripture, but that it was contrary to every worthy view of God's character,—that it was contrary to his justice and goodness, and utterly irrational and unnatural. Still there were many passages of Scripture, especially in the Epistle to the Romans, that seemed to countenance those doctrines. In the commentary of Adam Clarke those passages were generally explained: they were shown to refer to a very different kind of election and reprobation from those of Calvinism; and to teach a doctrine quite in harmony, and, in truth, illustrative of the goodness and justice of God.

The remarks of Adam Clarke on hired preachers in his notes on the 10th of John, in which he gives the marks of the true, good shepherd, who goes before his flock and leads them, and the false, hireling shepherds, who look for the fleece only, or come to kill and destroy, struck me a great deal, and prepared me to expect that amongst those who called themselves shepherds of Christ's flock in our day, all would not be found to resemble the chief shepherd Jesus Christ.

Adam Clarke's commentary also made me wishful to understand Greek, and consequently Latin as an introduction to Greek, and from that time I set myself to learn those languages. It was reading Clarke's commentary that first revealed to me the fact that the Scriptures, as we have them in the common English translation, were not perfect,—that the translation was defective, and in many places very erroneous,—that even the Greek texts are not all alike,—that Greek New Testaments and Greek manuscripts differed from each other, and in some cases differed very much. It was from Adam Clarke that I first discovered that there were various readings in the ancient versions and manuscripts, and that in some cases the Greek manuscripts had been corrupted. By reading Adam Clarke I also became acquainted with the names of many other books of the existence of which I had before no knowledge, some of which I afterwards procured and read. In short, Adam Clarke had a great deal to do in making me a heretic,—and in making me so great a heretic. He sowed in my mind the seeds of almost all the heresies which have since sprung up in me. My opinion of Adam Clarke is, that if he was not a heretic himself on certain points, he was very nearly one, and would have been a heretic outright, if it had not been for fear of expulsion and reproach. He had sense enough to be a heretic, and very likely was one, but lacked perhaps the courage to declare himself one. I cannot account for many things in his commentary on any other supposition. But there are many strange things which will never be brought to light in this world. People generally know very little of the world they live in, of the people with whom they are surrounded, or of the revelations which the future will make with respect to the hearts and histories of many men. What horror, and shame, and confusion,—what rage, and remorse, and torment await some people, if all that is now so carefully hid is to be brought to light,—if all that orthodox preachers say in corners, and whisper in the ears of their particular confidential friends, is to be published as on the house tops. Wo to the hypocrites; and they are very many: and alas for the timid, who, though they are not hypocrites outright, are almost hypocrites. How little will their laboured explanations and trimmings of their sentiments, and all their studied and unnatural accommodations of their thoughts, and feelings, and expressions to the prejudices or passions of men, avail them in the day of revelation. How happy are they who have thrown such fears to the winds! who have not only avoided the guilt of rank hypocrisy, but who have risen above the prudence of temporizing and trimming,—who have uttered both in deeds and words the secrets of their hearts,—who have revealed themselves,—whose thoughts and feelings have been what they ought, and whose talk and life have been in agreement with them. I say happy are they. They are worthy of their relationship to God. They are heirs of eternal bliss and fame. By mastering themselves, they have conquered the Universe, and won to themselves all the joys of eternity. Adam Clarke was a great man; but I would not be he. He was nobler than Bunting or Watson far, and he was worth a thousand such men as R. Newton; still I would not be he. He never revealed himself fully. His writings are not the true full likeness or expression of his soul. He gave himself to the world but partially: he kept back from his brethren part of what was entrusted to him by God for their sakes. Hence his writings are feeble and lame, and must soon die. God only can tell how far his errors and short-comings were sins; but whether sins or only frailties, I had rather not be he.

Another book in which I began to read about this time was a volume of Goadby's Bible, or illustrations of the Scriptures, printed or published by Goadby. It was the third volume, containing the New Testament: the other two volumes I had not then seen. I found this work in the work-shop of a neighbour and relation, and began to read it there. I read in it until I wished to borrow it and have it at home, that I might look at it more frequently. I had not read much, before many religious subjects began to present themselves to my mind in a clearer and more satisfactory light than before. Mysteries that had hung around religion from the beginning, began, in part at least, to fade away. The light began to pour itself in something like its purity upon my mind. Still my poor mind, so long accustomed to darkness, was slow to comprehend the light, and slower still to make a proper use of it in detecting and exposing anti-Christian errors and delusions. I began to see the Scripture doctrine of faith and justification in a clearer light than I had done before, and yet I was either unable or unwilling to part at once with the old erroneous notions that had been drilled into my soul. The subject of human nature also began to present itself to my mind in a different light from that in which I had been accustomed to view it before. I no longer looked on man as thoroughly depraved in consequence of Adam's one transgression. I no longer traced all man's wickedness up to natural, hereditary, irresistible depravity, introduced into his nature by God on account of the first offence of the first man. I began to look on men's depravity, not as the work or appointment of God, but as the result of their own unfaithfulness to the light and heavenly influences with which they had been favoured. The first chapter of Romans, when properly attended to, threw light on this subject. I saw that the depravity of the Gentile world was traced, not to Adam's transgression, but to the transgressions of the guilty parties themselves; and that their fall had not been an instantaneous fall in Adam, but a gradual fall in themselves, resulting from their abuse of the light and powers which God had given them. When they knew God, they glorified him not as God, neither were thankful; but turned aside from the Creator to worship the creature, and gave themselves up to vile lusts, and thus became reprobate, undiscerning in mind, enslaved to the various forms of cruelty and licentiousness enumerated in that chapter.

I also saw the passages in the third chapter of Romans, quoted from the Old Testament writings, in a different light from that in which I had been taught to regard them by the writings of Fletcher, Wesley, and Beveridge. I saw clearly that there was no reference to natural depravity at all. But that perhaps which relieved my mind most on this subject was what I read in the Epistle to the Romans, and in the Epistle to the Galatians, along with the notes in Goadby's Bible on those two Epistles, respecting the *flesh* and the *spirit*. I had been taught that the word flesh, in Scripture language, meant natural depravity, in-dwelling sin, or the sin of our nature, and that the word spirit, when put in opposition to flesh, meant the Spirit or grace of God, or something given to man, or to *some men*, to counteract or destroy the flesh. I now began to see that this orthodox view of the subject was without authority or proof. I saw that by the flesh was meant man's body, or the animal part of his nature; and that by the spirit was meant man's soul, or the intellectual and moral part of his nature. I began to see that man, to be accountable, must be free, and that to be virtuous, he must be tried. I saw that in the union of flesh and spirit in man's nature, provision was made for the discipline and trial of man. Flesh and spirit were presented to my mind as two great powers, both of them from God, and both quite right and useful in their places, yet differing in their tendencies: the flesh seeking after earthly, selfish, sensual gratification; the spirit perceiving something higher, holier, better, possessing glimpses of truth, and a consciousness of duty and obligation. The flesh, seeking to break through all restraints, and to indulge itself freely in its pleasures; the spirit discovering the law of God, approving of its purity, its holiness, its equity, its goodness, and consenting to its requirements. And here commenced the struggle; here was the trial; the flesh lusting against the spirit, the spirit lusting against the flesh, and these remaining contrary one to the other, so that man could not do as he liked. If he would act so as to have a consciousness of rectitude, the flesh must be denied; if he would have the pleasures which the flesh covets, the spirit must be resisted, and man must be convicted in himself of sin. Either the lusts of the flesh must be crucified, that the spirit may live and grow up to perfection, or the spirit must be overpowered and enslaved, that the flesh may live and revel, and satiate itself with its forbidden delights. When I saw this, there appeared no longer any mystery about the origin of evil: *liability* to sin was the natural result of man's constitution, of man's moral freedom, of the conflict between the spirit and the flesh, and sin itself was the natural result of man's neglecting to keep the flesh in its place of subjection to the spirit,—of his neglecting to regulate its instincts, and to limit its pleasures and indulgences by the spirit. Then also I began to see what constituted a life of holiness, and what a life of sin,—what it was that made man pleasing to God, and what it was that brought down on man God's displeasure. Nothing could be plainer than the teachings of the apostle on those subjects. 'To be carnally minded is death, to be spiritually minded is life and peace.' 'If ye live after the flesh ye shall die; but if ye through the spirit do mortify the deeds of the body ye shall live.' 'The minding of the things of the flesh is enmity against God.' 'Be not deceived; God is not mocked: for whatsoever a man soweth, that shall he also reap. For he that soweth to his flesh shall of the flesh reap corruption; but he that soweth to the Spirit shall of the Spirit reap life everlasting.'—Gal. vi. 7, 8. And again, 'Let no man deceive you with lying words, for because of these things,'—the pursuit of fleshly gratifications without regard to the dictates of the spirit, or the requirements of godly purity and charity,—' cometh the wrath of God upon mankind.' Right views on those subjects prepared my mind for better views on other subjects, and I consider that the work of which I am now speaking, Goadby's Bible, was the principal work in helping to clear away the errors of my earlier orthodox instructions, to remove the clouds of obscurity which had been thrown around religion, and to enable me in some measure properly to understand the truth as taught by Jesus. I never was thoroughly orthodox according to the common and false meaning of that word, after reading this book, whatever I might be before. I never could think afterwards, when I was reading what were considered orthodox writers, that they reasoned correctly and conclusively on their peculiar doctrines. And when I tested their arguments, they generally appeared to be unsound. I also found, when I referred to the passages of Scripture that they quoted in support of their notions, that they seldom quoted them fairly, or interpreted them justly and rationally. The passages quoted either did not refer to the subject to which they were applied, or their meaning was either doubtful or directly contrary to the meaning attempted to be put upon them by the advocates of orthodoxy.

After this my mind began to be less occupied for awhile with reading books on religion. As I have said before, I began about this time to turn my attention to Latin and Greek. I also began to learn a system of short-hand writing. I began to study Arithmetic also, and Grammar, Mensuration, Algebra, and the like. I also began to read something in History, especially the History of England, and Rollin's

Ancient History. The study of these things partly diverted my attention from subjects of controversy, but they tended to strengthen my mind, and give me closer habits of thought, and greater carefulness of judgment, and thus prepared me, when I returned to the study of religious subjects again, to study them to greater advantage.

I had at this time no school to go to, and I had hard to work, so that I was obliged to learn what I did learn during the short intervals of my usual labour. My work was spinning chiefly, but when I was spinning *warp* I could contrive to work, and to read and study at the same time. *Warp* had to be twisted or twined twice or thrice as much as the *weft*. When the thread had been drawn out to its proper length, I had to stand till I gave it from a dozen to twenty rounds more. While I was standing and giving it those extra rounds, I contrived to get a look at my book, which I had fixed up on the Jenny Gallows, and read a sentence or two each draw. I thought over what I read till I had drawn out the threads a second time, and while twisting *them*, I got another glance at my book, and read another sentence or two, and so went on. I also contrived to read a little even when I was spinning weft. When I was learning Latin, I was obliged to do more than just look at my book: I had to write exercises. I accustomed myself to write exercises on every part of speech and on every rule in Grammar. And I could not do that without leaving off my work for a short time. I therefore took this plan: I committed a rule to memory, and got to understand it fairly, and then stole a little time to write a single exercise, and in that way I went through a great part both of Valpy's exercises and of Turner's. I also found a little time for my studies in the morning. And the only instruction which I got from any one, I got in the morning. I used to go almost every morning to see Joseph Sutcliffe, one of the Methodist Travelling Preachers stationed at that time at Bramley, and, from five to six o'clock, have a few lessons from him in reading English, and in studying English Grammar, and then at six o'clock, I used to visit Joseph Hill, and a School-Master at Bramley, and a Methodist Local Preacher, and have a few lessons in Latin with him. Both Mr. Sutcliffe and Mr. Hill were very kind to me, and must have often put themselves to trouble and inconvenience on my account. And they not only gave me instructions, but helped me to books as well.

Joseph Sutcliffe gave me a copy of an English Grammar which he had published himself, and he also gave me a copy of the Vulgate Latin Bible. He also lent me Massilon's Sermons, and Horne on the Psalms, both of them books which I had never seen before, and which I read with a good deal of profit and delight. It is rather curious; I liked Horne on the Psalms best at that time; but when I read those books again at an after period, I liked Massilon best. Indeed Massilon became one of my favourite authors, and I yet regard him as one of the ablest writers of sermons in the world. Mr. Hill did not *give* me any books; I do not think he could very well afford to do so at that time; but he *lent* me books with the greatest liberality, and assisted me in the purchase of books. He lent me Watts on the improvement of the mind, which I liked very much, and read it twice through, though I thought there were rather more words in it than were necessary. He also lent me Watts' Logic which I read through. I liked those parts best which treated of the uses and abuses of words, the origin of errors, and the means of avoiding or of curing ourselves of errors.

It was at Mr. Hill's that I first heard Shakespeare mentioned. Mr. Lister Booth was talking to Mr. Hill, and asked him if he had ever read Shakespeare. Mr. Hill said he had. 'I am so glad to hear you say that,' replied he; 'and what did you think of him?' 'I am pleased that I read him;' said Mr Hill, 'I should be sorry not to have read him; yet the perusal of his works has left many images in my mind which I should be glad to be without.' A year or two after I met with a volume of Shakespeare's works, and read it with great delight. What pleased me most was the simplicity and beauty of his style. He had always a meaning in what he said, and you could easily see his meaning. He never talked at random, or lost himself in a mist. I had at this time been so accustomed to meet with dull, mysterious, and unmeaning stuff in many religious books as they are called, that I felt quite delighted to read something that was rational, plain, stirring, and straightforward. I have often read Shakespeare since then, and never without pleasure; though I am far from regarding him as some do, as one of the first of moral teachers.

Mr. Hill helped me to a Greek and Latin New Testament, Greek down one column, and a literal Latin translation down the other. This helped me in studying both Latin and Greek. He also helped me to a copy of Grotius on the truth of the Christian religion in Latin, and assisted me in translating it into English. He first lent me his own copy, and then procured for me a copy for myself. He assisted me in a similar way to a Latin Grammar, a Latin Dictionary, as well as other elementary works. Indeed I owe to the kindness of Mr. Hill almost every thing. While most of my fellow-townspeople neglected me, disregarded me, neither offering me instruction, nor supplying me with books, nor deigning even to converse with me on any branch of learning or on any subject in connexion with religion or science, Mr. Hill, a stranger just come to the town, was like a brother to me. He invited me to his lodgings, addressed me as a being designed by God to become a man, offered to instruct me in any thing which he understood himself, and poor as I was, and unattractive as I was both in manners and appearance, he treated me with the greatest respect, and was not ashamed to become

'My guide, philosopher, and friend.'

I shall never forget his kindness, so long as my powers of memory remain, and I can never cease to wish for opportunities of testifying my gratitude and of making some suitable returns for his kindness.

Nothing could have a happier or a more powerful effect on my mind than the kindness and respect which I received from Mr. Hill. Though Mr. Hill was but poor at that time, yet, being a stranger and something of a scholar, he was generally much respected even by the richer portion of the people. And when I found myself noticed and cared for by him, and even treated with brotherly respect, it made me feel I can scarcely tell how. I felt as if I had risen from the rank of nothingness to that of being: I felt as if I really was a man, or destined to be one, and as if the world had not been made in vain. I felt as if I had been an outcast from the world before, an outcast from the world of thoughtful, intellectual, honourable men, and as if I was now admitted within its circle. It was, in fact, a new era in my history; it was like the commencement of a new life to me, or of a new feeling of life.

When any of my townsfellows had spoken to me in the way of counsel or reproof, they had generally spoken harshly, unkindly, as if they thought I was good for nothing but to be kicked and cuffed. When a lot of young people were singing once, I innocently enough joined in, never dreaming but that I was singing tolerably well, when one of them, a sort of a leader among them said, 'Prythee hold thy *din;* thou puts every body out of tune about thee; thou art like a Jack-ass rawting, [braying.] Then again, when I told W. Windham that I had begun to learn Grammar, he said, 'Thou may as well give it up, for thou'll never learn it: I have been at it seven years, and I can't understand it yet: and I'm sure thou'll never make aught out in it.' So also when I told John Witson that I was learning shorthand, he said, 'You'd better learn to write long hand;' and when I told him that I was beginning to learn Latin, he said, 'You'd better learn English, I think.' And this is a sample of the harsh and discouraging manner in which I was generally addressed by my townsfellows. The greater part of them however seemed hardly to think me worth even a word of discouragement. Mr. Hill treated me quite differently. He gave me to understand from the first, both by word and behaviour, that he thought I might become a scholar, and do well in the world, and be of use in it. He encouraged me to learn every thing that I had a fancy to learn, and was ready to help me in learning. He always encouraged me to hope for success, and I did hope. If he reproved me, it was with gentleness; if he undertook to correct my errors, he did it with respectfulness. He treated me as if I was capable of becoming good for something, and he increased my desires and strengthened my determination to learn all I could, and to live as I ought. I shall never forget the gentleness of his reproofs. Like some others that I have seen in my lifetime, I had a disposition when in company to begin talking, before another in the company had done. I did so once in Mr. Hill's company. I began to speak while *he* was saying something. He instantly stopped, and, without either a word of reproof or a frown, began to listen to me. I saw at once I had done wrong, and stopped, that Mr. Hill might proceed; but he still waited for me to go on. I was quite ashamed of myself, and I never transgressed in that way again before him, and not often perhaps before any one else. One evening when I was walking with him I used the word *impious* putting the accent on the wrong syllable, as if it were sounded *impious:* he simply took occasion to repeat the word in a following sentence, and my error was effectually corrected. And this was the kind, the gentle and respectful manner in which he corrected me in all things.

Still, after all, I at one time gave this kind friend great pain by a piece of most unreasonable behaviour, which I have often and bitterly lamented. He knew that I wished to be employed as a teacher in a school, and very kindly used his influence to procure me a situation as usher in a boarding school at Market Weighton, kept by Luke Richardson, a very decent man, as far as I know. Mr. Hill, if I am not mistaken, had occupied the same situation before me. Both my obligations to Mr. Hill, who, besides all his other favours, had procured the situation for me, when he might perhaps have recommended a far better qualified person, and a respect to what was due to myself, to my employer, and to God required, that I should do my utmost to give satisfaction to my employer,—that I should even put myself to great inconvenience and loss rather than fail to meet the reasonable expectations of my friends. But I did not. I left my situation about the end of six weeks, and that under circumstances calculated to grieve my employer and my friend very bitterly. The affair was as follows. I had never been from home above a week at a time before, and that only while I was at school at Leeds, only four miles from home, so that I had never been weaned from home at all. The consequence was, that after I had been about a fortnight at Market Weighton, I began to feel home sick, and to long for a sight of my mother and father, my brothers and sisters, and all my companions and friends. Still I struggled with my inclination, and tried to be at ease, and contrived to get over another week or two. My feelings at length became almost uncontrollable. My longing for home became intense. I was miserable, in fact; almost intolerably miserable. And I had no idea that time would make me feel better, and enable me to be comfortable from home. So I asked for permission to go home and see my friends for a day or two. The request looked a foolish one to Mr. Richardson; he thought it quite unreasonable for me to think of going forty miles, after so short a period, merely to see my friends. But I was not to be satisfied with anything less. I felt as if I could hardly live unless I went home. My employer consented at last to let me go for a day or two, and I went. I stayed a day longer than had been agreed upon, and on my return Mr. Richardson looked very unpleasantly at me, and said something that made me feel uncomfortable. And I was not in a fit state to be vexed just then. Then other things were not to my taste, and much as I had suffered, I had not yet learned that patience under trials which is so essential to the perfection of the soul and the true enjoyment of life. The way of living too was very different from that to which I had been accustomed at home, and I quarrelled at that. Some of the scholars were not so orderly or manageable as I wished them to be, and I got into trouble by chastising one of them over roughly. I had always had *beer* at home, but I had none allowed me here; and this was a grief to me then. Then my home-sickness came on again after a while, and all these things together led me to resolve that I would stay no longer. I returned home. Mr. Hill was astonished, and so were others. Mr. Hill too was very much grieved, and well he might. He expressed his disapprobation to his friends, and I had no more sense of propriety than to charge him with evil speaking, and that even formally in the Quarterly Meeting of the circuit. I am ashamed of myself when I think of these things, but they cannot be recalled. I can only acknowledge my fault, and hope that I may never err so greatly again. Yet great and grievous as was my offence, Mr. Hill forgave me, and became my friend again. He rejoiced in my success when I was a travelling preacher, and always welcomed me to his house when I visited my native place. And even now, though my opinions are so different from his own, he still retains his gentleness of manner towards me, and never, either in word, or look, or deed, shows anything but a spirit of respect and love. God bless him, and return his kindness a thousand fold in blessings into his own bosom.

Joseph Sutcliffe was very much of the same disposition as Joseph Hill. Both of them showed the same desire that I should do well; both of them thought there was something in me, which, if cultivated, might make me a useful man; and both were condescending enough to stoop to become my teachers, and kind and generous enough to give or lend me books. Mr. Sutcliffe became interested in me in consequence of hearing me pray at a prayer meeting. When I went, according to his invitation, to see him at his house, he told me that I was to be a DIVINE. I did not understand at that time what the word divine meant, but I supposed it to mean some kind of a preacher, and was glad to hear such a prediction. He was very wishful to have me to become a travelling preacher, and did what he could to prepare the way for it; but he only remained in the circuit about a year, I believe, so that his plans were not carried out. I was greatly afflicted when he left the circuit; I felt as if I had lost a dear relation, and mourned bitterly for many days. He frequently wrote to me, and I wrote to him; and even after I joined the New Connexion he still addressed me as one of his children, and gave me his fatherly advice. He is still alive, I believe, though very old, and he still regards me with good-will, though he considers me as having gone fearfully astray. God bless him, and make his last days peaceful and happy.

The manner in which Joseph Hill was led to take so much interest in me was as follows. A number of young persons met on Saturday evenings to exercise themselves in *preaching*, and their meeting place was a chamber over one of Mr. Hill's rooms. I joined this company of young preachers, and took my turn in preaching. Mr. Hill, it seems, could hear our performances from his room, and had heard mine among the rest, and his attentions to me began from that time. Some time afterwards I was requested by a cousin of mine to write a letter to her brother who was dangerously ill in the Isle of Man. I wrote a letter of considerable length, urging him to direct his thoughts to religion. This letter was taken to Mr. Hill by my cousin before it was sent off. He read it with surprise and pleasure, as I was told, and after that he encouraged me to study Grammar, Latin, and the like.

While Mr. Hill was teaching me Latin, Mr. Sutcliffe was teaching me English Grammar. But Mr. Hill was not aware for a length of time, that while I was receiving instruction from him in Latin, I was receiving instruction in English Grammar from Mr. Sutcliffe; nor was Mr. Sutcliffe aware that while he was instructing me in English Grammar, I was receiving instructions in Latin from Mr. Hill. Both had begun to teach me, each in his own way, without any knowledge of each others plan, and I received the instructions of both, and made the best use of them I could. After awhile Mr. Hill told me I might now begin to learn English Grammar. I told him I *had* been learning it for some time. He was astonished at that, and began to examine me, and was delighted when he found how far I had gone. About the same time, Mr. Sutcliffe said I might now begin to learn Latin. I told him I *had* begun a good while ago. Mr. Sutcliffe seemed more astonished than Mr. Hill had seemed; and questioned and examined me at some length. After he had examined me, he said I was far enough advanced to begin to learn Greek, so I began that morning, and before the close of the day, though I had to spin all day, I read in some way the first chapter of Matthew's gospel through in Greek.

The study of English Grammar helped me to learn Latin faster, and my Latin exercises helped me to understand the English Grammar, so that I got more rapidly on with both than I should have been likely to do perhaps with either of them separately.

I went on learning Greek, but durst not tell my friend who was teaching me Latin, for fear he should think that I was attempting more than I could accomplish; but it was not long before he said he thought I had gone far enough in Latin to fit me for beginning with Greek. I told him I *had* begun with Greek. He then examined me to see how far I had gone, and seemed somewhat surprised at the proficiency I had made.

While I was thus learning English and Latin, and Greek and short-hand, and working at my business from twelve to sixteen hours a day, I was also occupied in preaching on Sundays, and in preparing sermons also during the week. Besides preaching, I regularly spent at this period, many hours on the Sunday in visiting, in company with two or three religious companions, several old and sick people, to talk to them about religion. I also taught at the Sunday School as well, besides attending, both through the week and on the Sabbath, prayer meetings, class meetings, fellowship meetings and preachings. So that I was completely and constantly occupied. At length I began to be unwell;—I mean more unwell than usual. My stomach was exceedingly disordered. I had the heart-burn almost all day long, as well as other symptoms of indigestion. I also felt a general weakness. I had frequent attacks of quinsey, and violent attacks too. Then I got the Erysipelas in my left hand, and nothing that I could do seemed to have any power to remove it. This so disabled me that I could not pursue my regular work. I had, in consequence, more time at my disposal for learning, and I made some use of it. I recollect the first time I had a full hour for writing Latin exercises. It seemed so great a privilege! And the hour seemed so long compared with the few moments I had been able to snatch from my daily labour at other times, that it seemed as if it would hardly ever come to an end. But I had now many hours a day for near a month together, and I got on with my exercises very rapidly. At length, when nothing seemed to have any effect upon my complaint, and when it was plain that my complaint would not allow me to go on with my regular work, my father thought he might as well let me go to school for a short time, and employ myself in study altogether. This was a delightful proposal to me. It was just the thing I wanted. I had often wished to go to school, but it had seemed as if there was very little prospect of having my wishes realised. We were, however, at this time in better circumstances than we had been before: my father was therefore better able to do something in assisting me in my learning than he had been at any former period. And harsh as he had often been to me, he was yet a kind-hearted father. He accordingly sent me to James Sigston's school, at Leeds. I was there as a weekly boarder. I had now nothing else to do but to learn, and I gave myself up very heartily to the work. I went on with my Latin; I studied Arithmetic, Mensuration, Geometry, and a little Algebra. I did something, though little, at Book-keeping; but as the Book-keeping was all theory and no practice, I did not understand it well. I did not, however, reap *unmixed* advantages from going to school. Some of my school-fellows were not all that they should be, and I sustained loss through my connection with them: and though I was very eager after knowledge, it was rather *too* great a change from hard and continual bodily labour, to entire bodily rest. I was not able to spend the whole day in close application to study, at least not always; and the intervals which I spent away from my studies were often, in consequence of my school-fellows, occasions of temptation to indolence and thoughtlessness.

Mr. Sigston had rather a large and good library, which was left at the service of the teachers and boarders. This was a great advantage to me. I never had had free access to any large quantity of books before, much less had I had any considerable amount of leisure for reading or looking over books. I had now both books and leisure, and I read a good many of the books, and looked over or looked through almost all the rest. It was here I first met with Baxter's Christian Directory. I was more delighted with this book than any I had ever seen. It was so full, so comprehensive, and, generally speaking, so clear, and so practical, and in all respects so adapted to my tastes and wants at that time, that I felt it to be an exceedingly rich treasure. I read in it almost continually in my hours of leisure, until I had read it through. I believe no book ever did more to store my mind with good religious thoughts and practical Christian truth than this book did. Perhaps no book ever exercised a more favourable and powerful influence upon my own mind than this, and no book contributed more to give me what preparation I ever possessed, for instructing, persuading, and edifying my fellow-men.

Another work which I met with here, was Lucas' Enquiry after Happiness, and some other practical works of his. I read these with pleasure and with profit; but the style was not so natural, nor were the thoughts so rich and practical, so level to my capacity as Baxter's were.

Another work which I met with in the library was Law's Serious Call to a devout and holy Life. I read this work also both with pleasure and profit,—but I have often wondered since I became better acquainted with the work, that I did not prize it more highly at that time. But I suppose my mind was not as yet *prepared* sufficiently to appreciate it. I now regard that work as one of the richest, best, most Evangelical, and truly Christian books in the world. It has its defects: it has its errors: and I wish what I say of the work to be applied to the work generally only, and not to every section or to every chapter. Some sections are objectionable: but as a whole I know no work superior to it, and in some respects, I hardly know its equal.

Another book that I met with in the school library was Downame's works, a large, thick, quarto volume. I met with many things in this work that pleased me and profited me. The perusal of it enriched my mind with fresh additions to my little store of religious knowledge. But Baxter and Law have improved on further acquaintance with them; while Downame and some others have gone down in my estimation.

It was in this library that I first met with the writings of any of the great English poets, and it was about this time that I first began to see any sense, or beauty, or worth, in works that were written in what is called blank verse. The first great poet that I got hold of was Milton. I read his 'Paradise Lost' at gallop. After I had begun I felt little or no inclination to rest, till I had got to the end. I also read a collection of small poems, on 'Death and the Grave,' by Porteus, Blair, Gray, and Young. I then read 'Young's *Night Thoughts*;' but I found it difficult to understand many parts of the book. Some parts I understood well enough, and relished them highly. Indeed, many passages seemed to be the pure result of heavenly inspiration. But I did not think quite so highly of Young afterwards, when I found that so many of his richest sentiments were borrowed from Seneca and others; that they were not so much the overflowings of his own soul, as translations from the writings of the classics.

It was about this time that I met with that volume of Shakespeare, of which I have spoken, the first book of plays I ever met with. I read this volume with great greediness, and my thirst for poetical reading was increased thereby. I then read Cowper, and Pope, and Dryden, and Goldsmith; Rogers, Akenside, Thomson, and a lot more that I do not particularly recollect just now. I also purchased the works of Byron and read them. I was so fond of poetry at one time, that I bought or borrowed, as I had opportunity, every poetical work that I could meet with. Some of them I liked very much; others of them I liked only middling; and some of them I did not like at all. I read Savage; but I never found anything in him that seemed to me to be worth anything. I read Shenstone; but his works seemed to me to be the most unprofitable and unsubstantial things I ever met with. I only recollect one verse in all his volume, that I thought worth remembering; the verse beginning,

'I have found out a gift for my fair.'

While I was at school I read Grotius on the 'Truth of the Christian Religion,' in Latin, and translated it into English. I read parts also of Virgil, Ovid, and Horace, Cicero, Florus, Justin, Sallust, Livy, Tacitus, Seneca the philosopher, and Seneca the dramatic writer; and some other Latin works. I was most pleased with Cicero. There seemed such a breadth, such a brightness, and such a fulness of soul about

Cicero, that I was quite delighted, and sometimes almost enraptured, while I was translating him.

The first time I recollect to have felt a strong relish for beauty of style and true eloquence, was while I was reading and translating one of Cicero's orations. Cicero's *thoughts* also appeared to me to be more natural, more true, more rational than those of most other Latin writers that I looked at. I liked many things in Seneca. I admired greatly many of his sentences: but there was a great deal in Seneca that I did *not* like. He often used arguments, when he was attempting to prove a point, which did not appear to me to be sound; arguments that I could see through clearly; arguments that rested entirely upon a play on words, or on some metaphysical conceit: and I always disliked such arguing as this from the very first that I recollect to have met with it. Perhaps I did not make allowances sufficient for Seneca; I cannot tell. But I thought that the arguments that *I* could so clearly see through, *he* must have seen through too, and that he must have used them, not because he thought them to be solid and strong, but merely to impose upon his readers.

I think it would be about this time that I read Richard Watson's Theological Institutes. Some things in this work I did not then well understand, so I read them and left them. Other things I *did* understand, and approve. Other things I understood but did not approve. I thought I found in Watson's work, even in those parts in which he was treating on the most important and solemn subjects, proofs of the same fault that I had discovered in Seneca, namely, the use of weak, unsound arguments, in support of his views. Even in that part of his work in which he endeavours to prove the existence of a God, he uses arguments that appear to me altogether inconclusive, and therefore worse than worthless; and the defect in the arguments seemed to me so plain and so striking, that it seemed a mystery how Watson himself could have overlooked it. I met with similar arguments in other parts of his works, employed in support of other principles; and though I did not come to the conclusion at that time that Watson was a dishonest writer,—that he made use of arguments which he himself did not believe to be sound and conclusive,—yet I had some kind of painful feelings, something approaching to suspicion, that such was the case. A while after, I was led altogether to suspect that Watson was guilty of that crime. I met with a Sermon preached by him at the formation of the Methodist Missionary Society at Leeds. In that Sermon he labours to make the impression upon the people that the heathen are all *lost*,—that they are not only in *danger, greater* danger than all other people, on account of the disadvantages under which they are left by God, but that it is, to say the least, altogether doubtful or uncertain whether any of them can be saved at all,—that it is exceedingly probable, if not quite certain, that unless the gospel of Christ be carried to them, they will every one be doomed to eternal life in torment. At the same time he seems almost afraid to speak his thoughts plainly out. He wraps his sentiments, (if I may call them his sentiments,) he wraps the sentiments which he wishes to convey to the minds of his hearers, in long, dark sentences, of doubtful and ambiguous signification, but still leaving the impression on the minds of the people, that he considered the state of all the heathens left without the gospel, as not merely doubtful, but utterly hopeless. I could not, when I read this Sermon, resist the impression, that he wrote it, knowing it to be false, and I never after could feel towards him that respect which I have always wished to feel towards a religious writer. I have read Watson's Institutes since then, but I do not think highly of them. He must of course have spent a great deal of time upon them, and they have the marks of considerable talent; but what respect can a man have for a book when he is obliged to believe that the author was not strictly honest,—that he wrote not from the perceptions of truth in his own soul, but from a regard to the favour of his patrons or masters, and that he studied more to accommodate himself and his views to Jabez Bunting and the conference, than to truth and to the wants of the children of men.

I think it would be sometime about this period that I read through the whole of Wesley's Christian Library so called, in fifty duodecimo volumes. Some of those works I liked very well, and others I did not like. Some of them I could not understand at all. Among those that I could not well understand were Arndt's True Christianity, Ambrose's Looking unto Jesus, some works by Preston, and some others of a similar stamp. I think in one or two cases I read from the beginning to the end of a volume without having a clear conception of any one thing that the writer said. I was too modest and diffident at that time to lay the blame on the writers, so I laid it on myself, supposing that the reason why I found nothing clear, intelligible, profitable in the books, was the weakness of my own mind, and my lack of ability to understand what I supposed might be the deep things of God. I have looked at some of those books since, and have found that I laid the fault on the wrong party; that the evil was not in me, but in the books themselves,—that the reason why I could not understand them was, that there was nothing to be understood,—that the books were made up of words, and common-place errors, and mystical and nonsensical expressions, and that there was no light or truth in them. Others of the works composing the Library I liked well. Law's Serious Call was one that I had read before. Baxter's Saint's Everlasting Rest was another that I had read before. The Homilies of Macarius formed another volume. Those I liked tolerably well, especially as they had been written so very early in the Christian era. The Epistles of Ignatius, Polycarp, and some other relics of antiquity contained in the library I did not like.

Jeremy Taylor's Holy Living and Dying I liked middling, but his style seemed too wordy. What impression was made by other parts of the Christian Library I do not now exactly recollect. I do however remember now that I was pleased with some of the works of Robert Bolton, as well as with some other parts of the Library.

Another book that I read some where about this time was Mosheim's Church History. This work opened almost a new world to my mind, and a strange, dark world it was. Oh, how I was amazed to find how what were regarded as the Fathers of the Christian Church, quarrelled, reproached, persecuted, abused, and murdered one another;—what trifles they made into essential articles of faith;—what foolish and nonsensical notions they put into their creeds as fundamental doctrines of Christianity;—with what fierceness they struggled for power,—with what craft they sought to supplant each other, and to enslave the people,—with what greediness of soul they grasped after wealth, and to what a fearful extent they succeeded in corrupting and perverting, in obscuring and almost destroying the religion of Jesus. My notions of religion at this time, so far as I had any notions of my own, were, that it consisted in the fear and love of God, in the practice of all goodness, and that its great rewards were the smile of God, the testimony of a good conscience, and the hopes and foretastes of eternal life. I had no idea that religion could ever be mixed up with political intrigues; that churches could have any thing to do with Government quarrels; that preachers and teachers of the gospel could ever dream of seeking political power, and earthly titles and dominion; and when I found from Mosheim that a great part of the history of the church, so called, was a history of political strife, of priestly persecutions, of covetousness and ambition under spiritual names, of wars, and insurrections, and political convulsions; when I saw religion first blending with the world, and then the world completely absorbing and swallowing up religion, and putting in its place false creeds and foolish rites, and priestly power, how strangely did I feel. I shall never forget the impression that was made upon my mind by reading this history of the church by Mosheim. I could not wonder, when religion was presented to men in such forms as it bore in Mosheim, that many should reject it as a priestly fable or political device, and loathe both it and its pretended ministers.

CHAPTER VI.

PREACHING, &c.

I stated that some time after I became a Methodist, I began to preach. It may not be amiss to give here a short account of my labours and trials and successes as a preacher. At first I supposed, according to the general doctrine, that every one whose duty it was to preach, should have some special, supernatural call to the work. I had an impression upon my mind from the beginning of my religious career, and even from the time I was only twelve or thirteen years of age, that it would sometime be my duty or my lot to preach and teach the gospel, and I accordingly began to look and wait for the special, supernatural call to engage in the work which was so generally considered necessary. In what form the call should come, I could not tell. I was therefore left to judge for myself when I had the call. One day when I was reading John Nelson's Journal, I was very much affected when I came to one part, and the impression that I was to preach the gospel was very strong upon my mind. I saw that the work was one of great difficulty and responsibility, yet it appeared to me that to engage in that work would be my duty, and I burst into tears. I regarded my feelings on this occasion, as the special or supernatural call, and began to prepare myself for the work of preaching accordingly. My views about a call to the ministry are now very different from what they were then. I now consider every man called to preach the gospel, who has ability to preach it, and who sees around him persons who are in want of Gospel instruction. The religion of Christ requires us to love God with all our heart and soul and mind and strength, and to love our neighbours as ourselves. It requires us accordingly to do all we can to promote God's glory and the welfare of mankind. If a man can promote God's glory and the welfare of his fellow-men by preaching or teaching the gospel, he is bound, by those general commands, to preach it. To wait for any special, supernatural call to induce him to engage in the work, is foolish. He ought to begin to teach as soon as he has learned the truth. He ought to employ all his powers in communicating to others that light and those blessings which God has communicated to him. The possession of ability therefore is a sufficient call to every one to preach the gospel. It is as foolish to wait for a special call to preach, as it would be to wait for a special call to teach our children, to learn a trade, to go a journey, to build a house, to make a bargain, or to get our breakfast. We have a general, a universal, an eternal call, to learn the truth, to live righteously, to do good, to make every body as wise and good and happy as possible, and he who waits for a further call is either foolish or something worse.

I cannot look back upon the steps I took in reference to preaching, with unmixed approbation and satisfaction. I did many things that I should not do now, many things which I should now regard as very unnatural and wrong. One of those things was this. There were several young men, members of the Methodist Society, as I have already intimated, who, before I had joined the Methodist society, had formed a meeting for the purpose of exercising themselves in preaching. They met on Saturday night, in an upper room, and each person was expected in his turn to deliver something in the shape of a sermon. They took texts, and divided them according to the usual fashion, and tried to talk a while on each division. They did not speak to one another for one another's edification; they simply spoke for the purpose of *practising*, or exercising themselves in the *art* of preaching. I was invited to this meeting, and went. I was requested to take my turn in preaching, and I did so. I fixed upon a text, and tried to prepare a discourse. My text was, 'Create in me a clean heart, O God, and renew a right spirit within me.' My sermon was to be on Sanctification, or Christian perfection. To prepare myself I looked at John Wesley's work on that subject, and at his sermons on that subject also. I met with another book also, a little old one, on the same subject. Who its author was I do not know. I also got Pike's dialogues on sanctification, and read them, and with these, along with my Bible, I contrived to collect a considerable amount of matter, and thus provided, I went to the meeting, and preached. I do not now recollect exactly what I said, nor can I recollect exactly what kind of notions I dealt out; but I suppose I must have got on tolerably well in talking, for the young men at the meeting spoke favourably of my performance, and encouraged me to go on. One of them even whispered in my ear that I should one day be a travelling preacher. I preached in this private assembly several times, and generally, if not always with what was considered tolerable success. Once I preached on eternal torments. On this occasion I read '*Watts' World to come*,' '*Benson's four sermons on Hell*,' and that part of '*Baxter's Saint's rest*' which speaks of the misery of those who lose that rest, as well as the Bible and some other books, to supply myself with descriptions of the miseries of the lost. My descriptions were sufficiently long and terrible, and my hearers were more satisfied than ever that I should make a preacher. What other texts I preached from I do not recollect. This was one thing that I would not do now. I feel the greatest repugnance to every thing like preaching in the way of *practice* or of trial of one's ability. It seems to me that men should never talk or preach but in good faith, from their own convictions, and for the purpose of teaching or edifying others.

The scenes at this preaching meeting were at times most ridiculous or pitiable. Sometimes a young person would get up to preach, give out his hymn, go through his prayer, and read over his text, and then stick fast, and stand dumb as a post. At another time the person would deliver a fine introduction, divide his text into three heads, then forget what his heads were. Sometimes the preacher would remember his heads, and repeat them over and over, without being able to add a syllable by way of a *tale* to his heads. And such ludicrous and pitiable looks they would wear in their embarrassment, as would have moved to a smile the gravest soul on earth. One night the preacher got on pretty well for a few moments, and then broke down completely all at once. He looked round for a moment or two, and then exclaimed; 'Friends, I'm fast, I cannot get on. I sometimes have my mind full of good ideas, and when I begin to talk they all fly away, and I have not one left. I'll tell you what, friends, I think my brains want taking out and washing. The meeting could hold no longer. We burst out a laughing in spite of ourselves, and it was a long, long time before we could so far recover our gravity as to think ourselves fit to conclude with singing and prayer. The preacher however was reproved, and I do not recollect that he was allowed to preach there any more. Such meetings, in my judgment, are calculated to do harm. I felt even then that they were not the right kind of meetings: and some time after I did myself form another kind of meeting, for mutual improvement in religious knowledge, where each one was required to bring a written article, on some particular subject, which was read and criticised expressly for the benefit of all who were present. More particulars about this meeting I may give hereafter. At present I only name it as better and more natural than the preaching meeting of which I have been speaking.

It was not long before I was invited to preach at one of our home missionary or out of the way country stations, in some one's place. I went and preached. My text was, 'Say ye to the righteous it shall be well with him, for he shall eat the fruit of his doings: but woe unto the wicked, it shall be ill with him; for the reward of his hands shall be given him.' My object was, I believe, to do good, and I laboured with all my might. It was in a private house, and the room was crowded, and the weather being very hot, I was, before I had finished, almost parched or choked with thirst. The place where I preached was between Pudsey and Bradford, and was called Gibralter. The object of my sermon was to persuade people to cease to do evil and to learn to do well, and the chief part of its substance was a statement of the happiness or advantages of being good, and of the miseries and dangers of being bad. It was altogether a simple, practical, persuasive sermon. It contained a sprinkling of orthodox errors, but much of it was no more than what I should preach even now. I do not recollect that any of the audience commended my performance, or gave me any encouragement to persevere, except a poor old aunt of mine that happened to be there. She, poor woman, thought I had done wonderfully well, and she invited me to go and preach at her house whenever I had an opportunity.

The next time I preached was at Jumble's Well, another place near Pudsey. My text was Ezekiel xxxiii, 11, 'Say unto them, as I live, saith the Lord God, I have no pleasure in the death of the wicked; but that the wicked turn from his way and live: turn ye, turn ye from your evil ways; for why will ye die, O house of Israel?' I really felt considerable concern for those that were neglecting religion, and urged upon them the unreasonableness of going forward in sin. I first showed them that the wicked would die, and then described to them the horrors of that death according to orthodox notions, understanding death to mean eternal life. I then showed them that God had no pleasure in the sinner's death, but would have all to turn from sin and live. This I proved by many arguments drawn from God's character, and words, and works. I also spoke of the blessedness of that future life which those who turned to God and live to please him should enjoy. I then entreated and exhorted them to turn. I noticed some objections they might have to turn, and tried to answer them. Even this sermon also contained much that I should feel free to preach at the present time.

The next time I preached was also at a place near Pudsey. The preaching place was a large room in the Work-house, next to the room in which the idiots and maniacs were confined. My text was, 'It is time to seek the Lord.' I spoke on the importance of seeking the Lord, and on the necessity of seeking him *now* without *delay*, and for anything that I can recollect, the address was plain and practical, and I do not recollect that there was anything in it either peculiarly erroneous or offensive. Yet some of the persons that heard me said, that I should have been more in my place if I had been in the *next room*, that is, the room where the mad people were kept, which was another way of saying I was myself a maniac or idiot. Others however thought differently, I suppose. The next time I preached was at Bramley, in my native place. This was in July, nearly a year after I had joined the Methodist society. I met with more encouragement here. I then began to preach more regularly, at a variety of places, and on the recommendation of some that heard me, I was put upon the plan as a home missionary, or exhorter. The places that I visited were chiefly out of the way country places, where the regular preachers were not accustomed to go. One place was called Alcoats, another Broadlane, another Farnley Moor Side, another Armley Hill Top, another Sodom, or Little More Side, and there were also a number of smaller places. I spent a year or two in visiting those places, along with a number of other young men, and preaching to the people that came to hear. I generally took a plain text, and my object in preaching was always I believe either to persuade sinners to repent and turn to God, or else to urge those that *had* given themselves to God, to hold on and persevere to the end. The following were some of my texts. 'Prepare to meet thy God, O Israel.' 'Let him that thinketh he standeth, take heed lest he fall.' 'Take heed therefore how ye hear.' 'He that believeth shall be saved, and he that believeth not shall be damned.' 'Because I have called and ye have refused, I have stretched out my hand and no man regarded; but ye have set at nought all my counsels, and would none of my reproof; therefore will I laugh at your calamity, and mock when your fear cometh.' 'The fool hath said in his heart there is no God.' 'My spirit shall not always strive with man.' 'Blessed are the pure in heart, for they shall see God.' 'Grow in grace, and in the knowledge of our Lord and Saviour Jesus Christ.' Another text on which I preached was from the parable of the supper, Matt. xxii, 'and he was speechless.' The object of that discourse was to show, that if men lived in sin, and died without securing the blessings of Christianity, they would be left without excuse :—that God wished all to be saved,—that he had done all that was needful on his part, in order to their salvation,—and that the blessings of salvation were offered on reasonable conditions, and might be sought and secured without any risk or inconvenience which the rewards of Christianity would not infinitely more than compensate, &c.

I went on preaching in this way for a length of time. I took fresh texts, and prepared fresh sermons. On one occasion I preached from 'Behold I bring you glad tidings of great joy, which shall be to all people: for unto you is born this day, in the city of David, a Saviour, which is Christ the Lord.' In this sermon my object was to show that men had reason to be joyful, very joyful, at the news of the birth of Christ, because the salvation which he came to accomplish was so great, so glorious. I showed that the work which he came to accomplish was calculated to make the whole human race perfectly and eternally happy. I observed that that from which Jesus Christ had come to save men was *sin*,—that sin was the greatest of all evils, and the fountain of all other evils,—that Christ, therefore, in saving us from sin, dried up the fountain of man's wretchedness altogether,—that in restoring us to holiness he restored us to happiness, and that if the end for which he came should be fully and universally accomplished, the days of paradise would be restored, or that even far happier days than paradise had ever seen would dawn upon the earth.

Another text from which I preached with much zeal was, 'Love not the world, neither the things that are in the world; if any man love the world, the love of the Father is not in him.' The object of this discourse was to show the evil of loving money. The substance of the discourse was taken partly from the Bible, but chiefly from two Discourses of Bishop Beveredge's, and from the Treatise of Baxter on the *Crucifixion of the world by the Cross of Christ*, and from his Christian Directory. I do not know how those sermons were received exactly. There was a great deal of truth in many of them, but there were also considerable mixtures of error, especially in some of them. Then my manner and pronunciation would be against me. And in addition to that, the impression, I imagine, would often be, that I was treating on subjects to which I was unequal on account of my youth. Many of my hearers would judge that I should leave those subjects to older preachers, and some, I suppose, began to believe that I was a dangerous person to be placed in the pulpit. In truth, I had begun thus early to be a reformer.

Another subject on which I preached was, John iii. 16, 'God so loved the world that he gave his only begotten Son, that whosoever believeth in him should not perish, but have everlasting life.' On this text I explained the word world, showing that it meant all mankind. I then showed that the world was in a sad, a perishing condition,—that God sent Christ to save it from perishing, and to bring it to eternal life,—that God did this in pure love,—that God's love, thus shown in seeking the salvation of the world, was very great,—and that all that was necessary on our part to secure our everlasting salvation was, that we should believe on Christ and obey the Gospel.

Another of my texts was, 'If it seem evil to you to serve the Lord, choose ye this day whom ye will serve.' Those were the principal texts on which I preached during the first three years of my labours as a preacher. I recollect another, viz., 'Ye must be born again;' and another, 'God is love;' and another, 'How shall ye escape, if ye neglect so great salvation;' and another, 'Ye are not your own, ye are bought with a price, therefore glorify God with your bodies and with your spirits, which are his.'

After I had preached as a home missionary for perhaps two years, it was proposed at a local preachers' meeting that I should come on the plan as a local preacher on trial. I was accordingly appointed to preach a trial sermon before one of the travelling preachers and two of the local preachers. I took for my text, 'Go ye into all the world, and preach the gospel to every creature; he that believeth shall be saved, and he that believeth not shall be damned.' The object of the discourse was to show that if men did not believe the gospel when it was preached to them and placed before them in its fulness of evidence, they *deserved* to be damned,—that God was perfectly *just* in thus punishing men when they rejected the gospel under such circumstances,—that they went in opposition to such clear light, and to such a vast amount of overwhelming evidence, that there was no excuse for them. I had at that time just been translating Grotius on The Truth of the Christian religion, and the subject was quite fresh upon my mind. And with translating the work first into

English, and then back into Latin, I had got nearly the whole of the book, as well as the whole train of its reasoning, quite fixed in my memory. The work of Grotius, therefore, with some additions, amplifications, and curtailments, was the substance of my sermon. It was on a week-night that I preached this sermon, and in a private house at Kirkstall. It was preached to a very small company, and perhaps there was not one person in the room that disbelieved the gospel. The sermon, therefore, to say the least, was out of place. But it was a *trial* sermon; a sermon to be preached for the sake of affording my judges an opportunity of deciding whether I was qualified for a place on the local preachers' plan or not, and as such they ought to have regarded it, according to their own principle of requiring trial sermons. Their decision, however, was against me. They listened to the sermon with a great deal of amazement, and wondered greatly where the wonderful discourse had come from. None of them gave me credit for having made it myself, nor even for understanding the subject to which it was devoted. They had no objection to make to what was said: they considered that the arguments were very conclusive and well arranged, and that the whole had been delivered with considerable freedom and ability, but they did not know whose the sermon was. The travelling preacher said he supposed I had taken it from Paley. I said, No. He asked, had I got it from Doddridge? I said, No. Where had I got it then? I told him that the *plan* of the sermon was my own, but that the substance of the arguments in proof of the truth of Christianity were from Grotius. However, I was not allowed to come upon the plan as a local preacher. About half a year or a year after this, I was appointed to preach another trial sermon, and I did so. The place in which I preached this time was the chapel at Farnley, and a travelling preacher, with some local preachers, were appointed to hear me. This time I preached from 'Say ye to the righteous, it shall be well with him,' &c. The sermon was plain, the subject was familiar, and it was nothing but what they could believe my own. I was approved this time, and my name was accordingly put on the plan.

Other six or twelve months afterwards, I was appointed to preach another trial sermon, to afford them an opportunity of judging whether I was fit to come on the Local Preachers' plan in full connexion. My text this time was, 'God so loved the world,' &c. The place in which I preached, was Bramley Methodist Chapel. The plan of the sermon I have already given. The sermon generally gave great satisfaction, but on one point I was considered to be heterodox. I had stated, according to the common notion in those days, that one part of Christ's work was to make atonement to God for sin, or as it is generally expressed, to make satisfaction to divine justice for man's sin. I observed, according to the common notion, that in order to enable Christ to make satisfaction for sin, it was necessary that he should be both God and man; man that he might suffer the punishment due to transgression, and God that his divinity might stamp his sufferings with an infinity of merit. All this was considered right enough. But in speaking on this point I happened to say something which was not common, and this gave rise to a charge of heterodoxy. I said that a man, if innocent, might have redeemed *one* man, or made satisfaction to justice for one man; but that as one man was only equal to one man, a man could redeem no more than one, and that he could redeem that one only by suffering the self-same torments that were due to the sinner, and that for the full length of the period threatened by the broken law, viz., for all eternity. So also, I said, an angel, supposing an angel to be equal to man in dignity, and supposing the angel to have no sins of his own to answer for, might redeem one man; but that he could only redeem him by sacrificing his own happiness, and submitting to bear the very same punishment due to the sinner, and that for all eternity; and that, I observed, would be no gain to the universe. The salvation of one would be the ruin of the other, and the number of the lost, and the amount of the torment endured, would remain the same. But Christ, I said, in consequence of his being both God and man united in one person, could redeem *all mankind*, and redeem them too without either suffering the *exact punishment* which had been threatened to the sinner, or suffering what he did suffer for ever and ever. In consequence of the connection of the divinity with the humanity, I said, a very small part of the punishment due to the wicked, and that small part endured but for a very short period, was equal, in worth to God, to all the sufferings due to the whole race of mankind, even if they had been inflicted, without intermission, for ever and ever. What gave the offence in this passage, was the doctrine that man, or an angel, supposing him to be innocent, could satisfy divine justice for any sin. I had overlooked, it seems, the principle that every sin committed against an infinite God, is infinite, and that one single sin does of itself require an infinite atonement, or an infinite satisfaction. When the case came before the quarterly meeting, I was objected to by the travelling preacher on that ground. He said the sentiment was neither Methodistical nor Scriptural. At that time I was not sufficiently well acquainted with Scripture to be able to say with confidence whether it was Scriptural or not, and as for what was Methodistical, I knew less perhaps about that than I did about Christianity. As I could not contend with the preacher, I said, I had not been aware that I had been saying any thing that was wrong, but that if it *was* anti-methodistical and anti-scriptural I would not say so any more. With the understanding that I should examine the subject, and that when I found that the notion was not Methodistical or Scriptural I should lay it aside, I was received upon the plan.

At present I regard the whole of these proceedings with disapprobation and regret, and the whole system of preparation for preaching, whether it be preaching trial sermons or subjection to human authority, appears to me to be both utterly anti-christian and horribly unnatural. I felt them to be unnatural at the time that I was submitting to those arrangements, and it was with pain and difficulty that I submitted to them; but my light was small, and my mind not ripe. I had not been accustomed to judge much for myself, though I had felt that all was not right in the common theology. I had no idea, no clear perception of what was wrong. Methodism was to me the whole of theology in a manner at that time. I regarded the preachers as something more than human, and it had not yet entered into my head to try the system by the simple doctrine of Christ, to see whether it was right or wrong. I took it for right as a matter of course, and submitted to it accordingly. I now look at the things through which I passed with horror, and I almost wonder that my mind was not shattered and broken by the treatment with which I met, so as to unfit me to go either after the discovery of truth, or the right performance of duty. God still remains with his people in the midst of their trials; he watches over them and preserves them from ruin in the midst of dangers, or none would be able to escape. Those priestly usurpations and sectarian snares are horrible beyond measure. But God still takes care of those whose wish it is to please him, and ever makes use of their trials for the accomplishment of his benevolent purposes. His name be praised.

I stated a little before, that I frequently met with discouragements from those amongst whom I went preaching. This however did not continue to be the case long. I had not preached long before I began to meet with very different treatment. At the place where I had been told that I should have better become the next room, the room in which the lunatics were confined, I became quite a favourite, and was frequently invited to visit them and preach to them when I was not appointed on the plan. My labours were more kindly received and more favourably regarded generally as I proceeded, and, in course of time, instead of being appointed merely to country places, to preach in private houses, I began to receive numerous appointments to the large chapels in the towns. It was not long before many began to talk of proposing to me to go out as a travelling preacher. The first person who had suggested such a thing to me was Joseph Sutcliffe. He told me very early, as I have already stated, that it was his impression I was to be a *divine*. What a divine meant I did not then well understand. I had never heard the word used that I recollect before. The only idea that I could affix to it was that of some kind of superior preacher or writer. He was wishful to have me out as a travelling preacher while he remained in the Circuit, but I was too young; nor should I at that time have been considered fit for the work by the Circuit generally. He therefore never brought the matter publicly forward. The preachers that followed Joseph Sutcliffe, were old John Farrar and James Etchells. John Farrar was a great drunkard, and had so little control over himself, so little care of his reputation, so little management, that his drunkenness became generally known. He would drink as much as a bottle of brandy in a day. He was sometimes so drunk in returning from preaching, that he could not keep the causeway, nor save himself from tumbling in the dirt. He was sometimes so drunk in the pulpit that the congregation could not help observing it. He was, in fact, a regular sot. His colleague, James Etchells, was far from being what he ought. He would drink ten or a dozen glasses in the course of a day, or even half a day; but he had more management; he contrived, if not to keep within the bounds of sobriety, to keep within the limits of decency with respect to appearances. I am not aware that he was ever found staggering, or reeling, or rolling in the mud.. These two preachers could not agree; they quarrelled greatly; and Etchells took occasion, perhaps for the sake of revenge, I do not know, to prosecute his superintendent for drunkenness, and Farrar was suspended. This made a disturbance in the circuit. Farrar was a bold, blustering, noisy, rude kind of a preacher, making use of queer words, quaint and low expressions, and frequently throwing the mass of his congregation into laughter. He was in consequence a great favourite with many. Etchells, though he was a man of considerable ability, and frequently delivered sermons containing a considerable amount of real practical religious instruction, was not an interesting preacher; so that he did not stand high with the circuit at any time. When he prosecuted Farrar and got him suspended, many people were very much enraged against him, and the circuit was divided into Etchellites and Farrarites. No business of any moment was in consequence attended to by the circuit, and during the stay of those two preachers very little was said about me going out as a travelling preacher. Mr. Sutcliffe wrote to Farrar about me, but he had enough to do about himself. The next two preachers that came were William Jackson and old William Harrison. By this time several in the circuit had begun to express a wish that I should go out to travel, and Harrison the superintendent came frequently to see me, and requested me to offer myself for the ministry amongst them. But it was now too late. I had found that none could be received as travelling preachers, unless they were willing to go to whatever part of the world the conference or the missionary committee might think fit to send them, and unless they could express their *willingness* to be so disposed of before they went out. This I could not do. It was my conviction that God had called me to labour in my own country, and to do good amongst my own neighbours. I had no idea at that time that it was my duty to go to any foreign country to preach the gospel, and I did not therefore feel at liberty to offer to go out on the terms required. On the contrary, I felt as if I should do wrong to expose myself to unseen dangers and unknown trials and difficulties in foreign lands, without a conviction that God required it at my hands. I could not think that I should be likely to succeed in missionary labours, unless I could enter on them with a belief that those were the labours for which God designed me. I considered that I should be likely to sink under missionary hardships and trials, if I exposed myself to them without a belief that God required me so to do. But there was another hindrance to my entering what is called the ministry amongst the Wesleyan Methodists. I found that Conference had made a new law, establishing a new test of orthodoxy, and that no one could be taken out as a travelling preacher now, who could not subscribe to the doctrine of the Eternal Sonship, as taught by Richard Watson and Jabez Bunting, in opposition to Adam Clarke. This test I could not subscribe. I cannot say that I altogether disbelieved the doctrine of the Eternal Sonship; but I was not in a state of mind to justify me in subscribing the doctrine. Whether the doctrine of the Eternal Sonship was right or not, I had not a firm belief in it: and this was reason enough why I could not subscribe it. This was the second hindrance to me becoming a travelling preacher. The next time that the superintendent preacher came to request me to allow him to propose me as a travelling preacher, I told him my mind on those subjects. He seemed rather put about, and tried to help me over my difficulties. He told me that though Conference required every young person that went out as a preacher to place himself in their hands, to leave himself at their disposal, and to express his willingness to go to whatever part of the world they might choose to send him to, yet Conference would not abuse its power, or send a man away from his native country, when it was his conviction that he was not called upon by God to go. He said they never *had*, to his recollection, sent persons to places to which they did not feel free to go, and that it was very probable that they would not do so with me,—that the pledge required was more of a *form* than anything else,— that it was necessary that they should *have* such a form for certain purposes which he did not fully explain, but that if I offered myself as a preacher, and left myself in their hands,

I should have no cause for complaint. I told him that what he said might all be true, but that it did not remove the difficulty. The Conference I said might not abuse their power, but it would *have* the power,—that I could not place myself in their hands with a comfortable mind,—that I considered it my duty not to give away my liberty, whatever probability there might appear to be that no advantage would be taken of it. In a word, I gave him to understand that however honest and well intentioned the Conference and the Missionary Committee might be, I did not feel free to declare my willingness to go to any place out of my own country, and that unless I could be taken out without giving the declaration which they required, I must remain at home. I also told him how I stood with respect to the Eternal Sonship test. He tried to help me over that difficulty also, but the substance of all he said amounted only to this, that I should submit to those that were older and holier than myself. This of course had no influence over me. He frequently came after this to request that I would offer myself for the ministry, and made use of various arguments to induce me to do so, but my mind was fixed, I could not do it.

About this time Conference passed some laws forbidding the teaching of writing in all Methodist Sunday Schools. I disapproved of these laws. I did not, at that time, call in question the authority of Conference to make laws for the government of the Connexion; I had no idea but that such authority belonged to Conference; but I thought the laws against teaching writing were *bad* laws; and on one occasion when the preacher came to see me, I told him my thoughts on that subject. It was not long after this that those disturbances took place in the Methodist society, in the Leeds circuit, respecting the introduction of an organ into Brunswick Chapel. Conference, through the importunities of some rich people, had broken through its own laws, and given authority for the introduction of an organ into Brunswick chapel, contrary to its established rules, as well as contrary to the wishes of a great part of the members, trustees, local preachers, and leaders. I, of course, disapproved of this proceeding on the part of Conference, and in one of my interviews with Mr. Harrison, I told him so. I had, on some occasions, heard Joseph Suttcliffe speak very seriously and with great and sorrowful dissatisfaction of the proceedings of those who were at the head of Methodistical affairs, and though I did not, at the time I heard him speak on those points, rightly understand him, events that took place afterwards, both brought his words to my mind, and partly interpreted their meaning. In consequence of what I saw, I began to be greatly dissatisfied with the manner in which things in general were carried on in the Methodist society, and stated my thoughts to Mr. Harrison. When I was speaking with him on those subjects on one occasion, he said to me, 'Brother, my dear brother, you do not understand these things; if you were only amongst us, you would soon think as we think.' I told him that was not very unlikely, but the question was, should I think right? It is common enough for people to approve of things when they begin to be mixed up with them, which they looked upon with great disapprobation when they saw them as the deeds of others only: but there is reason to fear that such parties do not change their opinions in consequence of having got more light, but in consequence of having lost part of their integrity.

I was, somewhere about this time, at James Sigston's school at Leeds, as a weekly boarder. While I was there the New Connexion of Methodists happened to have their Conference at Leeds, and one of my school-fellows, called the Honourable Charles Van Linden, a youth from India, who was very fond of getting to know all that was passing in the town, and who was especially wishful to find out the peculiarties of the different religious denominations in the country, and who had a great delight in hearing all kinds of preachers, got one of the Conference plans, and went to hear some of the New Connexion preachers. He told me where he had been, what he had discovered, and whom he had heard, and invited me to go along with him the next day. I went, and heard some of the New Connexion preachers, Simeon Woodhouse, and James Dunkerley, and some one else. In the evening I attended a meeting at which the young preachers, that had finished their probation, were received into full connexion. I heard them tell their experience, declare their belief with respect to matters of doctrine, and their views on the subject of church government. I recollect especially, that some of them spoke a good deal about an equilibrium of power in the Connexion, the rights and liberties of the people, &c. This was all new to me, and I did not, at first, understand it. Curious as it may seem, I was not aware at this time that there was any such thing in existence as a regular system of church government. I had no idea that there was any such thing as church government in connexion with the Methodist society, and had never thought of any such thing. And as to equilibrium of power, and rights of the people, it was all a mystery to me. I might have read something about church government in Mosheim; I do not recollect. But if I had, I had certainly either not understood it, or not attended to it. But whether it was before or after this that I read Mosheim's Ecclesiastical History, I cannot tell. If I *had* read it, I had gained no information on this class of subjects. Still I remembered what I had heard at the Conference, though I did not then understand it. A short time after this, one of my companions, Dan Sunderland, bought a volume of a Methodist Magazine, supposing it to be a volume of the Old Connexion Magazine. It turned out, however, to be a volume of the New Connexion Magazine. In this volume there was a rather full account of the history, and the constitution of the New Connexion, with a lengthy and laboured defence of its principles of church government.

At the end of the volume there was bound up with it a discourse by Thomas Allin, and some other articles bearing on the same subject. This volume opened quite a new world to me and my companion. We read with a great deal of interest what was said in reference to the New Connexion, and talked over the subject of its history and constitution very freely and frequently between ourselves. If I had not read any thing on Church History before, I certainly began to read on that subject now, and what I read both in Common and Ecclesiastical History, assisted me in understanding what I met with in the Magazine and in the other publications on the subject of Methodistical Church Government. The consequence of my reading and thinking and talking on these subjects was, that I began to think the Old Connexion all wrong. The preachers, the rules, the constitution of the district meetings and conferences, seemed all unscriptural and tyrannical. The misconduct of the preachers also tended to sink the Connexion in my estimation, and a number of palpable falsehoods and exaggerations which I heard at some missionary meetings in the neighbourhood, did the same. It became plain to me, that the preachers generally were a set of selfish, lordly men, who lived not for the good of the people or the public, but for their own unworthy ends. My mind was in consequence greatly alienated from the Connexion.

Another thing that tended to alienate my mind from the Connexion was, I began to pay more attention to what I heard from the pulpits, and to compare the preaching of the travelling preachers with the doctrine of the New Testament, and I found their preaching in general to be exceedingly unscriptural. When I attended missionary meetings, I became more and more disgusted with the speeches that I heard, with the everlasting begging, and the vulgar jests, and the low humour which were employed to please the people, and to dispose them to contribute their money. I began, and not without sufficient reason, to doubt altogether the honesty and fidelity of the ruling parties in the Connexion, and the whole system began to appear to me in a very unfavourable light indeed. I was also somewhat concerned on my own account. I thought that God intended me for a travelling preacher, and in truth I *wished* to be one. I was very desirous of knowledge; I wished to be a scholar; and I desired to be a travelling preacher in order that I might have my whole time to devote to reading and the like. This, I have no doubt, was one thing which led me to turn my attention the more readily and thoughtfully to the New Connexion. I could no longer labour in the Old Connexion with comfort. I had lost all sympathy with the ruling portion of the body. I no longer felt any great interest in its prosperity. *I* could not pray as I had been wont to do for a Methodistical revival. It seemed to me that every one who joined the Connexion became a slave to the preachers,—that the preachers took advantage of the increase of members to increase their own power, and to strengthen themselves in their evil ways, and I did not therefore feel at liberty either to pray or to take part in efforts which had for their object, so far as the rulers were concerned, the increase of their ill-used power, and the enriching of their ill-used funds. The increase of the body seemed the growth of a dangerous power, a power employed not to raise the people but to depress them, not to make them intelligent and independent, but to keep them in ignorance and slavery. It also appeared, that an increase of numbers and funds tended to increase the pride and intolerance of the preachers. I stated my feelings to some one, who soon made them known to others, and it was considered such an awful thing that I could not pray for God to revive his work in the body. I was supposed by many to have fallen entirely. The Methodists generally had no idea that religion could spread or souls be saved by any other means but Methodistical revivals, so that they concluded, I suppose, that I was opposed to the spread of religion altogether. This, however, was not the case. I was as anxious for the spread of religion and the salvation of souls as ever, but I wanted to see religion spread and souls converted apart from a corrupt and selfish priesthood. I wanted good to be done in such a way, that it might not strengthen the powers of evil, and so be rendered of no effect. My feelings at this time were often very painful and trying. Many a time did I lie waking on my bed hours together, amid the silence and darkness of night, pondering those matters in my mind, thinking what course I should pursue, and wondering what would be the results. One night I recollect well, while I lay waking on my bed I felt as if the point was settled, and I said, I shall do something to-morrow that will make a stir, and so it proved. Wearied with doubts and anxieties, I had at length formed the purpose to leave the Old Connexion, and, if I met with encouragement, to join the New Connexion. I told my purpose to one of my companions, and he approved of it. We went to Leeds that day, and heard Richard Watson preach a missionary sermon, and attended a missionary meeting in Brunswick chapel, in the afternoon I was not much displeased with Watson's sermon, though some things which he said appeared to me unscriptural and false; but with the missionary meeting I was very much dissatisfied; the falsehoods and the follies put forth were utterly disgusting; and before it was quite over I left, and went along with my companion in search of the New Connexion superintendent preacher. We found his house, and he invited us in, and bade us be seated. We opened our errand, and he talked to us rather freely, and before we left, we got a copy of the New Connexion general rules. We read and examined the rules, and we thought very favourably of them. We examined the doctrines, and we found little or nothing to blame, with the exception of one or two words or phrases. The doctrines were almost all expressed in Scripture language, and were plainly designed to allow of considerable variety of opinion. There was nothing about the trinity, or about justification by faith *alone*, or the *direct* witness of the spirit. The doctrines of justification, the witness of the spirit, and the atonement, were left almost entirely in Scripture language, without any Methodistical or Calvinistic additions. One article spoke of the *personality* of the Holy Ghost, and of the divinity of Christ; but I believed in the divinity of Christ at that time, and I had no objection to the phrase, *personality of the Holy Ghost*, provided only *one* Holy Ghost or Holy Spirit were designed, and that one spirit the one true God, and provided also that we were allowed to use personality in the sense of real being, conscious existence only, as distinguished from unliving, unconscious existence. In another article it was said, that Adam involved all his posterity in guilt and depravity. I believed at that time, that Adam involved his posterity in *depravity*, but not in *guilt*, as *I* understood the word guilt. So that I objected also to this expression. These were the only objections I had to the doctrines. I was now more fixed than ever in my determination to join the New Connexion, and my companion was the same. So we went again to see the New Connexion superintendent preacher, with the purpose of offering ourselves as members. The preacher that we had first seen, W. Ford, had left, and another, Thomas Styan, had come in his place. He was a surly sort of man, and he seemed at the time we called, to be in a rather uncomfortable state of mind. The Connexion or the Conference had not pleased him, and though he had not a particle of the reformer about him, he was disposed to complain of the Connexion. He rather dissuaded us from joining the Connexion than otherwise, but we were not to be soon discouraged. Some of the lay members of the New Connexion got to know that two persons had been visiting their preachers, and offering themselves as members, and they sought us out, and treated us very kindly. Through their instrumentality we got introduced to other members, and it was not long before we were invited to preach among them. I preached for them once or twice in Ebenezer Chapel, Leeds, and met with very great encouragement from them. I then got introduced to John Henshaw, the younger preacher in the Leeds circuit, who lived at Ripon, a distant branch of the Leeds circuit. I found him a person both of considerable intelligence and earnest piety. He encouraged me in the pursuit of truth, and was evidently wishful to open my way to extensive usefulness. I had not preached long amongst my new friends, before some of them were desirous that I should go out as a travelling preacher amongst them. To this I had no serious objections, though I had in part made arrangements for settling in another way of life. I was given to understand that I should have perfect liberty of judgment, of speech, and of action in the body, —that the New Testament was their sole creed and law,— that if a person believed the New Testament and lived aright, he was a suitable person for membership, and if, in addition to this, his abilities were sufficient, he was qualified for the ministry amongst them. I also found that the *perfection* of the Scriptures both as a rule of faith, and as a rule of life, was one of the first articles in the New Connexion creed or confession of faith, and I was also given to understand that though the works of John Wesley and Fletcher were referred to in the general rules for a further explanation of the doctrines laid down in their confession of faith, they were referred to simply as an explanation, and not as a standard of orthodoxy,—that each preacher was at liberty to receive and interpret every article according to his own views of the doctrine taught in the New Testament, and that he was to use Wesley's and Fletcher's writings, not as authorities, but simply as helps to his understanding,—not as fetters to enslave his mind, but as a means to enlarge his knowledge, his freedom, and to increase his spiritual strength and independence. Liberty was the great subject of conversation in every circle in the New Connexion. It was the great object of my search and of my wishes, and I believed assuredly that I had at length found all that my soul had sighed and sought after. I did not however meet with every thing in the New Connexion that I could have wished to have met with. I thought I saw a great lack of hearty religiousness and Christian excellence. I also soon found that the travelling preachers were not on good terms amongst themselves,—that the superintendents were jealous of those that were younger, and represented their younger brethren as lacking in point of respect for them, and as proud and wishful to be above their proper place. It was not long after I joined the New Connexion that I was invited to attend one of their quarterly meetings, the April quarterly meeting. Amongst the things which came before the meeting, was the filling up of the preachers certificates. The business passed off without much that was worthy of serious observation, until the meeting came to the business of the youngest preacher's certificate, who was a preacher on trial. This young preacher had married before the time of his probation was up, and it appeared from what was said in the meeting that he had not been able to support his wife so comfortably and respectably as some of the people in the circuit considered necessary to the credit of the Connexion. It was not objected to him that he had gone into debt, or that he had obtained money from any one either by fraud or honest begging; but he had not been able, it was considered, with barely forty-five or fifty pounds a year, to support himself and family in the same style as those who had one hundred and forty or one hundred and sixty pounds a year. There might be some other objections to the young man, but they were not mentioned in the meeting. His talents might not be considered so great as was desired, or his habits and disposition might not be thought so strictly Christian as they should be, but these were not things that were brought forward as charges against him. The great objection brought forward was that he had got married before the time, when he had not sufficient means to support himself in what the world would call a respectable style. This led to a good deal of unpleasantness. The meeting was divided into two parties, and terribly disturbed, and the discussion was ended at last in a very unpleasant way indeed. Some, who were aware that I and the friend who was with me, had lately joined the Connexion, expressed themselves as being sorry that we should have seen the system to so great a disadvantage as we had done that day, and gave us to understand that such exhibitions of strife and contention were not usual, and that they had nothing to do with the system. This, as I afterwards found, was not true; but it served its purpose for the time, and so the matter passed by, and I and my friend went on, expecting not soon to see any similar causes of dissatisfaction. But there were other things which I did not like, and which tended to give me uneasiness, though not so much uneasiness *then*, as they have done since, when I have looked back and reflected on them. I found, for instance, in the Connexion a complete division between the rich members and the poor members. The rich were a class or a caste to themselves, and the poor were another class or caste. The rich met at each others houses; they had their regular parties, many of which were very extravagant and expensive, while the poor were completely lost sight of, as if they had belonged to another race of beings, except when a poor person happened to become a preacher among them. The rich, along with the travelling preachers, formed one world; the poor, left all alone, formed another world; and between the two there seemed to be a great gulf fixed, so that those who lived in the poor world could hardly pass to those that lived in the rich one, and those that lived in the rich world would seldom pass to those who lived in the poor world, except to make collections among them. Then besides, as I have intimated, the rich were very extravagant. They were also generally unintellectual, sensual, and slaves to the world and to the world's fashions. It was their custom, as I have said, to have feasts or social parties, at which from a dozen to a score would be present. When one had invited a number, each one of the number was expected to invite the whole again, and thus the parties went round from week to week, occupying a considerable part of the year. At some of those parties five, ten, fifteen, or twenty pounds would be expended. There was not only a great deal of extravagance in eating, but in smoking and drinking. I have seen persons at those parties drink and smoke till they could neither govern their tempers nor their tongues, nor even steady their eyes or their limbs. The conversation at those parties was seldom if ever, on any literary, intellectual, or philanthropic subject: it was seldom instructive or edifying in any way. Sometimes the conversation would turn upon something connected with religion, but the subject would generally be the excellency of the New Connexion system of Church government over that of the Old Connexion, or accounts of some additions to the body from the Old Connexion. Nothing seemed to give greater pleasure generally to those parties, than tidings of disturbances or of probable divisions in the Wesleyan body. Party politics and slander and mere formal foolish talking, talk for talking's sake, with eating, drinking, smoking, with occasional singing and playing on the Piano, formed the whole business of those parties. They used to conclude those parties with prayer sometimes, when the travelling preacher was there, but not otherwise. These things shocked me a great deal at first, but with being frequently invited to those parties, and having a great deal of respect and attention paid to me, my dislike of them partially subsided. I came gradually to think less of those evils. I also entertained a hope, that as the New Connexion system was good, all those evils, as well as all other particular evils, might be removed in course of time, if suitable efforts were made.

I had many interviews with John Henshaw, one of the younger preachers, and I found him on the whole a superior man both in point of knowledge and piety. He was very communicative, glad to give any information he possessed, and equally well pleased to listen to others if they had any information to give in return; and I received some benefit from my intercourse with him. He introduced me to an acquaintance with some fresh books both on divinity and history. But the influence which my intercourse with him exerted on my mind was not good altogether. He was not a perfect character: far from it. His aims were not the highest. He had but little of the reformer about him. He had no idea of grappling with the great errors and evils which he saw prevailing in the Connexion or the world. He was rather disposed to leave great errors and evils as they were, though wishful to make the best of things as they were. As a preacher for instance, though he knew much which his hearers did not know, and though he could have liked to have taught his hearers something, yet he declined to attempt to teach them when he found that they cared less for instruction than for wild and passionate excitement. He preferred his own popularity among his ignorant hearers, to the consciousness of having faithfully discharged his duty. He chose rather to please his hearers by labouring to excite their feelings, than to risk their favour by endeavouring to make them intelligent, useful, and godlike. He told me one day that he had been preaching at Ripon on some subject of a practical nature, and endeavouring to lead his hearers to *think*, and to *understand* the subject; but he said I soon found out that it would not do,—that the people began to stare and look dissatisfied; so I accordingly began to address them in my usual way, appealing to their feelings, endeavouring to excite powerful and pleasant emotions, and they soon began to show signs of life then: they were satisfied.

This was the principle on which he acted generally, I believe. He knew a many things which he never attempted to teach his hearers; he saw many errors amongst them which he never attempted to expose or correct; he saw plainly that the people were far, very far below the proper standard both in knowledge and in religion; but when he found that he could not attempt to raise them to that standard without risking his reputation as a popular Methodist preacher, he gave up the attempt altogether, and left error, superstition, and selfishness in full possession of their power. He sold himself, in fact, whether he knew it or not, to the enemy of *true* religion, and preached with a view to keep up the numbers of the congregation and the society, and to secure their ignorant good-will, their selfish approbation and support. Whether he thought this way of proceeding right or not I cannot tell; but he recommended it to me; and my respect for the man, and his kind attentions to me, made me regard the advice with less feeling of disapprobation than it deserved.

It is a curious fact, that though John Henshaw was a great revivalist, and a very grave and solemn man when engaged in his *religious* duties as they are called, he was quite another person among his particular friends. He was exceedingly fond of Don Quixote, and some other similar productions, and he strongly recommended them to me. And he delighted in ridiculous stories. One hour he would be preaching with all the horror and solemnity imaginable about the eternal and infinite torments of the damned, and then in an hour or two he would be laughing at a ridiculous story as if his sides could hardly hold him together.

He was also very fond of Boswell's Life of Johnson, and of his lives of the poets, both of which works I read by his recommendation. Don Quixote I never did read. The only reason which he gave for recommending the work to me, was that it would make me laugh in spite of myself; and as I had no particular wish to be made to laugh beyond my usual measure, I never troubled myself to procure the book.

After John Henshaw left Leeds, he was stationed at Nottingham. Though he was a very lively man, he was not robust, and it was not long after his removal to Nottingham, before his constitution began to fail, and he was obliged to have some one to assist him in his labours for a short time. He wrote to me, requesting me to go and assist him, and being urged by the advice of some of the friends in Leeds to go, I went. I preached for him at Nottingham, Beeston, Derby, and some other places in the circuit; but before the end of a fortnight a letter came to Leeds, and through the friends at Leeds to me, requesting that I should be sent to Liverpool to supply the place of a preacher there that had resigned or been set aside; and as my friends, both those at Nottingham, and those at Leeds, concurred in urging me to go to Liverpool, I went. I travelled by coach from Nottingham, through Derby, Bakewell, Matlock, Buxton, Stockport, and Manchester to Liverpool in one day. Thomas Allin was the superintendent preacher in the Liverpool circuit at that time, and to him I was directed to go. I found my way to his house without much difficulty, and he received me very kindly. On the Sunday following I commenced my labours as a *supply*. I went very comfortably through my work for two or three weeks, and met with every encouragement from the leading friends in the church and congregation; but after awhile I began to find myself in serious difficulties. Thomas Allin was at that time the most popular preacher in the Methodist New Connexion: he was supposed to have neither equal nor resemblance in the whole body. I was comparatively ignorant and unpractised in the art of preaching: there were only five or six sermons in fact that I was able to preach with perfect ease and confidence. I *had* preached a many more, but I had not preached them sufficiently often to have them perfectly at command, so as to be ready to preach them without fear or embarassment. And there were only two chapels in the town, and the town was the whole circuit; and several of those who attended one chapel one part of the day, attended the other chapel the other part of the day, so that it was very uncomfortable and difficult to preach the same sermon twice over. Then there was preaching on the week night in the principal chapel twice every week. The consequence of these things was, that in about a fortnight or three weeks, my ready, familiar sermons were all preached, and I was obliged to begin with those that were neither so much at my command, nor so good in themselves as the others were; and this was a very great trial to me. I gave myself, it is true, rather closely to study, and I laboured hard to prepare and write out the substance of a fresh supply of sermons; but frequently when I had made a sermon, and even written it out in a great measure, my fears prevailed against me, and I was unable to deliver it with freedom. Many a time did I preach in complete agony. No one can tell the anguish which I endured at times, especially in the pulpit. After a while however I gained a little more confidence, and went on with a little more satisfaction, partly in consequence of the superintendent speaking to me very kindly, and giving me favourable accounts of the reception of my labours among the people, and partly in consequence of some of the people giving me great encouragement.

But alas, after awhile I was run down again. The stock of preaching materials which I had at my command, seemed to be almost exhausted. There were only certain kinds of subjects which I had at that time confidence sufficient to bring before the people, and these subjects I had now brought before them once. And it was painful to me beyond measure to be obliged to use over again the same materials, and to repeat before the people the same sentiments. Perhaps I had no need to be so scrupulous on this point: it is very likely that ninteen-twentieths of the audience had forgotten what I had said in my earlier sermons. It is very likely that I might have repeated whole sermons with new texts and a little difference in the arrangement, without any considerable portion of the congregation observing it. But I did not feel my mind disposed to do so, and this gave me even greater uneasiness than I had previously experienced before, in consequence of being obliged to preach sermons which I had not had the opportunity of making familiar to me by frequent preaching. My mind became almost distracted. Whether I was in the house or in the street, I was lost in thought, pensive and sad. I recollect, on one occasion, that I lost myself completely in a street which was either the next or the next but one to that in which I resided; a street that I knew almost as well as I knew any street. I was so completely lost, that I neither knew where I was, nor which way to go for a length of time. I must at this time have been nearly driven to madness by my anxieties. And I never could bring myself to relieve myself as many preachers do. I could have got plenty of skeletons and sketches of sermons, and I could easily have prepared them for the pulpit and preached them; but I could not bring my mind to do so. I could have committed sermons to memory and preached them; but I could not persuade myself to do that. I felt unwilling to tell the people any thing but what I really knew and felt; any thing but what had become my own by serious reflection and by a clear perception of its truth. And not only so; I felt unwilling to deliver sermons which did not appear to have a direct and special adaptation to the wants and circumstances of the congregation to which I had to preach. Such sermons I had not at command: and as I was still expected to preach the usual number of times, and to preach the usual length of time each sermon, I was distracted beyond measure. How I got through these trials I cannot tell. It was hard—it was killing work. When I look back upon what I experienced at that time, I feel such strong disapprobation, such horror and abhorrence of the system that placed me in such circumstances, and reduced me to such extremeties, as I can scarcely express. I have since then almost ceased to wonder that so many preachers are mere formalists; that so many make it a custom just to repeat sermons as they find them in books, or to dress up the sketches and skeletons supplied them through the press or by their friends. I have almost ceased to wonder that so few preachers have a real love for truth, or an eager desire to understand the Religion of Christ. I have almost ceased to wonder that preachers generally are amongst the most formal, and stiff, and ignorant, and irreligious of mankind. What I passed through was almost enough to have made any one either give up all thoughts of being a preacher, or else become a mere dealer in words and other people's sentiments. It was of God's great mercy that I was preserved from complete intellectual and spiritual ruin. I was however enabled to get through the year in some way; and oh how glad I was when I obtained permission from the Quarterly Meeting to leave the Circuit a single sabbath before my time was expired. It was such a relief! I felt as if I had escaped from the darkest and most dismal dungeon in which a poor soul could be imprisoned; as if I had been released from a rack on which my whole spirit had been stretched and tortured. It was like a transition from hell to heaven when I got my liberty.

While I was at Liverpoool, I was called away to supply the place of the superintendent preacher in the Chester Circuit for a few weeks, who had died very suddenly, under very peculiar circumstances. His name was Dunkerley. I was told by persons likely to know the truth, that he was very much given to intemperance,—that he had regularly indulged to such an extent in the use of intoxicating drinks as to deserve to be regarded as a drunken man. On one occasion, while he was over at Liverpool, he fell down in the Theatre Square, and had to be taken up and carried into a neighbouring shop. At first it was supposed a *fit* had seized him; but a little further attention to the case revealed the secret that he was drunk. On another occasion, on his return from Liverpool to Chester, he was observed, when he got off the coach, to stagger backwards and fall down. Some friends that were waiting for his arrival, ran and helped him up, and took him to a member's house just by. He was found to be drunk then also. The members spoke to him on the subject, and reproved him sharply, and then put him to bed. The Tuesday night following, the matter was mentioned at the leaders' meeting, when he was present. The leaders told him that such conduct could not be tolerated, and that unless a change took place for the better, the matter would have to be laid before the Quarterly Meeting. The preacher acknowledged his fault, and promised if they would forgive him that once, he would do so no more. I believe that from that time he gave up the use of intoxicating drinks altogether for a week or two; but shortly after, having to go to the Welsh side of the Circuit, he began to use them again. It seems that at one of the places the leaders were accustomed to have their meetings in a room in a public-house, near the Chapel, and were accustomed to lodge the preacher at the same place. Perhaps poor Dunkerley thought it would hardly look right for him to be accommodated at a public-house with a bed, and yet take nothing to drink; so he got some gin. It would seem that the relish for the gin must have returned upon him with great power when he began to taste it, for he drank very freely. He drank so much, in fact, that the publican himself, as was afterwards stated to me, began to feel alarmed for him. A short time after he went up stairs to bed the people of the house heard a noise of an unusual character in his room, and on going to see what was the matter, they found the preacher on his knees, in an apoplectic fit, and the blood gushing from his nose and ears. He died very shortly after, the same evening. There can be no reasonable doubt that he died drunk.

It was this man's place that I went to supply. I do not wonder now that Dunkerley and several other preachers in the New Connexion were drunkards, when I take into consideration the customs and habits of the people of the connexion at those times. I never met with any thing in any society, that I recollect, more at variance with the principles of Christian temperance, and more likely to lead both preachers and people into drunkenness and profligacy, than the habits and customs of many of the members of the New Connexion in the Chester Circuit. In the first place they were all users of intoxicating drinks, and all those that were in tolerable circumstances regularly kept spirits as well as milder, weaker kinds of intoxicating drinks in their houses. In the next place a preacher could never call at the houses of those people, whatever the time of day, without being urged to drink of either the stronger or weaker kinds of intoxicating drink. And he could hardly refuse to drink without seeming to slight the kindness of the people, and running the risk of giving offence. In the third place they were very much addicted to extravagant social parties, pleasure jaunts, &c. They were worse than the people of Leeds in this respect; unless they were worse than usual while I was there. I do not recollect that all the time that I was in Chester, there was a single day when they had not either some dinner-party or tea-party or both, or else some pleasure jaunt on the water or on land. And those pleasure parties and feasts were always occasions of wild mirth and extravagant eating and drinking. Besides abundance of flesh and game, and other luxuries, there was always a great, overwhelming supply of intoxicating drinks, and a great amount of different kinds was consumed. I have seen men on those occasions drink five, six, eight, or even ten glasses of wine or spirits, besides drinking ale or porter or wine at meals. I recollect very distinctly seeing a person, and that a preacher too, drink, in addition to what he consumed over his meat, ten glasses of port wine between dinner and tea, after which he went somewhere to preach. The conversation at those parties was anything but instructive, religious, or profitable in any way, and the manners of several of the people were what I should not consider seemly or decent in other respects. But several of the things which I witnessed during the few weeks which I spent at Chester are hardly fit to be described, so I shall pass them by.

Some of the preachers and members of the New Connexion have professed to wonder how it was, that they should make such little way in the world. I do not wonder at their lack of prosperity: I rather wonder that the Connexion has not ceased to exist, when I think of the lack of principle, the earthliness, the selfishness, the extravagance, the intemperance, and the profligacy prevailing in the body. When I think of the character and habits both of the people and of the preachers, especially of the richer kind of people, I wonder that God has had patience with the body. I wonder that he has not altogether destroyed it long ago. And if it had not been for the fidelity and purity existing among a few of the poorer and humbler members of the Connexion, it never could have continued to exist so long as it has. It is the want of principle and piety that has kept back the Connexion from prosperity.

The members of the Connexion at Liverpool were not much better than the members of the Connexion at Chester. One of the principal men was an attorney, and though I never saw much proof of piety or liberality about him, I never saw any thing much out of the way in his character. Since then however he has proved himself a very unworthy person, unless I have been greatly misinformed. Two others of the leading members were drapers, but drapers of a particular kind. Their business was chiefly amongst females of bad character, and their plan of doing business was to sell out goods to those persons on credit, and then go round to their houses or lodgings, and collect the money from them fortnightly or monthly as the case might be. They were accustomed to sell their goods very high; the profits would seldom, if ever, be less than one hundred per cent. I suppose they anticipated losses in their way of doing business, and therefore laid on extravagant profits, that those who *did* pay, might make up for those who did *not*. Such a business, even if it had gone no further than this, would have been bad enough; but those respectable members of the Connexion carried things still further. One of the parties, if not both, went so far as to take houses for lewd people, and furnish them, and even supply them with coals and the like, as well as with dresses and ornaments, and receive so much a week or so much a month in return, thus acting as wholesale bawds and panders. To make the matter worse, they regularly sent round their children, who were become young men, to those places of infamy, to collect the money. The consequence was that their children became profligates, and even while they professed to be religious, some of them were indulging in the grossest licentiousness. Yet these people, these wholesale panders to the grossest vices, were the people with whom Thomas Allin, the superintendent preacher in the circuit, was most familiar, at whose houses he most frequently visited, and at whose tables he most frequently ate and drank, and from whom he accepted presents of gold and silver and raiment. And I am very much mistaken if he did not encourage one of the sons of those people, a son who was employed in going round to collect money from those wretched profligates, to pay his addresses to his eldest daughter. Whether T. Allin was properly aware of the character of those people or not, I cannot tell. It is possible that people would tell me things which they would not tell him. I cannot tell.

There were at Liverpool, as well as at Chester, other persons of a very different character, persons that really feared God and worked righteousness; but they did not stand so high in the church, nor did they share so much of the preacher's regard as those whom I have just mentioned. The society generally which was connected with the principal chapel at Liverpool, was fearfully corrupt. Persons of all characters, some few of them good, but most of them bad and indifferent, had been raked together for the sake of making up a tolerable number of members, and collecting support for the chapel and the preachers. It cannot be wondered at that this circuit never prospered,—that though so much money was expended upon it by the Conference and the rest of the connexion, it should still be languishing, and low, and dying.

The Liverpool circuit recommended me to go out as a travelling preacher on trial, and the conference received their recommendation, and stationed me at Hanley, in the Staffordshire Potteries. The Conference was held at Halifax. I was present at Halifax during a considerable part of the conference time, and preached in the Halifax Chapel one Sabbath morning, in the place of one of the Conference preachers. W. Ridgway, who was the delegate to the Conference from the Hanley circuit, heard me, and was so well pleased with the discourse, that he requested to have me stationed in their circuit in consequence. I reached Hanley a week or so after Conference. From Congleton to Hanley I had on the coach with me James Ousey, one of the preachers then stationed in that circuit; but I did not find out who he was till after he had left the coach. . When I got to Hanley, there was no provision made for me, nor was there any friend waiting to receive me; so I went and took lodgings at the King's Head Inn. I found next day that my home was to be at Newcastle-under-Lyne; but it was some time before the place was provided for me. The preacher that had been there before me, had given no great satisfaction to the people with whom he had lodged, and they refused to take any more preachers. I might have stated that the same thing happened at Liverpool. The persons who had accommodated the preachers that had preceded me, were so tired of the job, that they would not have any thing to do with me. Lodgings were therefore provided for me at Benjamin Joseph's, a decent person, and the husband of a decent wife. But I was appointed to have a bed-fellow, and a bed-fellow too who was a snuff-taker, a whiskey-drinker, and even something worse. At length I left these lodgings and got better; but I lost the friendship of my bed-fellow's father thereby, who was a leading man in the New Connexion, and caused me much trouble. But to my affairs in Staffordshire. At length a place was found for me, but not one of the most comfortable places. I had but just one small room for both my bed and my study. The master of the house, as I shortly found out, was a drunkard, and the woman was a great tattler, and a very ignorant person. She acted the spy over me, and reported to the superintendent preacher and to others that were in the Connexion, all that she observed. She also took people into my room in my absence, (for there was no lock on my room door) to show them my papers, my books, &c. The superintendent preacher was Thomas Waterhouse. I found no great friend or helper in him, but much the contrary. The first Sunday, I preached at Newcastle in the morning. There was one person in the congregation that attracted my attention more than the rest, though I knew nothing who she was. As I was going from the chapel to my lodgings, I saw the same person passing through the Theatre Square amongst a crowd of others, who were all leaving the chapel and returning to their homes, and I went and shook hands with her, and spoke to her. The thought struck me at the time, suppose that female should become my wife. I had no intercourse with her for a length of time after, but she *did* become my wife sure enough, and I have had great cause to be thankful that she did. But more about that hereafter.

I met with a great deal of encouragement in this circuit generally. I had large congregations, and the people appeared satisfied with my labours, and many professed to be profited by them. I was also invited to preach occasional sermons at Cheadle, Lane End, and in the Dawley-green circuit. But this exposed me to difficulties which I had hardly looked for. My superintendent was jealous and envious, and so was his wife. They could not bear to see another, especially a younger preacher, have larger congregations than the superintendent, and they began to conduct themselves towards me in a very unpleasant way indeed. Both he and she began to use their influence amongst the people to prejudice them against me. They both began to try to find something that they might circulate to my disadvantage. He told people that I was idle, and spent my time in gossiping instead of spending it in study. He one day went to the house where I lodged, at Newcastle-under-Lyne, in my absence, and went into my room and examined my books and papers, and took account of a number of books that he considered were of an objectionable character,—that were such as *he* thought a young preacher ought not to use. Amongst the rest he had found the works of Lord Byron, and the works of Shakespeare, and some also of a theological character that he considered objectionable. He said nothing to *me* about these books. He gave me no reproof, no caution, no advice. He made no attempt to show me that I was in error, or to lead me to do better; but went at once to such as he considered had the most influence in the circuit, and told his discoveries to them. He had also heard something else about my attending a party where the people, or *some* of the people, had played at the trencher, and where one of the young persons had sung a song. A meeting was called of some of the leading persons in the circuit, and I was summoned to attend. I attended, and found John Ridgway, William Ridgway, my superintendent, and two or three others there. The possession of those objectionable books was the principal subject on which they spoke to me. They talked to me about the danger of such books, and told me that *my* business was to be a Methodist preacher, and that I had nothing to do with any other books than those that would qualify me for teaching, inculcating, and defending Methodistical doctrines, and for exercising Methodistical discipline in the societies. They advised me, by all means, to be sure and get rid of those books as soon as I could. I did not, at that time, think that their advice was good, and I therefore retained my books, and went on my way as before.

The superintendent preacher still continued his labours to injure me in the estimation of the people, and to a considerable extent he succeeded, especially at Newcastle. An attempt was made, at his instigation, by a number of the Newcastle people, to prevent me from having a perfect certificate; but it failed. My certificate was perfect, and I left the circuit with the affection and esteem, as well as with the best wishes, of nearly the whole of the people.

I left Newcastle with very peculiar and even painful feelings. For one thing, I had become exceedingly attached to the person before alluded to, and had made known to her my wish that she should be my wife. My intercourse with her had led me to form a very high opinion of her worth, and to entertain for her a kind or a degree of affection that I had never felt before, and of which, in fact, I had never formed any conception. I parted from her reluctantly and sorrowfully enough, but I had no alternative. I could not yet be married according to the rules of the Connexion, and I had, besides, no sufficient means of providing for the comfort of my wife. I was obliged, therefore, to submit to my sorrowful lot. The Conference stationed me at Halifax, in Yorkshire. The interval between leaving Staffordshire and going to Halifax, I spent with my parents and friends at Bramley, but I cannot say that I enjoyed their company as I had been wont to do on former occasions. Another affection had taken possession of my soul, which had almost swallowed up all others. I was glad, to be sure, to be once more in the circle of my friends, and to throw my eyes over the scenes of my childhood and early youth; but my heart was far away. What pleased me, pleased me only for a moment, and then my thoughts were clustering round the object of my affections in the scenes that I had left. I passed the time in great sadness and anxiety.

At length I removed to my circuit. Simeon Woodhouse and Thomas Batty were my colleagues. Simeon Woodhouse was rather fond of reading, and he was a tolerable preacher too. Compared with many he might be called a good preacher. He had collected a considerable amount of knowledge, such as it was; but it was chiefly a knowledge of curious and little things. He had nothing like largeness of soul, nor anything like a comprehensive view of religious and general truth. He was besides an irritable and an intolerant bigot. He never liked to be contradicted, and he never liked to be roused or troubled with anything new. He had adopted his creed; he had made up his mind; his sermons for life were all composed or compiled, and the idea of progression or improvement never entered his soul. He was a stereotyped sample of a Methodist preacher of the more creditable class. He had not a thought of learning anything more than what was contained in his creed, and he seemed to suppose that no one else should ever think of learning more. A Methodist preacher, in his judgment should take the creed and the discipline of the connexion just as he found them, swallow them whole, and never dream of altering or mending them in the least. He seemed to consider that it was perfectly right for a man, when he had once embraced a system of doctrine or of discipline, to lay aside the use of his judgment, and the exercise of his spiritual faculties altogether and for ever. He was at the same time a man of considerable kindness, and, I should judge, a man of order, of temperance, of truth, and of integrity. His faults were more faults of judgment and constitution perhaps, than any thing else. I occasionally gave Simeon a good deal of trouble. I had begun before this to think about religious matters myself very seriously. I had been led to suspect the truth of several notions that were generally considered orthodox and evangelical, and considerably to modify my views on other subjects. With respect to my style or way of speaking, I had altered it almost altogether, so that it had ceased, to a very great extent, to resemble the common theological and methodistical dialect. Many words and phrases in common use among Methodists and other orthodox professors I had entirely laid aside, and others I had greatly modified. There were many things which it was customary for the preachers to take for granted in their sermons and conversation, that I thought without foundation in the Scriptures, and when Simeon would be talking with me, I frequently was unable to say, Yes, when he expected me to do so, and sometimes I was obliged to say No, instead of yes. This instantly excited his displeasure, and his face would colour, and his eyes look strange, and he would seem as if he considered it the most fearful offence imaginable for a man to object to any of the prevailing notions or customary expressions about religion. Still his anger would generally subside pretty quickly, and he bore with me on the whole tolerably well. I never found that he tried privately to prejudice people against me. In that respect he differed very widely from my former superintendent, T. Waterhouse. And Simeon had a very different wife from Thomas Waterhouse. Thomas Waterhouse's wife was a very proud, lofty, haughty, jealous kind of a woman, and would never allow her husband to behave well to a young colleague, unless the young colleague would be entirely at her beck. S. Woodhouse's wife on the contrary, was a quiet, inoffensive, modest woman. She had nothing of the tattler and busy-body about her that I ever discovered; and I am not aware that she would ever have felt it an intolerable calamity, or even a serious affliction for her husband to have a colleague who stood higher in the estimation of the people as a preachar than her own husband. Thomas Batty, my other colleague, was a very curious kind of a man. Though a preacher, and with some people a very popular preacher, yet he hardly seemed to have intellect sufficient to make him accountable either for what he said or for what he did. He was one of the most ridiculous talkers and preachers that I ever heard. He was completely childish or something worse. Poor man. His sermons were just as they happened to be; sometimes he preached tolerably well, but at other times his discourses were the most ridiculous, nonsensical things imaginable. I heard him three or four times myself. One night he was talking about *fire*, and he was wishing to prove that fire would *burn*. He mentioned several fires spoken of in the Bible that burned, such as the fire that overthrew Sodom and Gomorrah, the fire that formed one of the plagues of Egypt, but at last, poor man, all unexpectedly, he stumbled upon the fire that enveloped the burning bush, and found it recorded that the bush did *not* burn. How he got over the difficulty I do not exactly recollect; but he either got over it or slipped by it in some way. Then he met with a great many fires that *did* burn, but again he came at length to Nebuchadnezzar's fiery furnace, which, though it would burn some that would not burn others. Then he talked about the fire of Moscow, and he said that fire gave as much light to the moon, as the moon gives to us, and added that the flame of the burning city was so great and so high, that we might have seen it even into England, if it had not been for the hills. And a lot of such talk as that formed the chief part of his sermon. I heard him again another week evening. He was not aware that I was there. I was sitting in the gallery which was not lighted, so that he could not see me. He seemed to be showing off wonderfully that night: but his sermon was such nonsense, such a jumble of absurdity and folly, that it seemed a mystery to me how any body could be so ignorant or so reckless as to talk such things, and it seemed a still greater mystery that people should be found willing to go from time to time to listen to such effusions.

The circuit was rather prosperous during the year. The congregations were good, and the societies increased in numbers, and the leaders' meetings, quarterly meetings, and local preachers' meetings were peaceable, and all things went on tolerably well. But during the former part of my residence there, I was very much occupied. My thoughts were fixed on a distant object, and I had no means, except by letter, of communicating with that object. I believed that the person who had become the object of my affection, was designed by providence to be my wife, and I was wishful, on more accounts than one, to take her away from the place where she lived, and have her for my partner and companion. But the laws of the Connexion were against me, and difficulties lay in the way arising from the prejudices of the people against any person that married before the time of his probation was concluded. Still I had good reason for wishing to be married. One reason was the inconvenience I found in being obliged to live in other people's houses. I was completely tired of that kind of life, and not without good reason. A great part of the time that I spent in Liverpool, it is true, I lived with decent people, but still I was very far from being comfortable. I was obliged to have a person of very indifferent habits for a bed-fellow, the son of Mr. M——, one, in fact, of those same young men that were accustomed to be sent up and down by their parents collecting the money from their unhappy customers. He was a great snuff-taker, and a drunken young man as well, and perhaps still worse. I stayed in these lodgings as long as I well could; but at length I made a discovery which made me resolve to sleep with my bed-fellow no more. I made myself a bed on the sofa for eight or ten nights, and at length succeeded in getting lodgings at another place. But my new lodgings were nothing extra. The people were kind and well disposed, but there were many things that prevented me from being so comfortable as I thought I ought to be. In Staffordshire my lodgings were not much better: in some respects they were much worse. The people were very disagreeable. They had a great many visitors, especially young women, who were encouraged by the mistress to frequent the house, from none of the highest motives. The manner in which my host and hostess betrayed me, by acting the spy, and reporting whatever happened not to please them to the superintendent, has already been described. These matters, and others of a like nature, made me resolve, that whatever was the consequence, I would have done with that kind of life as soon as I could, and have a home and a household of my own. At Halifax I had more comfortable lodgings. The people were very kind and free, the accommodations also were far superior to what I had had at Liverpool and in Staffordshire, and the family seemed to take delight in making me comfortable. Still they wanted me to be comfortable in their *own* way. They wanted me to throw away my own dispositions and habits, and take up theirs. They wanted me to cease to be myself, and to become something else, a being quite different from myself. And this I could not do. My nature rebelled against it. I could not even make the attempt to be any body but myself. If I liked a thing, I said I liked it; whether they professed to like it or not; and if I did not like a thing, I would not say that I liked it, whoever else might like it. If their pleasures pleased me, I would share them; not else: if mine pleased them, all the better; but if they did not, I still felt no inclination to give them up. If

I was melancholy, I would be melancholy, however frolicsome others might be; and if I was cheerful and gay, I would be so, and I would let my cheerfulness and joy be seen, even though others might choose to be in a pet at the time. I liked to do what I liked, or what I thought most reasonable, and not to act a part unnatural for any-body's pleasure. And this my host and hostess did not like. One or two of the preachers which had occupied those lodgings before me, had been accustomed to amuse the master and mistress and other inmates with merry tales, and especially with talking about their sweethearts, and telling courting stories. They had been accustomed it seems to keep few secrets, and to exercise very little restraint either over their tongues or their behaviour. I thought fit to take a different course, and that did not please them so well. I was more reserved. The treatment I had met with at my former lodgings had *taught* me a little reserve, and made me rather distrustful of strangers. Besides my mind was not in a state to be pleased with that kind of conversation. I was not only contemplating a most serious step, but I was besides very deeply engaged in religious inquiries, which were producing most serious effects on my belief. Still if I had gone to these lodgings when I went out at first, I might have been comfortable in them; but as it was, I could not be comfortable, and I should have been comfortable no where at that time in any one's house but my own. I resolved therefore at length to be married, and about twenty weeks after Conference, I *did* marry. I took a house and furnished it, and had a home of my own. And now I believed myself happy, and I *was* happy.

Nothing very particular took place during the remainder of my stay at Halifax. I gave myself more diligently to writing than I had been accustomed to do, and I also gave myself diligently to reading, and the consequence was, that I made considerable improvement, I believe, both in knowledge and in other things. Among the works that I read while at Halifax, were the Writings of Robert Fellowes. There were several things in his works which I liked, but I was not at all times pleased with his spirit. He appeared to be correct in censuring the orthodox systems of theology, but he appeared to be wrong in the use of sarcasm and ridicule. The substance of what he had to say seemed generally to agree with truth, but the manner in which he said it appeared to be too little in accordance with that tender and benevolent spirit which is inculcated so strongly by the religion of Christ.

While at Halifax I read over a great many books which I had bought during my residence in Liverpool. Many of them I found to be worthless, especially a lot of Calvinistic books which had been urged upon me by a man of the name of JABEZ BURNS, and recommended by him as particularly adapted to assist me in making good practical sermons. On going through them I found, to be sure, that they *were* sermons, but nothing more. There was neither much light nor much power in them. They were poor, barren, commonplace, orthodox Calvinistic compositions, and when I had looked them through, I devoted the most of them to destruction.

I also read, while at Halifax, some of the works of Flavel, Abraham Booth, and Thomas Watson, and I do not know what others. Most of these I found to be about as worthless as the sermons that I had from Jabez Burns, and after writing my disapprobation of different parts of them on the margin of the books, I devoted them also to destruction, except a few which I gave to a bookseller in exchange for other works. Still, though those books were worthless, the time I spent in reading them was not lost. They furnished excellent exercise for my reasoning faculties. In exposing their errors, I often made discoveries of truth. In writing down my criticisms on the works, I was improving both my powers of thought and discrimination, and my powers of utterance too. I was, without knowing it, becoming a critic and an author. I was correcting my own style; I was detecting my own errors; I was enlarging my own capacity of thought, and preparing myself for future usefulness. Indeed, I can hardly say whether I have got more good from true, good books, or from false and foolish books. This I am sure of; I have got much good from both.

While I was at Halifax I also read a good deal of poetry. I read the works of Lord Byron and of Shakespeare amongst the rest. I liked Lord Byron's works in some respects. I was pleased, for instance, with the freedom of his style of writing, with the fervour or passionateness of his feelings, and with the dark and terrible pictures which he seemed to take pleasure in painting. But I never liked his works so well after I was married as before. I could take no pleasure in his dark and melancholy pictures after I had been cured of the mad melancholy of my own soul. I do not now think very highly of Byron's works. Byron had great poetical powers, but he was not a worthy man. Nor was be a well informed man. He was not very learned, nor was he richly furnished either with religious or with general knowledge. He knew very little of human nature; he knew very little of the world in which he lived; and he knew very little of the universe at large. He had a soul naturally endowed for any thing good, and for any thing great; but he did not do justice to his soul. He neither cultivated his intellect as he ought, nor did he cultivate or discipline his affections. Hence his works are wanting both in truth and naturalness; they neither give men knowledge, nor tend to make men good. They stir men's feelings; but they often stir those feelings most which are best unstirred. They seldom stir or rouse those feelings whose activity is most friendly to goodness. His works are not all alike; but they are most of them seriously faulty. The faults are not equal; but they are generally serious ones. I do not look upon his works with dread, because nature and truth are too strong for them; but I cannot respect them or like them as I could have wished. It is a pity that a man of such great and glorious powers should have made such a fearful shipwreck of himself. We may truly say of him as he says of Wellington, 'Never man had greater opportunities or abused them more.'

I said I read Shakespeare also. I found very great pleasure in reading Shakespeare; much more in reading him than in reading Byron, or any other poet. Indeed, I can hardly describe the eagerness and life with which I went through *his* writings. And I read him oftener through then I ever did any other poet that I recollect. But Shakespeare also has fallen in my estimation, in some respects, since then. I never feel much inclination to look at his writings now. A great change has come over my views and my tastes in these things. Still, if I ever do look into his works, I always find something that is pleasing, and great, and good. He is certainly the greatest, the cleverest poet in existence. If his moral principles and lessons had been as high and holy as his poetical talents were great, he would have been the first of authors, if not the first, the greatest, the most glorious of all God's creatures. But his morality in general is low.

While at Halifax I read the Vicar of Wakefield through. I do not know what led me to peruse it, but I read it with a great deal of pleasure. But I never read it again, nor do I feel any inclination to do so. I feel very little interest in that kind of works now.

I read the life of Lord Byron also, by Thomas Moore, while at Halifax, but I do not know that I felt much interest, in it generally, but I recollect being very much struck with one thing that Byron said about Shelly's writings in opposition to religion, and about his endeavours to shake people's belief in the great doctrines of God, and providence, and immortality. Byron's words are to this effect, That whether a man believed in religion or not, he ought never to attempt to destroy the belief in religion in others; adding, that the hopes of religion, even if false, were worth more than all the world's best truths. It seemed a great thing for such a man as Byron to say. But every man that thinks or feels at all, must, I suppose, feel at times the necessity of religious consolation. But though pleased with this saying of his, I could not help but be disgusted at the looseness of principle and character which Byron unfolded in his correspondence, and I cannot but look on him with great pity, and on his works with great disapprobation. As I have already said, he was a great man without doubt, and *formed* to be a very great man. His writings give many proofs of genius and power. He might have been one of the first and best of poets. He might have served mankind and the cause of truth to a very great extent, and gained a fame both high and wide and permanent; but he threw his opportunities away, and he is doomed now, in my judgment, to go down with vast multitudes of other writers who have trifled with truth, with conscience and religion, to the regions of darkness and the shadows of death. The day will come, I have no doubt, when his memory will perish, and his works be all forgotten.

Byron appeared to me, in some of his letters, to speak extravagantly with respect to the extent of his moral and theological reading. He named a number of authors, such as Barrow, and Tillotson, and others, whom he speaks of as if he had read them carefully through. Now I do not myself believe that he had done any such thing. He could hardly have been so ignorant of the real character of the Christian religion as he manifestly was, if he had carefully read the works he mentions. He must, if he had read the works he enumerates, have been better able to distinguish between Christian truths and some of those orthodox follies and blasphemies which go under the Christian name.

While I was at Halifax I spent a good deal of time in reading over the New Testament, with a view to ascertain its doctrines on various points. The consequence was that my mind was more confirmed in its doubts of the truth of various portions of the orthodox theology, and more strongly inclined to receive those views which had generally been cried down by the prevailing sects as heterodox and heretical. While here I lost my belief almost altogether in the common notion of hereditary depravity, and of the accountability of mankind for Adam's first transgression. I began to believe, or strongly lean to the belief, that little children were God's own creatures,—that they were made by God just right,—that their constitution, though such as to make a conflict between good and evil inevitable, was still exactly adapted to the end for which human beings were created, and that in this respect, as well as in all others, God's work was perfect. I had before this ceased to believe that little children were born under the wrath and curse of God, or were reputed *guilty* on account of Adam's sin. My mind also began to get clearer and more correct and comprehensive views of the work of Christ, of the end of Christ's mission, and of the means by which he sought to accomplish that end. Indeed at this period I was led to believe, or at least to surmise, that the true character of Christ was that of a prophet or teacher, that his great work was to bear witness to the truth, to unfold or exhibit it in his example, to rouse and convince men by his miracles, and to move, and change, and transform the souls of men by the exhibition of God's love in his humiliation and suffering for the human family. I recollect proposing to myself this question, Was not Christ's great office the *prophetical* office, and was not this his great object and work, namely, by the manifestation and enforcement of the truth, to illumine and sanctify the souls of men, to change, to purify, and to perfect their characters. This I laid down as an hypothesis,—I regarded it as probable,—I was inclined to believe it to be the truth. I took the New

Testament and examined it on this hypothesis. I put down every thing that was said by Christ, or that was written by his apostles bearing on this subject. I first put down every thing that was plain, and that appeared manifestly to be in favour of my hypothesis or supposition; I then examined every thing appearing to bear on the subject that seemed in any way dark or doubtful, or which appeared to lean to the other side of the question. Those passages of Scripture which were in favour of my hypothesis, soon became a great multitude, and the evidence which they afforded of its truth appeared to be almost irresistible. The passages which seemed to be dark or doubtful were comparatively few, and those which seemed to bear *against* the hypothesis were fewer still: and the result was, that I ceased to feel any pleasure in representing the mission and work of the Messiah after the usual fashion. I preached some of my sermons with less confidence, and others of them I could not preach at all, and others of them I was obliged to alter greatly. I was also obliged to change my style of speaking and writing in general. Indeed my mind was at that time undergoing great and rapid changes; and I was becoming less and less orthodox, according to the common mode of talking, and more and more heretical or heterodox daily.

The New Connexion had a law against preachers getting married until they had either finished their probation, which never lasted less than four years, and which sometimes lasted five or six or more, unless they could obtain special leave from the annual Committee or the Conference. One of the reasons assigned for this law was the necessity of young men giving themselves up wholly to the improvement of their minds by study, and the like. It was intimated in the rules that after young preachers got married, they would not be able to attend to their studies so closely, or to make improvement so rapidly. I however found it quite otherwise. I proved the reason assigned for limiting the preachers' liberty to be a false one, so far as my own case was concerned. I studied more closely, and I improved more rapidly after my marriage than I had ever done before. And I studied with far greater pleasure too. I might have more cares after I was married, but I had many more comforts. I might have some new difficulties to contend with, but I had many more advantages. My conviction is, that the common plan of hindering young preachers from getting married for the first four or six years of their preaching life, is a very bad one, and that on more accounts than one. It both hinders their improvement in knowledge, and greatly endangers their purity and piety if they have any. The system is full of danger and mischief. It causes many unhappy marriages, and many fearful deeds of treachery and covenant-breaking. It has broken many a woman's heart, embittered and shortened many a woman's life, and in some cases ended in the suicide of injured females. It has a great deal to do in causing that terrible amount of licentiousness to be found among the preachers of the different denominations of Methodists, Baptists, Independents, &c., and in corrupting the sects in other ways. And the real reason why the law was upheld in the New Connexion, was not to secure to the young preachers better opportunities for study and general improvement, but to meet the wishes of the Circuits which would have hired preachers, and yet wished to have them at as little expense as possible. The Circuits could have a single preacher for forty, fifty, or sixty pounds a year less than a married one, and this was the real reason of the arrangement. The other reason, the reason published in the rules, was only a *sham* reason; a *made* reason; a means of imposing on the public only.

While I was at Halifax I scalded my foot very badly, and was laid up for awhile. Before my foot got well, I had a violent attack of diarrhea, &c. I was also repeatedly and violently attacked with sickness. My stomach was very much disordered: my health was very far from being good. But I was preserved alive, and I was, generally, able to attend to what were considered my duties as a preacher in the Connexion. It did however frequently happen that my labours were a tremendous task to me. I have more than once gone to preach when I have scarce been able to drag my legs along to my appointment, and when I have scarcely been able to keep my eyes open for the mighty pressure of sleep that fell upon them, or to muster strength sufficient fairly to utter or force out my words while I have been in the pulpit. But I was *appointed* to preach, I was *hired* to preach, I was expected to preach. The people at the place to which I was appointed would have considered themselves wronged if I had not preached, so I was obliged to try to preach. But when my body was disordered and weak, and my mind in consequence so unprepared for the work, it was dreadful drudgery. I feel exceedingly glad that I am now free from a system which made such drudgery, such forced, such unnatural efforts a part of my duty.

There was a good deal of luxury and extravagance amongst the members of the New Connexion in Halifax. There was a great deal of feasting, a great deal of extravagant eating and drinking, and I sustained some injury by being frequently invited to those eating and drinking parties. But I did not then properly understand the subject, and see the evils of those customs as I have done since

While I was at Halifax there was an oratorio in the parish church, and Braham was there, with a lot of other great popular singers and musicians. One of the members gave me a ticket, and I went. It was the first time I ever was at such a place or meeting, and I have never been at one since. I got severely rebuked for going by some of the members, and perhaps justly rebuked, though I hardly felt inclined to acknowledge myself in fault. I hardly recollect what I thought of the performance in general, but I know I was very much pleased with Chaos, the introduction to the Creation. I fancy I did not think much of the singing in general. Braham sang one verse of Luther's hymn; no more. This seemed almost like nothing. Some of the singers tried hard to do something out of the usual way; but to me they seemed to spoil themselves by so doing. I always liked something natural. Altogether I had but very little pleasure in reflecting on the meeting, and I think that the parties who blamed me for countenancing such a thing were right. It was all, or most of it, acting, hypocrisy.

The next conference was at Hull. At this conference a complaint was made against me for having broken the law of the Connexion by getting married during my probation, without the leave of conference, and the conference put me a year back on my probation, as a punishment. They never wrote to me for any explanation, nor invited me to attend to answer for myself. I never even heard that a complaint had been made against me on the subject until I received information of the punishment. I was accused, tried, and condemned all in my absence. This was the more unjust, as it so happened that I had not in reality broken the law; at least I had not, as they supposed, broken a law which I had promised to keep. When I went out as a preacher, I refused to give any pledge on the subject of marriage. But if I even had given a pledge, it would only have been a pledge to obey the law then in existence. Whereas before I was married, the law was altered, and another kind of pledge adopted, to which I was no party. The pledge which I had been requested to give, but which, in truth, I did not give, was now abolished. I had not therefore either broken an engagement or disobeyed the law under which I had gone out as a preacher. Yet conference punished me. And besides putting me back a year, the conference transported me to Blyth, in the Newcastle circuit, a distance of one hundred and thirty miles. I had of course to break up my house, and shift my furniture and family, and all at my own expense, and that too at a time when my wife was far from being well, and when she was in a state to render travelling both inconvenient and dangerous. But the members of conference cared nothing for these things,—they rather rejoiced at the thought of the trouble and expense they had caused me, and at the difficulties in which they had placed me. I hardly think it possible for a man to have to do with a more hard-hearted or unfeeling set of people than those which generally composed a New Connexion conference. One of these men, G. Beaumont of Halifax, was unusually cruel and unmanly. Not content in taking part with trying and condemning me in my absence, and subjecting myself and my delicate and unoffending wife to the greatest annoyance they could, he told my wife, after he returned from conference, a whole lot of frightful tales about the circuit to which we were appointed. He made her believe that the land was so full of pits, that my life would always be in danger, &c. I grant that this man was worse than his companions, but they were most of them very cruel and unreasonable.

I felt very much dissatisfied with my appointment, and was very reluctant to submit to it, but there seemed no alternative: go I must. I therefore set to work to make the best of my trials. We packed up our furniture and sent it off, and then set off ourselves. On our way we called at Bramley, my native place. There my wife was taken very unwell and continued unwell, dangerously unwell, for a length of time, and doubts began to be entertained both by the doctor and my own relations, that she would not recover. This was a greater trial still; but I was able to bear it. I was of course unable to proceed to my circuit; I could not entertain the thought of leaving my wife until there appeared to be some signs of improvement. This brought on another trial. The people in the circuit were grieved that they could not have their preacher as soon as they expected, and prepared to receive me, when I should arrive, with rebukes, and frowns, and ill-nature. At length my wife began to mend, and she was quickly so far improved that we were able to start on our journey, quite contrary to our fears. The journey did her good instead of harm. A violent cough that she had had, and which continued to the day of starting, gave way in the course of a few hours through the change of air, and by the time we reached Stockton-on-Tees, she was both relieved in her chest, and revived in her system generally. She was also able to eat a hearty meal, which she had not been able to do for weeks before.

Though stationed at Blyth, we stopped a short time at Newcastle. My labours happened to be in that part of the circuit at the time we arrived at Newcastle. As soon as I had opportunity, I went over to Blyth to take a house, and prepare it for my wife's reception; but I could not find a house unoccupied in the whole town; and we had to search a long time before we could find even two or three rooms that we could take. I however succeeded in obtaining some rooms at length, and glad I was.

The first text I preached from at Blythe was Isaiah iii. 10, 11,—'Say ye to the righteous it shall be well with him; for he shall eat the fruit of his doings.' The discourse was very well received, and it appeared to have a good effect upon the congregation. But I confess I preached the sermon as much for myself as for the people, and perhaps its principal effect was upon my own mind. I was very much comforted while speaking of the wisdom and goodness of God's providence,—of the assurance given us that all things work together for good to them that love God,—that all the changes in our earthly lot are under the direction of our heavenly Father, and that the painful, the dark, and the threatening, as well as the joyous, and bright, and promising, are all intended by God to promote our improvement, our perfection, and our blessedness.

After I had taken rooms, preached my sermon, and made

all needful arrangements, I returned from Blyth to Newcastle to fetch my wife, and in a few days we took up our residence at Blyth. I found the people at Blyth, generally speaking, a kind-hearted and well-disposed people, and I enjoyed much comfort in their fellowship. But they were not all alike. One was grieved that the young preacher did not live at her house; another was jealous and afraid that the new preacher would not be as pliant in his hands as the former young preacher had been. Still the people generally were affectionate and loving, and delighted to contribute to our comfort.

I preached regularly two Sabbaths in four at Blyth, and spent the other two Sabbaths in Newcastle and the surrounding villages. We received only about £40 a year from the circuit, so that we were somewhat straitened in our circumstances in consequence. We had besides to meet many extra expenses. But I never went into debt, and I never asked a favour from any one, nor did I ever complain of poverty or of hardship. This of course was owing in a great measure to the economy of my wife, who understood, as well as most good wives, how to create a great deal of comfort out of a scanty supply of materials. I had always plenty, and my home was always clean and comfortable; though I am sorry to say that my wife was never as attentive and kind to herself as she always was to me. My kind parents also supplied me with clothes, which lightened the burden we had to bear.

There were several of the members at Newcastle and in the surrounding societies, who were not so kind and well-disposed as the Blyth people were. Several of them seemed to take pleasure in crossing and trying the feelings of their young preacher. Amongst the worst of that class was Thomas Snowdon, an old local preacher, leader, and trustee. The first interview I had with Thomas Snowdon he took occasion to insult me respecting my marriage, and also gave me to understand that he should expect me to be in perfect subjection to him, if I wished to enjoy much peace or comfort in the circuit. It fell to my lot to be lodged and boarded for part of my time at this man's house, and to show his spirit and manner of his proceeding I may give the following.

It was T. Snowdon's custom to read a portion of the Scriptures to his family every morning, and as he past along he would make comments on what he read. When I was there, he would frequently stop in his readings and comments, to ask my opinion, and he seemed to expect that I must always coucur in what he said. However at times I was obliged to dissent from his sayings, and then would follow a little controversy. Those controversies were never very profitable, in consequence of his constant determination or desire to force his own opinions on myself, and to extort from me assent to his whimsical and foolish observations. Yet he still continued to force those controversies. He also took upon himself the office of perpetual censurer of my discourses. His censures however were generally proportioned to the goodness of the discourse. If I happened to be particularly at liberty in my discourse, and preach better than usual, he would blame almost every thing. If I preached indifferently, he would censure less; and if I preached poorly, if I were embarrassed in my discourse, and seemed troubled or sad on that account, he would scarcely censure at all. Then the things which he censured would be sure to be the best and truest parts of my sermon. And this was the way in which he acted in almost all things. He appeared to think that he was out of his duty, unless he was endeavouring to torture the mind of the young preacher, and to force him, if possible, into servile and absolute subjection to his will. I however could not allow myself to be forced into such subjection, and the consequence was, perpetual torture and persecution. If I could have agreed to all he said,—if I could have flattered him and told him that he was one of the best and wisest men I had ever seen, he would have commended me in every thing; but as it was there was no end to his annoyances.

There were two others that were far from being considerate or feeling towards their young preachers. They both appeared to have taken lessons from T. Snowdon, and to have profited by them in a certain way, though neither of them was equal to their master. One of them was T. Snowdon's son-in-law; the other was a doctor, an old, fast friend of T. Snowdon's. Yet both seemed to consider it their duty to prevent their young preachers from thinking, except in one direction, and from speaking except in echo to their own fixed orthodox opinions. The consequence was that I enjoyed but little comfort while on the Newcastle side, and I always took the first opportunity to leave that part of the circuit, and return to my home at Blyth.

At Newcastle a meeting was formed a short time after I came to the circuit, for conversation on religious subjects. R. Banks, a Baptist preacher, and J. Blackwell, S. Frost, J. Townsend, and some other members of the Methodist New Connexion were the principal members. I attended some of those meetings, and expressed myself somewhat freely on certain points of doctrine, especially on such subjects as the witness of the spirit. The other members talked about people *feeling* their sins forgiven, and feeling that they were in the favour of God. *I* said it would be better to use the word *know* instead of *feel*,—that men might *know* that their sins were forgiven, but could not *feel* it,—that they might feel joy in consequence of knowing or believing that they were accepted of God, but could not feel the acceptance itself. This startled some of them, and they seemed as if struck dumb. S. Frost, the doctor, asked what was the difference between knowing and feeling; he could see no difference. I explained the difference; showed that we know many things which we could not be said to feel. Another thought I was on dangerous ground, &c. And thus the members proceeded. I tried to enlighten them, but to very little purpose. Most of them were too old to learn anything new, especially from a youth. Yet I still continued to go to the meeting for a while, and to express my thoughts with a measure of freedom, but my sentiments were not over kindly received, and an intimation was given by some of the members, that a young man like myself, a preacher, supported by the Methodist community, should be careful not to run into Anti-Methodistical notions,—that, in short, he should not have opinions of his own at all, unless he could make the opinions of the *body* his own. I in consequence soon gave up my attendance at the meeting, and the meeting soon fell through.

The superintendent preacher in the Newcastle circuit was James Curtis, a little man both in body and mind, but a person of great importance in his own estimation. Like most of the preachers that I had to do with, he seemed to consider that a young preacher was guilty of rebellion and impiety if he happened to think or speak in any way that was not in accordance with the judgment or prejudices of his elders. The young preacher that had travelled with him the year before I went to Newcastle, had called Mr. Curtis *Bishop*, and he had conducted himself towards him, as I was given to understand, with the greatest servility. Little Curtis seemed to expect the same kind of servility and flattery from me, but I was not prepared to give him what he expected. I had no idea of flattering any one, or of being a slave to any one. At the same time I felt nothing towards him but what was kind and friendly. I often went to see him, and conversed with him, talking over matters with great freedom, laying down my objections to a number of words and forms of expression generally used in speaking and writing on these subjects. But he was far from being worthy of the confidence which I reposed in him. At first he did not reveal himself in his true character; he appeared for a length of time to be very friendly, and to be wishful to promote my comfort and my welfare, and to assist in making my way plain before me in the circuit. It was his professions of kindness that led me to speak with him so freely as I did. But I at length found reason to repent of the confidence which I had reposed in him. I conversed with him on the subject of the trinity, the atonement, the doctrine of original sin, regeneration, justification, sanctification, the witness of the spirit, and the like, expressing my dissent, also, from many of the common opinions held on those subjects, and stating what appeared to me to be the pure Scriptural doctrines on these and similar subjects. He seemed to concur in what I said in general, and expressed great pleasure in having those subjects stript of the mystery in which they had been wrapt, and brought into an intelligible and rational shape. I had not at this time entirely rejected the orthodox doctrines on those subjects; on the contrary, I considered myself a believer in them all, only I had, as I thought, discovered the true, the rational, the Scriptural explanation of them. I had no idea that I could be a heretic or heterodox so long as I kept so plainly to Scripture and to common sense. Nor was I aware that my sentiments approached so nearly to the doctrines of Unitarians as I afterwards found out they did. His conduct and conversation altogether led me to suppose that he was friendly to freedom of thought, and to spiritual improvement,—that he delighted in liberty himself, and was wishful to give liberty to others. I continued to entertain a favourable opinion respecting him, and to regard him as a friend, for a considerable length of time, for five or six months perhaps. At the same time I heard from different quarters that he had expressed himself privately to several members of the church, to the effect, that he was doubtful and suspicious with respect to my orthodoxy, and had fears that I might not turn out to be sound in the faith. But I took little notice of these hearsay tales. He seemed to be friendly and kind, and it never entered into my head to suspect him of insincerity and treachery. Yet false and treacherous he was, as I afterwards was forced to believe. It seems that his manner of proceeding was this. At first, when the people spoke favourably of my discourses, he would say, 'Yes, yes, but I think his sermons would be no worse if they had a little more Christ in them.' In this way he introduced further observations, saying how highly he respected me, but pointing out defects in point of doctrine, which, if remedied, would make my discourses all that a person could wish them to be.

My wife was convinced long before me that his profession of friendship was not sincere,—that the freedom of conversation which he encouraged in me, he encouraged for the sake of obtaining opportunities to betray me; and she warned me repeatedly against placing over much confidence in him. But I was always unsuspicious, and therefore neglected my wife's admonitions, and went on. At length he showed himself openly, and proved my wife in the right. The occasion of the revelation was as follows. I had objected to leave Blyth and go to Newcastle on one occasion at the appointed time. At that time the cholera was very prevalent in the district, and I myself was rather unwell; so I requested Mr. Curtis to take my place at Newcastle, and allow me to take his place at Blyth for a fortnight. It seemed most reasonable and desirable at such a time, that we should both be at our own homes, that if any thing happened to either ourselves or our families, we might be able to help or attend each other, and have each other's company. My superintendent however objected to the proposed change, and insisted that I should leave my home, ill as I was, and take my usual appointment at Newcastle and the neighbourhood. I refused to do so, and this brought him out in his true colours. He called a meeting, and laid the matter before the leaders and stewards at Newcastle, and expressed himself very violently. He would fain have had them to take measures instantly for my removal from the circuit. His haste and violence however defeated his purpose. He gave several of the people reason to suspect that his motives were not good—that he was influenced by jealousy, and not by a regard to the interests of the Connexion, and they refused therefore to do as he wished them. He then accused me of heresy as well as insubordination, which led to replies from others; and it then came out that he had for a long time been slandering me in private, and labouring incessantly to injure me in my reputation and influence. Nay it came out that even while he was professing all friendship towards me, he had gone so far as to propose to the circuit steward to call a circuit meeting to try me for heresy, and to have me laid aside from the ministry. These revelations went seriously against my accuser, and the storm which he had sought to raise against me, turned round against himself, and afflicted him terribly. Even those very persons who had been made his confidents, with the exception of one or two, turned against him; and when the April quarter day arrived, the whole circuit, with those one or two exceptions, united in petitioning the Conference to station me amongst them a second year.

My labours at Blyth were rendered very useful. The society there was about doubled in its numbers, and all things went on prosperously. Many young persons were brought to begin to be religious, and some that were rather advanced in years also were led to embrace religion. The people generally were improved in knowledge and in character. The influence exerted upon the congregation and the neighbourhood generally, by the principles which I inculcated, was of a truly beneficial character.

It was a great trial to me to be removed from Halifax, and sent so far away into a strange and unknown distrct. I considered my removal from Halifax and my appointment to Newcastle as one of the most painful events I had met with then, and I continued to regard it and to feel it a great trial for a length of time. It was nevertheless overruled for my good, and I have since been led to regard it, and I regard it now, on many accounts, as one of the greatest blessings of my life. For one thing I met with a great many books at Newcastle that I had never read before, which afforded me a great deal of instruction. Amongst those were the works of Dr. Campbell, his preliminary dissertations on the four Gospels, his translation of the Gospels, his discourse on miracles, and other discourses on important subjects, and his works on pulpit eloquence and systematic divinity. These I read with a great deal of pleasure. I both received much instruction from them, and was greatly confirmed by them in many of the opinions which I had been previously led to entertain. Another work that I read with some interest was Butler's Analogy of Religion, and his Discourses on Benevolence, &c. I also read Foster's Essays on Decision of Character, on the application of the epithet ROMANTIC, and on some of the causes why men of learning and taste rejected or neglected the religion of Christ. I was pleased with all these works, and especially with Campbell's and Foster's. Campbell's works seemed very clear and rational, and there was a spirit of liberty and rationality pervading the whole, which was exceedingly grateful to my mind. They both threw fresh light around me, and stimulated me to think and judge and seek after truth for myself. I was pleased also with Foster's Essays. I did not much like the style of the essays; it seemed laboured, harsh, and hard, and very un-English; but I liked the thoughts very much. They were new to me, many of them; but yet they commended themselves to my judgment as true and right. Others of his thoughts were not new, they were thoughts which had long been familiar to me, but they were no less pleasing on that account. His Essay on the causes why men of taste and learning frequently re-rejected Christianity were especially interesting to my mind. This was a subject on which I had spent much thought myself, and his views were in a very great measure in accordance with my own. His Essay on Decision of Character too had its influence on my mind, and tended to make me more firm in what I believed to be right, more decided in my opposition to error, and more resolute in my efforts to propagate truth than I had been before.

I also met with some works while in this circuit on the constitution and government of the Christian church, in which were many extracts from the writings of John Hales of Eton, afterwards called the venerable Hales. I read those works with very great pleasure. They gave me information with respect to church matters which was both new to me and very important, and which led me to think on that subject more closely and thoroughly than I had ever done before. They did, in fact, sow the seeds of my present thoughts and views on those subjects.

I met with another treat at Newcastle greater than all, it was the library of Doctor Tomlinson in St. Nicholas' church, consisting of from five to ten thousand volumes, on all subjects bearing on the history, the doctrines, the character, the evidences, and the tendency of the religion of Christ. The library contained the works of authors of all varieties of opinion, whether infidel or Christian, orthodox or heterodox, papist or protestant, dissenters or church of England men. This library was public property, and was open to the public three or four days almost every week. I went to this library frequently when I was on the Newcastle side of the circuit. I used to go there in the morning as often as I could, and spend the greater part of the day in looking over the books, reading such as appeared likely to give me the information that I was seeking, and often making extracts from the works. Among the works that I met with there were several of Baxter's which I had never seen before, the works of Cudworth, Locke, Newton, Whitby, Moore, Burnett, Norris, Tindal, Mead, Chubb, Machiavel, Goodwin, Hobbes, Milton, and a great many others which I cannot now enumerate. From some of those works I made considerable extracts, especially from the writings of Locke, Hobbes, Newton, and Milton. I had an opportunity of satisfying myself while reading those works with respect to a great many points of controversial Theology and Church history, on which my mind had been long in suspense. One effect which my reading in this library produced, in addition to storing my mind with a great variety of information, was, to make me resolve to be free. I saw that it was impossible for the soul of man to answer the end for which it was created, while trammelled by human authority, or fettered with human creeds. I saw clearly that if I was to do justice to truth, to God, or to my own soul, I must break loose from all the creeds and laws of men's devising, and live in full and unrestricted liberty. And this I resolved to do. That measure of bondage in which I saw myself placed in the New Connexion began to be exceedingly irksome to me, and I felt strongly inclined to throw off the yoke and to assert my liberty. But whither should I go? And what would become of me?

The darkness and dangers that surrounded me depressed and afflicted me, and reconciled me for awhile at least to move on in my accustomed path, in hopes that at length God would open for me a way of escape. I then resolved to attempt the reformation of the Connexion, and the hope sprang up in my breast that I might in time secure to myself, in the Connexion, the liberty that my soul required. I had been taught that liberty was the distinguishing principle of the body,—I had been promised when first received into the body at Leeds all the liberty that a Christian could enjoy; and I would try if that liberty could not be secured. I would try to bring the Connexion to carry out the principles of liberty to their full and proper extent. I soon found however that I could not do this without subjecting myself to great inconveniences. I found that not only were the preachers opposed to every thing like full and perfect Christian liberty, but that many leading and influential members of the Connexion were the same. If I expressed myself freely on religious subjects, fears were at once awakened in the minds of some with respect to my orthodoxy, my safety, and my future usefulness; and if I pleaded for greater Connexional liberty or toleration, it was at once suspected by some that I wished for liberty and toleration because my own views were heretical. It frequently happened that in my public discourse, I gave utterance to more truth than was supposed to be contained in the creed of the Connexion. When this took place, I was almost sure to receive admonitions, warnings, and rebukes, from some of the leading members. I found the preachers and the leading members to a considerable extent alike in this; all were afraid of anything new, afraid of any attempts at improvement, afraid of the progress of the mind. At the same time I have reason to believe that one ground of their fears of change, and of their opposition to opinions different from the common opinions of false orthodoxy, was not an idea that such opinions were unscriptural or false, but a fear of the injury which the Connexion might sustain by any attempt at change. Many of the laymen would have been glad to have had the whole subject of Christianity investigated, and the whole wide world of truth explored, if they had thought it could have been done without injury to their interests or reputation as a Connexion. But they saw that to allow such a thing would necessarily cause confusion, division, and perhaps the entire breaking up of the body, and the loss of property and popularity as well; so they could not allow truth to have its way. They saw, or thought they saw, that they could not allow the mind of man to move onwards in its natural and destined course of improvement, without inconvenience and risk; so they made up their minds to stand still, and keep things as they were.

And as they had decided not to go forward themselves, they were resolved that others should not go forward either. They began to persecute those who would not stand still with them, and keep them company in their conscious errors. And those who had once been themselves inclined to liberty and reform, but had started back through fear, were the most cruel and intolerant persecutors of all. The annoyance I received from some of those persons was cruel in the extreme. Many a time after I have been receiving private lectures and remonstrances from some of those leading men in Newcastle, have I climbed the Wind-mill Hills with a sad and anxious heart. In consequence of the feverish excitement which their rebukes and threats occasioned, I was often unable to take my usual supply of food, and night after night have I laid on my bed wakeful and troubled, pondering the sorrows of my situation, the difficulties with which I seemed to be surrounded, and the obstacles placed in the way of my improvement, my freedom, my usefulness, and my happiness. It was impossible for me to rest where I was, yet the results which seemed likely sooner or later to follow from the course which I felt bound in conscience to pursue, afflicted me at times beyond measure. Still I was supported and comforted in all these troubles. I had some trust in God, though not much. I had a little courage too, and confidence, though my heart often quailed, and I still went on with my studies and inquiries, and laboured to instruct others as well.

About this time I began to think of publishing a penny periodical for the expression of my sentiments. From conversations however that I had with some of the preachers and leading members of the Connexion, I was led to conclude that little or nothing new could be published without great opposition and disturbance,—that if I published my sentiments in my own name, I must expect persecution and perhaps expulsion from the body. Though the Connexion had been founded on the principle of liberty, it was plain that its rulers were not prepared to allow its members to act on that principle, unless they could act on it without endangering the reputation of the Connexion, and that, it was plain, was impossible. Much as the rulers were accustomed to boast of their liberality, they would allow nothing to be published but what was in accordance with the notions of orthodoxy entertained by or professed by the respectable orthodox world. I was led in consequence to postpone for a time the commencement of my periodical. But I felt very uncomfortable at being obliged to do so. I longed for free intercourse with the thinkers of the world, and should have felt it an unspeakable happiness to have had the opportunity of laying my thoughts before them, and of receiving their thoughts in return. Many a time did I wish that I could meet with some periodical through which I could reveal my thoughts with freedom, and in which I could have read the free and honest thoughts of others. I have since discovered, that there were publications at that time which I might have used for that purpose, if I had been aware of their existence; but I was not. I was not aware of the existence of such publications till long after I had commenced a periodical publication of my own. I was obliged therefore to live in a great measure alone. There were two or three with whom I could hold intercourse privately, one a brother, and another or two who were preachers, but as for the world of free and thoughtful men, I felt as if shut out from it. But why did I not break loose, and declare my thoughts without reserve? My thoughts were not yet ripe; I had not sufficiently examined things: and I was afraid of persecution,—afraid of injuring my reputation,—afraid of losing my influence,—afraid of many things. But my thoughts would have ripened faster if I had published them; my investigations would have become more thorough if I had boldly provoked discussion; and I should have found friends and every thing else that I needed, if I had just used my freedom, and left the rest to God. Yes, I know that now, but I did not know it then. I was a child then; but I am more of a man now. I see now that all my fears were foolish and vain; and that all my prudence was folly. I see clearly that if I had trusted God and set man's will and power at nought, I should neither have injured the cause of truth, nor destroyed my own influence. I see clearly that the world was ready for me, if I had been ready for it. I see clearly now that the wisest thing would have been to have had no wisdom at all, but the wisdom of simply obeying the spirit of truth within me,—the wisdom of allowing my soul to speak without reserve or delay,—the wisdom of disregarding or annihilating fear, and allowing my soul to pour forth with perfect freedom the inspirations with which I had been favoured. I say I see all this now: but I did not see it then. I was ignorant then and foolish: I was under the wisdom of the world and the flesh. I had not full faith in God. I had lost the sweet innocence and simplicity of childhood, which reveals itself freely and without reserve, and had got in its place a smatch of the spurious and infernal wisdom of the sects. And it took a long, long time to get rid of it. Thank God I ever did get rid of it. God grant that what I now am writing may help others to get rid of it too, or else keep them from ever being infected with it.

During my residence in the Newcastle circuit, I read several works on Mental Philosophy, on Rhetoric, and Logic. These works did me a great deal of good. I do not recollect exactly now the effects they had upon my mind, but they led me to attend to my style as well as to my way of thinking, and contributed thus both to my own improvement and my usefulness to others.

During my residence in that circuit, my views on many subjects became anti-methodistical to a very great extent indeed. I now no longer held the prevailing views with respect to the nature of Justifying Faith, the Witness of the Spirit, Regeneration, Sanctification, and the like. In reading Wesley's works I was astonished at the great number of unmeaning and inconsistent passages which I met with. In many of his views I perfectly agreed with him, but with a vast amount of what he said on other subjects, I could not help but disagree. I commenced a dialogue at this time between John Wesley and Jabez Bunting, on those subjects. Jabez Bunting I represented as the firm and undistinguishing advocate of Wesleyanism, as taught in Wesley's writings. John Wesley I introduced as a spirit from heaven who had gained better information on many subjects than he had had while he lived on earth. Jabez introduced himself as the staunch and indiscriminate defender of John Wesley's writings and of his institutions and laws. John Wesley kindly but strongly rebuked him, and directed him to a better and higher principle than that which led him to subject himself to the authority of men, and to a better and higher standard of truth and duty than his own writings. He pointed out to Jabez the folly of making imperfect and fallible man our measure; the duty of seeking after truth for ourselves in the words and the works of God, and of allowing our souls the liberty of seeking after truth and perfection without regard to the authority of any man whether dead or living. He then began to lament the errors of his mortal state,—to point out cases in which he had spoken and legislated ignorantly and inconsistently, &c. It was my intention to have led the two speakers through the whole field of Wesleyan theology and church discipline, but the matter dropped, and the manuscript was left unfinished.

About this time finding that there was little likelihood that I should be tolerated in the New Connexion unless I could allow my mind to be enslaved, and feeling that I should be obliged sooner or later to break loose from Methodistical restraint, and speak and act with freedom, I thought of visiting Mr. Turner, the Unitarian minister of Newcastle, and seeking an interview with him. I had heard something to the effect that Unitarians were great lovers of freedom,—that they did not bind their ministers and members by any human creeds, but left them at liberty to investigate the whole system of Christianity thoroughly, and to judge as to what were its doctrines and duties for themselves, and to preach what they believed to be true without restraint and persecution, and I thought if this was the case, they must be a very happy people. But from other things which I had heard respecting them, I was led to regard them with something of horror,—to look on them as persons who trifled with Scripture authority, as persons who had rushed from the extremes of false orthodoxy into the extremes of infidelity. I was in consequence prevented from visiting Mr. Turner, and I remained in comparative ignorance of the Unitarian body, in ignorance both of their principles and of their character, still shut up in the dungeons of orthodox slavery.

While at Blyth I met with some works that had been published many years before by a Joseph Cooke, a Wesleyan Methodist travelling preacher, on the subject of Justification, and the nature of Saving Faith. By reading these works I was strengthened in my convictions that the prevailing

Methodistical and Calvinistic views on those subjects were not correct. I found afterwards that Joseph Cooke had been expelled from the Methodist Connexion for his opinions. I was told also that he had become a Unitarian preacher in Rochdale, but this was not the case.

As I stated before that I spent nearly one-half of my time on the Newcastle side of the circuit, and visited my own home at Blyth regularly about the middle of the ten days that I used to spend on that side. I of course passed from Blyth to Newcastle and from Newcastle to Blyth twice every month. I almost always walked; for though coach-hire was allowed to the superintendant, none was allowed to the young preacher, and I could not afford to pay for riding out of my own short allowance. This long and frequent walk, a walk of fifteen or sixteen miles each way, seemed a hardship at first, but it proved, in fact, one of my greatest blessings. My journeyings to and fro on the rough and lonely road from Blyth to Newcastle and from Newcastle to Blyth were amongst the happiest and most useful periods of my life. I almost invariably found some new book to read on my way, and I generally got through a middling volume, or a great part of a volume, from the beginning to the end of each journey. I should think that during the year and a-half that I spent in the circuit, I read not much less than from fifty to sixty volumes on the high way. And I could read as comfortably and as profitably while walking slowly along the road, as I could while sitting in my library. Nay I believe I could read *more* comfortably and profitably on the road than in my library. And indeed to this day, I never read more comfortably, than when I read and walk along my path. Reading on the road has become so habitual, that it feels quite natural; and I should now feel very uncomfortable if I were obliged to go a journey without a book. Even if I know that I am to have a companion in my walk, I still feel as if I should not be properly provided for without a book.

While I was in this circuit I first became a father. My eldest child was born at Blyth, on the first of September, 1831. This event awakened feelings which I cannot exactly describe,—feelings of a very peculiar description. And strange as it may seem, some of those feelings were not of a pleasant nature. I was foolish in fact. I had not full faith in the wisdom and goodness of God's providence. I had not well learned that all God's ways are right, and that every thing which he appoints is for our good. Or if I had learned the lesson, my trials prevented me from deriving that comfort from the doctrine which I have often derived from it since.

Though my new relationship added considerably to my trials, yet it greatly increased the comfort of my life.

Twice or thrice my little child was sick, and near to death, and these things tried me. On one occasion all hopes of his recovery seemed to be gone, and yet, while the little one was in that state, I was obliged to leave my home, and visit the Newcastle side of the circuit. When I had nearly finished my labours on the Newcastle side, I requested the leaders at one of the places, Westmoor, to give me up, as I had received word that my child was not likely to live, that I might have an opportunity of visiting it and its mother in their affliction; but those hard-hearted people refused me the favour. I told them that I *must* go home, and that if the child was living and at all likely to recover, I would return and preach to them; but if not, I should *not* return, say what they might. I should stay at home, and take the consequences. I walked home, and happily found my child a little better. I returned almost immediately on foot to Westmoor, a distance of ten miles. I had walked seventeen miles already. From Gateshead to Blyth, and from Blyth to Westmoor again, made twenty seven miles. I was very much tired. I however got through the journey and preached, and early the next morning returned home, walking ten miles more. This cruelty of the Westmoor leaders made me feel most acutely. It was a terrible trial to me to be obliged thus to leave my poor wife with a languishing and an apparently dying child, and then to be refused the privilege to return a day before the appointed time, though I had heard that my little one was worse. I never can think of the cruelty of those leaders, without feelings of horror and indignation. But it did me good. It made me less happy in my priestly bondage, and did something towards leading me at length to believe that the hireling system was a bad one, and that Christians should keep themselves perfectly free.

The Conference appointed me to the Newcastle circuit for an additional half year. During this half year I published my first sermon, *The deceitfulness of sin,* or *The madness of procrastination.* I had published before that a small tract called *A few hints on various subjects*. I found the work of an author to be no easy work. I had written the sermon before it was preached, and for aught I knew it was tolerably correct; but when I formed the purpose of publishing it, and began to look over it again before sending it to the press, I instantly began to see or to imagine that I saw innumerable faults. This sentence seemed wrong, and that seemed wrong. This might perhaps be mended, and the other might perhaps be mended, and nothing seemed to be so good as it should be. I found it a very different thing to write so as to satisfy myself in my closet, and to write so as to be able with confidence to place a discourse before the eye of the public. I of course began to alter sentences, and the alteration of one part led to the alteration of other parts. I got at length perplexed. I had confidence in nothing. Part of the discourse had gone to the press, and was in type; the other part I began to fear I should never be able to finish to my satisfaction, and I became exceedingly feverish. I was at length unable to sleep, and for want of sleep at night, I was unable to work by day, and it seemed as if I should now stick fast altogether. My anxiety was truly dreadful. At one time I lay down during the day, and fell asleep, and dreamed that I had carried the last part of the discourse to the printer. And such was the disorder of my mind, that when I awoke, I went to the printers for a proof of that part, never imagining but that what I had dreamed had really taken place. The printer of course could not give me a proof; he had not yet seen the copy, and the terrible suspicion was forced on me that I had taken a dream for a reality. On returning to my room I found that so it was; the papers were there unfinished. This was terrible work for me. No one that has not passed through something similar, can conceive its painfulness. I did however succeed in getting through the discourse, and it was published. I have many times since then had great difficulty in preparing things for the press,—great difficulty in putting them in such a form as to be able to lay them before the public with confidence; but I have never had so much as then. The discourse was favourably received, and I received five pounds from it in the way of profit, which I foolishly gave towards the erection of the new chapel in Hood Street.

CHAPTER VII.

HISTORY OF MY OPINIONS.

Before I proceed further, I shall give some account of my religious opinions.

My religious opinions originally were exceedingly simple. The great doctrines that occupied my mind were the doctrines respecting God, his government, a future judgment, and my own accountability to God. A belief that there was a God, and that God was a rewarder of all them that diligently sought him,—a belief that there was a God, and that God would punish those who lived in opposition to his will,—a belief that the reward of the righteous and the punishment of the wicked would alike be great and everlasting, were the principal doctrines that occupied my mind, and that influenced my feelings and my life. It was under the influence of these doctrines that I was led at first to renounce what I believed to be evil, and to give myself to the practice of what I believed to be good. It was not till sometime after I had joined the Methodist society, that I began to think upon many other subjects, or to entertain any opinions with respect to what are called the peculiar doctrines of the gospel. What my first thoughts were on several of those subjects, I distinctly recollect.

1. With respect to the person of Christ, for instance, I was taught to regard him not as a perfect man, but as having only the body, the *case* of a *man*, and as having for his *soul* the infinite *Godhead*. I regarded Christ literally as an earthly tabernacle in which the Godhead dwelt. I considered the Godhead as occupying in Christ the same place as a human soul occupies in men generally. And this was the doctrine held by those who were my companions at that time,—the doctrine of an incarnate God.

2. With respect to the doctrine of justification, I was taught that God imputed to us Christ's righteousness,—that Christ had been righteous instead of us, and that his righteousness was imputed to us when we relied on him, and that it was on account of Christ's righteousness thus imputed,

that God accepted us. This doctrine I had got partly from the writings of Bishop Beveridge, and partly from the conversations of my friends. I was taught that God could not accept an *imperfect* righteousness,—that however good a man might be, if there was still one flaw, one defect in his conduct, however small or however unavoidable, that single flaw or defect would vitiate the whole, and render it unacceptable to God. As therefore we were taught, 1st, That no man could have a perfect righteousness of his own. 2nd. That God could accept nothing short of a perfect, absolute, unbroken righteousness, from first to last, we, of course, were led to believe, as Wesley phrases it, that we every moment needed the merits of Christ's death. It was plain that no man could pretend to have a perfect, unbroken, absolute righteousness of his own, from the first hour of his existence to the last; and as an imperfect righteousness was considered as bad as *no* righteousness at all, so far as securing God's approbation and eternal life was concerned, we were led to feel that we had nothing left on which to rely for acceptance with God, but the perfect righteousness, and the all-sufficient atonement of Jesus Christ.

3. The work of Christ we were taught to regard as consisting chiefly and almost altogether, first, in fulfilling all righteousness for us, in order that God might have something on account of which he could accept us and love us; and, secondly, in bearing the punishment due to our sins, in order that God might have a sufficient reason or inducement for forgiving our offences. Sometimes we spoke of Christ's sufferings and death as redeeming us from hell, and of his perfect righteousness as meriting for us heaven. Sometimes we spoke of Christ's sufferings and death as purchasing our pardon, or paying God the debt which we had contracted, and spoke of his righteousness as a price by which he purchased for us peace and everlasting life. His sufferings, as we supposed, delivered us from evil; his righteousness purchased us happiness and heaven. The *teachings* of Christ, his *miracles*, his *example*, his *resurrection from the dead*, and indeed almost every thing else connected with Christ's history, were almost overlooked, and always greatly undervalued. Christ's work as a *reformer*, Christ's work so far as it exerted an influence upon *man*, enlightening his mind, renewing his heart, reforming his life, was seldom thought about, seldom spoken of.

That which occupied our minds, and occupied them almost exclusively, was the influence Christ was supposed to exert upon *God*. Christ was regarded not so much as a Saviour from sin, or as a leader or guide to righteousness, or as the re-creator and perfecter of man's moral character; but as a kind of external, outward Saviour, whose great business it was, by exerting an influence upon God, and paying to God certain valuable considerations, to deliver us from danger of hell, to which God's justice was supposed to have doomed us, and to procure for us an admission to the blessedness of heaven, from all hope of which God's enraged and unsatisfied justice was supposed to have excluded us.

4. With respect to the trinity, I can scarcely say what were my earliest views. I was taught to use the *word* trinity, and the phrase 'one God in persons three,' and many similar phrases; and for any thing I know, I believed in the *doctrine* of the trinity as much as others believed in it. I knew no other than that I believed in it. I used to sing the Trinitarian hymns, such as

> 'Him three in one, and one in three,
> Extol to all eternity.'

But perhaps it would be almost considered profane by some, if I were to state what were my *thoughts* on the subject. Still, as I commenced this history with the intention of uttering all that I could recollect with respect to my religious experience and religious opinions, I shall state with perfect plainness and simplicity the exercises of my mind with respect to the doctrine of the trinity. The great point with me was to reconcile three persons with the idea of one God, or in other words, to make three persons into one person, and one person into three persons, and to have the three to be one, and the one to be three, at the same time. The word *person*, as a matter of course, at once suggested the idea of a *man*, an individual human being, and *three* persons, of course, suggested the idea of *three men*, three individual human beings. To imagine three men, three venerable individuals, was no difficulty at all; but to imagine them three and yet to imagine them one at the same time, *was* a difficulty, was an impossibility. To imagine a single individual human being was no great difficulty; but to imagine one single individual being to be one and three at the same time, was a great difficulty, was an utter impossibility. Yet this was the task which theology appeared to set me; and I laboured to accomplish the task. When thinking of the trinity, I used to imagine three aged venerable looking men, up in a chamber, gravely clad, and with broad-brimmed hats on their heads, quite silent, and looking solemnly downwards towards the floor. These three I used to endeavour to squeeze or compress close together, and if possible make them into one. It was hard work, to be sure, to make them one; yet still I partly persuaded myself at times that I had succeeded, and that I had only one man left. The next operation was to separate and divide this one man again, and make him into *three*, and place the three in their old position again. This I could do more easily than the former work of making three into one. But the moment I had got the three, I had lost the one; and the moment I had got the one, I had lost the three; so that to keep them three, and yet to have them only one,—or to keep them one, and yet to have them three, was a continual impossibility to me. Still I considered myself bound to believe that I had accomplished this impossibility, or else to entertain fears that I was not a true believer,—that I had not the full and proper Christian faith,—and that I was not in a safe or hopeful condition.

There were other difficulties connected with the Trinity. I was to believe that the three persons in the Godhead were all equal both in power and in eternity, yet I was taught that the first of them was the father of the second, and that the third was the product of the former two. I was to believe that the first person begot the second person, and that from the first and second proceeded the third person; yet I was to believe that the father was no older than the son whom he had begotten, and that the spirit was no younger than the father and the son from whom he proceeded. It was impossible to believe that God the Father had begotten God the Son, without believing that God the Son had once come into existence, and that before he came into existence, he of course was not. It was impossible to believe that the Spirit had proceeded from the Father and the Son, without believing that he too had had a beginning,—that with respect to him there was a period when he had no existence; yet I was to believe that the Son had always existed, and that the spirit also had always existed,—that the Son and the Spirit were both of them eternal, equally eternal as the Father,—that the

Father who *begot* the Son, did not exist before the Son whom he begot,—that the Father and the Son from whom the Spirit proceeded, did not exist before the Spirit that proceeded from them. The orthodox theology taught us these things, and required us to believe them on pain of eternal damnation. I therefore *tried* to believe them, or what perhaps amounted to the same thing, tried to *believe* that I believed them.

We were also taught to believe that Christ was the 'eternal Son' of God,—that he was 'eternally begotten,' and that the Holy Spirit had 'eternally proceeded' from the Father and from the Son. Hence we were led to use such expressions as 'eternal generation,' 'eternal filiation,' and 'eternal procession.' Again, those three persons in the Godhead I was taught to regard as entirely distinct and separate agents. One could send, another could be sent, and the third could stand by and neither send nor be sent. One could remain in heaven, governing the world as an almighty king; the second could come to earth, be incarnated, dwell in a body of flesh, could suffer and die; while the third could stand apart, occupying a position different from either of the former, applying the merit of Christ's death to the consciences of men, and yet all three, according to our belief, or our *professed* belief, be one God. One could sit upon a throne as sovereign of all; another could sit at his right hand, and a third be engaged with the souls of men upon earth; yet all be one being. One could pray to the other, the other give answers to his prayers, the third convey those answers to the souls of men, and yet all form one substance, one God. One could demand satisfaction to his injured justice; another could suffer and die to *give* satisfaction; the third could neither demand nor give satisfaction, but simply carry on the plan of salvation in a comparitively private capacity, yet all be one Jehovah. One had great jealousy for the honour of his law; another a great love for man, who had fallen under the condemnation of the law; the third could stand apart without feeling much interest either in the law or in unhappy man, yet all be one and the same eternal spirit. These I say were some of the things that we were required to believe,—some of the things that we were taught to regard as the great, the fundamental doctrines of the gospel. These were the doctrines which we were taught to believe every one must hold, if he would be accepted of God and obtain everlasting life,

These doctrines I tried to believe,—these imaginations often occupied my mind, and I considered myself as a true believer in these things,

5. With respect to Adam's state and relations, and the effects of his fall, my views were as follows:—I was taught that Adam at first was perfect,—perfect in knowledge, perfect in goodness, perfect in bliss; as perfect as it was possible for man to be. I supposed his knowledge to be as vast, or almost as vast, as the universe itself. I supposed him to understand the qualities of all animals, of all vegetables, and of all things else in the world in which he lived. I was taught that he gave names to all animals, and that the names which he gave to the different animals, exactly expressed their qualities. I was of course taught that his knowledge of *God* and of all *spiritual* things, was as vast, and as perfect, as his knowledge of earthly things. I was also taught that his goodness was as perfect as his knowledge,—that his love to God was unbounded,—that his love of goodness was unbounded,—that he was so good that it was impossible that any man now should either *equal* him in goodness, or make anything like a near *approach* to him in goodness. This was the doctrine which was taught from the pulpits: it was the doctrine which I found in John Wesley's writings when I began to read them. In his sermons on Christian perfection, he frequently guarded his hearers against the notion that he meant *angelic* perfection, or *Adamic* perfection. He was very careful to guard them against the idea that he thought it possible for men now to become as perfect, either in knowledge, in love, or in practical goodness, as Adam was in his first state. I was also taught to believe that Adam was the *federal* or *covenant* head of all the human race,—that God made a covenant with Adam, by which all his unborn posterity were bound,—that the particulars of the covenant were to this effect, that if Adam obeyed the law under which he was placed, he and all his children should be saved; but that if Adam disobeyed, he and all his children should be lost. I was taught that if Adam had obeyed the law, all his children would have been born in such a state, that they could never have erred, never sinned, never suffered,—that in consequence of Adam's *not* obeying the law, all his children are born so that they cannot *help* but sin, cannot help but err, cannot help but suffer. I was taught, in fact, that if

Adam had not sinned, we should have been born perfect as the angels,—but that now, in consequence of Adam's sin, all are born utterly depraved, thoroughly corrupt, unable to think a good thought, to speak a good word, to form a good purpose, to do a good thing. I was also taught, that not only are we born utterly depraved in consequence of Adam's transgression, but under guilt, under condemnation, under God's wrath, and liable to eternal damnation.

6. The next doctrines that I was taught to believe were that Christ came into the world to atone, or to satisfy God's justice, for the offence of Adam,—that in consequence of Christ's death, Adam's sin is forgiven so far, that children are no longer liable to eternal damnation on account of it. I was taught, that if it had not been for the satisfaction made to God's justice for the sin of Adam, by the sufferings and death of Christ, every little child born into the world must have been inevitably damned,—that when Adam had sinned, there was no alternative for God, but either to destroy the first man and the first woman, and so prevent the human race from coming into existence, or else to demand the sufferings and death of his own son, as an infinite sacrifice to satisfy his justice, and so make it possible for him to spare and save our race.

7. I was also taught, that in order to obtain salvation, *every man*, of every age and clime, must actually believe in Christ, and trust in him as the only ground of his acceptance with God,—trust in him as an all-atoning, all-satisfying sacrifice. I was taught, that from the beginning of the world to the present time, all that had been saved, had been saved by this one belief in Jesus; this one way of relying on his merits, or on his satisfaction to justice. With respect to those who lived before Christ came into the world, I was taught to believe that they were saved by believing in Christ as a saviour to come, while I was taught to believe that those who have lived since Christ's days, were to be saved by believing in Christ as a saviour already come. I was taught that the faith of all the ancient patriarchs, and prophets, and saints, differed from the faith of apostles and saints under the Christian dispensation, simply in this, that one was a looking *forward* to Christ as to come, and the other a looking *backward* to Christ as already come.

8. I was also taught, that all the ancient sacrifices of the

patriarchs, and all the sacrifices prescribed by the law of Moses, were *types* of Christ,—that they were intended to represent the great sacrifice which Christ should hereafter offer,—that those who offered those ancient sacrifices were taught to see in them a representation of the sacrifice of Christ; or in other words, that they were taught, and were accustomed to look through the victim that was before them, to the human or divine victim that should hereafter be offered for all mankind; to look through the sacrifice which they were presenting, to a greater sacrifice which should be presented by Christ at a future day. I was taught that in the blood of the victim which they slew, they saw the blood of Christ,—that in the agonies of the victim which they offered, they saw the agonies of the Son of God,—that the minds of the faithful of old looked upon the sacrifices which they offered, simply as emblems or figures, as illustrations or examples of that great, and universal, and infinite sacrifice, which Christ was hereafter to present to the justice of his offended Father. I was taught that it was by relying on this infinite sacrifice thus pre-figured to them, that they obtained forgiveness of sins and everlasting life. My idea was, that all other faith which the ancients might have, and all their obedience to moral laws, all their inward, and all their outward goodness, were, so to speak, of no avail with God whatever, could do nothing towards obtaining God's favour and blessing ; but that everything depended on their recognising the blood, the sufferings, the sacrifice of Christ in the victims which they presented, and on their relying upon the blood of the sacrifice thus pre-figured, as the sole ground of their forgiveness and everlasting salvation.

9. With respect to regeneration, I was taught that it was an instantaneous work ; a work accomplished by the immediate agency of the Holy Spirit, or the third person in the trinity,—that it took place at the same moment with justification,—that no one could be regenerated without knowing it,—that no one could be forgiven without feeling that he was forgiven,—that those who doubted whether they were born again and forgiven, did, by their very doubts, prove that they were not forgiven or born again, and that an unfelt pardon was no pardon.

10. I was also taught that education, whatever good it might do in other respects, could never change a person's

heart, never make a person holy. The idea that children might be taught the truth, and so trained from their infancy, that they would gradually become truly godly, and never need an instantaneous and complete revolution of their whole soul and character, was considered a dangerous heresy. We used to say, 'Parents may teach their children what is right, but they cannot give them grace.' We supposed grace to be something which came to the soul directly from God; some invisible influence, changing the heart, bending the will, purifying the whole soul, and making it entirely new, by its own almighty energy. This invisible influence, this grace, we supposed to be the sole agent in conversion, and we considered it to act apart, and to work in a manner independently of the teaching and training which children might receive from their parents.

11. Sanctification I was taught was another work, which followed regeneration. This also I was taught to believe was instantaneous, and wrought by the same direct invisible agency as the work of regeneration. Sanctification was spoken of as the *second* blessing, regeneration or justification as the *first* blessing.

12. That which gave men the knowledge of their forgiveness and acceptance was called the witness of the spirit. This witness of the spirit was supposed to be an impression made upon the soul by the Holy Ghost, rendering it impossible for a man to doubt his forgiveness and acceptance. It was frequently called the *direct* witness. As this witness of the spirit was supposed to be an impression made directly upon the soul, those who had it were said to *feel* that they were forgiven or accepted. It was not enough for a man to say he *knew* he was forgiven; he must say he *felt* that he was forgiven. Other means of ascertaining whether a man was born again, forgiven, or accepted of God, were comparatively slighted. Among my first Methodist companions, it was considered a *legal* kind of way of seeking assurance, for a man to compare his heart and his life with the requirements of the gospel, and *thence* to draw the conclusion that he was accepted, forgiven, or saved. By many it was considered impossible for a man to know whether he was forgiven or accepted by comparing his heart and life with the requirements of the gospel. The assurance which a man might get in this way was always considered to be doubtful, or alto-

gether worthless, because it was considered in general, that nothing but perfect holiness of heart and life could secure the approbation of God, and that no one could pretend to such perfect, absolute, inward and outward holiness. True, John Wesley taught, in one or more of his sermons, that a man might know whether he was accepted and saved in this way; and he also taught in one of his sermons, that no one could tell whether he had the witness of the Spirit or not, except by examining his own heart and his own life. *He* had taught that people might be deluded, and led to conclude that they had the witness of the Spirit when they had no such thing, if they did not attend to what he called the witness of their *own* Spirits, or to the tempers, dispositions, and habits of their own souls. But it happened in this case, as it happens in many other cases where the writings and the systems of men are adopted as the rule of faith; the *truer* and the *better* portions of Wesley's writings were overlooked or disregarded, and the more doubtful, or the erroneous portions of his writings were alone regarded as the true ones.

13. We were also taught to believe that no man had any right to commence the work of preaching, unless he had a special, supernatural call to that work. A man might give bread to the hungry, clothing to the naked, and medicine to the sick, and comfort to the sorrowful without a special call; he might do all these things on the common principle that he was bound, as a Christian, to love his neighbour as himself, and to do good as he had opportunity; but with respect to preaching, the case was different. *Here* he must *not* act on the principle of simply using his talents, and doing good according to his ability. He must have a special call, and to commence the work of preaching without such special call was considered an intrusion, a sacrilege, an impiety.

These were some of the principal notions that were instilled into my mind after I connected myself with the Methodist society. These were the principal doctrines which were taught, the doctrines which were represented as forming the great essentials of Christianity, and these were the doctrines which at one period occupied my mind, and formed my belief.

It was not long, however, before I began to entertain doubts respecting some of them, and in the course of time I began to entertain doubts with respect to most or all of them.

In what order I was led to call in question the truth of those doctrines, I do not exactly recollect; but I shall state my doubts in the order in which they at present present themselves to my mind.

In the first place I was led to doubt certain views of the doctrine of atonement or redemption. I had been taught, for instance, that Christ paid our debts. It appeared to me if that was true, that we owed God nothing,—that God had no claim upon us,—and that, therefore, he had nothing to forgive. I had been taught that our title to heaven was Christ's righteousness; it therefore seemed to follow, that if Christ's righteousness was complete, our title to heaven was complete,—that our obedience could not improve it, and that our disobedience could not invalidate it. It was however plain to me, as plain as any thing could be, that God *had* something to forgive, and that we *did* need something more than Christ's righteousness to entitle us to heaven. It was plain that we were taught to say, 'Forgive us our *debts* as we forgive our debtors.' It was therefore plain that Christ could not have paid our debts. It was impossible that he should first pay our debts, and then teach us to pray, *forgive* us our debts. It was also plain, that if we would obtain eternal life, we must ourselves obey God,—that our future and eternal salvation depended upon our own conduct, upon our own faithfulness. It was therefore plain that Christ's righteousness could not be regarded as our *only* title to heavenly blessedness. I was thus led to reject the doctrine of imputed righteousness, and to call in question the doctrine that Christ had paid our debts.

Again; I had been taught that Christ bore our punishment—bore the punishment due to our sins; but this also appeared to me at variance with Scripture, and with common sense. One part of the punishment of *sin* is a guilty conscience; but it was plain that Christ could never have endured this. Another part of the punishment of sin is God's anger or displeasure; but this, as it seemed to me, Christ could never share. The Scriptures taught plainly that God was *well pleased* with his Son. Christ himself said, his Father did not leave him alone, because he always did those things which pleased him. There was no proof that God was ever more pleased with his Son, then when he gave himself to death for our salvation. Another portion of the punishment of sin, as I was then taught to believe, was the eternal torments of hell; but it was plain that Christ could never endure those;—that if he endured the *elements* of those torments, or tasted of the *bitterness* of the pains of hell, he could never with propriety be said to endure *eternal* torments themselves.

This, however, was not the greatest difficulty with me. I could conceive how Christ should suffer something like the torments of hell, so far as those torments were the result of *fire;* but I could not conceive how Christ could ever bear those portions of the punishment of sin which consisted in a consciousness of guilt, and in the pains of God's displeasure. These views, therefore, of the work of Christ, I rejected. I recollect at a very early period of my Christian career, speaking to a young preacher, a companion of mine, on these subjects. He afterwards told me that he wished I had never mentioned those things, for I had spoiled some of his best sermons. I had raised in his mind the same doubts that occupied my own mind, and had made it impossible for him to preach the old doctrine with any degree of pleasure.

I had always been taught to believe that redemption, the redemption of Christ, was twofold; the redemption by *price*, and the redemption by *power*. The redemption by *price* was understood to mean the buying of our souls from the justice of God, by the payment of Christ's life to God; the redemption by *power* was explained to mean delivering us from the power of the devil, freeing us from our slavery to sin. I was led to doubt this two-fold character of the redemption by Christ. It appeared to me, that redemption was *one*, and that it was only the *manner of speaking* of redemption that was *two-fold*. Redemption by *price* appeared to me to be only the *figurative* representation of what was called redemption by *power*. Indeed it was plain to me, that the redemption spoken of in the New Testament, was a redemption 'from *iniquity*,' a redemption from our 'vain conversation,' or our foolish and wicked way of life; and that it was this same deliverance from iniquity, this deliverance from our own wicked way of life, this rescue of men from their sins, that was figuratively spoken of as the redemption by price, or as being bought with a price.

About the year 1830, I began to keep a record of my doubts, and of my disbeliefs. I put down a list of all those doctrines which were generally held and taught by Methodists, which appeared to me to be without foundation in Scripture, and it may not be amiss if I give some extracts from this list. The chief portions of this my negative creed, were written while I was travelling in the Halifax and the Newcastle circuits, in the years 1829, 1830, and 1831.

1. I do not believe that there are two kinds of redemption taught in the New Testament—redemption by price and redemption by power. I believe that the only redemption by Christ mentioned in the Scriptures, is a redemption from *iniquity*, deliverance from all sin; and this deliverance from sin is spoken of as a redemption by price, only by a figure of speech.

2. I do not believe that Christ died to redeem us from the guilt of Adam's sin. There is no proof that the work of Christ had any reference to the transgression of Adam.

3. I do not believe that Adam was so perfect in knowledge and in goodness when first created, as he is generally represented to have been. There is no proof that he understood the nature and the character of every kind of animal which God had created. There is no proof that the names which Adam gave to the different animals, expressed the natures, the dispositions of those different animals. There is no proof that Adam was more perfect in goodness than it is possible for people to be in the present day.

4. I do not believe that Adam was the federal or the covenant head of all mankind. I do not believe that Adam was entrusted with the destinies of the whole human race. I see no proof that God caused the welfare, the purity, and the happiness of all the human family, to depend upon the conduct of the first formed pair. On the contrary, I believe that every man is appointed by God to answer for *himself*, and for himself *alone*,—that every man's happiness depends on his own conduct, and on his own conduct alone,—that God entrusts the destinies of no man to the keeping of another man, but that every man stands or falls, is saved or lost, according to his own behaviour.

5. I see no reason to believe that if Adam had continued obedient, we should have been born in such a state as to be incapable of sin and misery. I see no reason to believe that if Adam had continued obedient, we should have been born either wiser, or better, or happier than we are.

6. I do not believe that children are born under the curse of God, or under the condemnation of his law.

7. I do not believe that Children are born guilty in consequence of Adam's transgression, as alleged in the list of doctrines. *(See Rules of the Methodist New Connexion.)*

8. I do not believe that any one is liable to everlasting destruction on account of Adam's one transgression.

9. I do not believe that children are born utterly depraved, thoroughly polluted, in consequence of Adam's sin.

10. I do not believe that those natural inclinations or leanings to evil which we see in children, and of which we are all conscious in ourselves, are the result of Adam's sin. For anything that I can see to the contrary, Adam himself had the same inclinations, the same leanings.

11. I do not believe that children are so born that they are incapable of thinking a good thought, of speaking a good word, of doing a good thing.

12. I do not believe that it can be truly said of any individual, much less of all individuals, that all the imaginations and thoughts of their hearts are evil, only evil, from their birth to the time of their actual and full conversion to God. On the contrary, I believe that every man born into the world has good thoughts as well as bad thoughts, has good feelings as well as bad feelings, and says many good words as well as bad words, and does many good deeds as well as bad deeds.

13. I do not believe that all the sin in the world is the result of natural depravity, caused by the sin of Adam. On the contrary, I believe that the sin which we see in the world is the result of men's own abuse of that power which God gives them ; that it is to be charged upon men's own unfaithfulness, and not upon the one transgression of Adam, or upon any depravity born with men in consequence of Adam's transgression.

14. I do not believe that when it is said that Adam was made in God's image, it means that Adam was more perfect in knowledge and in goodness than it is possible for people to be now ; for we are plainly taught that *Christians* now are created anew in the image of God.

15. I do not believe that when it is said Adam begot a son in his own likeness, that the meaning is that he begot a son with a corrupt nature. I see no proof that Adam lost God's image by his one transgression. And if he did loose

it, I see no proof that he did not recover it before he became a father. It appears to me, that when it is said Adam begat a son in his own likeness, the meaning is, he begat a son in that same likeness in which he himself was created by God.

16. I do not believe that Cain's wickedness is any proof that he received a corrupt nature from his father. I regard Cain's wickedness simply as a proof of his own unfaithfulness to the light God gave him, or of his own abuse and perversion of that nature, and of those powers with which God created him.

17. I do not believe that all the saints under the Old Testament dispensation were saved by believing in Christ; much less do I believe that they were saved by believing in Christ as a sacrifice for sin, or by trusting in his death as a satisfaction to God's justice.

18. I believe that the faith by which the ancient patriarchs, and prophets, and Old Testament saints worked righteousness, and obtained salvation, was a belief in just those truths which God revealed to them, whether those truths had reference to Christ, or to any other subject.

19. I believe that the faith by which the Old Testament saints lived, and by which they obtained salvation, was in general, 'a belief that God is, and that he is a rewarder of them that diligently seek him.'—Heb. 11.

20. I believe that the faith by which Noah became heir or inheritor of God's blessing, was a belief of what God said to him respecting the flood, and respecting the ark which he directed him to build for his own safety.

21. I believe that the faith by which Abraham obtained God's blessing, was a belief of what God said to him respecting his posterity, and the land of Canaan.

22. I do not believe that the ancient patriarchs and prophets generally had the least idea that Christ would ever die, much less that he would die as a sacrifice, and least of all that he would die as a sacrifice to satisfy the justice of God.

23. I do not believe that the ancient sacrifices of the patriarchs, or the sacrifices prescribed by the law of Moses, were, according to the common doctrine of types, types of the sacrifice of Christ. There is not the slightest intimation given in the law of Moses, that those sacrifices had any reference to the sacrifice of Christ whatever. Men are never commanded, when offering their sacrifices, to look through

them to Christ,—to regard them as figures of Christ's sacrifice, or to trust in the blood of the future sacrifice for acceptance with God. There is not the slightest intimation given, from the book of Genesis to the book of Malachi, that any patriarch, or prophet, or ancient saint ever *did* regard the sacrifices they offered, as figures or representations of Christ's sacrifice. In no case is any man commended for looking through those sacrifices to Christ; in no case is any man *blamed* for *not* looking through those sacrifices to Christ; in no case is the slightest intimation given that those sacrifices were designed to prefigure, or to represent to the offerers, the death or sacrifice of Christ at all. The whole theory of types, as laid down by M'Ewen, and as taught by orthodox preachers generally, appears to me to be a mere imagination, a pure fiction.

24. I do not believe that Abel, or Noah, or Abraham, or Isaac, or Jacob, or Joseph, or Job, or Moses, or Aaron, or Joshua were types of Christ, according to the common signification of that word. That is to say, I do not believe that those men were intended by God, to represent to persons living in their times, the character and the work of Christ.

25. I do not believe that the ark of Noah, the tabernacle, the temple, the brazen serpent, the land of Canaan, and other Old Testament things, were types according to the common acceptation of that word. That is, I do not believe that they were intended by God, to represent to those who saw them, certain other things, partly resembling them, under the *Christian* dispensation.

26. I do not believe that the ancient patriarchs and prophets had all that knowledge of the Christian dispensation, which it is generally supposed they had.

27. I do not believe that conversion is an instantaneous work; on the contrary, it appears to me to be gradual, beginning with the first dawn of light upon the soul, or the first belief of the truth made known to us, and proceeding by degrees, through many conflicts and struggles, to its completion.

28. I do not believe that men are regenerated by the immediate influence of the Spirit of God. On the contrary, I believe that men are regenerated by the power of *truth ;* by the revelations made to them of the character of God and of his will, and of all those great principles unfolded in the works of God, and in the teachings of his word. It appears

plain to me, that throughout the New Testament, the *truth* is represented as the grand instrument by which people are converted to God, are delivered from sin; the means by which they are sanctified, cleansed, or made free. The truth is spoken of as the seed of the new creature; as that by which men are begotten again, born again, and made holy. The truth, the gospel, is the power of God unto salvation, to every one that believes and obeys it. Hence the apostle says, 'Seeing ye have purified your hearts by the *belief of the truth,* unto unfeigned love of the brethren, see that ye love one another with pure hearts fervently: being born again, not of corruptible seed, but of incorruptible, even of the *word of God,* which liveth and abideth for ever: and this is the word, which, by the gospel, is preached unto you.—2 Peter i. 22—26.

29. I do not believe that every one who is converted *knows* that he is converted. There are some who do not know what conversion *is*, and who therefore cannot tell whether they are converted or not. If a man does not know what it *is* to be converted, how can he tell whether he be converted or not? Now many have been so mistaught with respect to the nature and signs of conversion, that they have no idea that they themselves are converted; when others that know them can see the clearest proofs imaginable of their conversion. Many have been taught that none are converted but persons who *feel* in a certain way, and experience a certain kind and a certain amount of pleasant or rapturous excitement. This notion is false; but *they* believe it to be *true.* They therefore do not consider that they are converted, because they have not experienced that kind or that amount of pleasant feeling which they have been taught to regard as *inseparable* from conversion. If people knew what conversion was, they would have no difficulty in ascertaining whether they were converted or not; but when people have been taught false notions respecting conversion and its accompaniments, they may easily imagine themselves to be converted when they are not, or think themselves *not* converted when they *are.* There are multitudes therefore, I believe, who think themselves truly converted, who are no such thing; and there are multitudes more, who *are* truly converted, who, nevertheless, think they are *not* converted.

30. I do not believe that every man who is forgiven, *feels* that he is forgiven. I do not even believe that every man who is forgiven, *knows* that he is forgiven. I believe that multitudes are forgiven who think they are not forgiven; and that multitudes think themselves forgiven, who are not forgiven.

31. I do not believe in the common doctrine of the Witness of the Spirit. I believe in the *Scripture* doctrine of the witness of the Spirit; but I do not believe that the Scripture doctrine of the witness of the Spirit, and the Methodistical doctrine on that subject, are the *same*. The Methodistical doctrine of the witness of the Spirit, as stated by John Wesley himself, is, that it is an '*impression* made upon the soul.' The Scriptures, however, say no such thing. The witness of the Spirit spoken of in the Testament, appears to be the testimony which the Spirit gave, first, to the truth of Christianity, and, second, to the great principle that all are received as the children of God, whether Jews or Gentiles, on the simple condition of faith, faith working by love. The Jews had the foolish idea that Jehovah was *their* God only, and not the God of the Gentiles. They had an idea that Christ came specially to exalt and to bless *them*, and not to exalt and bless in like manner the *Gentiles*. And even when they were cured of this notion, and brought to believe that God was the God of the Gentiles, as well as of the Jews, and that Christ was the Saviour of the Gentiles as well as of the Jews, they still contended that the Gentiles could not be allowed to enjoy Christian privileges unless they would be '*circumcised* and *keep the law of Moses*.' Against these false notions the apostles gave their testimony. The apostles testified, that Gentiles and Jews were equal before God; alike welcome to the blessings of the gospel; and that they were welcome to those blessings on the same conditions: that the Jews were not enriched with Christian privileges on account of any obedience of theirs to the law of Moses, and that the *Gentiles* were not to be admitted to share those privileges on any such condition; that there was *one* God, the God of the Gentiles as well as of the Jews, who received all, welcomed all his children on the simple terms of faith in Jesus as the Messiah, faith working by love. And the holy Spirit bare witness to the truth of this doctrine, by giving the power of miracles to the Gentiles, as well as to the Jews. This wit-

ness of the Spirit we all have: the witness or the testimony that we are all the children of God through faith in Christ Jesus, and that none are children of God through obedience to the law of Moses.

32. I do not believe that we have any Scriptural authority for speaking of the *direct*, the *immediate*, or the *indubitable testimony* of the spirit. These are all Methodistical forms of expression for which we have no authority in Scripture.

33. I do not believe that the testimony of the Spirit renders all for whom it was given, assured of their forgiveness and salvation.

34. I do not believe that every one knows what the witness of the Spirit is.

35. Hence I do not believe that every one who has the witness of the Spirit, knows that he has it.

36. I do not believe that the forgiveness of sins is always accompanied by some particular impression on the mind, or with any particular kind or degree of pleasant or rapturous feeling. I believe that every man is forgiven when he ceases to do evil and begins to do well; when he turns from sin to righteousness; from self to God: and I believe that many turn from sin and self, to righteousness and God, without experiencing, at the moment, any particular, overwhelming flow of rapturous feeling at all.

37. I do not believe that the first days of a man's religious life are the happiest or the best. On the contrary, I believe that if a man do as he ought, if he diligently and constantly seek after truth, and faithfully reduce it to practice as he finds it, he will continually become more happy; will experience a more perfect and stable peace, and will in all respects, notwithstanding the trials to which his faithfulness will subject him, and the reproaches and persecutions which it may bring upon him, enjoy life more perfectly from year to year to the last.

38. I do not believe in the doctrine of instantaneous full sanctification. I believe that sanctification, or the purification of a man's soul, and the perfection of his religious character, is a *gradual* work, and requires much time.

39. I do not believe that men are justified by faith *alone*. On the contrary, I believe that faith alone profits nothing; that if a man have *all* faith, and have not charity, he is nothing; that a man is justified by *works*, as James expressly

teaches, and *not* by faith only : that as the body without the spirit is dead, so faith without works is dead also.

40. I do not believe that a man is *sanctified* by faith alone. On the contrary, I believe that a man is sanctified by practice, and by painful discipline ; that man must perfect his soul and his character by diligent continuance in well doing, as well as by the belief of truth.

41. I do not believe that the faith by which a man is justified or saved, is 'a sure trust and confidence which a man hath in God that his sins are forgiven :' on the contrary, the faith by which a man is forgiven, must go *before* his forgiveness : and if the faith by which he is forgiven must go before his forgiveness, how can a sure trust and confidence in God that he *is* forgiven, be the faith by which he obtains forgiveness.

42. I do not believe that a man obtains forgiveness first, and then becomes good after ; but that he must become *good*, or begin to live right first, before he can be forgiven.

43. I do not believe that the faith by which we are saved, is a belief that God loves or approves us *as individuals in particular :* but a belief of Gospel truth in general, a belief of God's love, or good-will or kindness to mankind in general.

44. I do not believe that the faith by which we obtain forgiveness is a reliance on the blood of Christ, or an appropriation of Christ's righteousness to ourselves, or trusting in the merits of Christ as the sole ground of our acceptance. I believe that the faith by which we are forgiven, and the faith by which we live to God and obtain eternal life, is a belief in the truth generally, as revealed to us by Jesus Christ.

45. I do not believe that there are *two kinds* of faith, a *general* faith by which people are led to repent and turn to God, and a *special* faith by which people obtain forgiveness or sanctification. I believe that there is but *one* faith, and that that one faith is a belief of the truth, and that by that one faith we both repent, obtain forgiveness, live a holy life, and secure eternal blessedness.

46. I do not believe that Christ died to satisfy the justice of God. I believe that Christ died to redeem men from *sin*, and to make men holy, zealous of good works.

47. I do not believe that Christ came to dispose God to forgive men. I believe that God was *always* disposed to

forgive men; and that Christ came to dispose men to love and serve God, that they might be fitted for forgiveness, and be everlastingly saved.

48. I do not believe that Christ came to make it possible for God to forgive repenting and believing men. I believe it never was impossible for God to forgive man, however he might have sinned, who renounced his sins, and returned with full purpose of heart to obedience.

49. I do not believe that Christ died to purchase our pardon, or to buy our peace from God. I believe the following words of one of Wesley's hymns,

"Pardon, and peace, and heaven to buy,
My bleeding sacrifice expired,"

are quite unscriptural and false. I believe that Christ buys nothing from God; that God *sells* nothing. I believe that whatever God bestows upon men, he *gives*, freely, for his own mercy's sake, or because he delighteth to be bountiful.

50. I do not believe in the following words of a hymn often sung;

Hallelujah to the Lamb, who hath *bought* us a pardon;
We will praise him again, when we pass over Jordan.

Only to think of God selling blessings.

51. I do not believe in the doctrine of the *Trinity*. I do not believe that there are three persons in one God. I regard the word *Trinity*, and the expression 'three persons in one God,' and all similar expressions, as unscriptural and mischievous.

52. I do not believe that any man can understand God to perfection, or can comprehend the mode of his existence. I acknowledge there may be many things in connexion with God, as there are many things in connexion with his works, which we do not understand, and which, in our present state, we never *shall* perhaps understand: but it is very plainly taught in Scripture that God is one, and *only* one, and that the one true God is the Father: while it is never said that he is *three*, or *three in one*, or that in his one essence there are three persons.

53. I do not believe that the Godhead which dwelt in Christ, was a separate person from God the Father: on the contrary, I believe that the God who dwelt in Christ, *was* God the Father, and that there is no other God but he.

54. I believe that Christ is the Son of God; but I do not believe that he is God the Son: nor do I believe that he is a second person in the Godhead. Still I believe that Christ is God in *this* sense; that the true God, even the Father, *dwelt* in him: that he is the *tabernacle* or *temple* of the Deity: that in him dwelt *all* the fulness of the Godhead bodily.*

55. I do not believe in the *separate* personality of the Holy Ghost; I do not believe the Holy Ghost to be a third person in the Godhead. I believe that God is a Spirit, a *Holy* Spirit, and that the words Holy Spirit or Holy Ghost are at times used in Scripture as one of the names of God. In this sense I believe the Holy Spirit is God, because God is a Holy Spirit, and called the Holy Spirit: but I do not believe in the existence of distinct or separate persons in the Godhead.

56. I do not believe that Christ paid our debts.

57. I do not believe that Christ bore the punishment due to our sins.

58. I do not believe that Christ bore the wrath of God for us.

59. I do not believe that Christ stood in the sinner's *stead*, and bore the sinner's doom, or was regarded by God as the sinner's substitute or representative.

60. I do not believe that God imputed our sins to Christ, or that he imputes Christ's righteousness to us.

61. I do not believe that God forgives sinners *on account* of Christ's sufferings and death; but that he forgives them on account of their returning from sin to righteousness.

62. I do not believe that God hears men's prayers *on account* of what Christ has done and suffered for them. I believe that God hears and answers our prayers on account of our faithfulness to duty; or as John expresses it, 'because we keep his commandments, and do those things which are pleasing in his sight.—1 John iii. 21—23.'

63. I believe that God sees us all just as we are,—that he judges us to be exactly what we are, and not what we are not. Those who speak as if God looked upon us *in Christ*, and saw us to be different in him from what we really are in

---

* This was my opinion of the Godhead of Christ for many years. Indeed I still regard Christ as the temple of God, only I do not regard Christ himself as God on that account.

ourselves, talk neither Scripture nor common sense. God sees all things in their true character, and men amongst the rest. If there be iniquity in Jacob, he sees it; and nothing can hide it from him. If there be iniquity in professing Christians, he sees it; and nothing can hide *that* from him. He sees none to be righteous, but those who are righteous; those whose hearts are right, and whose lives are holy. The idea that God throws over men's iniquities the cloak of another's righteousness, and thus hides men's wickedness from his own eyes, is foolish; it is worse than childish; it is blasphemous and monstrous.

64. I do not believe that God accepts, or loves, or receives people at last to heaven on account of the merits, or sacrifice, or righteousness of Christ. If God approves one man, and disapproves of another man, it must be because the one is really good and worthy, and the other bad and unworthy. There is no respect of persons with God. If God takes one to heaven, and shuts another out, it must be because one is fit for heaven, and the other not fit. And this agrees with the Scriptures, which teach us, that to the faithful God will say at last, 'Well done, good and faithful servant; *because thou hast* been faithful over a few things, I will make thee ruler over many things: enter thou into the joy of thy Lord.'—Luke xix. 16, 17.

65. I believe that Christ's great object was to make people wise and good; that his work consisted, not in altering the character or disposition of the Almighty, but in altering the character of man.

66. I believe that Christ's great office was that of *teacher;* that the manifestation of the truth was the great means which he employed for the renovation and salvation of our race. It is as a teacher that he is chiefly set before us in the gospels: it is in the work of instruction that we find him chiefly engaged: it is as a LIGHT that he is figuratively presented to our minds. I regard his miracles as one means of instructing and regenerating men. The miracles both illustrate and prove the doctrines which Christ taught. I look upon Christ's life also as a lesson. His life is the comment on his teachings, the illustration, the exhibition, of his own doctrines. I regard his death as a portion of his example, and as designed, among other things, to set forth, to exhibit in its true light, that righteousness which God requires of men; that love

which is the soul and substance of religion, and which would lead us to lay down our lives for our brethren. I therefore look upon his teachings, his miracles, his life, and his death, as one great means of rousing, of instructing, of regenerating, and saving the human race. I look upon his teachings, his life, his miracles, his death, as designed by God, as well as every way adapted in themselves, to redeem or deliver men from all iniquity, to make them a pure and godly people, zealous of good works.

67. I am not aware that Christ is ever represented as a priest, except in one book of the New Testament, the epistle to the Hebrews. In the gospels, in the Acts, and in all the other epistles, he is chiefly set forth as a *teacher*, a lord, a judge, a saviour. There is not in all those writings, the slightest intimation given that Christ's work was designed to resemble the work of the ancient Jewish or patriarchal priests. On the contrary, he is set forth as a *prophet*, whose business it was to preach, to teach, to declare God's will, to reform men, to call sinners to repentance, to heal men's souls, to promote knowledge and true holiness amongst mankind.

68. I do not therefore believe that Christ came to reconcile God unto men, but to reconcile men unto God. God never needed reconciling, or turning into a friend to man. God was always man's friend. Man *did* need reconciling or turning into a friend to God; for men, generally speaking, had acted as *enemies* to God by wicked works. Christ's object therefore was, as I believe, not to make *God* more kindly disposed towards *men*; but to make *men* more kindly disposed towards *God*. In short, his object was to bring men to love God, to serve God, to love and serve each other; his object was to bring them, by patient continuance in well-doing, to secure to themselves peace and true blessedness on earth, and everlasting life in heaven.

69. When it is said that Christ bare our sins in his own body on the tree, I do not understand it to mean, either that our sins were imputed to Christ, or that the punishment due to our sins was inflicted upon Christ. I take it to mean that he bare our sins *away;* that he *freed men* from their sins and made them holy. So when Christ is called 'the lamb of God that taketh away the sins of the world,' I understand the meaning to be what the words literally express, that he

taketh *away* men's sins, so that men have no longer any sin left. I may explain this by reference to other matters. The doctor *takes away* a man's complaint, when he *cures* him. Medicine may be said to take away a fever, or inflammation, or a dropsy, when it *cures* the party, and makes him well. So Jesus, as the physician of souls, takes away our *spiritual diseases*, our evil tempers, our wicked habits; he cures us of them, and makes us spiritually healthy, spiritually strong, truly, inwardly and outwardly, righteous.

70. I believe that when the Scriptures represent Christ as a *teacher*, an *example*, a guide, they speak *literally;* but that when they speak of Christ as a *priest*, they speak *figuratively*.

71. I believe that when Christ's death is spoken of as a *sacrifice*, the Scriptures are to be taken figuratively; unless we understand the word sacrifice simply to signify what the word originally meant, a *sacred deed*, a *religious act*. In *this* sense all our deeds of charity, and all our expressions of praise and thanksgiving are sacrifices; that is, they are *sacred acts, religious deeds.*

72. I believe that when the writer of the Epistle to the Hebrews compares Christ's death to some of the sacrifices of the ancient law, it is chiefly to those sacrifices which were used as *purifications*, as means of *cleansing persons or things from their defilements:* hence the blood of Christ is spoken of as '*purging men's consciences*' from dead works, and his sacrifice is represented as the means of *purifying* or *sanctifying* men's souls.

73. It appears to me that the whole of Christ's work may be explained on the principle, that he was a TEACHER and REFORMER; it appears to me, that all he did and suffered may be reduced to this one idea, of a *means for enlightening and purifying mankind.*

74. I do not believe in the necessity or usefulness of human creeds. It appears to me that the Scriptures should be our only creed, and our only law book, if we regard them, *as protestants profess to do*, as a PERFECT and INFALLIBLE rule both of faith and practice. We should either alter our belief about the Scriptures, or have done with human creeds and laws.

75. I believe that creeds are injurious; that they tend to enslave the minds of men; to give some a power which man

ought not to have over man, and so deprive others of liberty and rights, which all men ought to enjoy.

76. I do not believe that a man's salvation depends upon the belief of any particular opinions. I believe that every man's salvation depends upon his *faithfulness in seeking after truth, and in reducing it to practice when he has found it.* It is not the amount of a man's knowledge which renders him pleasing to God, but his faithfulness in getting and in using knowledge. It is not the number of talents that a man has that secures his blessedness; but the use which he makes of his talents.

77. I cannot see any use there could be in preaching the common doctrines of the Trinity, of satisfaction to divine justice, of trusting in the merits of Christ, or of justification by faith alone, even if they were true. I see no tendency in such doctrines to make men holy. I see no tendency in them to make men uneasy in their sins, zealous in the performance of their duty, or patient and happy under afflictions. They are utterly useless.

78. I do not believe that by preaching Christ, the Scriptures mean preaching particularly on the subject of his death or sacrifice; much less do I believe that by preaching Christ, or by preaching the cross of Christ, we are to understand dwelling chiefly or exclusively on such doctrines as those of the trinity, the distinct Godhead of Christ, justification by faith alone, natural depravity, salvation by reliance on Christ's merits. In fact, those latter doctrines are no doctrines of Christ or of his apostles at all. They are mere inventions of men; not only without foundation in Scripture, but directly contrary to the plainest teachings of Scripture.

79. I believe that by preaching Christ we are to understand, preaching Christ's *doctrine*; just as by preaching Moses, or preaching the law, we are to understand preaching the *doctrine* of Moses, or the law as laid down in the writings of Moses. I believe that then a man truly preaches Christ, when he preaches what Christ preached; when he enforces what Christ taught by reference to Christ's life, to Christ's miracles, to Christ's death and resurrection, or by the use of such motives as Christ used.

80. I do not believe that Paul, or Peter, or John preached the common doctrines of the trinity, satisfaction to justice, total, natural depravity, or justification by faith alone at all;

much less do I believe that these doctrines were the *staple*, the regular subject, the sum and substance of their preaching. I cannot find, either in the Acts of the Apostles, or in their epistles, the slightest intimation, that they either preached those doctrines to the heathen, or taught them to the converts in the churches which they formed. On the contrary, *their* doctrines were the simple doctrines that there is a God,—that God is the Father of mankind,—that he made all men of one blood; that he formed us for righteousness; that he sent Christ to teach us the truth, to instruct us in righteousness, to bring sinners to repentance, and to improve and perfect the saints, &c. *These* doctrines, and the doctrines generally which Christ himself taught, formed the staple of apostolical preaching, and the sum and substance of the apostolical writings.

81. When Paul says, 'God forbid that I should glory, save in the cross of our Lord Jesus Christ, he does not mean, 'God forbid that I should glory, save in the doctrine of satisfaction to justice:' but, ' God forbid that I should glory, save in the religion of Christ,' the religion of self-sacrificing love; the religion illustrated by Christ's voluntary death upon the cross; the religion by which the world is crucified to a man, and a man crucified to the world; the religion by which men are led to live a life of piety, of purity, and of charity.

82. I do not believe that when Christ says, 'I came not to call the righteous, but sinners to repentance,' that he refers to the *self*-righteous, the scribes and the pharisees, who fancied they were righteous when they were not. On the contrary, I believe that he refers to the *truly* righteous; to those who did not *need* to be called to repentance or a change of mind; to those who did not need to repent or change their minds. If the words are taken as they are generally understood, they will not be true; for Christ *did* come to call *those* to repentance, who thought they were righteous, but were *not*. These were *sinners;* sinners of the first rank; and Christ came to call sinners to repentance. Some people talk as if there were no truly righteous people in the world when Christ came: as if there were no truly righteous persons to whom Christ could refer: but this is a great mistake. If we take the Scriptures for our guide, they will tell us expressly, that Mary and Joseph were righteous; that Elizabeth and Zachariah were righteous, walking in all the ordinances and

commandments of the Lord blameless; and they also give us to understand, that there were many other devout, religious, righteous people, who at that time were waiting for the salvation of Israel. And not only were there righteous people among the Jews, but among the Gentiles also. Cornelius, a Gentile, was a good man: he feared God and worked righteousness; and was accordingly accepted of God. And we have reason to believe that there were many others like him among the nations of the earth; many, who were acting according to the light with which God had favoured them; who were using faithfully the talents entrusted to them. In other words, we have reason to believe that there were many who feared God and worked righteousness, and were therefore as truly acceptable to God, as truly righteous in their measure, as the saints of the Old or New Testament. And those persons Christ did *not* come to call to repentance. He came to give them further light, and to raise them to a higher state of knowledge, and of religious excellency: he came to unfold to them truer views of life, and to give them fuller revelations respecting God and immortality; but he did not come to call them to repentance.

I take the following passages in the same sense, 'They that be whole need not a physician; but they that are sick.' Christ was a moral, a spiritual physician. There were some however that were not sick, and therefore did not need to be cured of any sickness. There were some that were spiritually healthy, truly sound: those did not need the physician. There were others that *were* sick; that were vicious, profligate, ungodly, unholy, uncharitable. These *did* need a physician; and these Christ came to heal, to cure. The occasion on which these and similar expressions were uttered by Christ, shows that he could not refer to the scribes and pharisees, who were righteous only in their own estimation. The occasion was as follows: Christ kept company occasionally with the publicans and sinners: he even went amongst the most disreputable and profligate of men; those who were generally considered as LOST. The scribes and the pharisees thought that he ought to keep better company; that mingling with such low, abandoned characters, did not *become* a person of such high pretensions as his. It was in answer to *this* objection that Christ said, 'They that be *whole* need not a physician, but they that are *sick*;' and

'I came not to call the *righteous*, but *sinners* to repentance;' and 'the Son of man is come to seek and to save that which was *lost*.' The scribes and pharisees seemed to think that Jesus, if he were a good and godly man, a special messenger and favourite of God, should associate with the *good*, the *godly*. Christ answers, in effect, 'If my object were simply to enjoy good society, I *would* do so. If I sought only my own pleasure, I would spend my time in the company of the enlightened, the pure, the elevated. But that is not the case. My object is *not* my own enjoyment. I came, not to do mine own will, but the will of my Father who sent me; and his will is that I should reclaim his lost and miserable children. I am a *physician*,—and a physician's work is not with the *healthy*, but with the *sick*. I am a *reformer*,—and a reformer's work is not with the *good*, but with the *evil*. I am a *teacher*; and a teacher's work is not with the *wise*, but with the ignorant. The physician would waste his *time* if he were to visit only among the healthy. The teacher might give up his office if he were to associate only with the learned or enlightened. The reformer would be out of his place if he were to mingle only with the good, the exemplary. So *I*, if I were to pass by the ignorant, the depraved, should be neglecting the great work to which God has appointed me: should be frustrating the designs of my Father that sent me. I therefore *leave* the good and the wise to grow wiser and better, and to enjoy the fruits of their knowledge and righteousness. *My* work is to make the *evil* good; the *ignorant* wise; the polluted holy; the miserable happy. I came not to call the *righteous*, but *sinners* to a change of mind. They that are *whole* need not a physician; but they that are *sick*. I leave the ninety and nine sheep that have not gone astray, to go to seek the one that is lost.'

83. I do not believe that those passages in Romans iii., which speak of all men as sinners, as unprofitable, as having gone out of the way, are to be taken and applied universally. —I believe there never was a time since men were multiplied on earth, when it could be truly said that there was *none* righteous, that *all* had gone out of the way; that *all* had become unprofitable; that there was *none* that did good; no not one. We are sure this was not the case in the days of Abel; for *his* works were righteous. It was not the case in the days of Enoch; for he walked with God,

and had the testimony that he pleased God. It was not the case in the days of Noah ; for God found *him* upright ; and on account of his righteousness, revealed to him his purpose respecting the flood. It was not the case in the days of Abraham ; for *he* was righteous according to his light. It was not the case in the days of Job ; for he was a perfect and an upright man ; one that feared God, and avoided evil. It was not the case in the days of David ; for he speaks of *numbers* that feared God and kept his law. It was not the case in the days of Solomon ; for he also speaks of men in his day who were wise and righteous. It was not the case in the days of the prophets ; for the prophets themselves were generally a righteous and a holy race of men, whatever the priests were ; and there were numbers in their days, who, amidst the greatest profligacy, refused to bow their knees to idols, or to pollute themselves with prevalent abominations. It was not the case in the days of Christ ; for *he* was righteous, and there were other righteous persons in his days ; persons that needed not repentance : persons who were spiritually healthy and sound, and needed not a spiritual physician. It is not the case *now*. There are righteous people on the earth at this hour. There are numbers who are not unprofitable. There are multitudes that do good. There are many that walk in the right way, and that turn not aside either to the right hand or to the left. And curious enough, even those who profess to interpret the passages literally, and to apply them universally, generally think that they themselves are righteous, that they themselves do good. It is especially true that there never was a time when every one's mouth was an open sepulchre ; when every man's tongue uttered deceit ; when the poison of asps was under every man's lips, when every man's mouth was full of cursing and bitterness, and when destruction and misery were in every man's way. What then is the meaning of those passages ? I answer, those passages are quoted from the Old Testament, which the apostle sometimes calls the law. Now at the close of his quotations he says, 'We know that whatsoever things the *law* saith, it saith to them that are *under* the law ;' that is the JEWS. What is said in those passages therefore, all of which are quotations from the law, was spoken of the *Jews;* and the meaning is, that the Jews, at the time referred to, were, generally speaking, (not universally,) a corrupt, a profligate, and wicked people; that lying, and deceit, and cursing, and cruelty were *exceedingly common* amongst them.

There are some who suppose that the passages mean that there are none good by nature; none righteous in their natural condition; but the words mean no such thing. The truth is, that no one is either good or bad by nature, or by birth; that no one is either righteous or wicked by nature or birth. It is he that *doeth* righteousness that is righteous; and a man by *nature*, by *birth*, or *at* his birth, does *not* do righteousness. It is he that wilfully sins that is wicked; but when a child is *born*, it does *not* commit sin; it does neither good nor evil. The apostle, therefore, could not mean to say that none were righteous, that none did good by *nature*, or at birth. Nor could he mean that none did good, or were righteous, while in their *natural* state, for in truth no one *remains* in his natural state. The state in which a person is born is that of *childhood;* a state without knowledge, without responsibility; a state in which the human being can neither do good nor evil; can neither go *out* of the way, nor walk *in* the way. That state continues but for a time, and then necessarily gives place to another state, the state of *youth;* and that gives place to another state again, the state of *manhood*. And it is when a person comes to something like *manhood* that he becomes *responsible*, that he begins to do good, or to do evil,—that he becomes righteous or wicked. In other words, it is *then* and then *only*, that a man can be said to be wicked, when he knows what is right, but will not do it; it is then and then only, that a man can be said to be righteous, when he sees his duty and performs; when he is tempted to sin, but refuses to sin.

It is also true, that those passages do not prove that all are depraved by nature: they would rather prove that men are *not* depraved by nature; that those who *are* depraved, have *become* depraved: that those who are out of the way, have *gone* out of it; not were *born* out of it. God makes all things *right;* all *his* works are *good*, are *perfect;* and if they afterwards become *evil*, it is not *his* fault, but the fault of the parties themselves. They *become* unprofitable or mischievous; they are not *made* so.

CHAPTER VIII.

DOUBTS, DISBELIEFS, ETC.

84. I think a great many of the words and forms of expression which are used by religious teachers and writers in our days, are calculated to bewilder or mislead people. People talk of coming to Christ, as if people could now come to Christ as they did when he was here on earth. They talk of people coming to Christ 'just as they are,' with all their sins and all their pollutions upon them; as if Christ were in some place, and they could go to visit him. Now it is true, that when Christ was on earth, people could go to Christ literally; they could go to him to hear him speak and to learn his lessons from his own lips. They could go to him to ask a favor, to solicit a cure. People *did* thus go to Christ; Christ invited them to go to him. 'Come unto me all ye that labour and are heavy laden,' said he, 'and I will give you rest.' And many that were heavy laden, that were burdened with affliction and calamity, went to him, and obtained relief. And many that were burdened and afflicted with spiritual maladies, many that were ignorant, unholy, and miserable, went to him, and found instruction, and received spiritual health and consolation. They listened to his words, they received his teachings, they placed themselves under his authority; they observed his example and followed it; they drank in his spirit, they imitated his virtues, and thus found rest to their souls. But people cannot go to Christ literally now. Christ is in heaven; we are on earth. He is no longer seen by men; he is no longer heard by men. He has finished the work which his Father gave him to do, and has gone to his reward. When people, therefore, exhort men to come to Christ now, they ought to *explain* themselves. The only way in which we can come to Christ now, is the way in which we may come to Moses, to Wesley, to Luther, or to Penn: that is, to their works, their writings, &c. We can come to the record of Christ's life; to the records of his teachings; and there we can learn his doctrines, discover his character, and thus be instructed, reformed, and perfected. But to talk of people

coming to Christ *just as they are*, is foolishness. It would often have been right enough to exhort people to come to Christ in the days of his flesh *just as they were;* that is, if people were sick, and wanted healing, it would have been right enough to tell them not to stay away in hopes of *curing themselves*, by a long and doubtful process of medicine, but to come just as they were, and seek a cure at his hands at once. It would have been right to tell them that if they tarried till they were better, they would probably never come at all; but such talk is out of place *now*. When we exhort men to come to Christ, we ought to give them to understand that our meaning is, that we wish them to *study his doctrine*, to *place themselves under his government*, to *live in obedience to God's will;* and instead of telling them to come *just as they are*, we ought to tell them *to lay aside every sin*, to *abandon every thing which they know to be evil*, to *begin at once to do all that they know to be their duty*, and to resolve to study the teachings of Jesus with a determination to reduce them to practice, and to study his spirit and his example with a determination to become as much like him as possible.

85. It is common for people to speak as if spiritual *light* and *knowledge* were two different things. This I do not believe to be the case. I believe that light and knowledge mean the same thing; that *light* is the *figurative* word for *knowledge;* that one word expresses figuratively, and the other literally, the same thing. When Christ is called the Light of the world, the meaning is, that he is the Teacher, the instructer of the world. When we are called 'the children of light,' the meaning is, that we are persons who have received instruction in religious matters; and when we are called upon to *walk* as children of the light, the meaning is, that we should reduce our knowledge to practice; live consistently with the doctrines which we have been taught, and which we have been led to receive as true.

86. I do not believe that all the heathens will be lost. The idea that God will save none but those who actually believe in *Christ*, whether they have heard of him or not, is a foolish, and unscriptural, and blasphemous idea. How can God demand impossibilities of men? How can God expect men to believe in him of whom they have never heard? to receive a doctrine that never was revealed to them? It is foolish and horrible to think any such thing. God is *just*,

and will deal equitably with his creatures: he is *good*, and will deal kindly and mercifully with them. He has no pleasure in the death of the wicked; how then can he make the life of any depend upon an impossibility? The heathen will be judged according to the light they have; they will be punished or rewarded according to their faithfulness or want of faithfulness. Those that have improved the light with which they have been favoured, will be rewarded and blest; and those that have either refused the light, or refused to walk according to the light, will be punished. '*This* is the condemnation; not that some are left in darkness and have no light; but that men *have* light, and love darkness better; because their deeds are evil.' I believe that the Gentile who uses his *one* talent, and the Jew who uses his *two* talents, are as acceptable to God as the Christian who uses his *five* talents. I believe that the Gentile is a law unto himself, and will be judged according to the law that is written upon his heart. I believe that the Jew whose only guide is the law of Moses, will be judged according to that law; and that the Christian, and the Christian only, who has the gospel law, will be judged by that law, that he only is expected to keep that law. I believe 'that in every nation, he that fears God and works righteousness, is accepted of God. I see no reason to doubt, but that in every nation there are persons who *do* fear God and work righteousness; persons who believe in God and serve him; who love their brethren and do them good as they have opportunity.

87. I do not believe that Unitarians or Socinians will be lost on account of their errors. In *many* things the Unitarians and Socinians are nearer to the truth than those who are called orthodox and evangelical. And even in those things in which they err, they may still be sincere and blameless in their error. I see no reason why a man may not as sincerely err on the side of *Unitarianism* as on the side of *Calvinism*. If a man may go to the *Calvinistic* extreme and yet be saved, why may not a man go to the *Anti*-calvinistic extreme,—to the *Unitarian* extreme, and still be saved. People generally acknowledge that men may innocently err on the *Calvinistic* side; what is there to prove that they cannot innocently err on the *Unitarian* side? I believe with John Wesley, that if a man can be safe who believes *Calvinistic* errors, a man may be safe, *whatever* errors he may hold. I

believe with John Wesley, that there are no errors under heaven, more unscriptural, more monstrous, more blasphemous, more mischievous in their tendency, than *Calvinistic* errors; and if an honest man can hold *those* errors, why may not an honest man hold errors on the opposite side? If a man can go to heaven and hold Calvinistic errors, who *may not* go to heaven, if he be an honest sincere man, whatever errors he may hold?

88. There are some who believe, that it is *possible* for people to entertain the errors of *Calvinism*, and yet be honest, candid, faithful seekers after truth; but that it is *not* possible for people to be honest, candid, faithful seekers after truth, and yet entertain the doctrines of Unitarianism. This I do not believe. I believe it is as possible for an honest man to be a *Unitarian*, as it is for an honest man to be a *Calvinist*.*

89. I do not believe that it is impossible for Roman Catholics to go to heaven. They hold many errors; they believe and practice many things which are nowhere taught or commanded in the sacred Scriptures; at the same time, I see no reason why it should not be believed that many of them are honest, truthful, God-fearing men. I see no proof that it is not as easy for people, under *some* circumstances, to believe all the follies, and to practise all the superstitions of popery, with as true a heart, and with as good a mind, as others believe the doctrines of Calvinism, and practise the ceremonies of many denominations of protestants.

90. In short, as I have said before, I believe that every man who is honest and faithful; who does the best he knows, and who labours to know more, that he may do better still, is pleasing to God, and will be received to heavenly blessedness hereafter, if he persevere.

91. I do not believe that the blessedness of heaven consists in what is called the '*beatific vision*.' I believe that the happiness of heaven will greatly resemble the happiness of the saints on earth,—that it will spring from the same sources, and will, in fact, be a continuation of that happiness

---

*Though I had begun to see much truth and reasonableness in Unitarian views at this time, I had no idea that they were so near to truth, and so far from deserving the reproaches and denunciations so commonly uttered against them, as I have since discovered them to be.

which they enjoy on earth, only heightened and perfected. As our happiness here results from the acquisition of knowledge, from the contemplation of truth, from the possession of health and vigour, from the exercise of our benevolent and religious affections, from the exertion of all our faculties and powers in good and generous and Godlike deeds, from our love to each other, and the love of others to us, from our social and friendly intercourse with each other, from our hopes of future improvement and blessedness to us and to our brethren, so will it be in the world to come. Our happiness there will spring from the discovery of fresh truths, from the detection and explosion of remaining errors and misconceptions, from the growth and exercise of our benevolent and social affections, from the possession of a healthy, sound, vigorous frame, from the exertion of all our powers in doing good, in carrying forwards the great work of universal illumination and improvement, from the anticipation of still further and fuller revelations of truth, from fuller developments of God's character and plans, from the freest and fullest intercourse with wise and good and Godlike souls, and from the ceaseless and everlasting growth and exercise of all our moral, and intellectual, and physical powers.

92. I do not believe that feelings, impressions, or anything of that kind, is the true and proper evidence of a man's conversion. The true and decisive proof to a man that he is converted, is that which John refers to when he says, 'By this we know that we have passed from death unto life, because we love the brethren.' And the proof of our Christianity to others is the same, according to the words of Jesus, 'By this shall all men know that ye are my disciples, when ye have love one towards another.' If I wish to know whether I am one of Christ's true disciples, I must ask myself, Do I receive Christ's instructions? Do I share Christ's spirit? Do I walk as Christ walked? Have I the same mind, the same disposition, that Jesus had? Do I live as Jesus lived? If I have not the spirit of Christ,—if I have not the disposition which Jesus had, I am not his true disciple. If I *have* the spirit of Christ; if the mind that was in him is in me, and if I walk as he also walked, or live as he lived, then am I Christ's disciple indeed; then have I the fullest proof possible that I am a new creature; that I am one of God's beloved children in whom he is well pleased.

It matters not what a man feels; it matters not what impressions he may have upon his mind: he may have experienced the greatest raptures; he may have felt his spirit melted into sorrow, or wrapt into extacy; his impressions, his persuasions, his assurances that he is a true Christian, that he is approved of God and sure of heaven, may be as strong as the strongest ever experienced by mortal man; still, if he disregard Christ's teaching, if he be a stranger to Christ's spirit, if he pay no respect to Christ's example, in short, if he does not love his brethren, and live to do men good, he is not a Christian; he is a hypocrite, or else a wild and mad fanatic.

93. I have no great opinion of the common plan of endeavouring to promote revivals. A *true* revival of religion consists in the promotion of goodness; in the promotion of love to God and love to man; and not in producing a great excitement amongst people, and bringing them suddenly to believe that they are accepted and forgiven. The common plan of promoting revivals, or of carrying on what are *called* revivals of religion, appears to me to have no countenance from Scripture; no countenance from any thing that we see in the history of Christ, or in the history of his apostles. Christ laboured to teach men the truth, to make plain to them their duty, and then urged them to respect the truth and to obey it. And so with the apostles; they instructed men, and by the manifestation of the truth to men, sought to bring them to renounce their idolatries, their superstitions, their crimes and abominations, and to live in righteousness, temperance, and Godliness. This was *their* way of promoting the interests of religion. This should be *our* way. Ranting and noise *may* do good, by rousing people's attention; but if people are to be truly converted, if they are to be made good Christians, they must be taught the plain principles of Christian truth and duty, and brought to square their lives according to those principles. That which seems most wanted at the present time is, that professors of religion should grow in *knowledge* and goodness, should come to be men in understanding, and men in purity and temperance, in zeal and charity. It is *improvement* in the churches that is wanted more than *increase*. If those who are already united in religious societies were as wise, and good, and Christlike as they ought to be, the world would be enlightened and converted

quickly, as a matter of course; and until those who profess to be ministers and followers of Christ do more justice to Christianity themselves,—until they study the truth as taught by Christ more thoroughly, and remodel their views, their tempers, and their lives according to its requirements, their zeal for the conversion of others is liable to suspicion, and must remind us of certain characters of old, who compassed sea and land to make one proselyte, while at the same time they were children of the devil themselves. Nor have I the highest opinion in general of those who are most forward in what are called revivals. Many who are most noisy and disorderly in their efforts to promote what they call revivals, are, as far as I can see, the least anxious to know the truth as Jesus taught it, the least careful to reduce the principles of the gospel to practice. They are, in general, as far as I can judge, amongst the least conscientious, the least creditable and worthy members of religious societies.

94. I do not believe that repentance consists in a godly sorrow for sin. I believe that repentance means a *change of mind*, a *change of purpose*, a turning round of the soul from foolish and sinful pursuits, to the pursuit of truth, to the discharge of duty. I believe that godly sorrow *worketh* repentance; but I do not believe that it *is* repentance. I believe that he who truly repents, *will* sorrow on account of his former sins; but sorrow on account of former sins is not itself repentance. Men may weep at the thought of their former transgressions,—they may weep especially at the thought of the troubles they have brought upon themselves by their wicked ways, and yet not repent at all: while others may repent, and yet sorrow comparatively little. They may especially repent, and not *manifest* much sorrow. Some who repent may be so eager to learn the truth more fully; so entirely taken up with endeavours to know and do all God's will for the future; that the past, for a time at least, shall occupy but little of their thoughts.

95. While I believe that godly sorrow is not itself repentance, I believe that repentance will more frequently be *followed* by godly sorrow, than it will be *preceded* by it. Some seem to think, that when a man has believed in God to the saving of his soul,—that when a man has obtained the assurance that he is forgiven and accepted of God, his godly sorrow ceases; that as Wesley himself expresses it,

'Sorrow, and grief, and sin expire.'

But this is not the case. Men may sorrow more *after* they have obtained an assurance of their forgiveness, than they ever did before. The longer men live, the more they learn, the purer and holier their hearts become, the more will they be grieved, at times, to think that they should ever have sinned against God; that they should ever have abused their own natures; that they should ever have violated their own consciences. The thought of past transgressions may be accompanied with shame and sorrow to the last; and even in heaven, for anything that I know, the recollection of our past misdoings may still mingle something like sorrow with our joys and pleasures for ever.

96. I do not believe that repentance, regeneration, and sanctification are three different things: they appear to me to be three different *words*, meaning, in general, the *same* thing. Repentance means, literally, a *change of mind;* a change from earthliness and sin, to God and righteousness. Regeneration is a figurative expression which means the same thing. Sanctification is a figurative expression also, meaning the same thing. There are *two* words that are translated sanctification, one signifying to become *unearthly*, and the other signifying to be *separated:* but both those words express no more than the single word repentance, or as it ought to be translated, *change of mind*, a change of mind from earthliness and sin, to God and goodness.

97. I do not believe that repentance goes before faith, but that faith goes before repentance. It is a belief of the truth which *leads* people to repent or change their minds; and it is a belief of the truth which leads people to renounce their sins, to give themselves to God, and to resolve to devote themselves to a holy, righteous life.

98. I do not believe that God requires impossibilities of any man. I do not believe that man is responsible for anything but what he himself receives from God. Some people talk as if God had a right, in consequence of Adam's transgression, to allow us to remain without the power to do right, and yet *require* us to do right: a right to require us to obey the same law under which Adam was placed, and to obey it perfectly; while at the same time we have not the power necessary to *enable* us to obey it. This I do not believe. Adam, and Adam only, was answerable for the power which Adam possessed; and *we* are answerable for

the power which we ourselves receive, and for that power only. Many talk of the human race, as if they were just one man; as if that which was true of one, was true of all; as if that which might truly be said of Adam, might be said of all his posterity. They say God made man upright; man sinned; man lost God's image; man incurred God's displeasure; man brought himself under condemnation; man abused his talents; man forfeited all right and title to God's regard; man rendered himself liable to everlasting perdition; man still continues under God's displeasure; man still remains under condemnation; man still is justly liable to everlasting perdition: &c., &c.; speaking all this time as if there had been but *one* man on the earth, from the beginning of the world to this hour. But every one knows that that is not the case. If people would use their common sense, they might see at once, that that which was true of Adam, is *not* always true of *me*,—that it might be perfectly true that *Adam* abused his talents, forfeited all right to God's regard, placed himself under condemnation, made himself liable to perdition, &c; while *none* of these things should be true of *me*. But preachers generally do not choose to consider those things. They choose to jumble all mankind together; to speak of the whole race as of one single individual; to make it out that because *man*, that is the *first* man, sinned, therefore *man*, that is *every* man, whether he has done good or evil, or done nothing at all, is equally under God's displeasure, and liable to condemnation.

CHAPTER IX.

FRAGMENTS.

Several events took place about this period of my life, or perhaps before this period, which have not been noticed in foregoing chapters. I must therefore notice them now.

I have mentioned Mr. Snowdon of Newcastle as a very singular man. There are two or three other matters connected with Mr. Snowdon that I ought to place on record.

When Mr. G. was appointed by the Conference to the Newcastle circuit, he went on his arrival at Newcastle, direct to Mr. Snowdon's house. Now Mr. G. was a little man, and had, at that time, a very youthful appearance. And how do you think Mr. Snowdon received the new preacher? He came to the door, and welcomed him in, but the very first sentence that he uttered was, 'Well, either Conference has a very *high* opinion of *you,* or a very *low* opinion of *us.*'

Another fact. I frequently slept at Mr. Snowdon's while in the Newcastle circuit; indeed their house was in a manner my home for a while. Mr. and Mrs. Snowdon frequently invited my wife, through me, to come over with me to Newcastle sometime, and spend a few days with them, and by frequently and earnestly urging and pressing their invitation, I at last succeeded in inducing her once to come along with me. And how do you think Mr. Snowdon welcomed her? The very first sentence that he uttered after he came in and found that we had arrived was, 'What has brought you here? addressing himself to my wife; I always think good wives are best at home.' And this is but a sample of his manner. It was quite a usual thing with him to teaze and torment people in this way. At the same time he was as kind in his way as a man need to be. He was, in fact, the most complete mixture of surly ill-nature, and, as it appeared to me, of real unaffected kindness, that I ever met with in my life. I never could help believing that he was, on the whole, a good man, and yet it seemed almost an impossibility for a man to be good, and at the same time to take such a pleasure as he did in annoying and tormenting people.

On one occasion he and I had nearly quarrelled. He had tried me till I could keep silence no longer, so I told him plainly exactly what I thought about his manner of proceeding. I spoke so plainly, that both he and his wife were seriously put about. Soon after that, on my visiting the Newcastle side of the circuit, I found that the people at whose house I was accustomed to sleep, had gone off, and closed the house, so that I was obliged to look out for other lodgings for awhile. I went directly to Mr. Snowdon's. He was the principal man in the Newcastle circuit, and it was his place to see that I was properly provided for while on that side of the circuit. His wife seemed astonished when I entered the house: but I told her how the matter stood; and I added, that I did not feel disposed to go, at that time of the night, (for it was getting rather late) to any other lodging; so that I hoped she would give me a bed: I also said, that unless I could be accommodated with a bed there, I would at once return to Blythe. She said, 'I should always be glad to see you, and to give you either bed or anything else, if you would not disagree and dispute so with our master.' I replied, 'It is your master that will disagree and dispute with me. I should be quiet enough, if he would let me alone. I never force my opinions upon him; it is only when he attempts to force his opinions upon me that I ever make any objections to what he says. You must yourself have seen that he will neither allow me to be silent, nor allow me quietly to speak my mind; that he *will* oblige me to speak, and yet always finds fault with what I say, if I say anything at variance with what *he* says.' She acknowledged that her husband was rather queer in that respect, but still thought that I might manage a great deal better with him if I would. I told her I had done my best, and that it was all to no purpose. 'He will ask my opinion' said I, 'on every subject that comes into his head, and then begin to complain whenever my opinion happens to differ from his.' I also added, that I thought he sometimes disputed with me merely for the sake of disputing, and contradicted me, not because he thought I was wrong, but because he thought that it would be too much of a compliment to acknowledge that he agreed with me on any subject. She thought I was too severe upon him. I said, 'Well, just wait and see to-night, and if it is not as I have said, you shall blame me as much as you like, and I will acknowledge myself in error.' Almost immediately Mr. Snowdon came in. 'What are *you* doing here to-night?' said he. 'I have come to sleep here,' I replied, 'and more than that, I *must* sleep here, or else return to Blythe. Mr G——'s house is closed, and it is too late to seek a bed elsewhere.' He made no objections, and things proceeded as usual. He soon took his Bible, called the family around him, and began to read. The lesson was in Isaiah. He had not read far before he began to explain a passage. 'This,' said he, 'refers to our blessed Lord Jesus Christ. It points out the glory of his character and of his person as the supreme God and Lord of all; exhibits him as the *Maker* as well as the *Saviour* of the world. Do you not think so M‑. Barker?'

said he. I remained silent. 'Is not that your view of the subject, Mr. Barker?' he added. 'I have no objections to offer at present,' I said. This did not seem exactly to satisfy him; but he went on, and read again. 'And so it is,' said he; 'we are all by nature as an unclean thing; there is no health in us. How deeply we are fallen, Mr. Barker! Do you not think so, Mr. Barker?' I made no reply. He wished to know why I was silent. I said I did not like to be always talking on those matters,—that I would rather he would read on, and allow us to think about the chapter at our leisure afterwards. All this time his wife was dreadfully fidgetty. She wanted to speak to him, but could not. She wished to control him by her looks, but to no purpose. The proof of the truth of what I had said was becoming too strong for her, and she could scarcely sit still on her chair. He proceeded: 'This,' said he, 'refers to the glory of the Church of Christ in the latter days, when the Gentiles shall all be converted, and the Jews brought back to their own land. This will be a glorious time, Mr. Barker. What are your views on this subject, Mr. Barker?' Then he added some further remarks, concluding with the question, 'Do you not think so, Mr. Barker?' I now began to laugh right out: I could hold no longer. 'And do you laugh at God's holy word?' said he: and a terrible lecture he would have read me, had not his wife broke out and said, 'Hinney, you are to blame, you are to blame. You won't let Mr. Barker alone: he would be silent if you would allow him: you are too bad.' He repeated his terrible rebuke of my levity, and I began to explain. I told him what had passed between his wife and me before he came in. I told him all that I thought about his way of proceeding towards me in those matters, and he, poor fellow, was completely confounded. I told him that it seemed to me as if he really took pleasure in tormenting people; as if he could not be happy unless he thought that he was making other people miserable,—that he seemed to begrudge those that were around him the least ease or quietness or pleasure, and to wish to keep them on a perpetual rack. It was his time now to explain and apologize, and what do you think was the reason he assigned for his proceedings? 'Hinney,' said he, 'Mr. Barker is a young minister, and I wish to inure him to hardness as a good soldier of our Lord Jesus Christ.' I told him there were painful things enough in the world to inure men to hardness without his making more, &c. After this he never annoyed me much in that way again. He did not allow me to rest altogether; that would have been too much; but he was a vast deal better; and if he ever after this began to be queer, I always felt greater confidence in refusing to talk to him, and in letting him know that I expected to be allowed to have a little of my own way in those matters.

I say I never could persuade myself but that this man was, after all, a good man. I believe he really feared God and loved his fellow-men. I think he was a man of conscientiousness and benevolence, of sobriety and purity. Among other proofs of his benevolence I may mention, that he took an orphan family under his care, and reared them. He made them *work*, it is true; he made *every* one work that was under *him*; but he fed them, and clothed them, and taught them in his way. He acted, in short, like a father to them.

Again, when my mother came over to see me at Newcastle, he invited her to his house. He showed her every possible attention. He was as kind as it was possible for a man to be. And when she had to leave for Leeds, he was up by four or five o'clock in the morning, to provide her a comfortable breakfast, and take her to the coach. But I observed that he was always kinder to old people than to young people. I suppose he thought that old people had had trouble enough, and that he had therefore no need to give them more; but that young people were in danger of being too happy, of having too little trouble, and that it was necessary therefore that he should be their tormentor. Or perhaps he thought it was too late for the old to receive much benefit from his annoyances, but that the young *might* be benefited thereby. But even to the young he could be kind on occasions, very kind; and if the young showed a disposition to meet his views, to receive his sayings as oracles, and always to consult his will, he would even caress and commend them. But he could receive no measured or limited subjection. They must be absolute slaves to him, if they wished to enjoy his favour. They must neither think, nor speak, nor smile, nor stir but in accordance with his will. The least imaginable opposition to his judgment or his pleasure, would instantly draw forth his rebukes.

Mr. Snowdon's manner of educating his children was as

objectionable as his manner of treating his young friends. He was a perfect tyrant to his children. He would neither allow them to think, nor to speak, nor to act but in perfect subjection to his authority. The instruction that he gave them was of the most orthodox and gloomy description, and was forced upon them with most absolute and stern authority. He required them to sit and listen to whatever he thought fit to read; and he read to them from his gloomiest and most fanatical books, till they were utterly overcome. His great object seemed to be thoroughly to break their spirits, to destroy everything about them like freedom or manliness, and to make them abject and unquestioning slaves. The character which he gave them of God was one of unmingled gloom and terror. God was always held forth by him as a dark and vengeful tyrant. He used the most horrible threats of God's wrath and judgments, and of eternal life in unutterable torments, to enforce whatever he chose to say or command. In short, the course he pursued with his children, was exactly adapted to make his children either infidels and profligates, or the most abject and crouching and miserable slaves. And this was the effect of his teachings. Those of his children who became religious, were superstitious, exceedingly superstitious; and those who did not become religious, were reckless profligates. With one of his children, one that became religious, I was very well acquainted. I frequently visited at her house for years. She had a great deal of her father's spirit. She was very masterful, very dictatorial, very impatient of contradiction, yet very kind in her way. She had a great deal of religious feeling, and under better treatment might have become a tolerably intelligent and useful woman; but as it was, she was neither happy herself, nor very agreeable to her friends. She lived on very bad terms with her husband, and had he not died suddenly, she would soon have been separated from him. When her husband was away, she was accustomed to plunder the business, in order to lay up a store against the time of separation. This increased her husband's difficulties, led him to defraud others to relieve himself, and brought upon him such shame, that he died very suddenly, in a most miserable way.

I cannot illustrate Mr. Snowdon's character better than by stating a few particulars in his conduct towards this his unfortunate son-in-law. His son-in-law had a mind and a will of his own. He would think and judge for himself. He was not all that he ought to have been, far from it; but his chief offence in the estimation of his father-in-law was, that he would not be entirely in subjection to his will. While I was at Newcastle, his son-in-law lost a child, and, at the time I refer to, it was lying dead in the house. This was a favourable opportunity, Mr. Snowdon thought, for making a salutary impression upon his son-in-law. He went to the door and knocked; his daughter opened the door to welcome him in, and his son-in-law stood by her side: but Mr. Snowdon would not go in. He held the door in his hands, and in his doleful and sepulchral manner observed, 'Ah, my hinnies, this is an awful visitation, a dreadful judgment from God for your disrespect and disobedience to his will.' When he had lectured them for a few moments in this style, he withdrew, and returned to his own home.

I say that his daughter very much resembled him; but she mingled a good deal of craft with *her* superstition. When she was robbing her husband during his absence, she used to write letters to him to say, that God was cursing the business because he had done this or that, referring to something in which he had not exactly pleased her. He refused to accommodate himself to her wishes in reference to religious or ecclesiastical matters, and she endeavoured to subdue him by the same means by which her father had endeavoured to subdue his children and other people to his will. If her husband happened to please her, she would write to him to say that God was prospering the business, and thus giving proof that he was well pleased with his doing as she had wished him. This woman was a first rate member of the Methodist New Connexion, and the ground of her complaint against her husband at this time was, that he had left the society on account of the tyrannical, unprincipled proceedings of the Conference, and joined with a company of reformers. But we may have to notice these matters at a future period.

A matter which I wish once more to notice, is the character of my poor father. I have spoken very freely of my father in a former chapter, making mention of his defects and errors very unreservedly. It is needful that I should make a few further remarks with respect to my father's excellencies. And first, He was remarkably honest; too honest, in fact, if such a thing be possible. He would any time sooner wrong himself, than run the risk of wronging another person. And many a time, I believe, has he paid a debt twice over, when he has had a doubt upon his mind as to whether he had paid it before. For many years he worked for other people in the woollen business, and had their work in his own house. But his care of his master's property, was always greater than his care of his own rights or interests, and he would often wrong himself, for fear of wronging his master. He would not only do always that which was strictly just, but would do more than justice could require. When people have work in the cloth-making line in their own houses, they have many opportunities of taking advantage of their employers; but my father would never take advantage of any one.

The man who has work given out to him at his own house, is required to spin the weft to a certain length per six pounds, and then to put a certain quantity into each piece of cloth. The master's orders are at times such, that if a man should spin the weft to the length named by the master, he would find it exceedingly difficult, if not impossible, to get the required quantity into the piece. In those cases the man must do one of three things; he must either set at nought his master's orders, and make the weft thicker than he was told to do, or leave a portion of it out, or make his job more difficult and less profitable than it ought to be. If he leaves any of the weft out, he must either carry it back to the master, and acknowledge that he has not done as he was ordered, or he must destroy it, or sell it and take the money to himself. In all cases of this description, my father would do as follows. He would first spin the weft to the length appointed by the master. He would then do his utmost to get it in; and if it took him, in consequence, ten days to do five days work, he would still, if possible, put in the required quantity of weft. If after doing his utmost, he was unable to get in all the weft, he would then take the remainder, and carry it back to the master, state the simple facts of the case, at the risk of provoking the master's displeasure and receiving his own discharge, and there let the matter rest.

It frequently happens that employers do not appreciate strict honesty in their men, so much as they ought. Hence while the man that cheats his employer goes on smoothly; the man that deals honestly with his employer meets with rebukes and scoldings. This was the case, to some extent, with my father's employer. Though a decent man on the whole, and one that had the highest opinion of my father's integrity, he was still passionate, and would frequently scold my poor father, and that most tremendously, when he found that he had not accomplished an impossibility. One of the rewards of my father's integrity therefore frequently was, most violent and terrible abuse.

Again; in spinning and weaving, it is impossible to avoid making some waste. Threads break when the man is spinning, and the readiest way for the spinner is, in all cases, to throw the broken ends aside, piece the thread, and go on with his work. In some cases it is absolutely necessary to throw aside a portion of the thread; but in others it is not. In some cases the thread breaks before it has been at all twisted, and then, with a little trouble, it may be preserved. At other times the thread breaks when it has been twisted sufficiently, or nearly so; and in this case also, with a little trouble, the thread may be preserved, and a little waste be prevented. The man who wishes to make a good week's work, will throw the ends of every broken thread aside, and thus save himself a little time, and make his job a little better at his master's expense. Another man will throw *some* threads aside, and others he will occasionally preserve. My father would never throw *one* aside, if it was in his power to preserve it. I have known him spend as much time in twisting a single broken thread, as would have been necessary to spin two hundred whole ones, thus sacrificing at the rate of three-pence a shilling of his wages, to save his master a penny in the pound. In fact, my father's anxiety to do absolute justice to his master, was such, that he was never able to earn as much at his business as other persons generally earned, though he generally worked much longer hours, and kept much closer to his work than others. There never was a man on earth that served another man more faithfully or conscientiously, than my father served the employers for whom he laboured. But in truth he never had many employers. Nearly the whole of the time that my father spent in working for others, was spent in one individual's employment; and though he and his master occasionally took the liberty to quarrel a little, they still contrived to make up matters, and to go on as before. The man for whom my father worked was an own cousin of his, John Haley of Bramley.

My father was as conscientious in other things as he was in reference to his work. For instance, he thought it was his duty to abstain from all work on the Sabbath day, and nothing could have induced him to work on that day. He thought it his duty to abstain from common conversation on the Sabbath, and nothing could have drawn him off his guard on that day: not a word would escape him from morning till evening, having the slightest reference to matters of trade, or any thing of a worldly nature. Again, he had at one time scruples as to the propriety of working after dark on a Saturday evening. He thought it was but right that work should be laid aside earlier on a Saturday evening, to afford an opportunity for preparing for the Sabbath. On some occasions however, people were almost under the necessity of working a little on the Saturday night. I recollect my father yielding to what appeared to be a case of necessity of this kind once. That night he spilled the oil, from the lamp by which he was working, upon the cloth, and the oil was of such a nature as to injure the colour of the cloth. This he regarded as an indication from heaven that he ought not to work on a Saturday night, and no one could have induced him to do it after.

In some cases he detected his children plucking up a hedgestake, stealing beans or turnips from the fields, and the like. Whenever he found out that his children had been committing any depredations of this kind, he would endeavour to find out the persons wronged, and make them restitution.

My father's virtue and integrity have been tried in other ways. There are occasions when temptations of the most dangerous description assail men. My father was assailed with such temptations; but he steadily resisted the tempter, and preserved himself unspotted.

My father's benevolence was very great. Though he was not always liberal to his own children, he was liberal to every one else. And if he had had a thousand a year he would have spent it in helping others: it never would have entered his thoughts to dispose of any portion of it selfishly; nor would he have employed it in exempting his children from the necessity of toil: it would have been all either wasted in trade, or applied to such purposes as he thought were likely to be most pleasing to God, and most useful to his fellow-creatures. In short, notwithstanding his defects, and they were such as caused his children great suffering at times, I question whether there ever was a man who had been similarly trained and circumstanced, or who had been as badly educated, that carried within him a greater amount of intellectual force, or of sterling Christian virtue. Notwithstanding his imperfections, he was a good man ; and in heaven, I doubt not, his reputation will be that of a great man too. And if to have strong intellectual faculties, great active powers, much patience and endurance, strict and unchanging integrity, ardent and overflowing benevolence ; in short, if to have great natural intellectual powers, a pure, exalted, and superior virtue, be greatness, then my father was great ; for few ever excelled him in those respects. He has deserved well, I believe, of all with whom he has had to do, and I question whether he has deserved ill of any one.

My father continued to learn even to his old age. He was willing to receive fresh light on religious subjects, from whatever quarter it might come. As an instance of the manner in which, even in his old age, he could give up a false notion for a true one, I may mention the following case :— About two years ago I was delivering a course of lectures at Huddersfield. My father, though between seventy and eighty years of age, and nearly blind, walked all the way to Huddersfield from Bramley, a distance of sixteen miles, to hear me. One of my lectures was on the doctrine of Eternal Life in Torments. On this subject my father had felt very strongly. He thought I and my brothers had all gone wrong, in rejecting the common doctrine on that subject. He had always been accustomed, from his youth, to believe that the doctrine of Eternal Torments was a doctrine of Scripture, and even one of the plainest and most undoubted doctrines of Scripture. He was, however, disposed to hear what was to be said on the subject. He heard my lecture ; he saw clearly that the doctrine had not the slightest foundation either in the Old or in the New Testament : he saw clearly that there was not a passage in the whole Bible that taught the doctrine of Eternal Life in Torments, and he gave up the doctrine at once, like a Christian. Next day, when I went to see him, he said, ' I'll tell thee what, Joseph, I've just been thinking how long a man may be kept in the dark on some points. I could not have believed, if I had not heard for myself, that the matter could be made so plain.' And thus he spoke, expressing his full conviction that the doctrine of Eternal Torments was an unscriptural, a horrible fiction of man's, and not a revelation of heaven.

CHAPTER X.

SUNDERLAND CIRCUIT.

I think I stated that after I had spent a year in the Newcastle circuit, I was appointed to that circuit again for six months longer. It was appointed by Conference that at the end of six months I should change with the Sunderland preacher who lived at Durham. As the period for my removal drew near, I went over to Durham, to look after a house or rooms, and had an opportunity of seeing one or two of the members of the Durham society. There I found that several were unwilling to part with the preacher that was with them, and that they looked on the exchange appointed to take place between him and me with very unpleasant feelings. I however made arrangements with respect to rooms, and at the appointed time, about the close of November, the change took place. The day that we removed from Blyth to Durham was an exceedingly stormy one. The wind was high, and carried along with it a perpetual fall of sleet and snow. Our furniture, which was sent off in the morning in an open waggon, was exposed to this downfall till night. The beds and the bedding were cold and damp, and parts of them quite wet. We ourselves also suffered from the wet and cold on our journey. Yet when we got to Durham no one invited us to their house. No one welcomed us for the night to a warm, a dry and comfortable bed. We had to take our things, damp and wet as they were, to our own rooms, lay the beds on the floor, and, at the risk of our health and our lives, I and my delicate wife, who at that time needed special attention and care, together with our little one, had to pass the cold night upon them just as they were. We all suffered in consequence in our health, but we all recovered, and we still remain alive. Next day we got our beds fitted up, and made our rooms as comfortable as we could. The mistress of the house, of whom I had taken the rooms, was a member of the society, but in no respect a superior or exemplary woman. She was a sycophant in fact, and entirely at the bidding of the leading member of the society in that place. And the leading member and his wife turned out to be by no means over friendly. She therefore showed us no great kindness. She was, in fact, a selfish, unsocial, disagreeable woman, full of deceit and hypocrisy. The wife of the leading member, (unless we call the wife herself the leading member,) employed this woman as a spy, and came and received her reports from her as to our manners and proceedings and the like. We, of course, were not likely to be over comfortable in such circumstances, and yet we were far from being unhappy. I minded my work, and found great pleasure in it, and my wife confined herself chiefly to the house, attending to her domestic concerns after her usual custom, so that notwithstanding our trials, we passed our time on the whole very comfortably and happily.

The first Sunday that I preached at Durham, I preached from Luke x. beginning at the 25th verse: 'And behold a certain lawyer stood up, and tempted him, saying, Master, what shall I do to inherit eternal life?' And then follows the beautiful parable of the good Samaritan. The object of this sermon was to show, that Christianity required all men to love their fellow-men, and to labour to promote their present and everlasting welfare;—that the man who did not love his fellow-men, and labour to promote their present and everlasting welfare, was not entitled to the Christian name, had no right to regard himself as an object of God's approbation, and had no just ground to hope for future and everlasting blessedness. The sermon was not at all of a character to meet the views of selfish people: on the contrary, it was calculated to give great offence to such; yet such, I have reason to believe, were the leading members of the New Connexion at Durham. Such, I believe, were the principal member and his wife. They had long been members of the Old Methodist Society, but had left and joined themselves to the New Connexion on account of some dispute between them and the preachers. They were afflicted with selfishness in various forms. They were not only fonder of money than it becomes professors of Christianity to be, but they were exceedingly ambitious, tyrannical, fond of power and domination, impatient of contradiction, or of any thing like freedom and independance of mind and manner in those with whom they had to do. They had besides been accustomed chiefly to preaching of a doctrinal and exciting character. To sermons on practical subjects, and especially to plain and faithful sermons on practical subjects, they were almost if not altogether unaccustomed. On these accounts my sermon was not at all calculated to give them satisfaction. But there was another thing, as I was afteswards given to understand, that rendered my sermon exceedingly offensive to the principal member. The principal member, Mr. Ward, was a *Lawyer*, and when I read over the text, ' Behold a certain lawyer stood up and tempted him,' &c., he fancied that the text was chosen on purpose for him, and that the sermon was designed especially and expressly for his case. It seems also that some others of the congregation got this fancy into their heads, that the sermon and text were designed for Mr. Ward, and that as soon as I read over the words, ' Behold a certain lawyer stood up and tempted him,' &c., their eyes immediately glanced on Mr. Ward, as if to say, ' The preacher is about to give you a lecture to yourself now !' And what might further tend to make Mr. Ward and some few members indulge those fancies, was the following. Mr. Ward had previously taken great pains in inquiring very particularly into my opinions on certain subjects, and had, in fact, been guilty of the crime of tempting or endeavouring to ensnare me in my words. He had, besides, made considerable opposition to my going to Durham, and had stated his objections against me to some of the congregation. It seemed therefore natural enough for them to think that my object in taking the text referred to, was to point out, or to hold up Mr. Ward, to the congregation, and to lecture him in their presence. At the same time no such thought had ever entered my mind. I had not at the time the least idea of what was passing in the mind of my hearers, nor had I the least idea that my text could lead to any such imaginations. The thought that Mr. Ward was a lawyer was never once present to my mind, that I recollect, during the whole of the service, nor had I at that time any idea that my sermon was particularly applicable to Mr. Ward's character. No matter, Mr. Ward felt very uncomfortable, and afterwards manifested his unpleasantness of feeling in his conduct towards me.

I had been told that Mr. Ward always expected the minister that preached there in the forenoon, to go with him to dinner, and that he would be very much offended if *I* did not do so. Unconscious myself of having given Mr. Ward any occasion to be displeased with me, I went to his house, and dined with him. I had been told by another preacher who had been stationed at Durham before me, that Mr. Ward was a very intelligent man, well read in Theology, and a most excellent talker on theological subjects. I was, in fact, given to expect that I should find in him quite a superior man, and should enjoy in his conversation a rich intellectual and theological repast. I had also been told that it was always his custom to spend the afternoon of the Sabbath in conversation with the preacher. I accordingly expected to find myself exceedingly comfortable at Mr. Ward's, and looked forward to the afternoon's conversation with a great degree of pleasing expectation : for I was all this while kept in ignorance of Mr. Ward's state of feeling towards me. It was not till long after, that I was made acquainted with those matters. I say I went to Mr. Ward's and dined, and after dinner looked for the rich and intellectual conversation. But Mr. Ward was dumb : he had not a word for me. He took up a book for a time, and began to read ; so I took up another and read too. After a short time he told me he must leave me, assigning some kind of reason which I do not now exactly recollect. He accordingly left me, and I saw him no more till tea time. At tea time he was no more communicative than he had been before, so that my expectations with respect to a rich conversation were altogether disappointed. I preached in the evening and called at his house again, according to directions that I had received from the stewards of the society. Still there was no free, interesting conversation. The only thing which he said, that I remember, was, that rhetoric was of very little use in the pulpit ; that if I lived to be older I should see that all rhetorical forms of expression were out of place in the pulpit, and that the simplest modes of address were the best. I understood this as a sort of censure upon my discourse, though I did not say so. The censure however seemed undeserved, for my study even in those days was to be as plain and simple in the pulpit as possible, and it seemed a mystery how any one could think that my discourses were chargeable with the fault implied in this censure. Here the day's intercourse ended.

A weekly prayer-meeting was held on the Thursday evening, and I attended it. I commenced the meeting as usual, and left the other persons that were present to give out a verse or a hymn and pray as they might feel disposed. In this it seems I gave Mr Ward additional offence. I was afterwards informed that it had been the custom of the preachers to request Mr. Ward to begin the prayer-meeting, and that in not conforming to this custom I had caused him great uneasiness. Mr. Ward did however engage in prayer during the evening, but he appeared to have very little liberty of expression; he seemed, in fact, to be exceedingly embarrassed. This made matters worse.

Still I continued all the time I was at Durham, whenever I preached at Durham in the morning, to go to Mr Ward's to dine. Sometimes he or his wife invited me; sometimes I was left uninvited; but in every case I went according to the instructions that I had received at the beginning from the stewards. Yet in no case could I ever induce Mr. Ward to enter freely into conversation on any subject whatever. On some occasions he would speak a few sentences, but never more. On one occasion the doctrine of natural depravity was the subject of a few moments' conversation. He had given me a French publication to read, and one of the first sentences that I met with spoke of all the wickedness in the world as being caused by the sin of Adam, and represented the prevalence of wickedness in the world as a proof of man's natural, total depravity. I remarked that that way of speaking seemed to me to be objectionable: that in the first place, the Scriptures never attributed all the sin that was in the world to the sin of Adam, but to men's own unfaithfulness. I observed in the second place, that the fact of people sinning could not, of itself, be a proof that they were naturally and totally depraved previously, for in that case the fact of Adam's sinning would be a proof that *he* was utterly depraved before his fall. He simply replied, 'If you had read the works of Fletcher and of Wesley, you would have found all those objections answered long ago.' I replied that I *had* read the works of Fletcher and of Wesley, but that I did not recollect that either of them had answered those objections, and I added, that I could not imagine myself how the objections could be answered. He intimated that it was no good sign when people began to cavil about matters of that description, and to raise objections to the leading doctrines of the gospel, and thus insolently did he put an end to the conversation.

On another occasion I succeeded in getting him into a few minutes' conversation on preaching. He had made some remark on the necessity of a minister of the gospel dwelling on the great peculiarities of the gospel in every sermon, meaning by the peculiarities of the gospel, such doctrines as those of the Trinity, Natural Depravity, Satisfaction to Divine Justice, and Salvation by trusting in Christ's merits. I remarked that Christ never dwelt on those points; that so far from making them the principal subjects of his discourses, he did not even mention them in his sermons at all according to the history contained in the gospels. He then remarked that Christ was not a preacher of the gospel; that his mode of preaching was not an example for us; that he had left it to his *apostles* who came after him, to preach the gospel. This was the first time I had heard such a statement as this, and it seemed quite unaccountable to me. I began to argue with him on the subject, but he soon cut short the conversation again, in his surly insolent manner, and left me for the afternoon to my own lonely musings again.

Curious enough, all this time I never suspected him of unkindness, or of coldness or antipathy towards me. Though his surly manner, and his reluctant conversation, and his abrupt and insolent manner of putting an end to conversation when it was begun, together with the general character of his looks and behaviour, would have been enough to satisfy most people of his unkind feeling in a single hour, yet they were not sufficient to satisfy me even in three or four months. There surely never was a mortal under heaven slower to take hints of unkindness, or to understand proofs of antipathy, than myself. What should be the reason of it, I cannot tell, but so it is, and it has always been the case. I have been for weeks and months, and in some cases almost years together, receiving one mark of unkindness after another, and yet never been able to understand them or to interpret them. If my wife had been with me at Mr. Ward's, she would have understood the matter at once: she would have seen the very first day that my company was not wanted by Mr. Ward; that it was a burden or an annoyance to him; she would have been struck with his manner at once, and would have understood and explained to me the mystery. But I could not understand. Even a post or a block could hardly have been more stupid and senseless than I was in those matters.

Before I left Durham however I was let into the mystery: the whole matter was explained to me through a conversation that I had with Mr. Ward with respect to a New Chapel. He had stated in this conversation that the people expected him to do everything; that they expected him to accommodate the preachers, to bear the responsibility of the Preaching-room, &c., &c., and he added that he was almost tired of them. I said, 'I did myself understand that you wished to have the preacher always at your house.' 'Nothing of the kind,' he said. I said 'I was told, when I came to Durham, that I should give offence if I did not go home with you to dinner;' adding, that it had previously been my intention to dine at home, and that I was prevented from doing so simply out of respect to his feelings, having been told by the stewards that it had always been the custom for the preacher to dine with him on the Sunday, and that it would be taken as a serious offence if I did not conform to the custom. He said the stewards had no authority for saying any such thing. And here the matter dropped. Next Sunday I went directly home after preaching. This caused a regular hubbub. It was considered such an offence as had never been committed. Mrs. Ward came to inquire what was the matter, and the outcry raised against me by Mr. and Mrs. Ward for the insult I had offered them, ran through the whole society. When the matter was mentioned to me, I stated, as my justification, what Mr. Ward had said to me, namely, that he never expected the preachers to dine invariably with him; that no one had any authority to say that he expected any such thing; that he expected to be at liberty to invite the preacher or not as he might think best. I contended that, under such circumstances, it would have been unreasonable for me to have gone to dine at his house, unless I had received a special invitation, and that no such special invitation had been given. No explanations however that

I could give could satisfy Mr. and Mrs. Ward, nor could any explanations that they could give, satisfy others but that I had done perfectly right. And here my intercourse with Mr. and Mrs. Ward for ever terminated. I never went to his house after, and I have never, that I recollect, exchanged a word with him anywhere since.

I ought perhaps to mention another matter which tended to prevent me from ever being a favourite at Mr. Ward's: it was as follows: Mrs. Ward was herself a preacher: every afternoon she had her congregation of females, and gave them a regular sermon. I was told that Mr. Ward was far from being pleased with his wife's fondness for preaching, but that he found it impossible to cure her of the malady. Mrs. Ward was, besides, the leading singer of the congregation, and, in fact, the great, the ruling person in the whole concern. She was, as you may perhaps by this time suppose, an exceedingly foolish, and an exceedingly vain woman; very fond of praise, and not at all particular with respect to the means she used in order to induce people to praise her. She was, at the same time, not one of the most praiseworthy people in many respects. She had some good qualities no doubt, and perhaps deserved praise in some respects; but the praise she deserved was not the praise she sought. She wished to be praised, and *expected* to be praised, for things in which she did not excel; for excellencies or gifts which she did not possess. She wished to be praised for instance for her vocal powers; but her vocal powers were, I will not say of the most *ordinary* description, for in truth they were very *extra*ordinary, but they were very far indeed from being extraordinarily excellent. I never in my life heard a mortal either drunk or sober, either mad or sane, that bawled in such an ugly or disagreeable manner. Her voice, it is true, was loud; but it was rusty and cracked. And she stretched it to the very utmost. Hence at times her singing was a loud ungovernable shout, at other times a dreadful squeak, and at other times a horribly jarring shriek, while at other times it was *all* these things together in a single line. At the end of a verse she would try to warble; and then she would give us a sample of the most ridiculous, horrible, and unendurable discord, that ever grated on a mortal's ears. Yet all this time she seemed to fancy that she was singing most gloriously, most delightfully; and of course she expected, that when the preacher went to dinner, he would pay some compliment to her musical taste and powers. I could not, for the soul of me, pay her any such compliments; and I never *did* pay her a compliment, however she might fish for one. I was either sturdily silent, or, if I spoke, I spoke in such a manner as plainly to indicate that I did not like to be questioned on such subjects. She also fancied herself a very excellent preacher, and though she professed to admit none to her services but females, yet she always made an exception in favour of the travelling preachers. She always caused it to be signified by one of her sycophants and tools, that she should like the minister to ask for permission to go and hear her. The minister, as a matter of course, always asked permission, and as another matter of course, always received permission, and even more than permission. But woe to the preacher after, if he was not prepared to compliment the sermon, and to praise the preacher. It was intimated to me that it would be very agreeable to Mrs. Ward if *I* would ask permission to attend one of her services, and to hear one of her sermons. Not having been fully initiated into the mysteries of my condition at that time, and not understanding, till later, the returns which would be required of me for the favour or privilege of hearing Mrs. Ward, I *asked* permission. Permission was most graciously granted. The plainest proofs imaginable were given, that my application was exceedingly grateful to Mrs. Ward. I went to hear her. She gave out her hymn and prayed. She gave out her hymn again, and read her text, and then she began to preach, and she *did* preach. Her preaching was as good as her singing. There was as much order and regularity in her discourse, if one may call it a discourse, as there was melody in her voice, or harmony in her song. In short, her sermon, as we must call it, was one of the most complete samples of random rant, and fanatical raving, bawling, sqeaking, shouting, and shrieking, and one of the strangest jumbles of error, inconsistency, and contradiction, that I ever heard. Well, next week I was asked by Mrs. Ward's spy, how I liked her sermon; but I refused to answer. Mrs. Ward then came and asked me herself, and I told her that I agreed with some things that she said, but that there were others that I did not think correct. That was quite enough; she never asked me to hear her any more, and she never asked me any more questions about how I liked her sermon.

Mrs. Ward occasionally went out to preach Anniversary sermons. This however was contrary to her husband's wishes I was told; but Mrs. Ward was not much accustomed, I fancy, to consult any one's wishes but her own.

The Durham Society was not a large one, nor was it an intelligent one, nor was it a good one in any respect. There were two or three persons connected with it of a worthy character, but there was not a single individual in the whole society that could with propriety be called intelligent or well informed, nor was there one that seemed a superior character in any respect. The society had originated in a separation from the Old Connexion, caused by a quarrel of some description, and it was either the inferior members of the old Methodist society that had left, or the members of the Methodist society in general at Durham must have been a very ignorant and inferior class of people. The latter was very likely the case. There are not many intelligent people among Methodists, and there used to be fewer formerly perhaps, than there are at present. Generally speaking, even the richer Methodists have but very uncultivated minds. Many of them are clever tradesmen; that is, they are clever enough to gain considerable wealth; but they are very seldom clever in any thing else. I can hardly call to mind, even at the present moment, a single individual among the members of the Methodist society, with whom I was acquainted, that has proved himself more than a child in understanding or in knowledge. I have no doubt but that Mr. Ward was one of the most intelligent and best informed in the Methodist society at Durham, but yet his information was neither very correct nor very extensive. He was but a child compared with a truly intellectual man, though many of the rest were but children compared with him.

The most influential man in the Durham society next to Mr. Ward was Robert Thwaites, a pawnbroker and a drinkseller. Mr. Thwaites and Mr. Ward, however, were always at variance with each other. They formed two parties, or stood at the head of two parties. What Ward did, Thwaites condemned; and what Thwaites proposed, Ward opposed. Mr. Thwaites was a local preacher. Six days in the week he sold intoxicating drinks, and the seventh preached temperance and religion. He did not sell drink by wholesale, but by retail. He had a place on purpose for people to go and sit in and drink. I occasionally went to see him and partook of his porter, which at that time I thought very good; but I now see reason to believe, from what I recollect of its influence upon myself, that such drink could never be used by people as a common beverage without both injury to health and danger to character. It had a terrible tendency to make one thirsty, and thus to tempt people to drink more. At that time, however, I saw not the great evil of his way of trade. It is true I could not regard it with perfect approbation, and I once held a conversation with him on the subject; at the same time, I was not then prepared positively to condemn it. I recollect that one thing which he said in justification of himself in following that calling was, that he kept many individuals from visiting *low* places, and associating with *depraved* company. I have heard of other Methodists making use of the same argument in justification of themselves in pursuing the same business. The argument, I believe, is a fallacious one. I very much question whether they *do* keep people from visiting worse places, and mixing with depraved company. On the contrary, I believe that what are called respectable public-houses or drink-shops, have a tendency to *lead* people to visit worse houses, and to mix with depraved company. They lead people to the formation of those habits, which ultimately prepare them for visiting the lowest houses, and for mingling with the most depraved and abandoned of men. Many people go to those respectable drinking-houses that would never think of going to a drinking-house if they were *all* low infamous houses. They go to those respectable houses, as they are called, and get *partially* depraved, and then they are emboldened to visit other houses afterwards of a more disreputable description. The respectable drinking-house is the first step downwards to the house that is not respectable. The respectable drinking-house is the entrance, the porch, the doorway to the low and disreputable house where drunkenness, gambling, and profligacy, in their most awful forms, are encouraged. I have no doubt myself but that these respectable drink-houses have been the means of ruining persons that never would have been ruined by drinking-houses of the common description. The respectable drink-sellers are like spiders of extra size and craftiness; they can catch stronger and more prudent flies than other spiders are able to catch. They draw into danger persons that would never be led astray by the common kind of drink-sellers and publicans. A Methodist New Connexion class-leader and preacher at Manchester opened a public-house. The consequence was, most of the leading members of the society, and even the travelling preachers, visited his house, drank together their social glasses, and spent the evenings apart from their wives and families. At first, no doubt, they drank their glass in moderation only, but they afterwards began to drink more freely, and so they proceeded from step to step, till nearly every leading man in the society became a drunkard, and several of them general profligates. And I have no doubt but this is the tendency of respectable drinking-houses generally. And I ought perhaps to remark, that Mr. Thwaites' house was *purely* a drinking-house. It was not a victualling-house, or a public-house in general, but simply a drinking-house.

Mr. Thwaites had no great amount of knowledge, either on religious or on general subjects. He appeared to have no disposition to inquire into religious matters, nor any idea that there was any thing to be known beyond the rude elements of Methodistical theology, He had taken Methodism as the absolute religion, and seemed not to entertain the least idea that there was either error or defect about it. This was the case with most others. I ought also to observe, that while they took Methodism as the only and absolute religion and theology, they were far from knowing what Methodism was. They had no acquaintance with Fletcher's or Wesley's writings, nor even with the writings of later Methodistical authors. They went to class, they asked or answered the common questions, they preached the common second-hand, third-hand, or thirtieth-hand kind of sermons, occasionally looked through the Methodist Magazine, and there their intellectual exertions ended.

There was another couple who attended the preaching-house at Durham that kept a drinking-house, namely, Mr. Thwaites' father and stepmother. *Old* Mr. Thwaites *had* been a member, but had ceased to be one: old Mrs. Thwaites continued a member. Old Mr. Thwaites was neither preacher nor class-leader, and never made any pretensions to know any thing about religious or theological matters at all.

All his concern appeared to be to go on in his usual way with his business, and neither think nor talk much about any thing else. His wife was a different person: she manifestly had strong religious feelings, and I believe, a great amount of benevolence as well. She was, I believe, far from being pleased with the business in which she was engaged, and she seemed exceedingly desirous to conduct it in the least objectionable manner possible. She was also wishful to make a good use of the profits of the business. I often heard of her liberality to people in distress, and I had proofs in my own experience of her kind-heartedness and liberality. She had understood that I and my wife had the same amount of income as Mr. Jones, the superintendant preacher. Some time towards the close of my stay at Durham, she found out that this was not the case, that I had only about forty pounds a year, while Mr. Jones had nearly a hundred and forty. It was not *I*, nor any one of my family, that enlightened her on this subject; but some other person; I don't know who. She spoke to me on the subject, and asked me if what she had heard was true. I said it was. Without more to do she poured me out a glass of wine, gave me a biscuit to eat, and while I sat eating it, came and put four sovereigns into my hand. A short time after she saw me passing by the door, and invited me in again, and gave me six pounds more; so that in less than a month's time, she gave me ten pounds. And from what I heard, her kindness to me was only a sample of her kindness to other people whom she believed to be in want of help.

There was another person lived at Durham, a member of the Methodist New Connexion, a very decent man, of the name of Dixon. He was a quiet, mild, gentle, and well-disposed person; but he was no great reader, nor any great thinker. Like most of the members of the Methodist societies, he made his business almost his only concern, and never extended his inquiries far beyond it.

Another person in the Durham society that I respected and loved was a Mr. Armstrong. He was a grocer, and lived with his sister, a person as affectionate and as good as himself. Neither of them was married, but they appeared to live comfortably together, and they were comfortable society and friends to us. But like almost all other Methodists, their minds were very little cultivated, I mean so far as knowledge was concerned. They lived, as almost all Methodists then lived, as if all truth were included in the first rude elements of Methodism, or at least as if all the truth beyond the first rude elements of Methodism was of no importance to them or to mankind. In short, there was not one single person in all that society at Durham, that had the least idea of living and labouring for the discovery of truth, and for the spread of truth amongst his fellow-men. There was not one that seemed to have the least idea, that it was any concern at all of his to compare Methodist theology with the teachings of Christ and his apostles, to endeavour to ascertain for himself what was truth and what was error, and to labour for the unlimited improvement of the understandings and hearts of his fellow-men. They were all alike in this respect.

Durham was in the Sunderland circuit, and Mr. Jones, the superintendant preacher, lived at Sunderland. It was my lot to go regularly round the whole circuit, preaching at every place in my turn. About one Sunday in three I preached in Sunderland,—another Sunday in the three I preached at Durham, and the other Sunday I spent at Houghton-le-Spring, Easington Lane, Hetton, Lumley, and Philadelphia. When at Sunderland I spent most of my time at Mr. Stephenson's. He was a free and friendly kind of man, but no way very intellectual. His wife was more free and friendly still, and perhaps the more thoughtful and intelligent of the two; but she had not passed beyond the common bounds. Among the persons who frequently came to his house were William Hardy and William Scott. William Hardy was one of the most trifling and laughing pieces of humanity that I ever met with in my life. Though a Methodist class-leader, he exceeded a buffoon in wild merriment. I believe he was exceedingly solemn in the class, as well as at the chapel, and in religious meetings generally; but in private, or in the fireside circle, his jests, his laughable stories, his puns, and other displays of wit and merriment, had neither bounds nor end. This was too much for me. I had no great objection to a little cheerfulness and relaxation at times, though my mind was generally occupied with serious subjects, and sometimes burdened with distressing cares: but William Hardy's utter levity, his continual merriment and laughter, were quite annoying to me, and many a time, both when in his company, and after he had left the company, I felt a wish that I might never be troubled with his presence more. William Scott was just about the opposite. He was a thoughtful, serious, sober, grave young man. He also seemed wishful to understand religion. Whether he ever had any thoughts that there was any religious truth beyond the boundaries of Methodistical theology or not, I can hardly say; but he certainly appeared desirous of cultivating his understanding, and of taking a journey into the regions of truth, to explore the spiritual world for himself.

There were two others friends that I met with at Sunderland, and in whose company I frequently spent a little of my time, that I esteemed more highly than the rest. Their names were Joseph and Grace Potts. They were both steady and exemplary Christians, and real inquirers after truth. They were members of the Old Methodist Society, but they were still of a liberal disposition, and could associate with those whom they thought lovers of truth and of religion, without regard to the sect to which they might belong. Though I belonged to the New Connexion, they showed me as much regard as they could show to a member or a minister of the body to which they themselves belonged. They took delight in rational and religious conversation. They were pleased to hear anything new that was true. They were also willing to have even their own peculiar opinions freely canvassed. They could both bear to hear what was to be said in favour of opinions which they thought erroneous, and in opposition to opinions which they thought true. Their spirit and manner were such as to make one feel perfectly at liberty in their presence, and to lead one both to open one's heart and to open one's lips in their society with the same freedom, as if one were sitting at his own fireside. They were both of them very tall people, and very straight as well; and I often thought their bodies were fair emblems of their souls. They had received no extra education in their younger days, nor had they been specially favoured with means of instruction afterwards; but they had naturally thoughtful, intellectual souls, and had made a good use of the few opportunities of gathering knowledge with which they had been favoured. I spent many happy hours in their society while on the Sunderland side of the circuit, and I have spent many still happier hours in their company since; and I think of them to this hour with the greatest satisfaction and pleasure.

They were worthy people, and I believe they are still as worthy as they ever were; I hope still worthier. They were true friends, and they have remained friends, while hundreds and thousands that have made greater professions, have failed me, betrayed me, and fled from me. They not only could love me and respect me when a minister in a Connexion that was at war with their own Connexion, but even when I was expelled from *every* religious denomination called orthodox, and disowned and denounced as a heretic and an infidel by the sects of the country generally. Though they never deserted the Wesleyan Methodists,—though they continued to the last hour of my intercouse with them both to attend the Methodist Chapel, and to respect and love many of the Methodist preachers, they still continued to read my publications, to receive me into their house when I visited Sunderland, and to show me, without any affectation or fuss, the truest kindness, the heartiest and most unsophisticated Christian good-will. God bless them. If it be our duty to pray for our enemies, it never can be wrong for us to pray for our friends. I say God bless them; and whether their thoughts and feelings towards me are the same as they used to be or not, I shall always remember my past acquaintance and intercourse with them with the truest pleasure, with the most unmixed satisfaction, and I shall ever feel disposed to believe, I imagine, that they were truly Christian people, real servants of God, true disciples of Christ, fair examples of Christian simplicity and purity, and of Christian love and gentleness.

Some tell me it is wrong to talk about other people in my life, but that is nonsense. How can a man write a history of himself, without giving, to some extent, a history of those with whom he has to do? What would be the history of Christ, without a history of his disciples and friends, and of the Scribes and Pharisees his enemies? Others say it does not look right to talk so freely of people as I do, till they are dead. But I think otherwise. I think it looks right enough, so long as a man speaks only the truth. Besides, it would be too late to write my life, if I were to wait till all that I have had to deal with were dead. I should be dead myself before that. But others might write it, say they. But *how* would they write it? *They* would be afraid of telling the truth, till the *children* of my friends and enemies were dead, and till my own children too were dead perhaps. I am doing just right, I believe, and I fancy I am likely to go on. I shall write whatever seems called for, whether it concerns the living or the dead, and I shall give people's names too in general. If I were to hearken to some people, I should never write my life. I must not write it now, while I remember things, lest I hurt people's minds; and if I wait till it is too late to hurt people's minds, nine-tenths of my life will be forgotten. I shall do nothing of the kind. I shall write now, and write with all freedom, as truth and righteousness may require, and leave results to God. And therefore I proceed.

Sunderland and Durham were twelve or fourteen miles asunder, and most of the country places where I used to preach, were from six to nine miles from Durham. I used generally to walk over from Durham to Sunderland, as well as from Sunderland and Durham to the various country places. On some occasions this was arduous work. My health was frequently not very good; my strength was not very great; so that I was frequently very much wearied and exhausted. Several times, while in this circuit, I had serious attacks of sickness and bowel complaint. I found that once or twice these attacks followed the use of Pork. I accordingly regarded Pork as the cause of these effects. I have since seen reason to alter my opinion on this subject. I now believe that the real cause of those attacks of sickness was the use of intoxicating drinks and tobacco. I have frequently used Pork since then; I eat it whenever it comes in my way; and it agrees with me in general as well as most other kinds of meat. At least it never causes any painful disorder in my system. In fact I have never once since I became a teetotaler, suffered from any such attack of stomach or bowel complaint on any occasion at all. My conviction therefore is, that the use of intoxicating drinks and tobacco so injured my system, and especially my digestive organs, as to make the use of things otherwise harmless and useful, injurious and dangerous. If my system had been in health, I should have digested the Pork, as I now do, and felt no inconvenience from it. But my system was *not* in health: the moderate use of intoxicating drinks, and the free use of tobacco, had *injured* the health of my system, and thus made me liable to sustain injury from things which would otherwise have been perfectly safe and even useful.

While I was in this circuit I had a most violent attack of

Influenza. On the April Quarter day I was taken with chilliness, and cold shiverings. Through the night I became exceedingly feverish. The next day I was much worse. I was even delirious, and obliged to keep to my bed. By the use of medicine I was relieved, but the weakness occasioned by this attack remained for some time. I was nevertheless expected to attend to my appointments in the country, notwithstanding my illness, and I was myself exceedingly unwilling to disappoint a congregation. I therefore set off a few days after the first attack of the Influenza, to a place about nine miles distant. I walked all the way, and preached when I got to the end of my journey; but I was dreadfully fatigued, and far from being well besides. I was so weak, in fact, that when I started on my journey, I felt as if I should be unable to walk a single mile: but I exerted myself to the utmost, and succeeded, as I have said, in reaching my appointment and preaching a sermon. But I should not do now as I did then: I would not now, on any account, place myself again in a situation in which I should feel myself *obliged* thus to act. The condition of a New Connexion Preacher was at that time one of very great slavery. The least omission of what was called his duty, might cause a charge to be preferred against him at the Quarterly meeting, and render it difficult for him to obtain his annual certificate to Conference. And the country people were so afraid of losing a travelling preacher's sermon, that they were very much inclined to believe that when a travelling preacher missed them, he did it without sufficient reason. Each country place paid so much at the Quarterly meeting, on condition of having so many Sunday, or so many week-night sermons from the travelling preacher, and what they paid for, they were very unwilling to lose. It seems a mystery to me now, how I could so long remain in such a situation: but I fancied that I had better opportunities of being useful as a preacher, than I could have in any other situation,—that the situation of a preacher afforded me more time to devote to study than any other situation would be likely to do; and this was the great inducement to remain in that situation. And it was best, very likely, that I *did* remain in it so long as I did. If I had left it earlier, I might have been less prepared for the labours and trials that awaited me. Even if I had exchanged my situation as a

Methodist preacher in the New Connexion, for that of a regular minister in some other body, I might have fallen perhaps under influences that would have unfitted me for much that I have since then been called upon to do, and led me into a way of life in which I should not have been so useful to my kind. I am inclined therefore to think, notwithstanding the painful feelings with which I look back on this portion of my life, that I was, while a preacher, in a situation that, on the whole, was best for me,—that I was gathering useful experience that I should not have been able to gather in another situation.

At Easington Lane, I used to stay at Joseph Love's. Joseph Love was the son of a Collier at Whitley, near Shields; and he himself, while a youth, had worked in the pit. By some means or other he contrived to save a little money, and began shopkeeping. He prospered in his new business, and now he had a large shop at Easington Lane, and was doing a good deal of business in other places besides. He had in fact become rather a rich man. He had had no education beyond being taught to read and to write a little, and even his ability to read and to write, I fancy, was not very considerable till after he became a man. He was a free, kind person, and his wife was as free and friendly as himself, and both together did what they could to make the preachers comfortable during the time which they spent in their house. They were both very kind to me. They took delight in spreading for the preacher a good table, in pouring out for him a good glass of ale or whiskey grog, and in supplying him with pipes and tobacco. They took care to give him a good, warm, comfortable bed; they laboured to make his stay with them agreeable by their kind and cheerful conversation, and they did what they could to secure for such preachers as they thought good for any thing, a large congregation. Their kindness to me I believe was even greater than to most. Both Joseph Love and his wife had got a very favourable opinion of me, and esteemed me very highly as a preacher. The first time I preached, the chapel was full, and it was full every time I preached afterwards. On Sundays the place used to be crowded, and people at times were unable to obtain admission. The sermons I preached were generally the subject of conversation with Mr. and Mrs. Love afterwards. They delighted in religious and theological conversation. They encouraged me to speak with the greatest freedom on every subject on which I had thought, and I told them in general all that was in my mind. We conversed on the prevailing errors of Methodistical theology, and on the foolish, the childish, and useless way of preaching which was generally in vogue. I pointed out to them in what particulars I thought the prevailing theology was false, what opinions were unscriptural and unreasonable, and what great truths and moral principles of Christianity were generally overlooked or misunderstood. They listened with as much pleasure as I spoke, and received with the greatest readiness whatever truth I unfolded to their minds. They did not pretend to agree with me while in truth they differed from me: they did not endeavour to draw me out in conversation for the purpose of taking advantage of my freedom of speech : they really *did* agree with me. They were truly wishful to learn the truth, as well as to bring others to understand it and preach it. They encouraged me to go on in my reforming labours, and were as sanguine as myself with respect to the success which would ultimately follow them. Still, kind as they were, they were the means of getting me into trouble. What I said to them, they as freely repeated to other people. I never told them to keep any secrets, and they never thought of keeping any. They conversed with the other preachers that came to their house, with the same freedom with which I conversed with them. This soon created an alarm in the mind of my superintendent, and the largeness of my congregations increased this alarm. He therefore began to use means to counteract my influence, and manifested a mean and persecuting disposition towards me, and to punish the country societies for showing greater respect to my preaching than to his, he refused to plan me at their places on collection days, that they might suffer a little in their finances. If he had planned me on the collection days, the people would have had larger collections ; while by planning himself on those days, the collections were reduced to a very trifle ; and thus he gratified his jealousy, by making it necessary for the societies to raise more money privately among themselves.

Mr. Jones also talked freely with Mr. Ward and Mrs. Ward of Durham, representing me as a dangerous young man, as a great heretic, and impressing upon them the necessity of doing something towards either lessening my influence, or bringing me to better views. Mr. Ward wrote to others in the Connexion, and endeavoured to spread the alarm respecting me amongst the leading influential members of the body; and it became manifest before the April quarterly meeting arrived, that efforts would be made by Mr Jones and his friends, both to prevent me from being stationed in the circuit for the following year, and to prevent me from being received into full connexion at the Conference. These things caused me and my wife considerable uneasiness, but we bore things patiently. We trusted in God, and believed that right and truth would triumph in the end.

While on the Sunderland side of the circuit, I was at times but indifferently provided for. At William Stephenson's I was always supplied with good and wholesome food; and if I slept there, I had a good and comfortable bed. But when appointed to take my meat or to lodge at other places, I was sometimes provided for very indifferently. One person that had agreed to take the preachers occasionally, treated me, the first time I went, to a piece of beef that almost filled the house with its bad odour : it was almost too bad to set before a dog. To this house I went no more.

A considerable portion of my time I was appointed to sleep at the house of a sailor. My bed was one of those little turn-up beds, and often disturbed me through the night with its creaking; but the mistress was a kind, decent body, and I was far from being uncomfortable.

There were a many curious persons in the New Connexion societies in the Sunderland circuit. Indeed, a very considerable number of the members of the Methodist New Connexion, and especially of the local preachers, were of a very indifferent character. One of them had had a large sum of money left him. When he got it, he bought a number of monkeys with part of it, I was told, and spent the other part as foolishly, and then had to live by keeping a gate on a railway belonging to one of the coal-pits. Another local preacher had made use of marriage as a means of raising himself above the necessity of working for his living. For a mean consideration, he had married a woman that he could not esteem; a person of whom he was ashamed. The consequence was, his wife and he were frequently quarrelling, and both tormented one another, and disgraced the society with which he was connected. Another man was an an endless talker, and with his talk mixed up a great amount of religious or irreligious cant. No one that knew him would trust this man; even the people that would come to hear him preach, never expected him to keep the truth in his private conversation. There was another, who lived at L——y. No one that knew him would have thought of trusting him: they knew that if he got into people's debt, he would never make an effort to get out: yet many would go to hear even him preach. There were others of a very different character; well-disposed, modest, virtuous people. But even these had very little information. They had no means of attaining the advantages of education while they were young, and the preachers made no efforts to give them instruction after they came to manhood. They were neither gathered into classes to receive useful instruction from the preachers, nor were they supplied with cheap and useful books. Indeed, the great object of the preachers generally appeared to be, simply to keep the circuits in such a state that they might be able to obtain their salaries: as for the diffusion of knowledge and the elevation of society, they appeared to have no concern whatever.

One man of whom I used to think tolerably well, was a plumber. One morning, while doing some work about a well, he fell in and was killed. He had a brother John, that I liked still better. Both John and his wife, I believe, were truly kind, religious people.

I ought perhaps to state one thing in reference to Mr. and Mrs. Ward, which did not come to my knowledge till some time after I left the Sunderland circuit. I stated that I was a smoker, that I smoked very freely. Some time after I left the Sunderland circuit, I was told that one reason why Mr. and Mrs. Ward did not like my company, was, that in consequence of my smoking habits, I carried about with me the odour of tobacco. At that time, I could hardly have believed that this could be a reason for people not liking one's company; but at present I can. The smoker carries about with him in general a smell which cannot but be disagreeable to persons who are altogether unused to tobacco; and I have no doubt that my love of tobacco would have its influence on the conduct of Mr. and Mrs. Ward. Still, they must have often had smokers before me, and snuff-takers too. Besides, if they could sit at table with a smoker, what should hinder them from sitting to converse with me after dinner was over, when placed at a far greater distance from them.

While I was at Durham, I joined the Temperance Society. The society at that time simply advocated abstinence from distilled spirits, allowing what was called the moderate use of wine and ale and porter. I attended one of their meetings in Claypath, but it was far from being a very interesting one. There was no speaking. One of the members read part of Dr. Beecher's sermons on Intemperance, and another read a little from another temperance publication, but no one delivered any address. The society was patronized by one or two Dissenting ministers of Durham, but those ministers seemed to take very little interest in its prosperity. I do not think any great good was done by the society. It might be the means of leading one or two persons to think a little on the subject of intemperance, but I fancy it never was instrumental in reforming a drunkard, or in exerting any perceptible influence upon the inhabitants of the city. The preacher that had been at Durham the year before me, (I mean the Methodist New Connexion preacher) had joined this society; but he had acted in such a way as to make himself and the society look very foolish and ridiculous. I said the society simply forbad the use of distilled spirits, while it allowed the moderate use of wine, and other intoxicating drinks. I ought to have said, that it forbad the use of distilled spirits as a *common drink*, but allowed them to be used as *medicine*. The preacher referred to, A. Thompson, illustrated the folly of this principle. He was very friendly with the Messrs. Thwaites, the drinksellers, and either the younger or the elder Thwaites had made him a present of a few bottles of spirit. He accepted the present, placed it in his cup-board, and I suppose used it occasionally; but he took care to paste upon each bottle a label with the word MEDICINE written large. This caused both him and the society, I say, to be greatly ridiculed, and well it might. What does it matter, if spirits *are* taken, whether they be taken in the name of *medicine*, or simply under the name of *brandy, whiskey, rum,* or *gin?* But Archibald Thompson was not remarkable for his regard to principle; he was always a temporizing young man. He would do right if it was perfectly convenient, but not otherwise, I imagine. He would be very *zealous* in doing right if there was much to be gained by it, either in the way of honour or pelf; but if ever he came to be tried, if ever he found himself in circumstances when equivocation or unfaithfulness to principle in any form seemed likely to prove safer or more gainful than truth and straight-forwardness, he would be sure to throw principle to the winds, and to accommodate himself to his interest. This at least always seemed to be his disposition.

It was while I was in the Sunderland circuit that I wrote the chief part of the discourse on the 'Character and Tendency of Christianity,' which I afterwards published. I used to ponder the subject on almost all my journeys, and write down such thoughts as struck me, whether on the road or in the houses of my friends, and when I got home I transcribed them into a book which I kept for the purpose. At this time, and indeed for a long time previous, the subject of this discourse was the principal subject that occupied my thoughts. It appeared to me to be a subject of the greatest importance, and I longed exceedingly to be able to explain it in such a manner as it deserved. It appeared to me that if it could once be clearly and fully shown, that the religion of Christ was calculated, if universally received and reduced to practice, to cure all the ills of life, and to raise society to the highest pitch of greatness and felicity, mankind could hardly *help* embracing it, and Christians hardly refrain from uniting together and employing all their powers for its universal diffusion. I imagined that if Christianity could be proved to be the enemy of every thing that was injurious to man, and the friend of every thing that was friendly to man's welfare, —I imagined that if Christianity could be proved to be the foe of all political corruption, of all war, oppression and slavery, of all craft, deceit and injustice,—that if it could be proved to be in all respects the friend of equity and liberty, of peace and prosperity, the hearts of men would immediately become enamoured of it, the objections of infidels be effectually overthrown, and the reformation and salvation of the world rapidly hastened. I therefore gave myself very diligently to the study of this subject. I made all my reading subservient to the illustration and proof of the great proposition which my discourse on the 'Character and Tendency of Christianity' is designed to illustrate and prove. Wherever I met with a book that promised to throw light upon the subject, I laid hold of it and read it with the greatest eagerness ; and whatever it might contain adapted to my purpose, I instantly made my own, and transferred it in substance to my common-place book ; so that before I left that circuit, I had covered a great amount of paper with my thoughts on that subject.

I also took a very lively interest in political affairs, at this period of my life. A little before this time, the Reform Bill had become the law of the land. From the passing of that measure, I, along with others, anticipated great good, both to Great Britain and the world at large. It was plain, however, that nothing could be done without good and faithful representatives of the people. The Reform Bill, it was plain, could be of no use to the country, except so far as it tended to keep out of the House of Commons corrupt and selfish men, and to place there men of equity and virtue, and of true and hearty good-will to mankind. I was therefore anxious to promote the election of men of equity and benevolence, and to exclude from the House of Commons corrupt and selfish men. The House of Commons appeared to me at that period, to be the greatest power in the universe, next to God. A good House of Commons appeared to me to be likely to accomplish the greatest possible good, both for our own country and for the world at large. It appeared to me that if the House of Commons could be made what it ought to be, the regeneration of the world would be effected soon. Only let the House of Commons, thought I, be thoroughly reformed, and the laws and institutions of our country might all be speedily and thoroughly reformed, and the nation at large be united in one great effort for the illumination, the reformation, and salvation of all the nations of the earth. I say I was, therefore, anxious to do something towards promoting the reformation of the House of Commons, and making it that instrument of good, which it seemed to me to be capable of becoming. At the same time, it had begun to be very plain to me, that if the House of Commons was to become a virtuous body, the electors, by whom that house was formed, must become virtuous. It had begun to be plain to me, that if the electors were corrupt, they would easily be bribed to return corrupt men to parliament. It was also plain, that though the electors might not be corrupt, they might still be easily deluded, unless they were well-instructed and intelligent. The first thing therefore, and the most important thing too, seemed to be to enlighten the public mind, to make the masses of the people intelligent and virtuous, and it was for this purpose partly that I wrote the discourse on the Character and Tendency of Christianity. I was in hopes that it would tend both to show people that Christianity was every way worthy of their acceptance, and to induce them, by convincing them of its loveliness and excellency, to place themselves under its authority. I can truly say, that at this period of my life, the great object that I had in view was to promote the happiness and welfare of the world, by the diffusion of simple, practical Christianity amongst the people. The reformation and welfare of the world by the reformation of the legislature, the reformation of the legislature by means of the reformation of the electors, and the reformation of the electors by the diffusion amongst them of the simple, practical, elevating principles of the religion of Jesus Christ, were the subject of my daily thoughts, and the object of my most earnest longings.

I must also acknowledge, whether I be smiled at for the thought or not, that at that period of my life I had a wish to take part in the legislative affairs of this kingdom myself. I had an idea that I might one day be qualified for such a work, and that if it should ever happen that a place in the legislature should fall to my lot, I might be of service there. I accordingly resolved to acquire what political knowledge I could, and also to amass as much as possible of such other kinds of knowledge as were calculated to qualify me for forming a correct judgment on matters of law and government, as well as on other questions affecting the interests of society. It was partially under the influence of these thoughts that I purchased *Blackstone's Commentaries, Montesquieu's Spirit of Laws, Grotius De Jure Belli et Pacis, Chateaubriand on Revolutions, De Lolme on the English Constitution, Gisborne's Duties of Men*, and a number of other works on Law, Government, and History. These I read with great attention and care, and the more I read, the more did I feel the necessity of great reforms, both in the laws and political institutions of the country. Still, even at this time it was plain to me, that no great reform could be effected in the country, unless the people *themselves* were instructed and reformed. To me it was plain even then, that the most important of all reforms was *personal* reform,—that the greatest of all wants was the want of individual knowledge and virtue, and that whether much was to be done by political action or not, it was plain that much was to be done for the benefit of our country and for the welfare of the world by the spread of knowledge, and the diffusion of righteousness, throughout society at large.

I may here observe, that my political feelings gradually cooled down from this period, and though the thoughts of future political action did not all pass away, they gradually became more and more like shadows, and less and less like realities. I gradually gave myself more and more to the promotion of *personal* reform, to the spread of truth and righteousness amongst mankind. I came to see more and more clearly, that the illumination and moral elevation of the people was not only the *greatest* thing, but *every* thing,— that personal reform included all reform, and that without personal reform, no reform of any worth or importance could ever be effected, and I gave myself accordingly to the promotion of personal reform with all my soul.

Before I bid farewell to Durham and the people, I may state, that one reason assigned by Mr. Ward for his opposition to Thwaites, was his opposition to R. Thwaites's business. On what grounds he was opposed to the drink-selling and pawn-broking business, I cannot exactly say. Whether it was because he thought them really immoral, or because he regarded them as disreputable, I cannot tell. I am rather inclined to think that it was their disreputableness that offended him more than their immorality; that he thought more of the light in which those businesses were regarded by certain people, than the mischief they were doing to the interests and morals of the community. Ward was a good deal of an aristocrat; his wife, I am told, was a member of the Gore family, and a relation of the Marquis of Stafford. He did himself, as an attorney, stand rather high, and anything that appeared low and disreputable would of course be an offence to him.

Mrs. Ward was frequently sent for from different places to preach anniversary sermons. The people who invited her, had no idea that she could preach well; but they knew that she would draw a large congregation, and offered them an opportunity of getting a larger collection than they would otherwise get. Almost all the sectarian congregations act on the same principle of inviting such persons to preach their anniversary sermons, as will draw the largest company together, and secure the largest collection. It matters not whether the man be a preacher of truth or of falsehood, whether he be a wicked hypocrite, or a truly Christlike instructor of mankind, whether he bawl and rant, or speak forth words of soberness, whether he be mad or of sound mind, whether he be a good, exemplary Christian, or an unprincipled immoral man, if he be likely to draw a large congregation, and to afford people an opportunity of getting a large collection, they will generally invite him. It was on this ground that they in-invited Mrs. Ward to preach their anniversary sermons; they knew that a woman would attract more hearers than a man, and that a woman who rode in her own carriage, and who was a distant relation of an aristocratic family, would attract a larger audience than another woman, and therefore they invited her.

Mrs. Ward was a great helper to some of the Connexion funds, especially the Missionary fund. She had an annual Bazaar, and the profits of it she divided between the Missionary fund of the Connexion, and some other fund under the direction of some other denomination. She generally raised about twenty pounds a year for each of these funds, and had, as a recompense, the pleasure of seeing her name in the public minutes of those bodies, with a published vote of thanks.

But to return to my own affairs.

It is the custom of circuits, at the April quarterly meeting, to appoint representatives to Conference. The common custom was for each circuit to appoint one preacher and one layman, as representatives. In case a circuit found it difficult to pay the expenses of two representatives, it was customary for them to send a preacher one year and a layman another. At this quarterly meeting the circuit appointed me to represent them in Conference. Among their reasons for so doing were the following. In the first place, they had not confidence in Mr. Jones: they did not believe that he would truly represent their wishes and interests in the Conference. They believed on the contrary, that he would endeavour to prevent them from obtaining their wishes; that he would set himself in opposition to what the circuit desired. In the second place, it was found that I should be obliged to go to Conference, whether appointed to go as a representative by the circuit or not; and as it was found that by appointing me as their representative, they would be able to save expense, I was requested to allow myself to be appointed as the circuit representative. This was no way disagreeable to me: on the contrary, I expected to be able to plead my own cause to better advantage, with respect to the restoration of my year, if admitted into Conference. Accordingly, I agreed to be their representative. This gave rise to fresh commotions. Mr. Jones was excited beyond measure, and besides endeavouring to stir up the circuit against me, he sent letters all round the Connexion, to excite the feelings of the superintendents and leading men in different parts against me. Things had come to such a pitch, that at the adjourned quarterly meeting it was thought necessary to appoint a lay representative to go to the Conference in *addition* to myself. The meeting accordingly appointed Mr. Joseph Love, of Easington Lane, a friend of mine, to that office. Mr. Jones was now more violent than ever. He declared his determination to go to Conference, whatever might happen, and intimated that the consequences of what the circuit had done, would be terrible enough, both to them and to me. Still the circuit persisted in its course, and I and Mr. Love remained its delegates to the Conference.

The Conference was held that year at Nottingham. Mr. Love and I reached Nottingham on the Saturday evening previous to Whitsuntide. It was the custom and the duty of the superintendent preacher of the circuit where Conference was to be held, to write to all the circuits to ascertain what persons were appointed by them as their representatives to Conference, to provide for them homes during their stay at Conference, and then to write back to the representatives to tell them where their homes would be, or at what houses they would be quartered. The superintendent of the Nottingham circuit however, John Bakewell, refused to provide homes for me and Mr. Love, and neglected altogether to write to us. He had received Mr. Jones's account of our election, and had taken upon himself to become both judge and executioner in the affair. He had chosen to decide a question that Conference alone had authority to decide; and he had chosen to decide it without hearing the accused at all. This was a most unconstitutional and criminal mode of proceeding, and in any man not known to be a thorough-going Conference man,—in any man suspected of having a particle of independence in his soul, it would have met with severe rebuke or punishment. But John Bakewell was known not to be a man of that kind. He was known to be a man ever ready to help the strong, to vote for the ruling party; hence his crime was allowed to pass uncensured. But to return, J. Bakewell's conduct did not altogether dishearten us, though we could not but regard it as exceedingly unreasonable and unjust. What right had he to take upon himself to decide that we were unduly elected? His place was to provide for our accommodation according to custom and law, and leave it to Conference to decide whether our election had been legal and constitutional or not. But John Bakewell knew which was the powerful and which was the weaker side, and knew that by his great zeal to mark his disapprobation of our election, he would gratify the leading or the ruling party in the Conference. Mr. Love and I, when we found that no place was provided for us by Mr. Bakewell and the committee, retired to an Inn, and provided ourselves with lodgings and with food. About ten o'clock at night a message came to request us to go to Mr. Sutton's shop. Mr. Sutton was a bookseller in Nottingham, and one of the leading members in the New Connexion. His son too was a very active and influential person in the Connexion there. When we got to Mr. Sutton's shop, we found Mr. Bakewell and some other preachers, along with Mr. Sutton, waiting for us. They instantly began to question us in the most insolent manner, and then proceeded to revile and banter us, treating us as if we were slaves or convicted criminals. We reasoned with them for a short time, but finding ourselves unable to make any impression upon them, we left them, and retired to our lodgings. Next day, Sunday, Bakewell and his counsellors began to be ashamed of their proceedings. They found that they had not only acted illegally, but that some of the Nottingham people were very much grieved at the idea that some of the delegates to the Conference had been obliged to seek lodgings and accommodations at a public Inn. After the morning's service in the chapel, Mr. Bakewell came to us, and showed something like repentance for his previous proceedings, and told us that if we thought well, we might have accommodations at the house of Mr. S——. We accepted the accommodation, and remained at Mr. S——'s during the Conference. When Mr. Bakewell had provided us a house, he then did me the honour to request me to preach at one of the chapels in the circuit, and I complied with his request. It now began to appear that the hasty, the unreasonable, and unconstitutional proceedings of Mr. Bakewell and his counsellors, had awakened considerable sympathy in our behalf, and that however strong the feeling amongst the Conference members was against us, there was still some portion of feeling in our favour.

On Monday morning, at the appointed time, I and Mr. Love went to Conference. After singing and prayer, the names of the circuits were read over, and the names of the delegates for each circuit called for. They had not gone far with this part of the business, before they came to a circuit which had sent the younger preacher instead of the superintendent. On other occasions this matter would not have excited the least discussion; it would have passed by as a matter of course; for each circuit was understood to have the right of sending which preacher it thought best to represent it in Conference: and indeed what would the right of representation be, without the right of choosing their own representatives? But on this occasion this case occasioned great discussion, and led to a considerable number of motions, amendments, counter motions, and counter amendments. It was known that my case would have to be decided afterwards, and the leading members of Conference, anxious to be able to decide against my election with some appearance of consistency and legality, were wishful to take advantage of this case, to pass some law or resolution which might furnish them with a pretext for excluding me. William Shuttleworth moved that a note should be placed on the public minutes, stating that in this case the superintendent minister was ill, or unable to attend Conference on account of some particular cause. This proposal however was founded on a palpable falsehood, and was rejected; so he made another, which met with a similar fate. James Dixon of Sheffield then came forward, and after blustering awhile in his usual style, proposed another motion more ridiculous than even Shuttleworth's had been, which was instantly set aside, or made to give place to another motion or amendment. How the matter was at last disposed of, I do not recollect; I believe no motion at all was passed, but that the appointment of the circuit was received as good and legal, without any qualification whatever. At length they came to *my* case. The first motion was that I should be excluded while the matter was discussed. This was both unusual and unconstitutional, but it was carried, and I was obliged to withdraw. If I mistake not, Mr. Love was not excluded during the discussion. The discussion continued for a length of time. Who spoke in favour of my election, and who spoke against it, I cannot tell; nor can I tell on what grounds the Conference at last came to its decision; but after a long discussion, they came to the decision to exclude me from the Conference, and to appoint Mr. Jones, the superintendent preacher of the Sunderland circuit, as the circuit representative in my place. This was still more unconstitutional. A person elected by the circuit as its representative, and elected according to rule, was excluded without any rule authorizing such exclusion; was excluded in *opposition* to all rule and to all custom; while *another* man, whom the circuit had *not* chosen, whom the circuit had *refused* to choose, because they believed, that so far from representing their views and seeking to obtain their wishes, he would altogether *mis*represent their views, and labour to *cross* their wishes; I say this man who was positively rejected by the circuit, was chosen by the Conference to be the circuit's representative in Conference, while the preacher chosen by the circuit, was excluded by the Conference. This was one of the most shameless and daring outrages upon the laws and constitution of the New Connexion, that it was possible for Conference to perpetrate. After all, they were afraid to carry out their decision. They therefore appointed a deputation to wait upon me and Mr. Love, *to ask our consent to the measure.* After thinking the matter over, and talking the matter over together, Mr. Love and I thought, that unreasonable and unconstitutional as their proceedings had been, it would be best to offer no further opposition to them, except to *protest* against them. We accordingly left them to pursue their course, but refused to sanction their proceedings, or to take upon ourselves any responsibility for them. Mr. Love and Mr. Jones were therefore admitted into Conference, and I was shut out.

After awhile the question of my admission into full connexion came before the Conference. The first point to be settled was, whether the year that had been taken from me, on account of my marrying before the close of my probation, should be restored to me. On this point there was a long and somewhat sharp discussion; but the decision of the majority of Conference was, that the year should be restored. The majority in my favour was not very large, but it *was* a majority. The next point for consideration was, whether I was a suitable person to be received into full connexion. The first question was, Were my abilities sufficient? That was decided unanimously. The next was, Were my labours acceptable to the people? That was also unanimously decided in my favour: and so was every other question, until the Conference came to the question concerning opinions. Here there was a lengthy discussion, and a warm one too. Some contended that I was heretical in my belief; others that I was sound: some contended that I denied certain leading doctrines of the gospel, others contended that I did no such thing; that I simply viewed those doctrines in a somewhat different light from others, and used a somewhat different phraseology in stating and explaining them. It was at length resolved that a deputation should be appointed to wait upon me, to ascertain from me personally what my views on the subjects under debate were. The deputation accordingly waited upon me, and they and I had a lengthy conversation on the doctrine of the Trinity, on the Godhead of Christ, on the doctrine of the Atonement. They were satisfied with my explanations on those subjects, but wished to have my sentiments on the *Trinity*, the *Godhead of Christ*, and the Atonement in writing. I accordingly drew up the following statement,

'With respect to the Divinity of Christ, I believe it is taught throughout the New Testament, and I know not how any one can question it, without questioning the truth of Scripture.

'3. I believe the sufferings and death of Christ were properly propitiatory, expiatory, or sacrificial; that they were *necessary as a satisfaction* in *some* way; that without them God could not forgive sin, so far as we can learn,—that through them 'God can be just, and yet the justifier of the ungodly that believeth in him.'

'4. On the TRINITY, I would say, that the Scriptures uniformly speak of the Father as God, of the Son as God, and of the Holy Ghost as God; and they uniformly speak of the Father, Son, and Holy Ghost, as we speak of three persons. But what mode of existence in the Divinity it is that gives rise to this manner of speaking, I know not—it is a mystery.

When this statement was submitted to the Conference, the discussion was renewed: some contended that the statement of my views was perfectly satisfactory, others that it was not satisfactory at all. One man contended that I had said no more than a Socinian or a Unitarian would say, another, Abraham Scott, replied, that a Trinitarian *ought* to say no more. At length the question was put, whether my statement of views on the subjects under question should be received as satisfactory, when the matter was decided by a large majority in my favour.

The next question was, Should I be received? That was decided in my favour by a still larger majority.

The next question was, Should I be *publicly* received? This also was decided by a very large majority. At this stage of the business Mr. Wall, the preacher appointed to propose questions to the young ministers that were to be received, before the public congregation, stated that he dared not undertake to propose the questions to *me*,—that he should be afraid of some *difficulty* arising, which might cause confusion in the public service. Other ministers told him that he had no need to be afraid,—that he would have no more trouble with me than with the rest. They were unable however to quiet his fears, and before he could undertake to question me publicly along with the rest of the young men that were to be received into full connexion, he must have an interview with me privately, and know from myself particularly what were my objections to the statement of doctrines contained in the rules, or to the wording of those doctrines in that statement. I met him and satisfied him that he need apprehend no unpleasantness. When the time came for the candidates to be publicly received, I answered the questions without making any particular remarks, contenting myself with having previously stated what words or forms of expression I considered objectionable, and in what sense I should use those words, if I *did* use them. And thus commenced my career as a travelling preacher in full connexion. Every day of Conference, from the first to the last, the feeling of the people assembled, became more and more in my favour. At first there was a mighty torrent of feeling against me, and but a very slender stream apparently in my favour: in a day or two the torrent that beat against me became weaker, and the stream that ran in my favour stronger. On the third day the feeling was on the whole in my favour, and my opponents were in the minority. On the fourth and fifth days the majority in my favour was very great, and the minority had fallen very low: and at the close I stood well with four-fifths of the people, and perhaps with more.

Now the question was, to what circuit should I be appointed. Several requested to have me, but none were so anxious or importunate as Mr. Love. He was exceedingly desirous that I should be returned to the Sunderland circuit. But I could not be returned to the Sunderland circuit as a married preacher, without being appointed the *superintendent* of the circuit. The circuit had but *one* married preacher, and one single one, and the married one must of course be superintendent; and to make me superintendent was an honour which many were unwilling to confer upon me. The superintendent had also an amount of influence with which they were unwilling, as yet, to entrust me. Though I had given them satisfaction in general with respect to the soundness of my belief, and though there had never been an objection raised against me on the ground of abilities and the like, they had had proof sufficient that I was accustomed to think for myself, and to speak and act for myself, and that I was therefore a dangerous man. The office of superintendent was in general reserved for persons who had been well tried, or who, whether well tried or not, had given abundant proof that they would yield implicit obedience to the orders of Conference, and devote themselves unreservedly, in all cases, to the interests of the Connexion, or to the will of the ruling party in the Connexion. Besides, there was a probability that if I was appointed the superintendent, I should have a place in the following Conferences; and this was a privilege not to be granted to one who had already awakened fears in the minds of many, both with respect to the soundness of his belief, and the regularity of his proceedings in matters of discipline. It was therefore decided that I should not return to the Sunderland circuit. I could not be returned as a *single* man, for now I was in full connexion, and entitled to a house and furniture, and quarterage for my wife and my child; and I could not be returned as a *married* man, because in that case I must be the superintendent of the circuit, and that was a thing not at present to be allowed. Mr.

Love did his utmost to induce the Conference to comply with his request, and with the request and wish of the circuit that had sent him; but to no purpose. His efforts and entreaties were all in vain, and when he found himself unable to accomplish his object, he left the Conference before the close of its sittings, and returned in grief and disappointment to his own home.

The next person who put in his claim for me was James Dixon, the representative from the Sheffield circuit; the man that had got up blustering at the opening of Conference, in order to propose some resolution that should have the effect of excluding me from the sittings of Conference. His conduct in Conference had given me but a very unfavourable idea of his character and abilities, though I had not seen much of him. A further acquaintance made me think worse of him. He was, in fact, an ignorant, forward, blustering, self-conceited, overbearing, vain and foolish man. And such was the light in which he was regarded by most, if not by all. Notwithstanding this, he was in great honour at Conference. He was *wealthy*, and the leading men of the Conference *wanted* wealth, to replenish their funds. He rode in his own carriage, and it seemed to reflect honour upon the Conference, in the estimation of many, to have a man among them who rode in his own carriage, whether he was a man of sense and principle or not. Besides, he had lately come from the Wesleyans, and many in the New Connexion prized him the more highly on that account. They always rejoiced greatly in a proselyte from the Old Body, especially if he were a man of wealth. I suppose they hoped that the acquisition of such persons would attract the attention of other persons in the Wesleyan body, and tend to draw them over in time. They therefore made James Dixon a great man in the Conference. They had already made him the first man in the Sheffield circuit, and now they were making him the first, or one of the first, in the Conference, and in the Connexion generally. Among other offices, he had, if I mistake not, a place on the Stationing Committee, the Committee for stationing the preachers. He came to me one day, and catching hold of me by the front of my coat, and staring me in the face through his spectacles, while the fumes of his wine came full upon me on the wings of his breath, he said, 'Well, my man, have you any objections to be my man?' I said I had no wish to be any one's man. 'Well, but you know what I mean,' he replied, 'have you any objections to go to Sheffield, and work under me?' I said, 'I have an objection to be under any body.' 'Well,' he said, 'but you know what I mean, have you any objections to be stationed in our circuit, to go with me to Sheffield?' I said, 'I had no particular objections, but I had rather go to Sunderland, if the Stationing Committee should think well to appoint me to that circuit.' 'Aye,' said he, 'but you won't go there; so you had better go with me;' and then left me. It was plain to me from this interview, that James Dixon considered himself the master of the circuit in which he lived, and the master of the preachers stationed there as well; and I afterwards found that he *was* so to a very great extent. He was especially the master of the preachers, just making use of them as he thought fit, for the accomplishment of his purposes. The preachers were his tools, his willing tools, of course, but no less his tools for that.

At that time Mr. Allin lived at Sheffield, as a supernumerary preacher; he lived in one of Dixon's houses, and was one of his near neighbours. Dixon, too, I was told, had lent him money, and had made him a present as well. Allin was therefore entirely at his will. And there were very few preachers in the Connexion but would be willing to follow Allin, in supporting any one whom he might choose to support. Well, my name was put down for Sheffield. I was appointed to be stationed there as a third married preacher. Now Sheffield had never had three married preachers before, and many of the leading members of the circuit were unwilling to have three married preachers. They had houses and furniture for only two, and they considered the income of the circuit to be unequal to the support of three. As soon, therefore, as a copy of the stations, as they stood at the first reading, was transmitted to Sheffield, a circuit meeting was held, and a resolution passed against the appointment of a third married preacher, and a person was sent to Conference to demand that the appointment should be altered. Mr. Ingleson, the person sent by the meeting, came and laid the decision of the circuit meeting before the Conference. The Conference, however, refused to alter the appointment. James Dixon insisted upon its remaining as it was, and, I am told, became answerable for the extra amount that would have to be raised for the third married preacher's support;

that is, he engaged that either the circuit should be brought to raise the additional sum, or that he would make up the deficiency himself. I was accordingly appointed to Sheffield. Andrew Ingleson, the person who had been sent to Conference by the circuit meeting to remonstrate against the appointment of a third married preacher, told me, that the circuit had no objections to *me*,—that it was not against *my* being stationed there that they objected; but simply against the appointment of a third married preacher, and the consequent additional expense that would be entailed upon the circuit: and when it was finally settled that I must go to Sheffield, he assured me that I should be most kindly received, and expressed his belief that my labours would be useful there.

The Conference closed, and I returned to Durham. As I have intimated, they had but two preachers' houses at Sheffield as yet, so that there was no house provided for me. An arrangement was therefore made, to the effect that I should remain one month at Durham, and that the preacher who was appointed to succeed me at Durham should take my place at Sheffield for a month, to afford the circuit an opportunity of procuring me a house and furniture. I accordingly returned to Durham with the expectation of remaining there a month. There was another reason why it was decided that I should remain a month at Durham. Every day we were expecting an increase to our family. My wife was not therefore in a fit or safe state for removing. It was hoped however that in the course of a month or five weeks, we should be able to remove without great difficulty. I arranged accordingly. But I had not been at Durham many days, when I received a letter from Mr. Dixon, stating that I must come to Sheffield immediately,—that the circuit was now just in the right state for welcoming me, and that if I did not go at once, there would be a serious disappointment, &c. He gave me to understand in his letter, that he was conveying the will of the circuit generally, and that the circuit would expect to see me in my place on the coming Sunday. This was quite unlooked for. I however was wishful to meet the views and wishes of the circuit, and therefore set to work, packed up my things, sent them off to Bramley, my native place, and started with my wife and my mother, who was at that time staying with us, for the same place. We reached Bramley late on the Wednesday evening. It was a most trying journey for my wife. She suffered very greatly. She however reached her journey's end in safety. Next morning our little daughter was born. The day after, or the day but one after, I most reluctantly left her in care of my parents and friends, and went to my appointment at Sheffield. After preaching on the Sunday, and doing what else I was obliged to do, I returned to Bramley, and spent the remainder of the week with my wife. On the Saturday I returned to Sheffield again, preached in my appointments on the Sunday and some other days, and then returned to Bramley again. And thus I continued to do for a month, going backwards and forwards a distance of about forty miles every week. On one occasion I walked the whole distance on foot, and on every occasion I walked a considerable part of the way. We had only had about forty pounds a year up to this time, with the exception of the help that we received occasionally from friends; so that our funds were very low. I was unable therefore to ride, without going into debt; and that was a thing I was not willing to do.

At length a house was provided and furnished, and my wife and children accompanied me to Sheffield. The house was near to Scotland-Street Chapel; it was a part of the chapel estate. It had been used as a ware-room or a lumber-room in connection with a foundry on the other side of the street. It was an inconvenient house, and in a very disagreeable situation; but we were glad to be in a house by ourselves, and we felt ourselves now very happily circumstanced. I met with the greatest encouragement in the circuit. The congregations were exceedingly large; the numbers in society were also large, and every week additions were made to the societies, as well as to the congregations. The chapels were generally crowded, and as to the principal chapel, in Scotland-Street, it frequently happened that numbers were unable to obtain admission in the evening. The preachers with whom I was stationed were at this time very friendly, and on the whole were agreeable colleagues. They were William Burrows and Andrew Lynn. Mr. Allin too was very kind, and so was Mr. Haslam, another superannuated preacher then living at Sheffield. All things, in fact, seemed now to smile upon us, and our lot was an exceedingly pleasant one. After awhile a better house was provided for us, in a more airy and agreeable part of the town ; this was an addition to our comfort. There seemed now scarcely anything left for us to covet or enjoy. Our cup of blessing seemed to be full and running over. I laboured with the greatest pleasure. I read, and wrote, and studied, and preached, with the greatest delight. I felt myself perfectly at home, both as it regarded my labours, and as it regarded the society, in general, amidst which I was placed. And my wife was as happy as myself!

There were three chapels then in use by the New Connexion in Sheffield, Scotland-Street Chapel, the oldest one of all; South-Street Chapel, a new one, built at the opposite end of the town, and Bow-Street Chapel, a large, substantial, well-built and commodious chapel, that had been erected by a body called *Independent* Methodists, a kind of Methodists who disapproved of hired preachers. This body had decreased, and their chapel had become a burden to them. Some of them, wishful to be rid of their pecuniary responsibilities, proposed a union with the New Connexion; and others, not prizing much, perhaps, the principle of an unhired ministry, acceded to the proposal. Several had stood out against the union, but they were overruled by the rest, and the union accordingly took place. The chapel was made over to the Connexion, and at this time the congregation attending there, though not so large as the congregations at the other chapels, were still very good.

As I have said, Scotland-Street Chapel was the *most* crowded; it was here that numbers were obliged from time to time to go away for want of room. It was not long before the *enlargement* of this chapel was proposed. Here disputes arose. Many were *for* an enlargement, but others were *against* it; and of those that were *for* an enlargement, some were for one plan, and others for another. Mr. Dixon seemed wishful to have the whole concern in his own hand; others were unwilling to trust him so far; and now became very apparent to me the existence of two parties in the circuit, one headed by Allin and Dixon, and the two preachers who were my colleagues, and the other headed by Andrew Ingleson, James Cutler, W. Birch and others. There were many meetings on the subject, but all of them ended unhappily. Many plans were proposed, but none of them met with general acceptance. Some were afraid of losing money; and others were unwilling to pull down the chapel which had been rebuilt at a considerable expense so short a time before. Some were afraid, that though the congregations were exceedingly great at present, they might not always be so, and that a larger chapel might involve them in serious difficulties: and others were afraid, that if the chapel were enlarged, the job would fall into the hands of Dixon, and would lead to an increase of his power in the circuit, and be made a means of profit to him. For now I began to discover, that Dixon was not that man of liberality which some had represented him. I began to discover, that though he had abundance of money, he was not very willing to part with much; that though he was very rich, he was anxious to be a good deal richer, and had no objection to make profit even by the erection of chapels. He employed his own joiner and builder in the erection of chapels, formed contracts like a master builder, taking care to secure possession of the chapel to himself till the money expended was paid to him. Suffice it to say, that after numberless meetings, and many unpleasantnesses, the proposal for the enlargement of the chapel was abandoned. The chapel never was enlarged; it is not enlarged now, nor is it nearly full. The New Connexion have now only two chapels in Sheffield instead of three; and they have only two preachers. And the two remaining chapels which they have are but very indifferently attended.

But to return. Dixon now proposed to build a chapel himself, on the Western side of the town. He proposed to build the chapel at his own expense, and to hand it over to the Connexion for a certain sum to be fixed by himself, after the chapel had been found to answer. Mr. Allin, Mr. Haslam, and the two preachers who were my colleagues, *favoured* this proposal. Others *opposed* it, and it ultimately fell to the ground.

Soon after I went to Sheffield, I commenced a new class, and soon had from fifteen to twenty members. Most of them were young people, and several of them seemed to be very promising characters. Some of them continue religious to this day, and one, at least, still ranks among my friends, and is a most zealous advocate of the simple, unsophisticated principles of the gospel.

I also proposed a meeting of the preachers for mutual improvement in religious knowledge, and in the ability to write or compose. The proposal was agreed to, and Mr.

Allin, myself, Mr. Burrows, and Mr. Lynn, together with my brother Benjamin, who had then come to reside with me, began to meet together accordingly. We used to meet from week to week at each other's houses. Our plan of proceeding was this. At the first meeting, I read an article on the Character and Tendency of Christianity: this article was criticised; its sentiments and its style of composition were all subjected to free discussion. At the close of the meeting a subject was given to each person present, and each one was appointed to bring a treatise on his subject in writing, and to read it at a following meeting. We had only one treatise at each meeting, so that each member had four or five weeks to prepare his treatise. My pieces were generally tolerably lengthy, occupying frequently an hour or upwards in reading. Mr. Lynn's also were frequently pretty lengthy, and so were my brother's; but Mr. Burrows' pieces were always exceedingly small. He never brought more than a few pages; his longest pieces could be read in ten or twelve minutes; and at times he brought scarcely anything at all. In fact, Burrows turned out to be a dreadfully idle man. And this was not all. He had other faults. He was an endless smoker, and a greedy drinker; and he made use of his pastoral visits as a means of indulging in those vices. He would begin his rounds in the morning, calling here and calling there, drinking his glass and smoking his pipe at almost every house. When he had drunk ale and porter till he was tired, he would then complain of his bowels, and ask the friends, in a half kind of whisper, 'Have you a little brandy in the house? My bowels are rather disordered this morning; and I am afraid I shall be very unwell, unless the disorder be checked.' Thus he would swallow his ale, his porter, his wine, and his brandy even in the forenoon, accompanying all with a ceaseless and plentiful consumption of tobacco. Of course, if he drank so freely in the morning, he would not be backward to drink in the afternoon and evening. These habits of drinking and smoking were no doubt one cause of his idleness; they disabled him in fact for regular study, and close, continuous, mental exertion. They were the very things to render spiritual labour and toil a weariness to him. The consequence was, that he made no improvement whatever in knowledge, or in abilities in any way. On the contrary, his knowledge diminished, and his abilities as a preacher became less. He had to preach his old sermons over and over again, and frequently his addresses were composed of little else but noise and empty rant.

Among other subjects that I treated at these meetings were the following: *What is meant by preaching Christ?* or, *When may a minister be said to preach Christ and him crucified?* In this discourse I controverted the common notion, that preaching Christ meant preaching chiefly about his sufferings and death, about his divinity and atonement, and about justification by faith and the influence of the Holy Spirit, and showed, that to preach Christ, was to preach Christ's *gospel*, to preach Christ's doctrines, to preach what Christ himself preached, and to explain and enforce what Christ himself enjoined. I showed, that *he* most truly and properly preached Christ, who best unfolded and enforced the whole Christian system, without addition, and without curtailment. This I proved from Scripture, and then strengthened my proofs by quotations from John Wesley, John Fletcher, and others.

Another subject was, *What is the reason that Christianity has not prospered more in ages past; and what is the reason that it does not spread and triumph more rapidly at the present time?* This subject occupied me several meetings. I stated that the reasons why the gospel had not prospered more, were to be found in the misconduct of the church and of the Christian ministry, as I then called the sectarian priesthoods. I pointed out a number of particulars in which professing Christians and preachers of the gospel had acted unwisely. I referred to the mixture of men's inventions with the doctrines of Christ; to the rejection of Christ's doctrines and the substitution of false doctrines in their places; to the improper language frequently employed in stating Christian doctrines; to the foolish way of preaching that had been so prevalent for ages; to the erroneous manner in which Christian doctrines had been set forth, even by those who had not *rejected* them, &c., &c.

Among other subjects which I treated at these meetings were the following also; *The Scripture doctrine of Justification,—The duty of Christians to seek the salvation of their fellow-men,—The end of Christ's coming into the world,—Growth in Grace,—Christ's sympathy with his brethren a source of consolation, &c., &c.*

In addition to these meetings, I found that Mr. Dixon and the preachers were accustomed to meet once a week, to talk over the business of the society and the circuit, and to agree upon the best plan of proceeding in the leaders' meetings, and in the quarterly meetings. This plan it seems had been acted upon during the previous year. Dixon and the preachers, foreknowing what matters would come before the leaders' meetings and the quarterly meetings, considered, first, what side they should take; secondly, what plan they should propose for the accomplishment of their objects; and thirdly, what means they should employ, before the meetings came on, to bespeak the votes of other persons, and secure their attendance at the meetings. By this means Dixon and the preachers were enabled to gain their object in almost all cases.

From what I have already said, my readers will have perceived, partially at least, that I could not act exactly as a party-man; that I was not able to identify myself with all the measures and plans of Dixon and the other preachers. Such was the case. I frequently took the liberty of making objections to Dixon's proposals, and of opposing the arguments employed in their favour by him and by my colleagues. This led them frequently to modify their plans, and caused them at length to give up their private weekly meetings altogether.

Their next plan was to consult among themselves, apart from me, and then to sound me afterwards, and see how far my co-operation could be calculated upon. The person who was generally employed to sound me was Mr. Burrows. He was always most forward to take in hand any matter of that description. He delighted to please Mr. Dixon: he said, in fact, that Mr. Dixon's house was the only house where he could get a throughly good glass of wine. And sure enough, Dixon *did* keep stronger wine than most people, and as he was exceedingly free with the use of it himself, it was but natural he should be tolerably free in treating his preachers to a little.

Burrows had a very wheedling and unmanly way of trying to come round people. I never used to like to see him, when he had any particular object to accomplish. He would smile, and look half on one side, and half upward, and throw down his head, and appear so affectionate; oh, he never loved you so much, and he never was so pleased with your house, and he never liked your tobacco so well, and he never tasted a drop of better porter than you were giving him, in his life; and the circuit was never in such a prosperous or hopeful way, &c. &c. And then, oh, by the by, he would say, what do you think of such a plan, or such a plan? and this was his usual way of introducing matters. Every thing was complimented; every thing was excellent: he was delighted with every thing; he smiled at you, blest you, loved you, was quite delighted with you, and all this as an introduction to the question, if he dared to have put the question right out, 'Will you join me, and Mr. Lynn, and Mr. Allin, and Mr. Haslam, in trying to secure to Mr. Dixon the pleasure of having his own way at the next leaders' meeting, or at the next quarterly meeting?' I used to take very little notice of his wheedling, and I seldom used to return any answer to his praises, and blessings, and compliments, and smiles, but waited till he put off the question to which I knew all these things were the introduction, Then, before answering his question, I should begin to discuss the matter, and if he was unable to satisfy me of its goodness, should decline engaging to support the proposed measure. Indeed I generally, if not invariably, refused to pledge myself to the measures they might have in contemplation, choosing rather to wait till I heard them fairly discussed in the proper meetings. By this means I frequently annoyed poor Burrows: and as for Dixon, I used to vex him dreadfully. He was a very proud man, and exceedingly impatient of contradiction. He was used to govern in his workshop with absolute sway, and he expected to govern in the same manner in the church. If one of his workmen had made the slightest objection to obey his will, or had manifested the least hesitation, he would have been at once dismissed; and he was disposed to act, as far as he could, in the same manner towards persons in the church. After I had objected to some proposal of his in one of the meetings, I called, on account of some business or other, to see him in his factory. He took me round, and showed me the extent of his works, and the number of his men, and said, 'See, I can govern all this concern; and it is a pity if I cannot manage a poor paltry concern like the New Connexion.' Yet Dixon had more patience with me, I think, than with most people, notwithstanding. Indeed he got into a way of expecting that I should not favour his measures, unless I was satisfied with them. Hence he set to work, whenever he had a measure in contemplation, to try to convince me that it was right. He did not argue with me much personally, but employed Burrows to do so, and never was a more willing or laborious creature in any mortal's service, than Burrows was in the service of Mr. Dixon. Idle as he was as to *writing*, he never seemed idle when about the work of Dixon. If, after all his efforts in person or by proxy, Dixon failed to convince me that his contemplated measures were wise and just ones, he would look exceedingly surly and sour at me when he met me, though he seldom ventured upon open rebuke.

Poor Dixon was an intemperate man, as well as a vain, a foolish, a proud and selfish man. He was very fond of wine, and very fond of brandy too. He would occasionally step into our house, when we lived near the chapel, and ask for a glass of brandy and water, when he had any business that detained him a little about the chapel. On one occasion, I saw him literally drunk in the Leaders' meeting. There had been an horticultural dinner that day, and he and Mr. Allin had attended it. After the dinner, they came to the meeting. I said a *Leaders'* meeting, but I am inclined to think it was an adjourned Quarterly meeting. As soon as Dixon had begun to talk, it was plain to many present that something was the matter with him; to some it was plain that the man was drunk, and could not get his words out distinctly, or could not string words sufficient together to make a proper sentence. He would begin a sentence as if he meant to say something about the business before the meeting, and end it in the most ridiculous manner; as you have heard drunken people do, I dare say. And when he was not drunk, he was seldom, if ever, properly sober; he was, in fact, almost constantly soaked. I should fancy, that on his most abstemious days, he drank as much as would have made most people drunk.

Dixon was a thorough old Methodist, and brought his old Methodist habits with him into the New Connexion. He was especially a great proselyter. All the means that he could use with any appearance of decency, he *would* use, and *did* use, to induce his work-people to come to one of the

New Connexion chapels, and to join the society. He especially laboured to induce them to go to Bow Street Chapel. He had had a good deal to do in *buying* that chapel, and was in some measure responsible for the debt upon it, and he urged them to go there, I suppose, in order, that by pew-rents and other contributions, they might render his burden lighter. He was a very ignorant man; and he was besides very insolent, overbearing, and proud: yet this man was honoured beyond measure by many in the New Connexion. Poor Thomas Allin would do anything for him, and allow him to do anything with him. Dixon was very fond of preaching, and he at times succeeded in getting the preachers to let him preach for them. He was fond of appearing in the pulpit even when he had not the opportunity of preaching, and often put in a claim to be allowed to give out the hymns, and to open the service for the preacher. He was especially anxious to appear in public on anniversary occasions; it was like meat and drink to him to be allowed to bawl out the hymn, and jumble out the prayer before a crowded audience. And then he knew that if he once got into the pulpit, he would have at least some little chance of getting in a word of exhortation, either before or after the sermon, and this he generally contrived to do. At times his exhortation, as he would call it, was most ridiculous. If it came before the sermon, the preacher had need to be a man of tolerable self-command, to prevent himself from being disqualified for the sermon; and if it came after the sermon, the people had need to be exceedingly thoughtful and recollected, if they were to be preserved from forgetting what the preacher had said, and losing the favourable impressions which they might have received under the sermon. The burden of his exhortations was generally something to the following effect:—' My friends, you should all be Methodists; you will never make much out till you are Methodists. What should I have been if I had not been a Methodist? A poor paltry working man. But what am I now? Glory be to God; I can ride in my carriage. I can come to chapel in my carriage. I can go where I like in my carriage. Look what a factory I have. It is all with being a Methodist. If you want to be rich, if you want to get on in the world, you must be Methodists. Bless your souls for you, come and join class, my friends, directly. Let's have none of your excuses. Look what privileges you will have. I belong to the New Connexion. We have all liberty here: no masters here; no tyrannical conference, no tyrannical preachers. Bless you; I had not been in the New Connexion a year, before they sent me to conference.' And thus he would go on. He once got into my pulpit; but never more than once: and even then I fancy he would not have got in, if it had not been at the opening of a chapel which he himself had built. He had arranged the services, and was in the pulpit before I got to the place. But Mr. Allin generally had him in the pulpit with him. Indeed I question whether he ever was without him in the pulpit from about a few months from the time that Dixon joined the Connexion, to the time that Allin left Sheffield. Allin was naturally a kind and easy sort of man, and when he had got laid under obligations to a person, his power of resistance was gone altogether. He was not the most remarkable man for maintaining his integrity under trials of any description perhaps; but when he was *dependent* upon a person, in *debt* to a person, or expecting *gifts* from a person, he was a complete slave. And this was the relation in which he stood to James Dixon: he had had *help* from him, and he expected more; so that he was as perfect a slave as if he had been sold to Dixon, both body and soul together. He was the more compliant with Dixon, in consequence of difficulties and embarrassments in his circumstances. He was very poor; he had got sadly into debt in consequence of some building speculations, and he was unable to extricate himself. Thus his independency of mind was entirely gone. Dixon therefore used him just at his pleasure, and employed his influence and reputation for the accomplishment of any project which he might have in contemplation. He used him as his hack, and rode him terribly. This was seen and noticed by Allin's friends, and many of them were sadly grieved that he should lower himself so much. Many of them ventured to speak to him on the subject, and some of them spoke very plainly to him. One man said to him, 'Mr. Allin, I have often seen a man ride on a jack-ass, but I never saw a jack-ass ride upon a man till now.' But Allin was not to be easily cured. Dixon no doubt did for him what other persons were not disposed or not able to do. When Burrows was complained of for his anxiety to please Dixon, he said he had *need* try to please him, for there was no one else that kept a glass of wine worth drinking but Dixon. And so Allin, no doubt, might say, he had *need* be at Dixon's bidding, for no one was better able to help him with a little silver or gold than he.

But Dixon was not generous after all. He was a selfish man, and was niggardly enough, except when he expected good returns for his money. If he gave Allin fifty pounds, it would be in the full expectation that by means of Allin's influence he would be able to obtain a job in chapel-building, or in some other way that would bring him in a few hundreds. If he let Allin have a house for a little less rent than another person would have let him have it, it would be because it was a new house, and one in a long range of new houses, and because he expected that Allin's residing there would make the house let better after, and tend to bring tenants to the houses still unoccupied. If he gave Burrows abundance of wine, it was in expectation of services to be rendered in another kind. He once told me he had plenty of money, and hinted what he could do for me if he thought well : in short, he proposed, in his own way, to bribe me : but suppose I had taken the bribe, I must then have been his slave, his absolute slave.

I say this man of pride and selfishness, this man of ignorance and vulgar insolence, obtained the highest honours that the New Connexion had to give. He could not be president of Conference ; none but a travelling preacher could be president ; but he was every thing else. They made him circuit steward ; they sent him to Conference as a delegate ; at Conference they placed him on the stationing committee ; then they placed him on the annual committee, the committee on which the government of the Connexion devolves from Conference to Conference. They placed him then on the Irish Missionary committee : they made him corresponding member of the annual committee ; the member of greatest responsibility and influence in the whole Connexion. They made him corresponding secretary of the missionary committee : they appointed him as a deputation to visit Ireland, to inspect the Mission Stations, and to attend the Irish Conference as a representative of the English Conference. They made him every thing in fact, and yet all the time the people that put those honours upon him, knew that he was a foolish, an ignorant, an ill-behaved man. The only difference between the conduct of those parties and Allin's was this, Allin was ridden by the ass, while many of the leading members of Conference hoped to ride upon the ass; but none of them regarded him, either in point of intellect or manners, as an average man. I fancy nevertheless that those who expected to make much of him, were sadly disappointed in the end. I never heard of him giving much, except when there was a prospect of something to be gained; and I fancy he never had an opportunity of gaining much, without making good improvement of it.

He showed his meanness shockingly in some cases. When he went as deputation to Ireland, he refused to stop at the house where his companions stopped, it was not good enough for him, so he went and took lodgings at one of the principal Inns in the town; but on his return he charged the Missionary fund with his expenses, and his expenses were paid him.

When he found that he was not able to make much of the Connexion, he retired from office, and if he continued in the Connexion at all, he continued simply as a private member: and when the leading men of the Connexion found that they could make no use of him, they ceased to heap their honours upon him, and left him to his retirement unmolested.

While I was at Sheffield, R. Carlile came to lecture in the town. It was not long after his liberation from imprisonment. He was advertised in large bills as the CHAMPION OF FREE DISCUSSION. A considerable number went to hear him, and amongst the rest, several members of the different Methodist societies. Some of my friends printed an edition of my small tract, called 'A Few Hints on Various Subjects,' and distributed it at the doors of his meeting-place. On a copy of this tract he made some remarks in his lectures, which, with other considerations, led me to take some part in opposing his views. Some wished me to go and oppose him in public discussion; but I was not, at that time, prepared for such a work, so I refused to go. The Independent minister advertised a lecture in opposition to his views, or rather in opposition to Atheism, which was his great leading doctrine, and he had an exceedingly large audience. But the lecture was a poor one. There were many good things in it, but there was nothing like order or force about it. The lecture bore proofs of the lecturer's ability to treat the subject well, but it also bore proofs that he was either an idle man, or that he had not had sufficient leisure to prepare for the occasion.

Thomas Allin took occasion from the excitement created, to publish a new edition of his sermons on Atheism, with notes, at a comparatively cheap rate. What effect these sermons had, I cannot judge; I believe they were not quite useless.

Carlile's friends laboured hard to bring about a public discussion between Mr. Allin and Carlile, but without effect. Mr. Allin, I believe, offered to meet Carlile; but Carlile declined the offer, and left the town.

After Carlile's departure, some of his friends published a brief report of his lectures. When I read this report, I was amazed at the folly with which the lectures abounded, especially with the inconsistency of the lecturer's mode of reasoning. He advised people, in reference to religious matters generally, to believe nothing without the strongest possible demonstration. In fact, he went so far as to advise them to believe nothing in religion without ocular demonstration, or, in other words, nothing but what they could see with their eyes. He did at the same time show, that he expected people to believe *him*, on his *bare word*. He had no wish that they should ask for ocular demonstrations, or for demonstrations of any kind, in favour of *Atheistical* views. Atheistical views he wished them to receive on his own unsupported testimony; Christian views he wished them to receive on no testimony whatever. This led me to write and publish a small tract, entitled 'ced *Carlile's Logic*,' in which I exposed his inconsistency. The tract met with a ready sale, and had, I believe, a good effect. It went through two editions.

The objections which Carlile brought against Christianity, and the objections on which his followers chiefly dwelt in their conversations with others, were objections against its *tendency*. They charged Christianity with being the cause of oppression, persecution, bad government, and the like. They represented it as a religion of uncharitableness, intolerance and blood. They contended that the prevalence of Christianity was inconsistent with the peace and happiness of a nation, and that Christianity ought therefore to be exploded as a means towards national prosperity. On this subject I took up arms against them. I delivered a course of lectures in reply to their objections, and also published my work on *The Character and Tendency of Christianity*. In this work, and in the lectures which I delivered, I showed, that Christianity was *not* a religion of intolerance, of persecution, or of blood,—that it did not favour oppression or tyranny, despotism or slavery,—that, on the contrary, it was the friend of liberty, of right, and of brotherly equality,—that it was a religion of gentleness, and peace, and charity,—that its tendency was to bring oppression and persecution, war and slavery, as well as every other form of evil, to an end, and to establish freedom and peace, and to promote purity and joy, among all nations.

Another objection which was brought forwards against the religion of Christ was, that though it might be good in its *teachings*, it was wanting in *efficiency*,—that it had not *power* to cure the evils of society, or to reform mankind. On this subject also I lectured, and on this subject I wrote, though I was not able, at that time, to finish and to publish what I wrote.

About this period some followers and friends of Carlile commenced a periodical, called the 'FREE INQUIRER.' It was a poor thing in every respect. The talent of the Writers, and the workmanship of the Printers, were of the lowest order; and the principles it advocated were of the worst description. It did, nevertheless, promise and prophesy great things in behalf of itself. It spoke in great swelling words of vanity of what it would do. It was not long, however, before the work was brought to a close. It would not sell. It did not pay. After sending for it two or three times one Saturday, and being unable to procure it, I began to suspect that it was dead, and immediately prepared its funeral oration, and sent it to my Printer, with instructions to advertise it for publication on the following Tuesday. The 'FREE INQUIRER' *was* dead, and on the following Tuesday, the Oration came out. It was soon sold, and a second edition was called for. In this work I used strong language in speaking of the principles, the characters, and the conduct of those unbelievers who had published the '*Free Inquirer;*' but not stronger language than the occasion seemed to call for, nor stronger language than truth itself would justify. Neither this work nor the review of Carlile's logic has been republished since I left Sheffield, though the larger work on *The Character and Tendency of Christianity* has. Perhaps they may be reprinted bye and by. They would, both together, hardly make a penny tract, though they were then sold for a penny each.

This controversy with the unbelievers of Sheffield had a favourable influence upon my mind. It impelled me to greater diligence in study, and obliged me to write more freely and fully on several subjects. It also led me to see and to feel more fully than I had done before, the necessity of laying aside, and of separating from the pure doctrine of Christ, all human inventions. I saw clearly, that the strength of infidelity was in the errors and inconsistencies of theology, and that if Christianity was to be effectually defended against the assaults of unbelievers, it must be defended apart from all peculiarities of orthodox systems. It was plain to me, that in free and fair discussion between infidelity and orthodoxy, infidelity must have the advantage, and orthodoxy suffer a terrible defeat. This controversy therefore tended to strengthen my heretical leanings, and to prepare me more fully for becoming an evangelical or a theological reformer. It did at the same time tend to strengthen my faith in the truth of Christianity, and to increase my esteem and love for it. The more I examined Christianity, the more lovely and perfect did it appear, and the more truthful and divine did it prove itself to my mind. The more I was led to contrast Christianity with infidelity, the more did I feel, that infidelity was at least a terrible misfortune, if it was not a grievous crime, and that a firm, decided faith in Christian principles, was both rational and an exceedingly great consolation and blessing. My mind was therefore perfectly satisfied both of the truth and the infinite value of the religion of Christ, and a fresh impulse was thus given to my zeal for its universal spread through the world. I did, accordingly, in my sermons and speeches, at public and social meetings, exert myself to the utmost, to induce those whom I addressed, to use their influence, their talents, and their wealth, to the utmost, for the spread of the religion of Christ through the world. Whether I attended meetings of Tract Societies or of Sunday Schools, of Bible Societies or Missionary Societies, the great object of every address was, to impress people with the infinite worth of true religion, and to make them sensible of their obligations, as professing Christians, to use their best endeavours to confer that infinite blessing upon all mankind. My thoughts of the world's conversion were at this period exceedingly vivid. Often did I look forward with unspeakable delight and joyous anticipation, to the period when the various forms of evil afflicting the human family should pass away,—when the bright revelations of truth should chase error, and ignorance, and superstition, and crime, from all lands,—when the peaceful influence of the Gospel of Christ should hush the din of war, and stop the effusion of blood, and end for ever the cruelties of hate and strife,—when the liberal principles of the Gospel should break the fetters of the slave, dissolve his chains, and set him free,—when all diversities of sects, and all the various schisms of humanity, should lose themselves amidst the prevalence of brotherly love, and ardent universal charity. I say I laboured, at this period of my life, to the fullest extent of my ability, for the spread of the Gospel, and for the illumination and salvation of my fellow-men. I laboured, in fact, till I injured my health; and had it not been for a merciful Providence, who placed me in the way of a wise counsellor, I might long ago have perished from the earth. The particulars I may name hereafter. But though I injured my health, I increased my enjoyment of life. My thoughts, my visions, and anticipations were, at this period, of a truly delightful character, and they were to me as so many realities. I lived in the hopes and forethoughts of a happy future, as in a world of realities, and scarce a day passed, scarce an hour, in fact, in which my soul was not blessed in the thought of blessing others.

At this period of my life, I exerted myself very much to obtain a clear and powerful style of writing and preaching. I was exceedingly pleased whenever I met with a truly clear and powerful writer, whatever might be the subject of his works. The works of Cicero and Virgil in Latin, as well as some portions of the works of Ovid, and the works of Massillon in French, and the works of Robert Hall, and of Shakespeare, and of Milton in English, yielded me very great pleasure. I read them with the utmost relish, and most eagerly did I long to be able to express myself with something like the freedom and fulness, the clearness and the power of these great writers. I was especially fond of Shakespeare, Massillon, and Hall. Though I could not agree with their sentiments on many points, their manner of writing was exceedingly delightful to me. There seemed to be such a naturalness about them, such an indescribable charm, laying hold of the soul, and bearing it along in spite of itself, that I felt as if I never could read their writings too much. Since then my regard for what may be called the beauties of language, and the arts of rhetoric, has partially subsided. My only concern, for a long time past, has been to speak the truth with plainness and power. Every thing like art or ornament my soul has been disposed to spurn. Its wish, its effort, has long been to express itself with perfect nature, without regard to any particular rules, or to any particular examples of style.

While I was in Sheffield circuit, Joseph Rayner Stephens, who was a travelling preacher amongst the Wesleyan Methodists in the Ashton circuit, was suspended, on account of his connection with an Anti-state Church Association; and Doctor Warren was expelled on account of his opposition to Jabez Bunting in reference to the theological institution. These acts of the Wesleyan conference caused a great excitement throughout the Wesleyan body, and vast numbers began to be alarmed for the safety of the Connexion. An association was formed, with Dr. Warren at its head, and meetings were held in various parts of the kingdom, for the purpose of calling the attention of the Methodist people to the perilous condition in which the usurpations of the conference had placed the body. A meeting of the association was held at Manchester. Thomas Allin, a leading minister in the New Connexion, addressed a letter to the members of the Association, recommending them, in case of separation from the Old Connexion, to unite with the New Connexion, and not to form a separate body. This address of Thomas Allin's gave great offence to the Methodist preachers, and one of them, John M'Lean, of Sheffield, expressed himself from the pulpit in a most violent manner in reference to Mr. Allin. He was reported to have prayed, 'that God would palsy the arm that was lifted up against their body, and the tongue that could speak against it.' Thomas Allin wrote to M'Lean on the subject, and the private correspondence was followed by a public controversy. Mr. Allin published a number of letters addressed to M'Lean, justifying what he had done, and exposing the corrupt and popish principles on which the Wesleyan Conference was proceeding. He spoke of the Conference as a society of Jesuits, of the Old Connexion system of church government as an embryo or infant popedom, and of the proceedings of the Conference as a mass of fraud, injustice, and cruelty. He detailed a number of Conference acts in support of his statements, many of them of the most atrocious and outrageous character. This brought out young Waddy, another Wesleyan preacher in the Sheffield circuit, in reply, and the town of Sheffield was all excitement. I was myself led to take part in this controversy. I published first, '*Two Dialogues between William and John; William representing a New Connexion preacher, and John an Old Connexion preacher.*' In these I stated my views with respect to the comparative merits of the two systems of church government established in the New and the Old Connexions, and endeavoured to answer the arguments by which the Wesleyan preachers were accustomed to justify their principles and proceedings, and to assail the principles of the New Connexion. I did at the same time publish another piece, entitled, '*An Appeal to the Wesleyan Methodists on the present crisis.*' I submitted it to Thomas Allin, who sent it off immediately to the *Christian Advocate*, (a newspaper at that time published in London, by parties favourable to Methodistical reform) in the columns of which it first appeared. From the *Christian Advocate* it was transferred to the *Leeds Times*, and to a number of other provincial papers. I then enlarged it, and published it in the form of an eight page tract. It was extensively circulated, especially in the town and neighbourhood of Sheffield. It has never been reprinted since, but it *may* be reprinted hereafter, in connection with the review of 'Carlile's Logic,' and the 'Funeral Oration' on the death of the 'Free Inquirer.' Ebenezer Elliott, the Corn-Law poet, was very much pleased with the appeal. He spoke of it in the highest terms, and expressed a great desire to see its author. I accordingly visited him, and had some very friendly conversation with him. He repeated his high opinion of the appeal, and presented me with a copy of all his own poetical publications as an expression of kindness and respect.

I wrote, about this time, several letters in the 'Christian Advocate,' in connection with the Methodistical controversy.

But I cannot say of the part that I took in the Methodistical controversy, what I have said with respect to the part I took in the controversy respecting the Character and Evidences of Christianity. I have no doubt but that the part I took in this latter controversy did me good, but it had not so happy an effect upon my mind as the former controversy. It did not exert upon me the same cheering and elevating influence that the former controversy did. Besides, the New Connexion was not in a position to contend with the Old Connexion. The New Connexion was not sufficiently distinguished from the Old. It was both a small and feeble body, and had no great distinguishing principles to recommend it to public attention. It was, besides, terribly wanting in efficiency. It had done but very little good. It had neither distinguished itself by publishing cheap books, nor by forming or supporting liberal institutions. Hardly a preacher in the body had proved himself, either an original thinker, or a liberal-minded man. Its principles had been too sectarian. One of the ablest of its ministers, old G. Beaumont, had been expelled, because he was *troublesome*. The Conference had forgotten the principles on which the Connexion was originally founded, and had gradually adopted the narrow, sectarian, intolerant, and exclusive principles of the very body which it was assailing. It was impossible, therefore, for a minister of the New Connexion to write or speak to advantage, against the Old Connexion. He could scarcely condemn the *Old* Connexion, without partially condemning the *New*. I have therefore but few recollections of pleasing feelings in connection with this controversy; while I have many recollections of very painful feelings connected with it.

Dr. Warren came to lecture at Sheffield while I was there, and the New Connexion lent him one of their Chapels for the occasion. After the Lecture, M'Lean rose up in the gallery to reply, though discussion had not, at that time, been either invited or offered. This led to great confusion. The people in general were determined not to hear M'Lean, yet M'Lean was bent on speaking, and several were wishful that he should be heard, hence the meeting was thrown into a terrible state of confusion and excitement. At this period of the proceedings, some of the members of the New Connexion, who had been opposed to the loan of the chapel to Dr. Warren, began to reproach the others for what they had done.

This added to the unpleasantness. Besides, Dr. Warren himself did not prove himself equal to the work which he had taken in hand. He had no broad principles of Christian liberty to advocate, nor had he any superior views of theology to unfold. A great deal of what he said was merely personal, and much of the rest was but weak. The results of the meeting were therefore on the whole unpleasant. I have no doubt that the New Connexion suffered in consequence of the part it took on this occasion, as well as in consequence of the part it took in this controversy generally. The leaders of the body manifested too great an anxiety to injure the Old Connexion. Their eagerness to proselyte disgusted and enraged the members of the Old Connexion, and rather injured than helped the cause of Reform in that body. It would have been better for Methodistical Reform, if Mr. Allin and the New Connexion had taken no part in the disputes that agitated the Wesleyan Connexion. It would especially have been better for Methodistical Reform, if the New Connexion had *previously* taken a proper position,—if it had carried out the principles on which it was originally founded,—the principles of unrestricted Christian liberty advocated by Kilham in his publications. But this the New Connexion had not done. It had shrunk from its duty. It had foreseen the reproach that it would bring upon itself by acting honestly, and had therefore given up reform. The Conference had gradually conformed itself to the likeness of the Old Connexion in all things, except the single principle of lay representation in Conference: in every other respect it had anxiously laboured to obtain a good repute for orthodoxy and strict Methodistical order. It had been guilty, in fact, of double dishonesty. For it had, in the first place, tolerated a considerable amount of heresy, and yet, at the same time, endeavoured to make the impression upon the public that it was strictly orthodox. The Old Connexion had repeatedly charged it with Latitudinarianism, and the charge was true, and the leading preachers and members of the New Connexion knew it to be true; yet they denied it. Their anxiety to obtain proselytes caused them, first, to abandon the principles on which the body was founded, and, secondly, to tolerate an amount of what was generally called heresy inconsistent with their reputation as an orthodox body; and, thirdly, to deny their toleration of heresy. All these things unfitted the New Connexion for the position it had assumed as a body of Methodistical Reformers. If the New Connexion had been what it ought to have been,—if it had openly, as it did in effect, set aside the writings of Wesley as the standard of orthodoxy, and substituted in their place the teachings of Christ, leaving each one to interpret these teachings according to the ability given him by God; if it had set at nought the reproaches of the Old Connexion, and dared to sacrifice its credit with other orthodox denominations,—if its ministers had been men of true piety and talent, and if, instead of making it their great object to obtain a quiet livelihood, they had done their duty as true-hearted Christian people, the controversies in the Old Connexion would most likely have ended more favourably for truth, for human progress, and for the universal good.

Since the controversies between myself and the New Connexion, or rather between Evangelical Reformers and the old orthodox sectarians of various denominations took place, the New Connexion has taken another course; it has given up fighting with the Old Connexion altogether. Allin and his friends have in fact retracted their charges against the Old Connexion; the Old Connexion has forgiven the opposition of the New, and friendly correspondence has taken place between the Conferences of the two bodies, and attempts are made to bring the two bodies together. And thus it must always happen. If men do not go forward in Reform, they will go backward to the point from which they started, and become the persecutors of Reformers. In many cases they will go farther back than they ever went forward, as has been the case with some of late. They began with Methodism: they proceeded a few steps towards simple Christianity: they are frightened at the prospect of reproach and persecution, desertion and loss, which opens before them. They are alarmed too at the principles which they are led, one by one, to relinquish, and at the doctrines which they find themselves called upon to embrace in their stead. They find themselves verging upon the grosser forms of heresy, and know not how much further their principles of liberty will oblige them to go. They turn back to their Methodism, but stop not there. They move backward still, until they lose themselves amidst the horrible and licentious blasphemies of Antinomian Calvinism.

During most of the time that I spent at Sheffield, my brother Benjamin resided with me. It was my wish that he should become a circuit preacher, and it was his wish too. I thought he would be useful as a regular circuit preacher; more useful as a circuit preacher than in any other way of life; and this was my reason for wishing him to become one. He came to reside with me for the purpose of improving his mind and gathering knowledge, and thus preparing himself the better for his contemplated labours. His residence with me was a very great comfort to me. I took pleasure in teaching him all that I knew, and all that I learnt from day to day. As we walked along the way from time to time, to the places where I was appointed to preach, I opened to him all my soul, and freely imparted to him its most valued treasures. He also heard all my sermons, read all my manuscripts, and perused many of the same books that I perused. He shared all my thoughts, and was familiar with all my projects, all my anticipations, all my hopes and fears. He was, in short, the sharer of my whole spiritual life. I say it was a great comfort to me to have my brother for a companion. The manner in which my confidence had been abused by others, had begun to cause me generally, in my intercourse with people, to shrink from that perfect freedom of expression to which I had been previously accustomed. The natural sociableness of my disposition was thus checked. I was driven, in spite of my nature, into a kind of reserve in my intercourse with people. I was unable to speak all that I thought, to utter all that I felt; to open my soul, and to reveal my wishes, with perfect, unrestricted freedom. I knew that in some things I should be misunderstood, and that in others I should be misrepresented. I had also reason to fear, that some who should even be convinced of the truth of my sentiments, and of the goodness of my plans, would betray me, and join with the strong ones in seeking to restrain me, to injure me, to thwart me, to persecute me, and to subdue me to the will of the ruling party. Under such circumstances I found it an unspeakable relief to have one, with whom I could continually associate without fear; in whom I could place unbounded confidence; one who, I had reason to believe, would both properly understand me, and fairly represent me; and who would only love and esteem me the more for those very things, which would have converted others into enemies, slanderers, and persecutors. Many a happy hour, and many a happy day have I spent on the road, and at the different stations in the circuit, in conversation with my brother. We always thought of attempting a thoroughly Scriptural reform, both in the Connexion to which we belonged, and the world at large; and our conversation generally referred to this subject. We investigated all questions in theology; we sifted all the books that came in our way and analyzed and tested every sermon or speech that we heard. We examined every principle that we heard brought out in conversation; we tried every custom, every institution, every system, and every form that met our eyes, or that came across our path, whether in church, in state, or in private life. We discussed the merits of preachers and of sermons, the characters of laws and of men, and expressed ourselves on all those subjects with the most perfect freedom. We hesitated not to say what we believed and what we disbelieved; what we loved, and what we hated; what we wished to have established, and what we wished to have abolished; what we purposed to attempt with respect to the future, and what we should do for the present; what we should oppose in the management of the Connexion to which we belonged, and what we should favour; what plans we should follow in order to accomplish our objects, and what hopes and anticipations we had with respect to success. We had the freest and fullest intercourse that friends and brothers could have. We were as perfectly one in soul, as friends and brothers could be. We were fully bent upon effecting a reform, both in the theological creed, and in the theological dialect of the professing world. We contemplated nothing less than bringing back the religious world, both in opinion, in language, and in practice, to the perfect simplicity of the gospel. We were also wishful to improve the order of preachers. We lamented greatly over the absence of talent, of knowledge, of integrity, of energy, and of zeal amongst the mass of preachers, and were exceedingly anxious to secure a better class of persons as preachers for the time to come. Many a happy hour, and many a happy day did I pass in contemplating the happy changes which future years were to behold: for at that time I imagined it possible to accomplish all the reforms that I contemplated, and that without serious convulsions, without the destruction of sects, and without the revival of those shameful deeds of persecution which had marked all previous reformations. Though I expected opposition, I still anticipated victory. I expected to be able to raise a party in the New Connexion itself, that would be strong enough to secure the needful reforms in that body ; and then I expected, by means of the influence possessed by the New Connexion, to secure the needful reformations in other religious bodies. I say I expected to be able to raise or to form a party in the New Connexion which should be able to effect the needful reforms in that body. My thoughts were particularly directed to the young circuit preachers, and to such as were candidates for the circuit preacher's office. I hoped to be able to lead the young preachers, and the candidates for the preacher's office, to a freer exercise of thought, to more liberal reading, to more diligent application to study, and to a more faithful discharge of duty generally. I hoped to be able to lead them to renounce the foolish and antiquated forms of speech by which theology had been beclouded, as well as to separate from theology all the additions which had been made to it since the days of Christ and the Apostles, by ignorant or ill-designing people. I had no idea at that time that the principles which I had embraced would lead me so far as they have led me. The reforms that I contemplated were much more limited than those which I have since been led to attempt. Yet my views even then would have been thought extravagant by many. I wished to have the Bible established in *deed*, as it was already in *name*, as the only rule both of faith and practice. I hoped to be able, by the help which I expected to receive from others, to bring the younger preachers, and the candidates for the preacher's office, to try their opinions by its simple teachings, and to remodel their creeds accordingly. I wished to bring them to form the habit of expressing all their thoughts and feelings on religious subjects, in the simplest possible language, so that all the old scholastic terms, and all the cant and unmeaning forms of expression in use amongst Methodists and Calvinists, might gradually fall out of use, and a natural and universally intelligible kind of language take their place.

With this view I encouraged the young to visit me at my house, and to converse with me on religious subjects. I also formed a meeting for the mutual improvement of the young in religious knowledge. The plan of the meeting was the same as that established amongst the circuit preachers in the Sheffield circuit. Each person had a subject given him, on which he was expected to write his thoughts at full length; and each one was expected to bring what he had written, and read it to the meeting. All the members were encouraged to take notes as the article was read, and to make observations on its style and sentiments at the close. When the rest had made their remarks, I was accustomed to make mine. I used great plainness and freedom in my criticisms, and at times gave no small pain perhaps to the youthful writers. The whole of them, or nearly the whole, were accustomed to bring the thoughts of others instead of their own thoughts. They collected whatever they could find on the subject on which they were expected to write, from such books as happened to be in their possession, or within their reach, without using anything like discrimination in their selection of materials. They appeared all to go on the principle, that whatever they found in religious books was true, provided it was not most palpably Popish or Calvinistic. Hence they would bring long extracts of error and folly from *Cruden's Concordance*, from *Brown's Bible Dictionary*, or from *Dwight's Sermons*, and read them without the least modification or variation, as though the whole were palpable truth. I had, in consequence, enough to do in the way of criticism. My young pupils were strangely astonished at times, when they saw their language and sentiments so severely handled. And I perhaps was too particular and severe. I used to notice almost every word and expression that appeared seriously objectionable, and every sentiment that appeared unscriptural. I noticed every false or partial quotation of Scripture, and every defect in argument or arrangement. While I pointed out what I conceived to be erroneous, I endeavoured to make the truth on every point as plain to them as possible. I noticed their misinterpretations and misapplications of Scripture texts, and by reference to the place from which the texts were taken, endeavoured to make clear to them their real meaning. I did my utmost to present to them the religion of Christ as taught by Christ himself, and to bring them to use such forms of expression as were best calculated to unfold its real character and glory. At times the whole article produced at the meeting would be one unmingled mass of error and inconsistency. In those cases my task was both difficult and painful. It was difficult, or toilsome at least, to unravel a whole discourse, and expose all its errors and imperfections; and it was painful to criticize the productions of my young friends so severely, especially when there was nothing in the piece on which to ground a little commendation by way of encouragement. Still I went through my task, and dealt faithfully with my charge. One member of the meeting had been out for a short time as a travelling preacher. The piece which he brought to the meeting, was almost one unvaried piece of error and folly. There was neither truth nor utility about it. The whole of it was borrowed, and it had been borrowed without any judgment. He had taken a lot of Calvinistic nonsense here, and a lot of Methodistical delusion here, and had joined the whole together without the least attempt at reducing any portion of it to the simplicity of the gospel. His piece was one great mass of cloud, revealing nothing, but obscuring all things. Another brought an article still worse, if possible. Its errors and inconsistencies were more gross and palpable. The former was a cloud of vapour; this was a blacker, a thicker cloud; a cloud of smoke. The authors of those two pieces appeared not to have thought that they were called upon to exercise any discrimination in preparing their pieces. The idea of proving all things by the simple teachings of Christ, of rejecting what they found to be at variance with Christ's teachings, and of holding fast only that which they thought to be in agreement with them, seemed never to have entered their minds. They acted on the principle of collecting a lot of materials wherever they could find them, without regard to the character or truthfulness of the materials, and to retail them without consideration. Or perhaps they went on the supposition that what was printed in books, must be true. As preachers, their object must have been simply to fill what was considered a higher place in the church, to occupy the time of a congregation for an hour or so in talking, and thus to gain the honour and respectability attached to the preacher's office. They were, properly speaking, neither teachers nor learners. They had never once set to work to learn what were the teachings of Christ and his apostles. They were the simple retailers of the idlest traditions of the elders.

Others of those young people took a somewhat better

course. They manifested something of intelligence; but they were very slow to learn. Still I was full of hope. I had no idea but that a little effort on my part, would make them as eager for the truth as I was myself; and that, with a little help, they would soon be able to distinguish between the dreams of men and the truths of revelation, and so be brought to be able and useful ministers of the truth as taught by Jesus. But my hopes were too high. It proved no easy matter to bring such people to think and understand. I am not aware that of all those youths who attended those meetings, one single individual has proved a real thinker, an intelligent Christian, a clever preacher, or a truly rational man. They had been spoiled, in fact. Their previous training had almost disabled them from thinking on religious subjects. And then their powers were not of the highest order.

I used to think, at this time, that men generally were born equal in point of spiritual power and capacity, and that the difference in men was wholly, or almost wholly, the result of education, or of personal application. I held the notion that people in general, if they chose, might equal the highest and cleverest of their kind. I hold a different opinion now. I am satisfied that all men cannot be clever,—that the difference between different men is, originally, exceedingly great,—that the capacties of men differ from their birth, and differ almost endlessly,—that some can learn almost everything, while others can learn comparatively little,—that some can learn very quickly, and others only very slowly,—that some are naturally quick in discerning, and others naturally dull,—that some bring into the world with them powers or constitutions naturally fitting them for the work of critics, and that others bring with them constitutions strongly disposing them to follow in the steps of others. I have no doubt but that all are capable of obtaining a considerable amount of intelligence, and that most might obtain much more than they do, if they would use their powers and opportunities as they ought. But I am thoroughly persuaded, that no efforts or training would ever bring men generally, to a level with the great ones of our race. No one could find a thousand O'Connels in Ireland, or a thousand Bacons in England. No one could find a thousand Channings in America, or a thousand Newtons in Europe. All the culture, all the helps, all the advantages and encouragements in the world, would never enable some individuals to obtain the knowledge, the discretion, the discrimination, the spiritual powers possessed by others of their race, whose culture has been defective, and whose outward advantages have been exceedingly few. I have no doubt but that the young men that I had under my charge at Sheffield, might, if they had been encouraged by the other preachers, and by the leaders and elders of the society, have been made far wiser and abler creatures than they were; but I have no idea that any considerable portion of them were capable of becoming great, clever, powerful men. They were all capable of becoming intelligent and rational to a considerable extent, but not of being prodigies either in knowledge or in power.

For a length of time I had a person living with me in the house, of the name of Jochin. He came from Whitehaven. He had wished to get out as a travelling preacher amongst the Old Methodists, but had not succeeded. Having heard that it was easier to get out as a preacher amongst the New Connexion, he wrote to Mr. Allin, the corresponding secretary of the annual committee, offering himself as a preacher. Mr. Allin, and other members of the annual committee, invited him over to Sheffield, to preach before them, to afford them an opportunity of judging of his qualifications. His performances were not to their liking. There were several good thoughts in his sermon, but his manner was very objectionable. He also hesitated a great deal. He frequently seemed as if he were at a loss for words, or as if his thoughts had entirely escaped him, and he had to wait and shake his head, or wring his hand, or stammer, till the looked-for words presented themselves, or the run-a-way thought, returned to his recollection. And this awkwardness of manner continued through the whole of his discourses. By some of his judges this was attributed to timidity, or to the embarrassment naturally occasioned by the preacher having to address a strange audience, under peculiarly trying circumstances, and by others it was attributed to a bad habit, which it was thought might easily be overcome. The decision was, that he should not be received as a travelling preacher at that time, but encouraged to apply himself to study, and to exercise his talents as a local preacher, and thus qualify himself for the place which he sought. It was arranged that he should live with me for awhile, have the use of my books, and have the whole of his time for pursuing his studies, for gathering knowledge, and for exercising his talents as a preacher. I accordingly received him into my family, and treated him as a brother. I gave him access to all my books, and even to most of my manuscripts. I supplied him with pen and ink and paper, and left a room at his disposal. I offered him any instruction that I was able to give, whether in Grammar, Religion, or anything else, and had hopes that he would ultimately prove a useful and able minister. I also encouraged him to read over to me what he wrote, that I might have an opportunity of suggesting improvements, or of giving him useful counsel. He frequently came to me with pieces to read; and I heard them, and made my remarks on them. With some of them I was tolerably well-pleased; with others I was not. Most of them, in fact, seemed to be pure pieces of plagiarism, or what, in common language, is called cabbage. He took long passages from a variety of books, and read them over without the least acknowledgment. Passages too that were far from true he adopted, and read them over with the utmost confidence, without the slightest manifestation of any idea on his part, that there was anything irrational, unscriptural, or contradictory in them. I offered my remarks, and urged him to diligence, especially exhorting him to write down his *own* thoughts on all subjects, and especially to put everything that he wrote, in his own words, to express it in his own way. I urged him to take nothing from others till he had fairly made it his *own*. 'Be sure,' said I, 'that a thing is true and right, and then write it down in your own,—your natural style.'

This, however, he did not choose to do. He went on in his usual way, taking from any one whatever he could lay hold of, and reading it over to me as his own. Sometimes he took whole sermons and read them over to me as his own, and what was more astonishing still, he actually, on one occasion, brought me a great part of a discourse of my own, that he had taken from one of my manuscripts, and read it to me as his own. And in this case he had taken the matter from a manuscript that I had placed out of his way, in a box, to which I had given him no access. How it came to pass that he read this to me as his own, I cannot tell. I imagine he had forgotten where he had got it, and was not aware that it was mine at the time. I questioned him on the subject after he had read the piece, and he was a good deal ashamed and confounded, but still he showed no disposition to give up his plundering, and to set himself to write and preach from his own soul.

At length I began to suspect that he had never used himself to serious thinking, that he had in fact no knowledge of his own, but that every thing he said on religious subjects, was the unthinking repetition of what he had gleaned from others. I one day asked him, if he ever *did* think; and he seemed not to understand what I said. I tried to explain myself, and asked him if ever he found, while he was reading, or walking, or sitting alone, certain thoughts on religious subjects rising in his mind, and if ever those thoughts led to other thoughts, and those to others again; and he said, No. Then you have no thoughts of your own on those subjects, have you? He said, 'No, I cannot say that I have.' And it was a fact, the man never *had* thought. He had never once, I believe, in all his lifetime, let his mind go freely after truth. He had never once thought of the distinction between truth and error; and of course never exercised his own faculties in endeavouring to separate truth from error, or to compare truth with truth, and to pass from things already known, to the discovery of things yet unknown. All he had cared for was, to be able to preach,—to be able to put together a certain amount of theological stuff so as to make a sermon, and to be able to preach that sermon in such a way, that it might so far satisfy the people as to dispose them to employ him and pay him as a regular minister. When I found out this, I gave up all hopes of doing him any good, and longed for an opportunity to get well rid of him. I may further remark, that he got no better in his manner of preaching. He still stammered and hesitated as much as ever, and shook his head, and wrung his hands, to help him through, just as he had done at the beginning. And the cause, I imagine, was his entire lack of all ideas; his utter ignorance of what he was preaching, and the consequent difficulty of recollecting the unmeaning words and discordant sentences that made up his sermons. I believe poor Jochin returned to his work as a carpenter at length, but not till he had made another attempt or two to obtain a place as a salaried preacher.

Before I went to Sheffield, I had frequently spoken at public meetings, and spoken with considerable freedom and power: yet notwithstanding this, when called upon to speak at a public meeting on the subject of slavery, in a strange chapel, and before a strange audience, I was so confused and fluttered, that I was not even able to read the resolution entrusted to me, without the greatest difficulty, and was altogether unable to speak. I have frequently found myself in this situation at different periods of my life. After I have so far mastered myself as to be able to speak without the slightest hesitation or embarrassment before my usual audiences, and in my usual places, I have still found myself, when brought into a new place, before a strange audience, unable to proceed at all without the greatest effort. I should go into one pulpit, in the morning, with the fullest composure, with the greatest assurance of being able to declare my thoughts and my feelings with perfect freedom, and on going into another, belonging to another denomination, in the afternoon, should tremble and falter to such an extent, as to be unable to preach without the greatest pain and difficulty. And I often failed on such occasions. This was a very great trial to me. It frequently caused me most grievous suffering. And it was not because I thought such failures would injure my reputation. I was not indifferent to my reputation, for I regarded reputation itself as a means of usefulness; but the chief cause of my distress on such occasions was, I believe, a concern for the interests of truth and religion. I was grieved and troubled that I should thus, through weakness, cause the interests of truth to suffer. But I was not to blame for it. The fear which overpowered me was a weakness only, and not a crime. It was partly the result of my constitution, and partly of that depressing kind of training which I had in earlier life. This self-same weakness remains in some degree to the present day. I still find it difficult to speak in any new position, especially if the occasion be unusually important. If I am called to speak before a humble audience, in a small room, I speak with the utmost freedom, let the place be ever so strange, or the position ever so new. But if called to speak in a strange place, before a large and important audience, my spirit flags, my heart beats, my tongue falters, my lungs become unsteady, my voice is tremulous, and it is with the greatest pain and difficulty that I can so far master myself as to be able to speak at all. And it very seldom happens that I can go through my work on such occasions with satisfaction. Many a time have I been bathed in sweat from head to foot, as if I had been dipt in the stream, so great has been my excitement, and so severe its influence upon me. I sometimes get blamed in consequence of this weakness, but it is all of no use. Neither blame nor counsel can cure it. It is a part of my nature, and will remain as long as I live. And I am not certain that it is on the whole an evil. If I had not had this weakness, I should probably have had something worse. This weakness has often led me to more serious thoughtfulness, to a closer examination of my sentiments, to a stricter regard to my motives, and has thus tended, I have no doubt, to preserve me both from levity and error. And it has never led me to shrink from what I believed to be my duty. If I have thought it my duty to speak on any occasion, I have always *attempted* to speak, notwithstanding the difficulty which this weakness has thrown in my way. If I have suffered from a partial failure, I have still returned to my task when duty has recalled me, and continued to speak as I was able, till I was able to speak as I wished. In no case have I been prevented from making a second or a third attempt, by any thing like a failure in my first attempt. I have gone on till I have felt myself equal to my place, and able to do something like justice to the subject which I had in hand.

In the chapels in which I usually preached, and before audiences which I was accustomed to address, I found no difficulty in speaking. On those occasions my mind, in general, felt perfectly free, and all its powers and resources were quite at my command. On some occasions I felt exceedingly happy in my labours. I was able, in a great measure, to deliver myself even to my own satisfaction, and on some occasions the effect upon my hearers was exceedingly great. I believe I stated that while I was speaking at a Missionary meeting once, in the Sunderland circuit, the whole audience rose from their seats in an ecstacy, and joined in a loud, involuntary acclamation of praise to God. Something partially approaching to this once happened in Scotland-street Chapel at Sheffield. It was a meeting of the Tract Society. I was speaking on the Character of the Religion of Christ, on its wonderful excellence and glory, on its beneficent power and tendency, and on its perfect adaptation to the wants of humanity. Christianity had presented itself to my mind as bearing the same relation to the spiritual or moral universe, as the laws of God's eternal and universal providence bore to the visible creation; and in this light I was presenting it to the minds of my hearers. I spoke of the harmony, the beauty, the glory, the grandeur which everywhere prevailed throughout the visible universe; of the order observable in the heavens above, and in the earth beneath; of the regularity with which the heavenly bodies performed their motions and imparted their influences; of the regular return of day and night, one friendly to rest, and the other giving light for labour; of the revolutions of the seasons, and the infinite advantages which we and all created living things enjoyed thereby. I then supposed the laws of providence to be suspended,—the order and harmony of earth and heaven to cease,—the sun, and moon, and stars to lose their light,—the planets wander from their orbs,—the earth to lose its course, and all the other laws of providence to fail or be suspended, and pourtrayed, in colours such as presented themselves to my mind, the terrible and universal disorder and ruin that would follow such a catastrophe. And thus, said I, it is in the spiritual world. When the laws and revelations of the religion of Christ are unfolded and obeyed, the spiritual world has harmony, has peace, has joy, has blessedness. The knowledge and practice of the religion of Christ makes the spiritual world a heaven. But let religion perish; let its laws and influences be lost; let the souls of men be left without illumination, without the heavenly influences of truth and love, and all things run into disorder. Wars prevail, and rumours of wars; slavery, and wrong, and cruelty, and fraud, intemperance, licentiousness, and all abominations fill the earth. Hence personal, domestic, and general happiness is lost, and earth becomes a dungeon or a hell. The words I used, and the order in which I expressed myself, are of course no longer recollected. But my mind was at ease. I felt myself at home. My spirit was full of light and power. My subject was glorious, and I felt myself equal to it; and the effect was such, that the meeting was greatly excited, and after the conclusion of the address a request was made that it should be published without delay. But the speech had not been written, and I never was able to write it. I had delivered it, and it was gone beyond my control. I might have written something a little like it, so far as the matter was concerned, but nothing of equal power: so the speech was never made public.

I may add, that part of the speech had been probably suggested by a beautiful and striking passage in the first book of Hooker's Ecclesiastical Polity. The passage is as follows:

'The world's first creation, and the preservation since of things created, what is it, but only so far forth a manifestation by execution, what the eternal Law of God is concerning things natural? And as it cometh to pass in a kingdom rightly ordered, that after a Law is once published, it presently takes effect far and wide, all states framing themselves thereunto; even so let us think it fareth in the natural course of the world: since the time that God did first proclaim the edicts of his Law upon it, heaven and earth have hearkened unto his voice, and their labour hath been to do his will; "he made a Law for the rain;" he gave his "decree unto the sea, that the waters should not pass his commandment." Now, if Nature should intermit her course, and leave altogether, though it were but for a while, the observation of her own laws; if those principal and mother elements of the world, whereof all things in this lower world are made, should lose the qualities which now they have; if the frame of that heavenly arch erected over our heads should loosen and dissolve itself; if celestial spheres should forget their wonted motions, and by irregular volubility turn themselves any way as it might happen; if the prince of the lights of heaven, which now as a giant doth run his unwearied course, should, as it were, through a languishing faintness, begin to stand, and to rest himself; if the moon should wander from her beaten way, the times and seasons of the year blend themselves by disordered and confused mixture, the winds breath out their last gasp, the clouds yield no rain, the earth be defeated of heavenly influence, the fruits of the earth pine away, as children at the withered breasts of their mother, no longer able to yield them relief: what would become of man himself, whom these things do now all serve? See we not plainly, that obedience of creatures unto the Law of Nature is the stay of the whole world?"

There is another beautiful passage, at the conclusion of the Book, as follows:

'Wherefore, that here we may briefly end: Of Law there can be no less acknowledged, than that her seat is the bosom of God, her voice the harmony of the world: all things in heaven and earth do her homage, the very least as feeling her care, and the greatest as not exempted from her power: both Angels and Men, and creatures of what condition soever, though each in different sort and manner, yet all, with uniform consent, admiring her as the Mother of their peace and joy.'

These passages, I have no doubt, had suggested the comparison employed in my speech.

I may add, that I cannot boast of absolute originality, either with respect to my sermons, my speeches, or my writings. I can trace a great deal both of my thoughts and my illustrations to other writers. Even those thoughts and forms of expression which have no exact resemblance in other writers, have frequently been suggested by what I have read in them. Books have frequently *inspired* me, when they have not supplied me with *thoughts;* and they have often supplied me with thoughts, when they have not been the means of inspiring me. How much of what I have written is original, and how much has been derived from other writers, I cannot tell; but I have certainly been indebted to other writers for a great deal. It is not however a matter of much importance, whether a man's thoughts and expressions are strictly and thoroughly original, or not. If a man be careful to utter only that which he himself believes and feels to be true,—if a man's expressions be such as exactly fit his thoughts and feelings,—if his mode of speaking and writing be strictly natural, be properly and truly his own, it does not matter much what amount of help he has received from others. The evil is, when men cease to be themselves, and become the mere imitators or echoes of others; when they take up another's thoughts without ascertaining whether they be just and true; when they make use of another's expressions without ascertaining whether they are fit and proper; when they allow their own judgment and their own taste or consciousness to sleep, and parrot-like, just mimic what they hear or read. The evil is, when men take the thoughts and expressions of others, not to *help* them in their labours, but as a substitute for their labours. And this was never my case. I never allowed myself to make use of thoughts, or forms of expression, till they had become truly my own. I never made use of another's labours as a substitute for my own labour, but only as a help to my labours. I have very seldom made an exact quotation from any writer, whether prose or poetical. I scarcely ever could find a passage of any considerable length in any writer, in the sentiment and expression of which I could perfectly concur. I have often begun to make extracts from books that have very much pleased me, but I have seldom gone far before I have met with something that did not agree with my own thoughts or feelings, something that did not fall in exactly with my plan, and I have in consequence left the extract unfinished. In those cases my plan has generally been to take so much of the writer's thoughts as were in full accordance with my own, and add to them my own thoughts, expressing the whole in my own way. When translating passages from the Latin or the Greek, I have generally been led to act in the same manner. I have generally found, in the passages which I admired, something that was not exactly to my taste or purpose. In those cases I have laid aside the plan of making extracts, and have written down my thoughts and feelings in my own style. The passage thus written has borne a resemblance to the passage which I had proposed to extract, but it has not been the same, nor has it, strictly speaking, been an imitation.

It has frequently happened that one single sentence in a book, has given birth in me to a whole host of thoughts, to a whole lecture, a whole sermon, or a whole book. I have laid aside my book to put down a thought suggested while reading: that thought has been followed witn another thought: the second thought has been followed with a third; and the third with a fourth, and so on, till I have written, before rising, the substance of a lengthy tract. It has also frequently happened when reading, that fit and happy forms of expression have suggested themselves, on subjects not connected with the book in my hands, but on subjects on which I had been previously writing. But no one can give the history of his mind in full. No one can relate the connection between his thoughts and the thoughts of others; the relationship existing between his own writings and he writings of others; between the development of his own mind, and the development of the minds of others. The history of a man's mind can be known in full to God alone. A man may know *much* about the history of his mind, but he can never know all. And even that which he knows, he cannot always relate. That which he has experienced in the course of his life is, to a great extent, forgotten, and that which is remembered cannot always be described; so that the history of a man's life, of a man's soul, must necessarily be exceedingly defective, exceedingly imperfect. Still, if a man record all that he *does*, recollect, it may be sufficient so to set to work the imagination of his reader, as to enable him to conceive the rest. A biographer can draw an outline, and fill up some small portions of it; and this, if it be done truly, may enable others to fill up, in their own minds, the rest of the outline, and so give them a tolerably correct image or picture of the individual.

While I *am* digressing, I may as well put down a few other matters connected with my mind's history. At one period of my life, the period at present under consideration, I frequently read in Shakspeare, and made considerable use of him. No one's form of expression seemed to me so perfect, so excellent, as Shakspeare's ; and if ever I attempted to imitate any one's style, it was his. Frequently, when reading him, have I laid aside the book, on purpose to write down thoughts of my own, in expressions suggested by his expressions ; and a thousand times, when I have not laid aside the book, and begun to write, has my mind been led to place its materials in forms of expression somewhat similar to those contained in Shakspeare. I seldom quoted Shakspeare. His words and thoughts seldom fell in exactly with my plan. Still in expressing my own thoughts and feelings, I have frequently spoken more or less under an influence exerted by Shakspeare's writings. How great that influence might be, and what might be the exact effects produced by it, I cannot tell ; but I can state the fact, that the influence was exerted and felt.

But to return. While I was at Sheffield, we commenced preaching at Ecclesfield, a village about five miles from Sheffield, near the Barnsley road. At first we had but few to hear us ; but afterwards we had a greater number, and before long we had crowded congregations. A revival, as it is called, took place, and a considerable number of persons were formed into a society, and steps were taken towards the erection of a new chapel there. A chapel was at length erected and opened, and preaching regularly established. But the revival soon ceased, and most of the members fell away, and I am not certain whether the society was not at length altogether broken up. The history of this revival furnished abundant proof to me, that the Methodist plan of proceeding in revivals is altogether wrong. The people at Ecclesfield were exceedingly ignorant. They therefore needed instruction ; and the preachers who preached to them should have *given* them instruction. But this was not their plan. Five out of six of the preachers that visited them, sought simply to excite their feelings. They gave them no information whatever. They *succeeded* in exciting their feelings, and brought several of them, as I have already intimated, to profess religion, to declare themselves converted. But they, poor creatures, had nothing to occupy their spiritual faculties; nothing to engage their thoughts. They had no lessons to learn, no subjects to ponder, no books to read. They were put in no way of gathering knowledge. They were not even taught that to seek after knowledge was their duty. They were not given to understand that to seek after knowledge, and to reduce knowledge to practice, was the great business of life. They were simply urged on to excitement. They were encouraged to pray in public, to tell their experience, and the like; but little more. Even my own addresses were not so full of instruction as they ought to have been. And the effect produced by them was little only compared with the effect produced by the perpetual preaching of the other preachers, or the wild excitement of the revivalism. To this neglect of instructing the people at Ecclesfield, I attributed the failure of our mission there; and the failure of Methodist societies in scores and hundreds of places, might be attributed to the same cause. Methodist societies generally are failures. The amount of knowledge and true religion in Methodist societies is exceedingly small. The number of apostates is exceedingly large, and the Methodist churches generally have a name to live while they are dead. And the great part of all this evil is to be attributed to the Methodistical mode of preaching; to the neglect, on the part of the preachers and teachers of the Methodist body, to feed the people with knowledge, to supply them regularly with solid instruction, and to help them forward in their spiritual progress towards intellectual and moral perfection. The wild excitement which people frequently experience in what are called revivals, cannot last. The spirit of man was not made to endure such wild excitement continually; and unless the people when roused, awakened, or converted, can be brought to read, to think, to gather knowledge, to be really scholars in Christ's school, students of his revelations, seekers after all truth; unless they can be trained to the proper exercise both of their intellectual and moral faculties, their conversion will prove a curse instead of a blessing; they will not only fall away, but their last state will be worse than the first.

We have nothing to say against excitement itself. Excitement is natural to man. God meant man to be excited. Man cannot help being excited. The principal part of all the excitement experienced by people in connection with Methodist revivals, is all right, is all natural; it cannot be prevented, and it ought not to be prevented if it could. The evil is, that this excitement should not be joined with proper intelligence; that the excited soul should not be led to learn the great and glorious truths of revelation. The evil is, that the excitement should not be regarded as sent by God to prepare the soul for receiving important lessons in religious truth and duty, and for more readily forming all those habits of self-denial and beneficence, which are necessary to the perfection of the Christian character.

I say excitement is natural to man. It is as natural in religion as it is in love. It is as unavoidable in religion as it is in love. It is calculated to be as useful in religion as it is in love. No one doubts its usefulness in love. It causes that perfect melting or dissolving of the soul, which enables two souls to mingle and become entirely one. It is that which enables a man to give himself up entirely to his beloved one, and which enables a woman to devote herself entirely to her husband; which renders it perfectly easy, perfectly natural, and even an exquisite delight to a man to serve his beloved, to minister to her pleasure, to labour for her well-being; and which renders it the highest bliss, the earthly heaven, of a woman, to minister to the pleasure and welfare of her husband. If there were not this excitement in love, true marriage could never be completed. That perfect and indissoluble union of soul between man and wife, which constitutes true marriage, could not be formed, and the happiness of marriage life could never be secured. If it were not for this excitement in love, marriage would become a sort of business transaction, a matter of prudential accommodation. It would seldom take place, compared with the frequency with which it takes place at present, and it would still seldomer prove a blessing to the parties concerned. But this wild, this almost boundless excitement which the souls of men and women experience in their first love, is a source of unspeakable delight, of boundless satisfaction, and tends to render marriage, not only more common than otherwise it would be, but infinitely more delightful and more conducive to man's welfare than otherwise it would be.

So with excitement in religion. Religion may be considered as a marriage between the soul and universal truth, between the soul and universal duty, between the soul and God, between the soul of the individual and mankind, between the soul and the infinite, unmeasured present, and the everlasting and incomprehensible future. This union cannot take place, in general, without excitement. Excitement, causing a perfect dissolution or dissolving of the soul, is necessary, in order to prepare the soul for taking a new form, for uniting itself to new beings and new worlds, and to enable it to enter upon a new life. Where this excitement does not take place, there is little prospect that the religious character of an individual will be completely decided. Where this excitement is not felt, religious duty will be more difficult, the pursuit of solid truth will be less interesting. The union of the soul with the souls of other men, its sympathy, its benevolence, its interest in the welfare of mankind, will be defective.

It is true there is no fixed amount of excitement which is necessary to man in religion, any more than there is in love. All men do not feel the same excitement in love. Some feel a greater amount of excitement; some experience a less. In some men it takes one form, in others it takes another. In some men it shows itself in one way, in other men it shows itself in other ways. In one individual it is milder, and is spread over a larger space of time; in other individuals it is more violent, but occupies perhaps a smaller period of time. In some it is like a fit, an ecstacy; in others it is only a high state of exhilaration. In some it is an uncontrollable passion; in others it is only the life and quickness of the imagination. In some it is an unspeakable and almost intolerable anxiety; and in others it is a delightful, pleasurable, but mild emotion. But it exists in all. It is felt by all. It is essential in all.

So in religious matters. The excitement naturally connected with religion, the excitement essential to religion, I mean essential to the commencement of the religious career, is felt by every one; but not by every one alike. It is awakened in every one; but it does not assume the same form in all. It varies endlessly, as the excitement of love varies. But to quarrel with this excitement is to quarrel with man's nature. To quarrel with this excitement is to quarrel with the law of God. Our business is not to quarrel with it, but to welcome it; to be pleased when we behold it. Not to quarrel with it, or to check it ; but to accompany it with instruction ; to take advantage of it for the purpose of laying the formation of the Christian character in those who feel it; to make use of it as a means of more readily uniting the man who feels it, to truth, to duty, to humanity, to God, and to the universe of being in which he lives. It is caused by God on purpose to render religion more easy ; to render more sure, more complete, more happy, man's spiritual marriage with truth, with duty, with mankind, with God.

Those who revile excitement, and discountenance it, know not what they do. While they are censuring the ignorance of Methodists, they are betraying ignorance as great and so mischievous in themselves. The men who scout excitement, who frown upon it, or who dread it, are as foolish as those who idolize it, and who make it their only study to awaken and perpetuate it. I have no doubt that while the Methodists have rendered their societies exceedingly shallow, unintelligent, and morally defective, by encouraging excitement so unduly, other religious bodies have driven people away from their circle, and obliged them to seek an asylum amongst the Methodists, by not giving to excitement its proper place. We will take some Unitarian congregations as instances. Here you see no excitement. The minister is not excited. His hearers are not excited. Every thing like religious excitement is discouraged. If a son or a daughter of a leading Unitarian manifests this excitement in any form,—if a daughter should at any period appear to be melancholy,—if her spiritual constitution should seem to be failing or dissolving, —if great and solemn thoughts should fill her soul,—if her feelings should begin to flow out in tears,—if the visible world should appear to be almost annihilated, and the spiritual world to occupy her whole soul, her whole feeling ; in a word, if she should experience that which the Methodists would call a work of grace, a thorough awakening of the soul, her parents would be alarmed. If a dozen or a score young people in such a congregation were to experience such a religious awakening, such a general dissolving of the soul, it would be regarded as a most terrible calamity, as a most fearful or alarming event. Physicians would be sent for ; amusements would be recommended ; change of air, change of scene, change of company, would be urged. Efforts of all descriptions would be made to check the excitement, to terminate the imagined spiritual danger. Now when such a thing happens amongst the Methodists, it is hailed with delight. The parties thus awakened, thus dissolved, are considered as in a most hopeful condition. The work of regeneration is in fact considered more than half accomplished in such cases, and the aim of the preacher and of their members is to help forwards this excitement to its consummation, to the height, under the false impression that this consummation is true conversion, true salvation, true regeneration. The error in both cases is about equal. The conduct of Methodists, in making it their great, their chief, their only study to help forward such excitement to its height, and the conduct of Unitarians, in endeavouring to check, to allay this excitement, as a dreadful calamity, are both unnatural, both irrational, both terribly injurious to the interests of religion and men's souls. The middle way is the right one. The Unitarian ought to regard such excitement, when it shows itself, with pleasure, like the Methodist; though not wthout some mixture of fear. The Methodist, when he sees such excitement manifesting itself, should regard it with fear, like the Unitarian; but not without mixtures of joy and thanksgiving. The Methodist and the Unitarian should both rather encourage such excitement than check it. In no case should recourse be had to medicine or change of scene in order to check it, except where the constitution is so feeble, and the temperament so nervous, as to give just ground for apprehending brain fever.

I am satisfied, that if the middle course, between that of the Methodists and the Unitarians, had been pursued at Ecclesfield, a great amount of lasting good would have been done. Not only would numbers of persons have been led to abandon their evil associates, and their old bad ways, but they would have become intelligent, pure, and useful characters. Among the persons converted at Ecclesfield, there were some who were endowed with no small measure of intellectual and moral power, and who had a clear perception too, in many things, of what was right and what was wrong. And they had a great desire and a strong determination to shun what was evil, and to practise what was good. And I have no doubt but that they would have become exemplary and useful characters, if they had been properly instructed. But the thoughtless and unwise treatment which they received from the generality of the preachers, spoiled all. One of the persons that was converted at Ecclesfield was a keeper of an alehouse, a drinking house of a low description. No sooner were his religious and moral faculties awakened and brought into action, than he began to regard his business as an unlawful one, and formed the purpose of abandoning it. At a love-feast in Scotland Street Chapel, when telling his experience, he began to confess some of the bad arts which were employed in connection with his business. He spoke of the adulterations that were used in making ale, describing the deleterious character of some of the things they mixed with it. 'And as for gin,' said he, 'it is real poison. If you only knew how gin is made, you would never taste a drop of it again.' And he was about to explain the manner in which gin was manufactured by publicans, and the manner in which gin had been manufactured by himself, I suppose; but this kind of talking was not according to the common plan of love-feast talking: it was too moral; it was too rational and instructive; and some of the preachers therefore urged him to stop, or else confine his remarks to his *experience*, as they called it, or, *as I should call it*, to a description of his feelings, and bursts of excitement. If this man had been treated as he ought, he would, in my judgment, have become an excellent reformer. He was a sagacious man, and a man of great power and determination; and if he had had parties to take him by the hand who were themselves reformers of the proper stamp, he might have been the means of incalculable good.

Another person from Ecclesfield, a female, rose and spoke at the same love-feast, but she confined her remarks entirely to descriptions of her feelings, mingling what she said with passionate exclamations. She seemed to have taken a lesson from the rebuke administered to the speaker who had gone before, for she avoided all reference to moral matters whatever. Her speech was listened to with delight, and loud and many were the shouts of 'Glory,' and 'Praise the Lord,' with which it was received. This female, however, soon fell away. And the man, poor fellow, became so disheartened, that he never looked comfortable after. Things generally went wrong, and the chapel at Ecclesfield soon became a burden to the Connexion. What became of it afterwards I do not know.

There was a regular increase, both in the congregations and societies in the town of Sheffield, during the whole of the first year that I resided there. Scotland Street chapel was crowded on Sunday evenings, and a plan that had for some time been in use, of inviting people to attend the chapel, by distributing around the neighbourhood small notes announcing the texts to be preached from, was obliged to be discontinued on account of the crowd. South Street chapel was also well attended. On Sunday evenings it was generally filled. And even Bow Street, the worst-attended chapel of all, was often filled. And additions were made to the society every week. New classes were formed, and the members in the old ones became more numerous. I did myself form a new class, which soon numbered upwards of twenty members, most of them young and very promising people. A measure of prosperity also was experienced by some of the societies in the country, though none of the country societies kept pace with the societies in the town. And the members of the society, as well as the congregations, were generally, I believe, improving in knowledge. My constant endeavour was to impart some clear and useful information to my hearers in every sermon; and in meeting the classes to give them their quarterly tickets, my object was the same. I never preached a ranting sermon. I always endeavoured to place before my hearers some one great truth or moral principle, and unfold it and enforce it in the clearest and most powerful way I could, endeavouring, in every sermon I preached, to make the people wiser, and better, and happier. And even my companions were often led through my influence, to preach more usefully and practically than they had previously been accustomed to preach. And had things been allowed to go on in this way; had proper encouragement been given to plain and practical preaching, the good done in Sheffield would have been immense. But many were anxious for what they called a revival. They were not content with people being added to the church, and with the members of the church becoming gradually more intelligent, religious, and useful. They wanted a spiritual explosion; a burst of religious excitement. They wanted to see scores and hundreds converted in a night. They imagined, that if protracted or revival meetings were held, ten or a dozen might be converted where one was converted on the rational plan on which we had been hitherto proceeding. Besides, Conference was coming; and the superintendent preacher was wishful to make a great appearance at Conference. He was wishful to have it believed that he had been the means of enlightening and electrifying great multitudes. Preparations were therefore made for getting up a revival. Meetings were appointed, and parties were fixed upon to take part in them. I was myself urged to take part in those meetings; but I hesitated and objected. I was afraid that harm would be done by them, and I *stated* my fears. My opinion was, that we were already going on very well, and that the plan which they proposed, would mar instead of mending the state of the societies; and I *told* them my opinion. No matter; they had formed their plan, and they were determined to carry it out. They accordingly commenced their revival meetings, and the preachers began to preach revival sermons; and their labours appeared to be attended with very great success. The body of Scotland-street chapel was crowded at the prayer-meetings, and scores in a night professed to be converted. I was in doubt at times whether I was right in standing aloof from the revival services, and more than once I went into the revival meetings and took part in them, endeavouring to master my objections and repugnance to them; and at times I partially succeeded: but it was only for a time. My objections and repugnance to the wild uproar and confusion attending those meetings returned upon me, and I was obliged to content myself with going on in my usual course. At times I thought ill of myself on this account. I thought Burrows and Lynn had a kind of goodness, or a measure of holiness, that I had not; and many a time I wished that I was something like them. At other times however I was more content with myself, and more disposed to regard my colleagues as in error. Meanwhile the revival went on. Burrows prayed and shouted with all his might, and Lynn, with his bulky frame, almost as tough as iron, and with lungs like leather, shouted, and sang, and ranted with all his powers. Their manner of proceeding was truly dreadful. They jumped over the forms,—climbed over the pews,—kneeled down and prayed beside such as they supposed to be penitents,—whispered in their ears,—urged them to believe,—talked in sterner ways to such as they supposed to be unawakened, thundering in their ears the horrors of damnation and eternal wrath, scores of them joining together to raise the wild excitement to its highest pitch. The screams, the shouts, the jarring songs, the disorders and indecencies were at times quite horrible. On many occasions three, four, or five, and at times even ten or twenty would be praying and shouting together. While some were praying, others would be singing. While some were moaning and groaning, crying or shrieking, others would be shouting with all their might, Glory, Glory; He is coming, He is coming, He is coming; He is here, He is here, He is here; while others would be exclaiming, I believe it, I believe it, I believe it; I *feel* Him, I *feel* Him; He is knocking at my heart; He *will* save, He *will* save; He *is* saving; Glory, Glory; He has pardoned my sins; I am saved; my soul is set at liberty. No sooner would the last expression gain the ears of any of the preachers or leaders in the meeting, than they would call out at the highest pitch of their voices, Another soul is saved! Another soul is pardoned! Let us praise God; and at once they would strike off the Old Hundred;

'Praise God from whom all blessings flow,' &c.

And while some scores would be singing this verse, some scores or hundreds more would be still groaning, shouting, whispering, screaming, leaping over the forms, falling down on the floor, climbing over the pews, whispering in people's ears, or lifting up the loud voice of warning to some apparent triflers who had come to gaze upon the awful scene. At times two or three lots would be singing together, while six or eight groups more would be praying or talking in other parts of the chapel, all at the same moment. Occasionally Burrows would retire into the vestry, to recruit himself with a glass of wine, or a little brandy and water, and then return to his labours again in the chapel. And thus would things go on for two or three hours, till the leaders of the revival were utterly exhausted and their voices gone, and then, after awhile, they would dismiss the meeting.

These meetings were held almost every night for several weeks, and it was stated that in the course of a month or two some hundreds had found peace, or got into liberty, at these meetings.

All the converts were invited to meet in class, and it was

customary for persons to have paper and pencil in readiness at those meetings, to put down the names and residences of the converts, and the class to which they were invited and urged to go. When a person professed to be converted, the paper and pencil came out, the name and address were put down, and some one was afterwards appointed to wait upon the converts at their houses, and lead them to their respective classes.

At the following quarter day the number of members in the circuit was considerably greater than it had previously been, but not so much greater as the reported number of converts had led some to expect. Out of the three or four hundred converts, not more than a hundred or a hundred and fifty could be found. Many of the converts had already fallen away. Some that were converted at night, were converted back again before the morning. Others of the converts were found to have been converted and counted several times over. Some of the converts were drunk at the time of their conversion, and when the influence of the drink and the excitement had passed away, they were as far from God, and as far from meeting in class, as they had been before they attended the revival meetings. Others of the converts turned out to be persons who had begun to meet in class before the revival commenced, and who had given every sign of a determination to learn and do God's will. They had not however experienced a sudden and miraculous conversion. They could not tell the time and the place where their souls were set at liberty. Hence they were called to the penitent bench at the revival meetings with the rest, and some of them were wrought into the necessary state of excitement, and made to believe that they were converted. But as these had been numbered before, they added nothing to the increase of the society.

I may also observe, that after the revival had subsided, the societies began to diminish in numbers. Instead of being gratified by the continuance of that regular increase which I had witnessed previous to the revival, I was doomed, now that the revival was over, to behold a perpetual falling away, a continual diminution of numbers. The revival had caused no increase of religious feeling; it had only occasioned a sudden and a premature *explosion* of that feeling. It had not improved the character of the congregations; it had only hurried some to a premature step, and ruined others by driving them, first, into wild excitement, and secondly, into hypocritical professions. The revival, as it was called, had, in fact, done infinite mischief. It had suspended all rational operations for the spread of truth and the promotion of righteousness. It had interrupted all rational and deliberate thought, and involved the religious feelings and rational principles of many in disorder, if not in ruin. It had, besides, interrupted the meetings for business and discipline. Its disorders and indecencies had disgusted many of the congregations, and driven them farther from connexion with us. It had strengthened false notions about religion and conversion in many, and increased their inability to understand the truth. It had thrown some good people into needless alarm about their spiritual state, by making them fear or fancy that they had not been rightly converted. It did harm in many ways; incalculable harm. And it is a fact, that from that period to the present, the societies in Sheffield have never recovered from the bad effects of that revival. They have gradually, and I believe continually, gone down. Before the revival commenced, there were in the Sheffield societies, and in the country places, somewhere about sixteen hundred members. That number had dwindled down to six or seven hundred some years ago; and I question whether it has not continued to dwindle to the present time.

Some of those who took a leading part in the revival meetings sustained a serious loss in their own characters. They became worse men. Some of them were far from being what they ought to have been before the revival commenced, but many of them appeared to be seriously worse after the revival was over. One of the most active revivalists of all, one that made the greatest noise and the greatest stir at the revival meetings, called Matthew Lindley, became a drunkard and a profligate, and died a few years after, the victim of his vices, as I was told. He was a young, strong, healthy looking man, and seemed one of the most likely men to live that I was acquainted with. But alas, he perished in the midst of his days. Among the parties who professed to be converted at the revival was a young woman, a prostitute. She had no home, or professed to have none, and Matthew Lindley took her to his house. I saw her there once or twice when I called upon him. I had very great doubts as to the soundness of her conversion, and I remember very well that I was not without fears as to the effect that her residence with Matthew might have upon him, nor without concern for his wife. How matters turned out with respect to this female, I never was told; but the account I heard of poor Matthew's apostacy and miserable end, brought forcibly to my mind the fears and anxieties which I had experienced when I called on him, and saw her at his house.

Another person that took an active part in the revival meetings, and who was almost as noisy as Lindley, became quite indifferent to religious matters afterwards. He was neither disposed to read nor to attend the meetings, nor to take part in the Sunday schools. He seemed to have *worn himself out*, so far as religious feeling was concerned, and to have spiritually expired. Others appeared to be much the same after the revival as they had been before. They were not, that I could see, either much better or much worse. But some of them were more disposed to quarrel with each other after the revival than they had been before, and there never was the same amount of peace or harmony in the Connexion after the revival, that we had experienced before it commenced. Even those who were as regular in their attendance on meetings, and as active in the schools as they had previously been, were, I have reason to believe, less affectionate and less happy in their labours than they had been before. They seemed to be something like people who have accustomed themselves to intoxicating drinks, till the excitement caused by them has become in a manner essential to their comfort; till the absence of excitement is painful and almost intolerable to them. What a pity that Methodists should close their eyes and their hearts to the truth on these subjects. What a pity that their views of religion, and of the way to promote the spiritual improvement and welfare of their fellow-creatures, are not more in harmony with truth, with Christianity, with human nature. If they understood things rightly, how much more rational would be their movements, and how much more happy would they be in their labours. And their labours would then tend to promote their own improvement and welfare, as well as the improvement and welfare of others. In teaching the truth, and in inculcating virtue, they would be strengthening their own minds, expanding and storing their own understandings, improving and perfecting their own best affections, as well as increasing and heightening their own enjoyments. They might go on doing good in this way without weariness. Instead of exhausting themselves by wild excitements, by violent and disorderly exertions, by shouting and brawling at the extremity of their voice, and holding their meetings so often, and continuing them so long, they might labour according to their strength, take rest when their bodies and souls were weary, increase their power both of body and mind by their moderate exertions, and go on *increasing* their efforts instead of *diminishing* them, and be constantly *augmenting* their pleasures instead of *exhausting* them. They might find a hundred times more happiness in the calm and peaceful pleasures accompanying the pursuit of truth and rational labours for the good of others, than men can ever find in the wild uproarious proceedings of Methodistical revivals. Besides, how much more creditable would it be to religion, how much better calculated to win the hearts of rational and thinking people, how much better adapted to cure the prejudices of unbelievers, and to win the esteem and reverence of people generally, would such efforts as we recommend be, than the wild and irrational proceedings of Methodistical revivalists. But revivalism,—I mean the wild and disorderly kind of revivalism just described,—is not near so popular among Methodist societies as it once was. Both the preachers and the leading members have discovered, that it is not only unchristian, but injurious; that it not only does harm to the interests of religion generally, but that it does injury to their own societies. They have found out that the good done in such revivals is more apparent than real, while the evil that is done is both real and extensive. They have found out that those revivals are generally followed by a decrease greater than the increase which they caused, and that after a year or so, the societies that had experienced those revivals were in a lower and weaker state, than the societies where such revivals were unknown. There have always been some amongst the Methodists who have disapproved of those revivals. The most rational and intelligent of the members have almost invariably disapproved of them. But their objections have been little regarded, and frequently the leading revivalists have treated such persons as unconverted and ungodly, and even prayed for their conversion in the revival meetings. The number of this class of persons is increasing among the Methodists, and their influence also is increasing. Their objections are more attended to, and the time is probably not far distant, when the wild and disorderly kind of revivals which we have described, will be generally discountenanced among the Methodist societies. Then besides, it is now not so easy to get up a revival as it formerly was. There are a greater number of persons, in most places, that read and think on religious subjects than there formerly were, and it is found that where any considerable portion of persons have begun to exercise their judgments on religious subjects, it is next to impossible to get up a revival. The spread of knowledge and of spiritual freedom is fatal to revivalism. The presence of two or three intelligent persons in a revival meeting, if those persons are known to the leading revivalists, paralyzes the revivalists, and destroys the excitement. In several cases I and my friends have gone into revival meetings of late, and the effect has been astonishing. The effect of a water-spout upon a fire could not be more effectual in extinguishing the fire, than the effect of our presence was in destroying the mad excitement of the meeting.

My class continued to prosper. Most of the members seemed desirous of obtaining religious knowledge. The greater part of them were young people, and most of them appeared to be of a somewhat intelligent character. My mode of leading a class differed considerably from the common one. My object was to awaken and cherish in the minds of the members a desire for knowledge, and to impart to them as much important religious information as I could. I proposed to them no questions respecting their *feelings*. I never asked them, whether they knew or felt their sins forgiven. I never asked them whether they could tell the time or the place where God spoke peace to their souls, or where God set their souls at liberty. I paid but little regard to mere feelings. My object was to lead my members to a *knowledge of the* TRUTH, and to bring them to *act in accordance with its requirements*. I knew that if they sought after knowledge, and reduced the knowledge they acquired to practice, all would be well. I knew that they would never lack the necessary amount of *feeling*, if they *lived* and *laboured* as they ought; and that *no* amount of feeling could be of *use* to them, if they did *not* thus live and labour. We therefore never had a noisy, ranting, turbulent meeting. The conversation was calm and rational, though tinged to some extent with Methodistical delusions. My knowledge of truth was not sufficiently great, nor was my confidence in its safety sufficiently strong, to enable me to give my class that clear and full and thoroughly rational instruction, which I now see would best have met their case, which would most effectually have brought them onward in knowledge and righteousness, and which would have bound them most firmly in attachment to religious pursuits. Still, my knowledge of religion was such, and my freedom in communicating it such, as to render my class very different in character from the rest of the classes; and my number of members I believe was constantly increasing. The time I spent at class I generally spent very happily. I enjoyed my conversation with the members very much; and had the state of my own mind, and the spirit of the body with which I was connected, allowed of greater freedom; had my situation as a preacher in the Connexion not exerted a cramping influence upon my soul, I should have enjoyed the society of my friends in class still more, and have proved a greater help and blessing to them as well.

One of my members was a Scotch woman, a modest, unassuming, thoughtful, and religious person. She seldom spoke at class, and when she *did* speak, said but very little. And here I may observe, that I never made it a rule, as most other leaders did, to require each member to speak. When the members showed a backwardness to speak, I left them to their own way. Hence a considerable number of my members were silent. I either never asked them a question, or if I asked them a question, soon passed on to something else, endeavouring to avoid embarrassing or distressing their minds, either by waiting for an answer when they were unprepared to give one, or obliging them to answer against their own feelings.

Another of my members, the only elderly man that met with me, so far as I can recollect, was a butcher, and had lived in Southampton, but had been driven away by persecution on account of his political principles. He thought fit to vote according to his conscience, without consulting the will of his customers, or of the ruling party in the place. His enemies succeeded in ruining his business, and obliging him to seek a home and a living elsewhere. He appeared to be a hearty, conscientious man, though perhaps too far advanced in life to learn many new lessons in religion.

Some of the young people who were members of my class, continue my friends to this day. One of them, Stephen Bacon, is an active man and a lecturer in the cause of truth and righteousness at this time. Others have got out of my sight. Where they are, or what they are doing, I do not know. I should be glad if I could meet them once again, and speak to them what now is in my heart.

While I was in Sheffield, I became a teetotaler. This was one of the most important steps I ever took. The effect of teetotalism upon my constitution, my character, my pursuits, my usefulness, and upon my enjoyment of life, has been most beneficial and delightful. Previous to my becoming a teetotaler, my health was very indifferent indeed. I suffered very considerably, and that in various ways. I was frequently subject to toothache, and had submitted to the extraction of two of my best teeth, and others seemed likely to decay. Indeed, the process of decay had begun. I suffered also in my chest and throat. I was very subject to colds; and a cold invariably caused soreness or slight inflammation in the wind-pipe or the lungs, and the effects of this soreness or inflammation were such, that I was frequently unable to finish my discourse on the Sunday evening. I had, for a length of time, made use of pitch plasters to relieve my chest or throat; but these had almost lost their power. I was therefore obliged to use hotter plasters. I had to have blistering flies mixed with the pitch; and the first year and a quarter that I spent in Sheffield, I preached almost every Sunday with my chest almost entirely raw. I regularly put on a blistering plaster on Friday and Saturday, to enable me to go through my labours without interruption on the Sunday. Scores of times have I preached with my chest all blistered or raw. Yet even this seemed to lose much of its effect at length. The inflammation or irritation became more violent, and on one occasion I suffered severely from a sturdy cough.

I also suffered greatly from the heart-burn. I had the heart-burn most violently; and I had it very frequently and long together. I was seldom free from it a day together. At times I found relief from the heart-burn by eating ripe apples, but at other times I could find no relief. I recollect having the heart-burn so violently on one occasion, that I felt as if I should be suffocated with it. I took magnesia; but it did me no good that I could perceive.

I had, in addition to the heartburn, a most distressing pain at the bottom or under part of my stomach. I imagined that it came from the same cause as the heartburn,—that it was, to the *bottom* or under part of my stomach, what the heartburn was to the *top* or upper part! The pain seemed to be limited to a very small space. I imagined that I could have covered the whole with the end of my finger. But it was exceedingly distressing. Sometimes I compared it to the sensation which might be occasioned by a red hot ball, about the size of a marble, pressing against the interior of the stomach, and burning it; or some living thing gnawing at the place, and eating its way through my stomach. This pain greatly weakened me. I was almost unable to stand or sit upright in consequence of it. I felt as if I should be bent almost double.

I had also other symptoms of a deranged system. About the month of April or May, 1833, which was towards the close of my first year in Sheffield, a strange change came over the natural secretions. The colour was perfectly black, and the consistence was like that of melted pitch. This continued for a length of time; for several weeks in fact. I began to be alarmed, and applied to the Doctor, who told me that I was suffering from *inspissated* or *thickened* bile; and he prescribed accordingly. I took his medicine, and found relief for a time; but still I continued unwell. The pain at the bottom of my stomach soon returned, and I still continued to be grievously troubled with irritation or inflammation in my chest. The heartburn also returned. My nights were much disturbed with dreadful dreams, and at times I suffered from horrible forms of night-mare. In the morning, when I awoke, my tongue would generally be parched, and sometimes would be so dreadfully hard, that it felt more like a piece of a brick, than a piece of flesh. I soon took cold, and a cold took dreadful hold of me. I frequently had a cough, though never but once did my cough appear to be in danger of proving a fixed, immoveable cough. In this state I continued for a length of time. I still went on with my work, preaching twice or thrice every Sunday, and three or four times through the week besides. I also continued to write, to some extent, though I was unable to get forward with my writing as I wished.

About the end of July, or the beginning of August, I was invited to preach some anniversary sermons at Boston, in Lincolnshire; and though I was far from being well, I went and preached. While I was there, I became worse, and was obliged to have medical assistance. The person who attended me was Dr. Small. He looked at me, felt my pulse, asked the usual questions, inquired into my habits of life, &c., gave me some medicine, and left me. The medicine afforded me relief, and though very unwell, I was enabled to proceed with my labours. During one of Dr. Small's visits to me, he began to converse with me in a very free and friendly way respecting my general health, and my habits of life; and after we had conversed for a length of time, and after I had told him all I thought or knew respecting myself, he told me that my health was in a very precarious state, and that unless I took great care, I should die in eighteen months, or in two years at the farthest, of *consumption*, brought on by *dyspepsia*, or *indigestion*. I, of course, asked him what means I should employ to *turn aside* the danger; and he gave me the following prescription:

First. You must study less, read less, and write less; and take more exercise in the open air.

Secondly. You must give up the use of all intoxicating drinks, and become a teetotaler.

Thirdly. You must give up smoking.

Fourthly. You must go to bed without supper; or if you take any supper at all, let it be simply a dry crust of bread, and a draught of cold water.

He assured me that unless I followed this prescription, I should have no right to expect to remain long in this world.

This was a serious prescription for me; and though I was very wishful to live, I felt as though it were impossible for me ever to observe it. The first part of it, which required me to read, and study, and write less, seemed the most difficult. I had always blamed myself for not reading, and studying, and writing *more*. Reading and studying and writing appeared to me to be the proper business of my life, the only matters, comparatively speaking, that deserved attention. I had long lamented that I got on so slowly with writing. I resolved therefore never to read, or study, or write less, if I could possibly obtain health and avoid a premature death by any other means. I secretly hoped to read and write much more.

The second part of the prescription I had very little objection to. I had already had thoughts of becoming a teetotaler. I had joined the *old* temperance society when at Durham, and had given up the use of spirits as a regular drink, never tasting them except as medicine. And before visiting Boston, I had received from John Andrew of Leeds, who had been a school-fellow of mine at Mr. Sigston's, and who had become one of the first advocates of teetotalism, a copy of the *Temperance Advocate*, by Joseph Livesey, of Preston, the originator of the teetotal system. What I found in this Advocate had made a great impression upon my mind, and led me to think rather favourably of teetotalism. And my mind in general was predisposed to think favourably of it. I had often lamented the prevalence of drunkenness, and had grieved over the drinking habits that prevailed in religious societies. The drunken habits of the country generally, and the drinking and drunken habits of preachers and professors of religion, had given me great concern. They appeared to me to be the greatest obstacles to man's welfare; the greatest foes both to plenty, to knowledge, and to piety. I had looked on drunkards as almost incurable, and had feared that the vice of drunkenness could hardly ever be driven from society. The *Temperance Advocate* had opened to me happier views; it had inspired me with new hopes. It had shown me that drunkards could be reformed, and it had proved to me that if teetotalism were universally practicable, the world might be delivered from drunkenness altogether. I had doubts, it is true, as to whether teetotalism *were* universally practicable. I had fears that it was *not*. I fancied that some individuals could not *live*, or at least could not enjoy *good health*, without a little ale, or porter, or wine. I even imagined that *spirits* were in *some* cases necessary as *medicine*, that to *some* constitutions *they* might be essential to the enjoyment of *good health*. I was strongly inclined to believe that a little ale, or porter, or wine, was essential to *my* health; that it was necessary sometimes, especially after preaching in hot and crowded rooms, to protect one against the effects of cold on exposing one's self to the night-air, or to wet and stormy weather. I had also an idea, that the use of intoxicating drinks might, in many cases, be essential to people's health and safety when they had used them a very long time, though those same people might have done without them, if they had never been accustomed to use them. It was with me, therefore, almost a settled point, that all who had been accustomed to use intoxicating drinks till they began to be rather old, would have to *continue* to use them, and that teetotalism would have to be preached to the young and to children only; and that the practice could never become general, till we had raised a new generation. I had set it down for granted, that most *old* drunkards, as well as most habitual free drinkers that were old, would have to continue their drinking and drunken habits to the last, or run the risk of losing their lives. I had never, up to this time, heard a teetotal lecture, nor had I ever read a teetotal work, except the single number of the *Temperance Advocate* already mentioned; nor had I ever had any conversation with a teetotaler on the subject of Teetotalism. I was therefore exceedingly ignorant on the point: but these were my thoughts, my fears, my imaginations. It was in this state of mind that I went to Boston. I was in this state of mind when I received the prescription from Dr. Small. I was, however, resolved to *try* the principle. I returned home to Sheffield with that determination. I spoke to my brother Benjamin on the subject, and he favoured my plan, and was disposed to join me in making the experiment. I resolved, therefore, to make the experiment at once. I ventured on the experiment with great fear, I might almost say, with fear and trembling. I imagined, in fact, that I was risking my life. I thought it very doubtful whether I should survive the experiment or not. Such thoughts and fears may seem ridiculous to some people now; they almost seem so to myself; but they then seemed rational enough. I felt as if I were venturing on an untried path, through an unknown region; as if I were setting my foot where foot of man had never trod before. And they do not understand human nature, who cannot account for my fears. Who ever ventured alone for the first time, into a dark wood without fear? Who ever ventured for the first time, and alone, upon the sands of the sea shore without fear? Not I. I remember well when I first ventured alone into a distant wood in which I had never been before. I felt as if I were treading upon dangers at every step, and as if I were liable to attacks of evil on every side. I recollect too when I ventured for the first time upon the sands of the sea-shore. I was then alone. And I had never seen any one walk on them before in all my life. I had also heard of quicksands. The sea was roaring at a short distance, in its terrible and solitary majesty. No one was nigh. And all things but the noisy sea were silent and still; and I felt, as I tremulously moved on in my conscious weakness and helplessness, as if the sand beneath me might in a moment give way, or swallow me up alive. And at the time when I experienced these fears I was a man. It was not when I was a mere child that I first ventured alone into the strange and distant wood. Nor was it when I was a child that I ventured alone upon the sands of the sea. It was when I was a man. And my fears were *natural*: I *know* they were. The nature of all men is the same in general, and that which *one* man fears, *another* man will fear; and that which produces solemn and vague and awful apprehensions in the mind of *one* individual, will, to some extent at least, produce the same emotions and affections in the minds of *all*. And this experiment in teetotalism was, to me, a venturing on an untried path; an entrance into regions unexplored; an exposure of myself to unknown dangers; and I cannot describe the solemn terror with which I ventured for the first time to reject my customary allowance of porter, ale, or wine. I *did* however reject it. I took my stand, resolved to drink no more, unless some strange and terrible necessity should compel me to do so. I went without my customary glass of ale at dinner; I refused my customary glass at night; and I refused my customary glass of wine after preaching on the Sunday morning. I cannot say that I found any great difficulty in giving up the use of intoxicating drinks, except the difficulty already described, arising from my fears of what might be the consequence. Still I experienced a *little* difficulty. I do not remember that I experienced any difficulty in taking water instead of ale to my dinner and supper; but when I came down out of the pulpit on Sunday, and found the chapel-keeper with his glass of sparkling sherry on his little tray waiting for me as usual, I *did* feel a little difficulty in refusing to drink it, especially as it was already poured out. But I *mastered* the difficulty. I refused the wine; and I never, that I recollect, experienced any difficulty in refusing it after.

And now, though my *fears* were not all gone, they soon began to be mingled with delightful hopes. I began to feel, as I usually do, when I have fairly entered upon any new course, great and lively expectations, and vast and gladsome anticipations of what would probably be the result. I began to think thus with myself; 'Well, if teetotalism *does* answer, I will let the world know of it, and I will do my best to bring others to try it. If it *does* answer, and become general, it will be a glorious thing for mankind. What numbers of drunkards will be reformed! What numbers of religious people will be preserved from apostacy! What mischief will be prevented in the church! What happy families it will make! What a change it will produce throughout the country generally! It will cure the greatest evil that afflicts society! It will remove the greatest curse that rests upon the church. And I should not wonder at all if it *does* answer. I begin to feel as if teetotalism will turn out to be safe and practicable.' It was thus I thought, I say; and it was thus that I talked with my brother on the subject. My spirit began to kindle, and my tongue began to move, and whenever my brother and I were walking together to my country appointments or back, teetotalism was still the subject of our conversation. As we walked along the road, or crossed the pleasant fields, all that I thought and felt, I uttered. All my hopes, all my anticipations, all my joys and pleasures, came forth in free and unrestrained expression.

Still I had no idea of becoming a public advocate of teetotalism for a good long time to come. I used to think of trying teetotalism till I was *forty years of age*, and *then* beginning to tell the results. I was then about twenty eight. I had no idea that the experiment which I was making, would satisfy me of the safety and practicability of teetotalism so soon as it did. Hence in my conversation with my brother, I well recollect saying, as we were crossing the fields from Walkley to Sheffield, 'Well, if I live till I am forty years of age, and find teetotalism practicable, I will let the world hear about it; I will make a stir about it.'

Well, time went on. I kept to my purpose of giving teetotalism a trial. And I had not tried it a fortnight, before I began to believe that the principle was a good one, that for me at least teetotalism was likely to answer very well. Instead of taking any *harm* by the experiment, I found myself *better*. Instead of getting *worse* colds in consequence of not taking a little intoxicating drink, I found myself freer from colds than I had been before. Instead of growing *weaker*, I found myself growing *stronger*. Instead of being *less comfortable*, I found myself *more comfortable*. I had not tried teetotalism above a month, before I found myself better in many respects. I had no heart-burn; and though I lived in fears of its returning every day, it never *did* return, and it never *has* returned. The pain at the bottom or under part of my stomach too was gone. My sleep was sounder at night, and I was more refreshed with my sleep in the morning. The unpleasant taste in my mouth on awaking in the morning was gone, and my tongue was moist and comfortable. I was less heavy and dull through the day. I was more cheerful and comfortable in company. I had a better appetite for my food. I relished it better; I digested it better; and it did me more good. I began to experience feelings of health and pleasure that I had never experienced before for years. I could read with more pleasure; and I could study and write with more pleasure. Instead of being obliged to adopt the former part of Dr. Small's prescription, respecting reading, and studying, and writing *less*, I found myself able to read, and study, and write considerably more. And I could read, and study, and write, so far as my feelings went, without sustaining injury.

I say, I did not take cold so soon; and I may add, that if I *did* take cold, the cold did not affect me so much as it had been accustomed to do; and when it *did* affect me, it sooner passed away. My chest was less subject to irritation or inflammation. I was not so soon hoarse in speaking. I had no longer any need of the hot or blistering plaster. I never but once used the hot or the blistering plaster after. It is now nearly fourteen years since I became a teetotaler, and I have never had a plaster of any description on my chest during the whole of that period, except once; and I question whether the plaster was necessary even then; but I had found it necessary to have such plasters so long and so frequently before I became a teetotaler, that I could hardly imagine it possible for me to be perfectly safe all at once without one.

From the time I became a teetotaler, I have never had one half hour's tooth-ache; I have never had five minutes' tooth-ache. The teeth which had begun to decay fourteen years ago, have made no progress in decay, that I can perceive, to this hour. My teeth are as good as they were when I first became a teetotaler, for any thing that I know. I can eat with them as well as I could then, and better. My teeth have become more clean. They require less attention to keep them clean. Their very appearance is changed. And this of itself is a proof that my general health is better.

I used to imagine that a little ale, or porter, or wine, was necessary when people were weary or exhausted. I have now found out the contrary. I used to think that a little ale, or porter, or wine, imparted a certain amount of strength to the system, and enabled persons to do a greater amount of work than they could otherwise do. But I have found out this to be a delusion. I am stronger now without intoxicating drinks, than I ever was with them. I not only enjoy better health, greater freedom from disease, but I feel myself in possession of a greater amount of strength. I find myself able to do a greater amount of work than I formerly could. I can work *harder*, and I can work *longer*. I am not so soon tired either in body or mind; and when I *am* tired, I am sooner rested.

Before I became a teetotaler, I had frequently slight attacks of *rheumatic* pains; but I have scarcely ever felt a touch of rheumatic pain from that day to this. And I have had infinitely more exposure to weather, and an incalculably greater amount of labour, and far more painful trials to pass through, since I became a teetotaler, than I ever had before. Where I used to write one page in a day, I have, since I became a teetotaler, often written two, three, four, and at times even ten or twenty. Where I used to lecture once, I have lectured twice or thrice. Instead of preaching twenty-five minutes, half an hour, or forty minutes at a time, I have, since I became a teetotaler, often preached fifty or sixty minutes, or spoken an hour and a half, or two hours at a time. The improvement that has taken place in my health since I became a teetotaler is incalculable, indescribable; and the increase of enjoyment which I have experienced has also been indescribable.

After I had been a teetotaler a month or so, I heard a teetotal lecturer of the name of Pollard, and after the lecture, which abounded in humourous and instructive stories, I signed the teetotal pledge. Pollard had two kinds of pledges, a *teetotal* pledge, and a *moderation* pledge, and he gave his hearers the liberty to sign which they liked best. *I signed the teetotal* pledge. My *reason* for signing the pledge was, partly, to induce *others* to sign. I had not, that I know, any need of the pledge *myself;* for I had become a teetotaler *without* a pledge: I had got over the *principal difficulties* of teetotalism without the pledge, and my purpose to continue a teetotaler was fixed. And I should have *continued* a teetotaler if I had never *heard* of a pledge, for anything I know. But I saw others around me, young persons, that were in danger of falling a prey to drunkenness, and that *did*, as I imagined, need a pledge. At least, I saw some around me whom I wished to become teetotalers, and to encourage and induce them to become such, I signed the pledge in their presence at this public meeting. Some of them signed the pledge after me, and I have reason to believe that my example, in this case, was the means of good to them, and may prove the means of good to them for ever.

A short time after this, I was invited to attend a teetotal meeting in the town, and when I went I was voted to the chair. I said a few words in favour of the object of the meeting, and that was my first teetotal speech. It was a very short one, and very far from being a thorough-going one. I was not, at that time, satisfied that teetotalism would answer for *every* one. I was therefore not prepared to *recommend* it to every one; much less was I prepared to speak strongly against those who had doubts or fears as to its general practicability. I thought it probable that teetotalism would answer for *many* people, perhaps for the *generality* of people; but I was not quite sure. And my speech was in accordance with my thoughts. I had at that time an idea that men's constitutions might infinitely vary, and that that which would answer exceedingly well for many, might answer very badly for others. I was a believer in the old proverb, that '*One man's meat was another man's poison.*' I believed the proverb in its literal sense. I had read a few of the arguments of teetotalers in favour of universal and absolute abstinence from intoxicating drinks; but I was far from being satisfied of their soundness. I had heard of the *chemical* argument; the argument which goes on the principle, that alcohol exists in all intoxicating drinks, and that alcohol is to all constitutions a poison. But this argument I thought extravagant. I questioned whether alcohol *did* exist in all the different kinds of intoxicating drinks in use amongst us, and I also questioned whether alcohol was a *poison* in all cases, or operated as a poison on all constitutions. I thought there might be stomachs that could derive nourishment from alcohol, or that could convert it into nourishment. I thought there *might* be constitutions to which alcohol might prove a *cordial* rather than a poison. In short, though I had begun to believe in the practicability of teetotalism to a *considerable extent*, and though I had begun to hope that it would ultimately prove practicable to *mankind generally*, I had not come to the belief that teetotalism was practicable in *all* cases, much less had I come to the belief in the soundness of the *arguments* made use of by teetotalers in advocating their principles. And as I have said, when I spoke at the teetotal meeting, my speech was in *accordance* with my thoughts. The doubts which I *felt* I *expressed*. Being uncertain whether teetotalism would *answer* for every one, I hesitated to *recommend* it to every one. I was however desirous, that as many as possible should make the *experiment*, and that those who found, on making the experiment, that teetotalism did them no harm, should join the teetotal ranks, and help on the teetotal cause. My doubts however were not agreeable to the teetotal leaders who attended the meeting, and I met with a little opposition and rebuke. But the opposition and rebuke were of a gentle and moderate character, and did me perhaps no harm. I was not however prepared, at that time, to receive much *good* from them.

After I became a teetotaler, I met with a good deal of annoyance in my visits to friends' houses. They all brought out wine, or ale, or spirits, and wished me to take a little: and all, or nearly all, seemed disappointed when I declined taking any. Some were very much grieved. They thought themselves insulted. Others however were more moderate and gentle; but most were disappointed. Some became my *enemies* on account of my teetotalism; and amongst the rest, a person of the name of Parkin, who kept a spirit-shop. Before I became a teetotaler he had generally given me something, whenever I called on him, towards the funds of the Connexion; but after I became a teetotaler, he would give me nothing but shy looks. Some of my friends, when I visited them, would begin to reason with me on teetotalism. With those I reasoned. I stated my views, my wishes, my hopes, and described the happy effects of teetotalism in my own case; and some of the more reasonable ones were satisfied. A few of them resolved to try teetotalism for themselves; but a greater number of them considered it a piece of folly or madness, and some even spoke of it as wickedness and blasphemy. I however went forward, resolved to give the principle a thorough trial.

W. Burrows, my superintendent preacher, did not like teetotalism at all. Still, he had not the manliness to oppose it in an open and straightforward way. Thomas Allin was more friendly to teetotalism, and said, on one occasion, when I and W. Burrows were talking to him on the subject, that he believed that if he had continued to take a glass or two of wine every day for some time past, as he had formerly been used to do, he would, by that time, have been a dead man. Thomas Allin had had two or three slight attacks of paralysis, and had been induced, in consequence, to give up the use of wine and spirits, and to become almost a teetotaler. His abstinence had proved beneficial to him, and he was, in consequence, at that time friendly to teetotalism. I am myself inclined to believe that the paralytic shocks from which Mr. Allin had suffered, had been brought on by his over free use of wine and spirits. He was what was called a very sober man: he never drank much; but he drank a little regularly. He could take a few glasses of wine in a day, and one or two glasses of spirit and water in addition. He had, I understand, previous to those attacks of paralysis, got into the habit of sitting and drinking a little extra with James Dixon; and the wine which James Dixon used was considerably stronger than the wine commonly met with. What Burrows said, was true to some extent, namely, that no one kept a glass of wine worth drinking but Dixon. Allin had suffered by drinking; he had had an hair's breadth escape from death; hence he took my side in general when teetotalism was the subject of conversation, and he joined me on this occasion, in recommending Burrows to become a teetotaler, and in endeavouring to convince him that the complaint under which he then laboured, was probably, to some extent at least, the result of his use of intoxicating drinks. Allin afterwards fell back in some measure into his former drinking habits, and spoke less favourably of teetotalism.

It was thus things went on while I remained at Sheffield. I became a teetotaler about the month of August, and I remained in Sheffield till the Whitsuntide following. During that period I had greatly improved in health, and my faith in the safety, the general practicability, as well as the vast importance of teetotalism, had greatly increased in strength.

At Whitsuntide the Conference stationed me at Chester. On my way to Chester with my family, teetotalism became the subject of conversation on the coach. One person spoke in its favour, and another spoke against it. I put in a word or two in favour of the teetotaler. The opponent of teetotalism then became abusive, and insinuated that no one would advocate teetotalism, unless he had some selfish motive for so doing. He talked and conducted himself in such a manner, as to rouse my indignation a little. But I made no show of what I felt. I kept my soul in subjection. But I said within myself, If *this* is the spirit of anti-teetotalism,—if it has come to *this*, that teetotalism cannot be tolerated,—if teetotalers and teetotalism are to be abused and insulted in *this* manner, it is time for me to come forward and see if I cannot do something in its favour. I resolved from that time to stand forward as a public advocate of teetotalism.

Before I went to Chester, several young persons connected with the Chester congregation had become teetotalers. These, when they heard that the preacher appointed to them by Conference was a teetotaler, were exceedingly glad, and looked forward to my arrival amongst them with a great deal of joyous expectation. They had previously been very much despised; they now thought, that when they should have a *preacher* on their side, teetotalism would be treated with a little more respect. They had also met with a good deal of opposition from their foolish fellow Citizens, and now they hoped, that when they had a teetotal preacher, he would aid them in publicly advocating the cause, and meeting the opposition with which they were assailed. When I arrived at Chester, those young teetotalers soon visited me, and made known their principles, and told me their thoughts, their wishes, and their hopes. The insolent and unmanly conduct of the opponent of teetotalism that I had met with on the coach, prepared me to listen to them with a great deal of favour, and to hear of their plans and labours, their wishes and their hopes, with no small pleasure. I gave them at once to understand, both that I was a teetotaler myself, and that I wished to promote the spread of teetotalism among others. I gave them to understand that I should be glad to co-operate with them in any way I could, and to assist, according to my ability, in publicly advocating teetotalism in their meetings.

It was not long before I had an opportunity of declaring my views on teetotalism to the public. Soon after my arrival in Chester, the teetotalers had their first anniversary I believe, and I was invited to attend. They took tea in the Cheese Market, and I addressed them after tea in the open air. My speech was not a long one, nor was it a very strong one. I had not yet thoroughly studied teetotalism. My knowledge on the subject was but scanty. My acquaintance with facts was very limited: and even the knowledge that I had, was not exactly at my command. It requires *more* than knowledge to enable a man to speak well on a subject. It requires a man to be *familiar* with his subject. It requires a man to have been *accustomed* to speak. A man will often have a good deal of knowledge on a subject, and yet not be able to speak well on that subject. His thoughts may not come when he wishes them: and even when his *thoughts* come, the fit or necessary *words* may not be just at hand. Good speaking depends much on *practice*. And a man may be an excellent speaker on some subjects, and not be an excellent speaker on others. I know a hundred things that I cannot communicate with ease and freedom, simply because I have never been *accustomed* to communicate them. I know the meaning of all the words that I might wish to use; but I have not been accustomed to *use* those words; and should therefore find some difficulty in commanding their services when I wanted them. A man's thoughts and words are something like a regiment of soldiers, useful according to the *drilling* or *discipline* they have had. If a man has not *drilled* his thoughts; if he has not used himself to *command* them; and if a man has not frequently used his words, and employed them frequently in expressing the proper thoughts, they are like an *undisciplined* regiment. The captain *commands* them, but they do not readily obey. He *commands* them, and they are *willing* to obey, but they do not understand their movements. Their movements are in consequence slow, irregular, disorderly. It is when a man has been accustomed to make *use* of his thoughts, and to express his thoughts in *words*, in conversation, and in writing, that he is able to do justice to a subject, to speak on a subject with freedom, with clearness, with order and with power.

I say my speech on this occasion was neither a long one nor a powerful one. It was both shorter and feebler than was agreeable to me. Still, it was plain and true, and it gave satisfaction to my teetotal hearers, and did some good I believe. I briefly stated my reasons for *becoming* a teetotaler, for *continuing* a teetotaler, and for *advocating* teetotalism. I told them that I had found teetotalism *practicable* in my own case, and not only so, but that I had found it very *useful;* that it had done me *good;* that it had improved my *health;* that it had increased my *comfort;* that it had enabled me to do more *work*, and to get through my work with greater *ease and satisfaction*. I also told them that teetotalism had been the means of reforming several drunkards; that it was calculated, as it spread, to be the means of reforming others; that it was sure to preserve *sober* people who embraced it from *becoming* drunkards, &c., &c. But I was, as yet, a teetotal child. I had to *grow* into a man. I had neither that fulness of confidence in the truth and goodness of teetotalism, nor that deep strong feeling of its vast unutterable importance that I afterwards experienced, and that I now experience.

From this time I began to study teetotalism more attentively. I read every work on the subject that came in my way. I bought all that Joseph Livesey had published, and borrowed all the publications on the subject that I found in the possession of my friends. I also read a number of American publications on temperance. I had previously read a number of works on abstinence from *spirits*, and now I began to find that almost every thing which had been previously written against spirits, was applicable to the use of intoxicating drinks generally. My reading supplied me with arguments in favour of teetotalism in abundance, as well as with a number of facts illustrative and confirmative of all that I had to say on the subject. Then the oftener I spoke on the subject, the more familiar did the subject become.

The more frequently I made use of the materials I had collected, the better able was I to make use of them to advantage. I also began to collect fresh materials myself. Almost every day's observation and conversation supplied me with facts tending to show the evil and danger of the drinking system, and the advantages of teetotalism. The conversation too which was almost constantly taking place whenever I went into company, increased my ability in advocating teetotalism. Wherever I went, some person was sure to oppose teetotalism; and as sure as any one began to oppose it, I began to defend it. And almost every individual had some new objection, and to every new objection some valid answer was suggested. Thus by conversation, observation, experience, and public speaking, the subject of teetotalism became perfectly familiar to me. It was almost constantly upon my mind. I studied the subject thoroughly. I left nothing unread that had been written on the subject. I left nothing that I heard unpondered, whether it was for teetotalism or against it. Hence in course of time I felt myself able to defend teetotalism, and advocate it, in a way very much to my own satisfaction. I now spoke very frequently on the subject. I attended all the meetings in Chester and the neighbourhood, when my other engagements would allow me to do so; and at all the meetings I spoke. I also held meetings in the country round about. I lectured at Hawarden, Dublin, (Wales,) Holywell, Greenfield, Northop, Wepre, Aldford, Tarvin, and a number of other places. I soon had invitations to attend teetotal meetings in other parts of the country; and as far as I could, I accepted those invitations. I lectured at Nantwich, Northwich, Liverpool, Warrington, Manchester, Stockport, Ashton, Staleybridge, Sheffield, Leeds, Ripon, Denbigh, Mold, Gresford, Pentrobbin, Ruthin, Wrexham, Overton, Oswestry, Broughton, Bretton, Ruabon, Newtown, (Wales,) Dudley, Stourbridge, Shrewsbury, and a number of other places too many to be mentioned. During one year I attended about a hundred and fifty public meetings, and delivered about two hundred addresses. I frequently lectured during the middle of the day when I had to preach at night. I lectured both in public buildings and in the open air; in the market-places, and on the tops of mountains. My audiences were generally large, especially after the first few months, and the converts to teetotalism were frequently very numerous. At a meeting that I held on Buckley mountain, about a year after I first went to Chester, seventeen persons signed the pledge, several of whom had been wild and lawless, turbulent and dangerous characters, and most of them, I believe, continue to act on the teetotal principle to the present time. In some cases upwards of a hundred signed the pledge at one meeting, and sometimes several hundreds signed in one day in Wales.

The effects produced by the spread of teetotalism in Wales, were truly delightful. They were glorious and blessed beyond all that I could have anticipated. Crime was diminished beyond all previous example; and in some places, where crime had been unusually prevalent, and where it had been increasing for a length of time, it appeared to be brought entirely to an end. This was the case in the neighbourhood of Mold and Ruthin. In the neighbourhood of Mold a proposition had been made before teetotalism was introduced, to appoint a fresh constable, to assist in suppressing public disorders and disturbances. The meeting however separated without coming to any decision on the subject, adjourning its farther consideration to the following monthly meeting. When the adjourned meeting took place, and the discussion was commenced afresh, one of the farmers observed in broken English, that 'they needed no other constable now, that they had got a new constable, and it was his name that was Teetotal.' The fact was, that the spread of teetotalism in the neighbourhood had put an almost instant and complete end to all those disorders and disturbances, which had led them to contemplate the appointment of an additional constable. The improvement that had taken place in the neighbourhood led the authorities to say no more about the matter. They left the preservation of the peace and order of the neighbourhood to teetotalism, and teetotalism did the work well.

It was in the August of 1834, that I first introduced teetotalism into Ruthin. I lectured in the Town Hall, and the Mayor of the town was chairman of the meeting. We had a tolerably numerous meeting, and the lecture was favourably received. Several signed the pledge, and a teetotal society was formed. The society set to work in earnest, and by public meetings, and the distribution of tracts, and personal influence, they succeeded in spreading the principles very rapidly, both through the town and neighbourhood. The beautiful vale of Clwyd, in which the town of Ruthin is placed, was regularly teetotalised. Twelve months after my first lecture there, I was invited to attend the anniversary of the teetotal society. It was held in the largest chapel in the town. The mayor was again in the chair. On opening the meeting, the mayor observed, that though he was no public speaker, he must state a few facts from his own knowledge, tending to show the beneficial effect of teetotalism on the morals of the people. He then referred to the meeting when teetotalism was first introduced into Ruthin. He stated that at that time crime was very prevalent in the town and neighbourhood; that a great many cases were brought before him as chief magistrate of the town; that for some time previous to that, the number of criminal cases brought before him had been on the increase, and that the increase had been so great as to make it necessary for him both to require one or two other magistrates to assist him in hearing them and disposing of them, and to oblige him and his colleagues to sit twice as often as they had formerly been accustomed to do. But he added, that since teetotalism had begun to prevail in the town and neighbourhood, crime had gradually and rapidly diminished. Instead of sitting twice a week, the magistrates were soon enabled to get through the business that was brought before them with sitting once a fortnight. In course of time they were enabled to dispense with one of their fortnightly sittings,—once a month being found sufficient; and *now*, said he, for a length of time we have not had a single criminal case brought before us. The spread of teetotalism had so far regenerated and purified the neighbourhood, as to make the office of the magistrate a sinecure.

The happy effects of teetotalism upon individuals and families were truly delightful. Hundreds and thousands of people in the different towns and villages of Flintshire and Denbighshire, blessed God that they had ever heard a teetotal lecture, or been brought to adopt the teetotal pledge. Numbers of people came to me, from time to time, to thank me for my labours in the teetotal cause. Sometimes a father would come and tell me, with tears, that through my labours in the cause of teetotalism, he had been cured of drunkenness, and changed from being a curse and a torment to his family, to be a blessing and a comfort. Sometimes mothers would thank me for the influence of teetotalism upon their children. Sometimes children would thank me for the influence of teetotalism upon their parents. Sometimes wives would thank me for the influence of teetotalism upon their husbands; and frequently husbands and wives would join together to invite me to their houses, to partake of their cheer, to see the comfort in which they could live since teetotalism had come to their deliverance, and the plenty with which they were blessed since they had been reclaimed from their foolish and intemperate ways.

At first I was the only advocate of teetotalism there was in Wales: but I had not laboured long, before some of the Welsh converts took the matter in hand, and began to preach it to their countrymen in their own language. When the Welsh began to advocate teetotalism in their own tongue, it spread more rapidly, and in the course of a year or two, it had overrun the whole of the principality. All the preachers amongst the Welsh Methodists embraced the principle, except one, and a very great number of them publicly advocated it.* In some towns the drinking system was completely brought to an end. The public houses were shut up; the beer-shop signs were pulled down, and teetotalism became the general custom of the place.

I might mention scores of individuals who were reclaimed from drunkenness through the influence of teetotalism, who continue steady and exemplary characters to this day. I might mention scores of cases in which husbands and fathers, who, by their drunkenness had reduced themselves and their families to wretchedness, were reclaimed by teetotalism, and became a comfort and a blessing to their families. Some of those cases were of the most interesting and cheering description. But to give those cases at length would be too long a story. Besides, some of them have been already published, and may be found in others of my writings. One poor creature, a shoemaker, called Job Thompson, had brought himself down to absolute want. He had sold his furniture. He had disposed of most of his clothes. He had changed his hat for a paper cap, and in a drunken fit a day or so before he heard me lecture, he had lost his miserable

* The Welsh Methodists were the most numerous body in Wales. They were not the followers of Wesley, but of Whitfield. They had no hired preachers.

cap. He had stuck quite fast in his business. He had nothing with which to buy leather, and he had no credit. Nobody would trust him. A brother of his had helped him till he found that his help was of no use; and now he was given up by every one, and left alone, in absolute wretchedness. He heard my lecture; he signed the pledge, and became a sober man. He got a job, and set to work. By some means he obtained sufficient, after a while, to make a few shoes on his own account. He got paid for them, and made more. He soon was able to support himself and his wife. By-and-bye he got a little furniture. His business extended; his means increased; people were disposed to aid him, and he now got settled in a little, clean, comfortable house. He one day invited me to go and take tea with him, and I went. His house was a very small one. It had only one room, and that was so narrow that I could almost stretch my arms from wall to wall. Still it held their bed, and his cobler's seat, and a few chairs. And every thing seemed clean and comfortable. And the table was spread with all that was needful, and the happiness of the inmates, and their thanks for the benefit they had received from teetotalism, made our meeting a very agreeable one. Job still went on increasing his means, and employing them wisely, and giving God thanks for his blessings; and the last time I called on him, he was occupying a larger house, and a good front shop, and was doing a very good business in the little country town in which he lived. This is only one case out of scores and hundreds that came to my knowledge, illustrating the happy working of teetotalism.

At Chester I commenced a new class, which soon numbered twenty members or upwards, and no less than fourteen of those members were reformed drunkards. To hear the stories which some of those reformed drunkards told of what they had suffered from drinking, and of the benefits they had experienced from teetotalism, was truly affecting. Many a time have I wept while listening to them, and given God thanks in my tears, for the great and glorious change which teetotalism had effected in their characters and circumstances.

Notwithstanding all these things, there were many professors of religion, and many who professed to be ministers of Christ, that looked on teetotalism with an evil eye; that regarded it with great disapprobation, and madly employed their powers in opposing it. There were several such in the Chester Circuit, in the Methodist New Connexion. One of my colleagues, James Ousey, was of this class. He hated teetotalism, and its prevalence seemed to distress him very much. He used all his influence to obstruct its spread; and when he found that any whom he knew had become teetotalers, he did what he could to induce them to renounce it, and to return again to the use of intoxicating drinks. With *some* he *succeeded*, and the effects, in some cases, were truly awful. One man, a member of the New Connexion, of the name of Downs, had become a teetotaler. Downs had repeatedly been overcome by drink. He was a sober man on the whole, but having to visit the markets at Liverpool, and being obliged to do business occasionally at public houses, he was frequently, though perhaps unintentionally and unexpectedly, overcome. He saw no means of securing himself from continued falls, but by becoming a teetotaler. He accordingly signed the pledge, and seemed secure. James Ousey, the preacher, *ridiculed* him for becoming a teetotaler, and reasoned with him, to convince him of his folly in doing so. The man was rather simple, and was persuaded by the preacher to renounce teetotalism. He began to drink again, and soon got drunk. But now his condition was truly awful. The reproaches of his conscience were more terrible than ever, and he was dreadfully miserable. I called one morning to see him, not knowing that he had broken his pledge, much less that he had again been drunk. On going into the house, I found him sitting by the fire, in a most woful and miserable state. His looks were wild and dreadful. His wife stood by him, weeping and sobbing as if her heart would break. Her eyes were inflamed with weeping, and she seemed almost distracted. What is the matter? said I; and the horrible story came out. He had been drunk the night before. He had been *seen* drunk by some of the members of the church. He felt himself disgraced. He felt besides that he had sinned against his God and against his conscience. He was ashamed of himself. He abhorred himself. He wished himself out of the world; and he had that very morning, only an hour or so before, been attempting to put an end to his existence. It had been with difficulty that his wife had prevented him from perpetrating the horrible deed. At the very same moment that I entered the room, he had been declaring to his wife that he could not live, and that he *would* not live; and his wife was wild with terror, and full of grief. I talked to him; I reasoned with him. He at length became calmer, and his purpose of self-destruction was abandoned. He resolved to be a teetotaler again. I urged his wife to join with him in teetotalism, and exhorted them to help each other to keep the pledge inviolate to the last; and they signed the pledge together that forenoon.

There was one person in the New Connexion at Chester in whom I felt more than usual interest. He was a local preacher and a class leader, and a man in tolerable circumstances. He was besides a somewhat clever man. He had a good sound mind. He had a considerable amount of knowledge, and very considerable talents; and was of a free and generous disposition. He was made in fact to be something great, and nothing was wanting to render him great, great in intellect, great in goodness, great in usefulness, but fidelity to his own nature, and superiority to the low indulgences of sense. But he was fond of what is called good living. He was also fond of his gun. He was fond of company besides; and if not fond of drink, he *used* it freely when in company. His love of drink had grown upon him. Drink had had an evil influence both on his body and his mind. It had had an evil influence on his body. It had made him enormously fat. He had become a very unwieldy, bulky man. Walking had become a wearisome task to him, and working was not over pleasant. His love of drink had had a bad influence on his mind. It had weakened his desire for improvement. He had, to a great extent, lost his taste for books. He had lost his pleasure in preaching; and though people were still delighted to hear him, whenever they could get the opportunity, he seldom gave them the opportunity. And his course was downward. He was getting worse. I was very much concerned for him, and exceedingly desirous of rescuing him, if possible, from his dangerous career. I succeeded at length in persuading him to become a teetotaler. He tried the principle for a good long time, and found it to answer exceedingly well. He lost, in the course of a few months, from twenty to thirty pounds weight. But what he lost in weight, he gained in strength. His breathing became better. He could walk better, work better, talk better, do anything better.

He was more cheerful, more happy. He was in a fair way, in fact, to become a new, a regenerated character; an exemplary and useful man. But mark what followed. My envious, malignant, or my foolish and unhappy colleague, visited him, ridiculed teetotalism, talked to him of its folly, spoke highly of moderation, preached loudly enough against excess, but spoke much of the childishness of intelligent and religious men signing pledges, and running to such wild extremes. He also dwelt largely on the inhospitableness of teetotalism, and said something about its impiety and blasphemy. I heard of his arguments, but I cannot remember them all. No matter; he succeeded in inducing my friend to return to his drink: and the last case of this man was worse than the first. The accounts I have heard of him since are most sad and humiliating; and whether he still be living, or whether his vices have carried him to a premature grave, I cannot tell: but his apostacy proved a dreadful matter both to himself, his family, and his friends.

There were some violent opponents of teetotalism on the *Welsh* side of the circuit, and one of them continued an opponent to the last. His name was Charles Shone. When I first went over to Hawarden, a town about seven or eight miles from Chester, I called at his house, as the preachers were accustomed to do, and there were assembled there, as was usual when the preacher came, a number of the leaders and members of the New Connexion society in Hawarden. Charles had heard of teetotalism, and soon began to talk about it. He ridiculed the idea of people living without ale, porter and wine; and some of his friends who were present, joined him in his ridicule. He said to me, 'You don't *believe* what you teach about teetotalism, Mr. Barker. You can't. Now tell us honestly,' said he, 'are you not making fun of the people. Do you really think that working people can do without ale or beer? Do you really think that wine, spirits and porter are of no use? Nonsense,' said he, 'you can't.' I felt little disposition to talk with him, so long as he kept in that strain; for reasoning against ridicule is like swimming, not against a stream, but against a rushing, headlong, overwhelming torrent. The most effectual answer to ridicule, is silence; and *I* was silent for a while. At length we came to reason. Charles now had no chance. The tide went against him. I had neither the stream nor the torrent to swim against.

After he had heard a great deal of what I had to say, he replied, 'Yes, you can talk against anything. You can argue on any subject. You can make anything look foolish, if you like; and you can make any thing look reasonable, however foolish it be. But,' says he, 'what could you do if you were to argue in favour of *a little drink?* You could say still *more* on that side, if you chose.' And in this style he went on for several minutes. Thomas Bennett, at that time one of Charles's companions, took Charles's side; but he was far more rational than Charles. He laughed hard enough occasionally, to be sure; but he used no banter, no insolence. His talk was not insolence or ridicule. He had something like fairness and honesty about him. Both Charles and Bennett were local preachers and class leaders; they were, in fact, the leading men in the New Connexion, on the *Hawarden* side of the circuit. Their opposition to teetotalism had its influence on many; but it did not prevent the people generally either from hearing the lectures, or from adopting the principle advocated. Bennett became a teetotaler at length, and began to advocate the cause which at first he had opposed. But Charles Shone, as I said, continued to oppose it to the last. Some thought Charles was vexed that he had not himself the honour of introducing teetotalism into the neighbourhood. Some thought that he had gone so far in opposing it at first, that his pride would not allow him to embrace it and advocate it after. But others told me that he was very fond of drink; that he had a very bad custom of visiting the public house, and drinking in company with a number of indifferent characters, and that it was probably his love of drink, and his love of his drinking companions, that held him in slavery. Whatever it might be, his drinking did him very great harm, and his *advocacy* of drinking, after teetotalism had proved itself so infinitely beneficial, went far towards destroying his influence, and putting an end to his usefulness.

There was another person on the Welsh side of the circuit that opposed me very zealously for a while. He kept a beer shop. He lived about two miles or so from Hawarden, on the way to Holywell. They called him John Astbury. He had heard me lecture at Wepre, and after the meeting, walked on with me towards Hawarden, where I was appointed to spend the night. He soon introduced the subject of teetotalism, and began to defend the use of intoxicating drinks. He told me that he kept a beer shop, and spoke of the traffic in drink as perfectly lawful and proper. I observed, that the prosperity of his business, must be the adversity of his customers,—that the better customers his neighbours were for his beer, the worse and more miserable they would be likely to become. And I asked him this question,—'When you rise in the morning, do you pray to God to bless you with plenty of custom through the day? and when you go to bed at night, do you give God thanks for all the drinking that there has been in your house through the day? Can you ask God's blessing on your buisness, and pray to Him to prosper it? Would you not, in praying for the prosperity of your business, be praying for the prevalence of drunkenness?' He remembered those questions, and thought about them seriously, and it was not long before I heard that he had pulled down his sign, and had given up his business as a drink-seller, and was resolved to support himself by the business to which he had been brought up, and which he had still continued to carry on. He became an advocate of teetotalism before long, and remains an advocate, I believe, to this day. He was a hearty, generous, well-disposed man.

I met with one opponent to teetotalism at Hawarden, of a more malignant description than any of those I have mentioned hitherto. His name was Kent, a farrier. He was a Methodist and a local preacher; but was a low, unprincipled man, and very fond of drink. At the time when teetotalism was spreading very rapidly in Hawarden and the neighbourhood, Kent told a story to the following effect,—'That he was at Chester early one morning, and saw me near a coach, and heard me ask a female on the top of the coach, if she would have a glass of brandy and water.' Now, on the morning in question, I *was* at Chester, and was at the *coach office*, by a coach, setting my mother-in-law, who had been with us for a while, off home. So far there was some foundation for the story. But, in the first place, my mother-in-law was a very abstemious woman, and never used spirit and water. In the second place, it was early in the morning, and my mother-in-law had only just come from the breakfast table, not having walked more than two or three hundred yards. In the third place, it was a hot summer's day. In the fourth place, my mother-in-law had only about twenty miles to ride. In the fifth place, I was known to the population of Chester generally, not only as a *teetotaler*, but as a *public teetotal advocate*, and the idea, that at a public coach-office, in the midst of a crowd of people, I should speak aloud, and ask my mother-in-law to have a glass of brandy and water,—that I should thus publicly and recklessly throw away my reputation, and expose myself to deserved reproach, was out of all character. In short, the story was a foolish as well as a wicked fabrication. It did however cause a great excitement. Many believed it. *Every* slander is believed by *some*, and slanders generally are believed by *multitudes*. This was believed by considerable numbers, and a terrible noise was made about it. When I first heard of it, I treated it as a matter of no importance, and was unwilling even to contradict it in a public meeting. I soon however found that the matter *was* of importance, and that it required to be carefully dealt with. I therefore instantly proposed that two parties should be sent off to ask my mother-in-law, whether I had ever asked her to have either a glass of brandy and water, or a glass of any intoxicating drinks whatever, either while she was with us at our house, or when she was on the coach to go home. I offered to pay one-half the expense of the journey. To this the adversary would not agree. Let it be spoken to Charles Shone's credit, that when he found I was assailed by a wilful falsehood, he zealously took my part, though an opponent to teetotalism, and offered himself as one to go and propose the question to my mother-in-law. My mother-in-law was no teetotaler. She hated teetotalism. But she was one that would tell the truth, and I had perfect confidence in her in the matter. When my first proposal was declined by the adversary, I announced my intention to expose the slander at a public meeting, and challenged the slanderer to attend. He declined attending; but a friend of his, Edward Parry, attended to see how things went on, but said little in opposition to any thing I had advanced. This same Edward Parry, at a later period, became a teetotaler, and laboured as a teetotal advocate. The excitement caused by Kent's slander soon died away after this meeting, and Kent, instead of injuring me or teetotalism, only brought disgrace upon himself. Kent never was highly respected in the neighbourhood where he lived, but he was less respected after this unprincipled attack on me and on teetotalism, than he had ever been.

During the first seventeen months after my appointment to the Chester circuit, I lived in the city of Chester, but during the following seven months I lived at Ewloe, in Flintshire, Wales, about a mile beyond Hawarden, on the Chester and Holywell road. From this time, the principal part of my labour was on the Welsh side of the circuit, though I regularly preached at Chester as usual. This left me more free to advocate teetotalism, than I should have been, had I lived in Chester all the time,—for on the Welsh side of the circuit teetotalism was very much in favour, and the societies there were more ready to give me up to attend teetotal meetings at a distance, than the society in Chester, or the societies in the neighbourhood, would have been. I should besides have been, to some extent, though not under his control, yet subject to annoyances from my colleague, during the *second* year I spent in Chester circuit, as my colleague for that year, as I have already stated, was a very great enemy to teetotalism. I had been a good deal annoyed by the opposition of certain members of the society, on the Chester side, before my opposing colleague, James Ousey, came into the circuit. On one occasion they actually called me to an account at a leaders' meeting, for taking the liberty to advocate teetotalism oftener than they thought allowable. They invited me to attend the meeting. I went, not knowing beforehand the business that was to come before the meeting. When I found that the object of the meeting was to prefer complaints against me for lecturing too often on teetotalism, and to pass, if possible, a vote of censure or admonition upon me, I briefly told them what I thought of their proceedings, and left them to themselves. What happened at the meeting after my departure, I either never learned, or I have since forgot. I believe they allowed the matter to drop.

On one occasion, I took the liberty of delivering a teetotal lecture in the New Connexion chapel at Chester, on a week evening, instead of preaching. This also gave offence to some, but I paid but little regard to their opposition.

The society at Chester was very corrupt, and drinking had had no small part in corrupting it. This made me the more resolute in my efforts to oppose the drinking system, and to promote the spread of teetotalism. One of the preachers that preceded me at Chester, the superintendent, was a regular drunkard. I found, as I went round the circuit, that he had the reputation of a drunkard, or a very hard drinker, at almost every place. At one house, at Tarvin, the servant girl had actually complained at being required to fetch up drink for him so frequently, and was so provoked on one occasion, that she actually spoke aloud, as she was going down the cellar steps, saying, 'He'll be drunk.' The mistress of the house told me, that it was no uncommon thing for him to be drunk, and that he regularly drank as much as *ought* to have made him drunk, as much as would have made *two or three* people drunk, that were not so much accustomed to drink. After preaching, he would sit and smoke, and drink glass after glass, empty pitcher after pitcher, for hours, and then tumble into bed. In the morning he would be coughing, and spitting, and retching, and unable to eat anything to his breakfast.

At another place I was told, that he was so drunk one time, that he could not find his way out of the garden, nor see his road before him, nor walk along it steadily when they had put him safely into the road. At another place I was told that he regularly drank a half-pint of gin, besides all the ale and wine that he could get, every time he came, though he spent only one or two nights with them at the utmost. This preacher used to complain of a lightness in the head, and he pretended to take gin to cure this lightness. The probability is, that his lightness in the head was *caused* by his gin, and that if he had been a teetotaler, he would never have been troubled with such a complaint. This same man was afterwards stationed at Bolton, and while there, was often seen drunk, and was one night found rolling in the street, too drunk to be able to help himself. He was, in fact, a regular sot. Yet he stood rather high in the Connexion, and at one time was ranked amongst the first, the best, and the most useful of its ministers. And I am inclined to think that he erred through ignorance, rather than sinned through wickedness; that he really believed that ale and gin were essential to his health, and to the preservation of his life, and that he drank, originally at least, from no bad motives. But drink had gradually gained power over him, until it had made him at length its slave. When I was first stationed at Chester, I went to live in the same house in which he had lived the year before, and in the cup-board were several pots smelling strongly of ale, and with a portion of that coloured matter in them that remains at the bottom of pots, after ale is dried up.

Another preacher, who had been stationed in Chester circuit five or six years before, as I was credibly informed, died drunk, after preaching one night at a country place on the Welsh side of the circuit. His name was Dunkerley. An account may be seen of him in my writings on temperance subjects.

Jackson, the man that had preceded me, had been accustomed, I was told, frequently to accompany certain members of his congregation to the public house, and to drink with them there; and one of those members, named Harrison, who was also a trustee, had failed in business, and left the city in disgrace, a short time before I was stationed at Chester.

I say, the society at Chester was very corrupt, and that drink had a great deal to do in *causing* that corruption. I may add, there were several persons at Chester, who were not exactly members, but who still were regarded as leading friends of the cause, who appeared to delight in nothing so much as eating and drinking; whose highest pleasure it seemed to be to attend parties, and who would sit and smoke and drink at such parties for six or eight hours in succession. As I have said elsewhere, I saw, at one of those parties, a preacher of the Methodist New Connexion, drink ten glasses of port wine between dinner and tea, besides what else he had drunk, of other kinds of drink, at dinner. I saw another preacher, who was present on the same occasion, but who was not a Methodist preacher, drink several glasses of spirit and water, besides drinking spirit and water at his dinner. And these were common things.

At some of those parties the people would stay till twelve o'clock at night, smoking and drinking nearly the whole of the time. And even the ladies, who drank only wine through the evening, were expected to take each a glass of spirit and water on leaving the house, to protect them against the cold night air. One of these leading patrons of the drinking system, called Welshman, refused to invite me to any of his parties, on the simple ground that I would not engage beforehand to drink a little wine with him. I had frequently been at his house before I was stationed in Chester, and had taken my glass of wine or ale, like other people, and he had professed to be exceedingly fond of me; but now, since I had adopted the principle of teetotalism, he could not endure me at a party.

There was another person of a similar character, but fonder of drink than Welshman, who had often invited me to his house when visiting Chester before I was stationed there, but he never invited me now that I had become a teetotaler. The patrons of drinking could not endure the presence of a teetotaler; they could not enjoy themselves if a firm teetotaler was present. The presence of a teetotaler spoiled all their pleasure. A teetotaler had as great an influence in parties like those which were so common at Chester, as a rational, intelligent man has in a Methodistical revival meeting. In the one case virtue, and in the other case intelligence, frightens the mad excitement out of existence.

During the two years that I was stationed in the Chester circuit, I received two presents, as public testimonials of gratitude for my labours in the temperance cause. One was a medal and a chain, which were presented to me in the Town Hall, at Chester; another was a beautiful pocket Bible, which was presented to me in Peter-street Chapel at Manchester. The chain I afterwards sold, as I wanted the money to help me in printing. The medal my wife got, and she keeps it still. The Bible I myself retain, and I prize it very highly. It has been of very great use to me. I used it in all my discussions with the Socialists; and I have used it in all my discussions with my orthodox opponents. One person, who observed with what readiness I opened this Bible on any passage that I wanted, requested me to get him one like it; he was foolish enough to think there was something particular in the book itself, and that it opened at any passage that I was wishful to find.

I must now return to Sheffield affairs. While stationed at Sheffield, I was frequently invited to preach anniversary sermons in other circuits; and in every place I had large congregations. I attended the missionary anniversary at Nottingham, and preached at the opening of a new chapel at Beeston, in the Nottingham circuit. I preached at the opening of another new chapel in Halifax, and attended chapel and school anniversaries at Ashton, Hurst, Hollingworth, &c. I had, in fact, become popular in the Connexion, and, at every following Conference, most of the circuits were wishful to have me stationed with them. The favour thus shown to me excited fresh jealousies in the minds of some of the preachers, and caused them to use their influence against me. Yet I still went forward in my labours, indulging a hope that the time would come, when persecution would cease, and when I should find myself in a position to effect such reforms in the Connexion, as would render it more effective, and make it a blessing to the world at large.

When the April quarterly meeting came, the societies of the Sheffield circuit had to decide upon what preachers they would ask for the coming year. The quarterly meeting consisted of representatives or delegates from all the societies. The representatives were divided about the preachers to be asked for. Most of them were wishful that *I* should be requested for another year; but those who were wishful that *I* should be stationed with them again, were not equally desirous that *Burrows*, the superintendent, should be stationed with them again. But Burrows was exceedingly *anxious* to be stationed at Sheffield again; and Dixon, and Allin, and two or three others, were also desirous of his re-appointment. Yet no one had courage to *move* that Burrows should be requested for another year. Dixon and Allin and their party were afraid to propose it, as they knew that the mass of the meeting were against them. And many of those that were wishful that *I* should be requested another year, were equally unwilling to propose *that* to the meeting, for fear of giving offence to Burrows. At length a zealous friend of mine, but one that cared little for hurting the feelings of his opponents, moved openly that Conference should be requested to appoint me to the circuit a third year, and that Conference should also be requested to re-appoint *Burrows*, provided *I* were made *superintendent*. He stated as one reason for his motion, that Burrows had been frequently unwell, and had in consequence been unable to attend to the business of the circuit; that I had been more active in the circuit than Burrows, and seemed likelier to manage the affairs of the circuit to advantage than he. This was enough, and too much, in fact. It caused a terrible stir, and great confusion. Dixon, and Allin, and Haslam were thunderstruck, and Burrows was dreadfully distressed. How matters went on after, I do not distinctly recollect; but I know that when Burrows addressed the meeting towards its close, he made woful complaints against the members of the meeting for the treatment which he had received, and talked in a most doleful and melancholy way. This was his farewell address. After he had done, it was my turn to take my leave of the circuit and the meeting. I told them that *I* had no complaints to make against them whatever; that I had received much kindness from them; that I had met with a hearty co-operation from them in my labours to do good; that I had spent two happy years amongst them, and that I should leave them with many pleasing recollections, and be glad whenever I might have an opportunity of meeting them again. I was so disgusted with Burrow's address, that in my own, I unhappily spoke of his as a *funeral* address, instead of as a *farewell* address. The temptation so to describe it was too strong for me at the time to be resisted. This made things worse. It grieved Burrows, and Dixon, and Allin, and Haslam immensely; and a short time after the meeting, perhaps a week or a fortnight, or it might be more, I was invited to attend a meeting at Thomas Allin's. I attended, not knowing beforehand what was the object of the meeting, nor what was the matter that was to come before it. When I got there, I found that it was a meeting of Allin, and Haslam, and Burrows, and that the object was to find fault with me for the manner in which I had spoken and acted at the quarterly meeting, and for the manner in which I had acted in the circuit generally. The substance of their complaint was this, that I had not acted in concert with my colleagues; that I had acted as one of a party, and that the party with which I had acted, was not the party with which my superintendent was identified. I say, this was the substance of the complaint. The complaint itself was a long one, and had many particular parts. I replied to the complaint, and reasoned with my accusers, and endeavoured to show them it was not *I* that had acted in the spirit of party, but *they*; that I had identified myself with *no* particular party, but had kept myself free from *all*; that I had simply preserved my independence; that my fault was, if I had *committed* a fault, that I had *refused* to be a party man; that I had refused to be the tool of Dixon, and to act with him in opposition to the circuit generally. They attempted to reply, but all that they said amounted to nothing, and I told them plainly at length, that they had all of them, in my judgment, got a Broom-lodge napkin over their eyes.

Broom-lodge was the name of the house in which Dixed lived. I told them that, in my judgment, they had sold both themselves, and the circuit, as far as they had the power, into Dixon's hands, and had gone a great way towards ruining the interests of the circuit, in foolish subservience to Dixon: and thus the meeting ended.

It was somewhere about this time that I called at the house of Burrows, and his wife refused to speak to me : and Burrows and I were never on the best terms after, nor were Allin or Haslam and I. I regard this occasion, in fact, as a sort of breaking up of the friendship existing between me and some of the preachers, or rather, as the open breaking out of the preachers' enmity, and as a step on their part towards my final separation from the Connexion. I was sorry afterwards that I had spoken of Burrows' address in the way I had done. It seemed a pity that I should have used a word in describing his address, so calculated to give him offence. But what could I do ? I hated his servility, and I hated his underhand mode of proceeding. I was disgusted with the whole of his party ; their conduct was so mean. They never could accomplish their objects without my help, and yet they never could seek my assistance or co-operation openly. Even when they had an object in view that was honourable, they must seek to attain it in a dishonourable way. I say I hated such proceedings, and I was utterly disgusted with them, and out of the abundance of my heart, my mouth inadvertently spoke ; and I cannot say that I am sorry for it now. If I am sorry for anything, it is that I bore with their meanness so long ; that I did not, from the first, speak freely whatever was in my mind, and break with them and with the Connexion altogether.

Some of the societies in the Sheffield circuit lay in Derbyshire, sixteen or seventeen miles from Sheffield. One of those societies was Clay-cross, a well-known station on the Leeds and Derby railway now. Another was Hanley, a place about a mile and a half, or two miles from Clay-cross. When we went to Hanley, we had our meat and lodgings at a farm house a little further into the country. In this part of Derbyshire, beans and bacon form a very common dish at dinner. Bacon is almost the only animal food which the people use, and those of the farmers that are not either richer or more liberal than usual, seldom like to bring out any other kind of meat, either for their families or their visitors. And the people who lodged and boarded the preachers at Hanley, were neither rich nor liberal to any great extent. They delighted therefore to supply the preachers with bacon every dinner time. But preachers, in general, don't like to make dinners of bacon; they had rather have mutton, or lamb, or veal, or beef, or chicken, or turkey. Burrows was especially fond of a comfortable dinner; but Burrows was not truthful and candid. I cared comparatively little what I had to dinner; still, I never liked bacon very well. I always preferred other kinds of meat, if they were easy to be had. When Burrows went to the house of which I am speaking, the people, as usual, placed bacon before him, but made, at the same time, the customary apology, to the effect, that they had not any other kind of meat at hand, but that if he wished it, they would get him something else.' 'O no, thank you,' says Burrows, 'I am fond of bacon;' and that was enough, for from that time to the day that Burrows left the circuit, they *gave* him bacon, and *he* never, I imagine, got any thing else but bacon. When *I* went, they placed bacon before me, but made the customary apology, to the effect, that they had not any thing else at hand, but that if I had rather have a little mutton, or any thing in that way, they would try to get it me. 'No thank you,' said I, 'I will take a little bacon; I cannot say that I am *fond* of bacon, but I always feel thankful for it when there is nothing else at hand.' That was enough; I never had bacon brought after. I had no intention of putting the people about. I could make a dinner without *any* kind of animal food, and many a time had done so; but when I was called upon to say what I *liked*, I *told* them what I liked, and left the matter with them. Burrows often complained about the bacon, and when I told him that they always gave me something different, he seemed astonished, and could not tell how it was. I told him that the people told me that he was *fond* of bacon; that he had told them he *liked* bacon very well. Burrows shook his head. He remembered very well that he *had* told them so, but he had no idea that they would *believe* what he said; or at least he had no idea that they would *act* on their faith so steadily and constantly as they did. This is a trifling incident, but it serves to illustrate the character of Burrows, as well as to show how it got him into difficulties occasionally.

While I am speaking of Burrows, I may mention another incident. At one of the Conferences, the delegate from Stalybridge was very anxious to have Burrows stationed in his circuit, while Burrows was equally anxious in his heart to go to another circuit, where, as he understood, the preacher had four shillings a week more allowed him for board. When the Stalybridge delegate spoke to Burrows, Burrows professed to be wishful to go to Stalybridge; but when Burrows was called into the Stationing Committee, he gave the preference to the other circuit that paid, as he understood, the most board. The other circuit however was coveted by another person, and this other person succeeded in getting stationed there. Burrows now began to look after the Stalybridge circuit; but the way to that circuit was now shut up. The Stalybridge delegate had found out how Burrows was acting, and refused to have any thing more to do with him. Hence Burrows had to look for a circuit where he could find one.

During the second year that I was stationed at Sheffield, my second colleague was Robert Henshaw. Lynn had been removed at the Conference preceding. Robert was an exceedingly quiet, inoffensive kind of man, disposed to learn, but endowed with only moderate abilities. He was exceedingly silent in company; he would sit for hours together and never speak. Yet he manifestly took an interest at times in what was said by others, and seemed disposed to *learn* something from what he heard. He was a middling preacher, perhaps rather better than middling, compared with most Methodist preachers; but he had very little power. No one, I should imagine, would ever be greatly moved by his preaching, either with hope or fear, with sorrow or gladness. I should fancy that he had not an original thought in his head. He appeared a perfectly *second hand* man; a man made and fashioned, both with respect to his creed and his habits, by the external influences to which he had been subjected. He had very little power to do good, and little or no disposition to do harm. If he did good, it would rather be by accident than on purpose; and if he did evil, it would be more through the incitement or instigation of others, than through any ill-will of his own. He could never become a heretic, I should think, but by mistake; and could only be orthodox in consequence of the circumstances in which he was placed, and the manner in which he had been brought up. He certainly approached as near to the *Socialist's* man, whose character is formed *for* him and not *by* him, as any one I ever knew. He never offended me by his conversation; nor did he ever please me. He never opposed me; nor did he ever favour me. He threw no obstacles in my way; nor did he afford me any help. He was neither a friend nor an enemy; but a perfect absolute piece of indifferentism or neutrality. I believe he is a preacher still. I have heard of him speaking against me in some parts of the country since my expulsion; but he would have spoken against any one else, if he had happened to be expelled, or had happened to be spoken against by those with whom he was connected. If I and my friends had been the ruling party in Conference, and had expelled the parties who expelled us, Robert would have been as true and faithful to us, as he now is to them. Of all the men in the world, I know no one so well calculated for a Methodist preacher as Robert; no one that would ever be less likely to be troubled with scruples of conscience, or no one whose conscience would feel more easy in adopting the general good, or the general interest, as his rule,—meaning by the general good, or the the general interest, the good or the interest of the ruling party in the body to which he might belong. I could never call Robert a bad man, and yet I could hardly regard him as a good man. I could not call him a *bad* man, because I think he had no bad principle, no bad purpose, no malignant disposition; yet I could not call him a good man, because I could hardly regard him as possessed of sufficient knowledge of good and evil, of sufficient power to discriminate between right and wrong, or of sufficient mental energy to enable him to adopt any general moral principle as the rule of his conduct, or to adhere to such rule, even if he happened by accident to adopt it for a moment.

Lynn was a man of a very different character. He had plenty of energy, but little intellect; and the intellect which he had, had been very little cultivated. Lynn never could have become great in point of intellect, but he might, if his intellect had been cultivated, have been great in other ways. He had considerable dramatic power. What he understood, he could represent, at times, in a very lively way. He had the power of making his thoughts visible and striking. His thoughts were often low, and his style was also low; but still, to such as were not easily offended with bad taste, bad grammar, bad logic, and foolish notions, Lynn was a powerful, engaging, interesting preacher. He had a good deal of wit, such as it was, and could make such people as were insensible to his defects, laugh exceedingly, and keep them on a laugh for a length of time. I have known him keep his hearers laughing for nearly half an hour together. He could, at the same time, represent in lively and striking colours, some of the awful things connected with religion. He could pourtray the character of God, describe a coming judgment and the torments of the damned, in such a manner as to excite great terror in the minds of those who were uncultivated enough not to be shocked with the horrible character of his notions, his vulgar language, and his unchristian manner. But his power was greatest when treating of things that were ludicrous. He could on these occasions make both himself and his subject look as ridiculous or laughable as any one could wish. He had, besides, strong lungs, and a good voice, though he had a nasty intolerable way with him of squeaking, squalling, and making a curious clicking sound with his nose. He had besides a very fair share of that other kind of power, which I call the power of affection or of sympathy. He could feel, and he could talk so as to make others feel. Hence he could carry along with him at his pleasure an uncultivated and vulgar audience, and produce on them a powerful effect. In prayer he was more powerful than in preaching. He was a clever revivalist, according to Methodistical notions of revivalism. But even in his prayers he could seldom refrain from vulgar witticisms. He was at times as vulgar and ridiculous when conversing with God, as he was when talking to men; and, in fact, he frequently made use of what is called prayer, as a means of talking to men. He was clever at praying *at* people. While pretending to talk to God, he would be lecturing those that were about him for five or ten minutes together.

Lynn had nothing that could be called knowledge. All that he had, that could go under that name with any one, was simply a bundle of incongruous notions and phrases, some of them great and some of them little, some of them false and some of them true, some of them ridiculous and some of them rational; and the false and the foolish, and the low and the little, and the absurd and ridiculous, formed by far the greater portion of his bundle of mixtures. He had never examined any matters for himself. I question whether the thought of examining into any matter, of inquiring into the foundations of any doctrine, ever entered into his mind till after his acquaintance with me; and even then he had no idea of entering upon such a task. He looked half horrified when I told him that so long as he neglected to inquire into matters for himself, and to search the Scriptures carefully, and test his opinions one by one by what the Scriptures taught, he knew nothing which of his opinions were Scriptural, and which were unscriptural; which of them were doctrines of Christ, and which of them were inventions of men. That which appeared to me to be the most rational thing in the world, seemed to him to be out of all character. What! a preacher, a revivalist, a man who had been a preacher and a revivalist for ten or fifteen years, begin to inquire into the foundations of his notions, into the soundness of his creed. A man who had preached anniversary sermons, and who had been petitioned for by most of the circuits in the Connexion, call his doctrines in question, and compare them one by one with the Scriptures, to see whether they were agreeable to Scripture teaching or not! It seemed to him out of all reason. And then again, where should he begin? How should he proceed? By what means should he ascertain what the Scriptures *did* teach? How should he get to understand the Scriptures? The idea of understanding the Scriptures had itself never entered into his mind. He thought the proper way was, to read them occasionally with eyes uplifted to heaven, and to receive as divine revelations, as the true and proper meaning of the Scriptures, whatever imaginations arose in his mind while engaged thus in reading them. The idea that the Scriptures had just one meaning, was an idea that he had never entertained. He considered that the Scriptures might have three, or four, or ten, or a dozen meanings, and that every meaning of a passage was right that he could either get *out* of the passage, thrust *into* the passage, or connect *with* the passage in any way. He was a man of dreams and feelings, and not of ideas and reasoning; his creed was built upon fancy, and not upon truth; his religion consisted in emotions, in passions, in feelings, and dreams, not in knowledge and benevolence, not in light, and love, and power. Hence he knew nothing, properly speaking. His theology and his language were alike patchwork; there was no originality, no order, no consistency, no rationality about them. Yet he chose, when the question arose respecting my orthodoxy, both to talk to me when I met with him, and to write to me when absent from me, on the necessity of guarding against error. He said I was a noble fellow, a clever and wonderful man, with the exception of those crotchets; referring to what he considered my un-Methodistical notions. And again he said, 'you would be gloriously useful if you could only get those cobwebs cleaned out of your upper story.' A man that had never spent an hour in seeking after truth; that had never read a book since he was born, with any idea or intention of testing its contents; a man who had never, from the day of his birth, proved any thing, much less proved all things; a man who had taken up whatever came to hand under the sound or semblance of religion, provided it did not shock his prejudices; a man in whom no very great power of reasoning dwelt, and in whom the rational power that dwelt in him had never been cultivated; a man that could not give a rational account of any single portion of his creed, or explain a hundredth part of the phrases which he commonly used; a man who would himself have acknowledged himself a perfect child in comparison with me, if he had not been told by others that some of my opinions were heretical; this man could lecture me both in word and writing, with the most ridiculous solemnity and apparent gravity. When I used to interrupt him in his lectures, and ask him a question as to what he meant, or as to the reason which he had for the statements which he made, he would say, 'You know I can't reason; I am no scholar. All I want is that you should keep to the simple Gospel of Christ, and get your soul full of the love of God, and preach like a good hearty Methodist preacher.' This man, from the depth of his ignorance, and from the thickness of traditional darkness in which he was enveloped, would call aloud like an oracle from his mysterious hiding place, to warn children of light against rushing into dangers, and to exhort them to beware lest they should err from the truth.

Still, he was not without affection. He really loved me, so long as there remained any prospect of my permanent union with the body, or so long as there seemed any hope that I might be brought to restrain my inquiries and investigations, and keep myself within the bounds of blind Methodistical belief. But when the prospect of my continued connection with the body was gone,—when his hopes of keeping me within the limits of blind Methodistical belief were utterly cut off, he then stood forth as a decided opponent, and was the first to get up in Conference to declare, that he should vote for my expulsion. He rose in Conference and declared, even before I had been tried, that he should vote for my expulsion. And why should he not, poor fellow? For he knew as much before the trial came on, as he would ever be likely to know when it was over. He voted by feeling, and not by facts. To attend to the details of a trial would have been most grievous and wearisome to him. It was as well therefore that he should make known on what side he intended to vote before the investigation commenced, as after it was closed.

I have seen Mr. Lynn once or twice since my expulsion: he never attempted to reason with me. He never gave himself credit, in fact, for being *able* to reason. Thus far he proved himself superior to some; for some can neither reason, nor find out their inability to reason.

During my second year at Sheffield, Lynn was stationed at Nottingham. He laboured there, as usual, to get up a revival; and succeeded to some extent. During this revival, he prayed and shouted at such a rate, and for such a length of time together, and for so many nights in succession, that he became unwell. Strong as he was, and he seemed the very image of strength; strong as he was, he utterly disabled himself. He could scarcely stand steady on his feet; he had painful and distressing symptoms towards the back of his head; and surgical and medical aid became necessary. If I remember right, he was cupped and blistered; but these means afforded him but doubtful or slight relief. He became dreadfully nervous, and horribly miserable. He doubted the truth of religion, and was tempted, most horribly tempted, to doubt the existence of God. His soul was in perfect disorder; his thoughts were all confusion; the sandy foundations of his faith were all disturbed, and his fears and anxieties were unutterably dreadful. How long he continued in this state I do not recollect; but he suffered for a length of time.

At length his health was partially restored; his mind recovered its tone, and he was able to preach and labour a little in his usual way. Some time after his recovery, he visited Sheffield, and I recollect meeting with him at Thomas Allin's, and remember him telling his story. Thomas Allin attributed his fears, and doubts, and temptations about the truth of religion, and the existence of a God, to a want of knowledge; to a want of acquaintance with the evidences of natural and revealed religion. Lynn attributed the whole to the malice of the devil. He thought that the devil had done it to stop the revival, and to prevent the salvation of souls. He looked upon himself as one whom the devil had particular reasons to dread and to hate, on account of his skill and power in snatching immortal souls from his jaws. He considered that the devil had held him a grudge a long time, and that he had taken this opportunity of avenging himself. Mr. Allin thought otherwise, and said that the devil would never think of tempting *him* in that way, nor of tempting any one else in that way, that was acquainted with the evidences of natural and revealed religion. Lynn could not believe that philosophy, as he called a knowledge of the evidences of religion,—he could not believe that philosophy would protect a man from the devil; so that though he had an infinite reverence for Thomas Allin in general, he took the liberty of differing from him in opinion on this occasion. He thought, no doubt, that the devil had obscured Thomas Allin's spiritual vision, by a few of his infernal, philosophical cobwebs. Neither Allin nor Lynn was quite right, in my judgment. Wiser men then T. Allin have been harassed with foolish doubts and horrible fancies when under the influence of disease, and people as ignorant as Lynn may escape such doubts, if favoured with continual health.

From what I hear now, I should suppose that Lynn has nearly worn himself out as a preacher. I never hear of him being employed in preaching anniversary sermons. I never hear of him getting up any remarkable revivals; while I have frequently heard of his disgusting his congregations, and making himself look infinitely ridiculous and foolish. Poor fellow; he might have been happy and useful, if he had been properly trained, and put in his proper place: for there is a place for every body; a place which every one can fill to advantage, both to himself and others: but Lynn never got into his proper place. His place would have been in the midst of a number of rational and enlightened people, and his work would have been to assist them in promoting the improvement and welfare of the masses of mankind. The enlightened and rational would have set him to work, and supplied him with tools for his labour. He would have roused people's attention, excited their feelings, and brought them under moral and religious influences; and the rational and well-informed with whom he was connected, would have taken the awakened and excited by the hand, and led them forward in the ways of knowledge and righteousness. Lynn would thus have done, for numbers of poor creatures, what more rational and enlightened people, with less of dramatic power and sympathy, could never have done; but rational and enlightened people would have been able to do for them afterwards, what Lynn could never have done. What a pity that men of all talents cannot join and work together. What a pity that bigotry and intolerance, and faith in human creeds, and the idolizing of traditions, should separate men so needful to each other, so fitted for co-operating, so adapted, when working in harmony, to rouse, instruct, regenerate, and bless mankind. If Lynn and I had been permitted to work together, without any efforts on the part of my opponents to prejudice Lynn against me, we should have been both happy in each other's society, and useful to those amongst whom we might have laboured. And in truth, all men might mix together, hold intercourse with one another, and labour in unison in the cause of truth and righteousness to advantage, if they could only get rid of intolerance and bigotry, and get a proportionate increase of benevolence in its place. I never expect to see all men perfect, much less do I expect to see all men alike. I do not even *wish* to see all men alike, nor do I wish to see all men perfect at once: but I do wish to see men loving, and tolerant, and agreeable; disposed to respect each other's worth, to appreciate each other's excellencies, to bear with each other's defects and peculiarities, to join together to make the best of each other in all things, and to do the best in all things for the welfare of the world at large.

While I was at Sheffield, there was a split in one of the Independent Churches in that town. Some of the members were rather more liberal and zealous than the pastor and the rest of the members. They wanted to be doing something for the good of their neighbours; and their pastor, and some of the members, were wishful to go on in the old quiet way, doing nothing out of the usual course. The younger members were determined to do something more than they had been doing; while the older members with their pastor were determined that they should not. Hence a division followed. The leader of the seceders, Mr. Gatley, came to me to ask for information respecting the regulations and working of Methodist societies. I had frequent conversations with him on the subject, and more than once he came to my class. He and his friends were wishful to adopt whatever there was in Methodism of good, and incorporate it with what was good in Independency. Mr. Gatley too was somewhat liberal and rational in his theological sentiments; more liberal and rational at least than Calvinists generally are. He frequently came to hear me preach, and I repeatedly visited at his house. At length the party appointed meetings of their own, adopted rules and principles for their government, and began a subscription for the erection of a chapel. I attended their social and public meetings at their request, and spoke at them. I delivered an address at the laying of the foundation stone of their chapel; I also delivered an address at the interment of one of their friends; I was in effect their pastor for the time. At length they got their chapel erected. The expense was great, and the chapel was likely to become a burden to them. They were obliged, or *thought* themselves obliged, to ask the aid of the regular Independents,—the people who had persecuted and abused them heretofore. They also had Independent ministers to open their chapel. They applied for a minister to the Independent College, and became, I believe, in course of time, a regular, unreformed Independent congregation. I have never heard to this day that they have made any progress either in knowledge or in virtue; that they have done any thing for the cause of truth, or liberty, or righteousness, more than the other Independent congregations around them. It is dangerous for Reformers to encumber themselves with chapels; it is dangerous for them to incur expenses which they are unable of themselves to meet: it is dangerous to render it necessary for them to ask the aid of the timid, the compromising, the enemies of reform. If a man do justice to truth and righteousness, to God and humanity, he must preserve his freedom entire; he must make himself dependent on no one; he must either be content to be outdone by the anti-reformers in chapel-building, music, and show, or at least take care not to go into debt, and render necessary the help of his opponents in order to keep pace with them in those things. If the Reformers had built a public *room*, that could have been used or let as a school, a lecture room, &c., they might have done well; but *chapels*, holy places, are always bad things; they are the graves of reform.

I was more than once invited to preach in Independent Chapels while in Sheffield, but in no case did I feel myself at liberty in preaching in them. Indeed I seldom felt at liberty in speaking for the first time in a strange chapel, to people of a different denomination from those I had been accustomed to address; but in a *Calvinistic* chapel, before a Calvinistic audience, I felt *less* at liberty than usual. My sentiments were exceedingly *anti*-Calvinistic; yet in accepting an invitation to preach in the Calvinists' chapels, I had in effect engaged not to attack their opinions; not to hurt their feelings. My position was therefore not a happy one; it was not a natural one. I had no business to place myself in such circumstances. I ought, when invited, to have given them plainly to understand, that I could neither preach a Calvinistic sermon, nor a sermon which Calvinists could fully approve: I ought, in fact, to have refused those applications for my services, except on the understanding that I should endeavour to instruct them in the errors of their creed, and bring them from the traditions of men, to the pure revelations of heaven. This I did not do, and I therefore *deserved* to be embarrassed. I did however learn one thing by going to preach at one of the Calvinist chapels, Garden Street. I learnt that they not only gave the minister a glass of wine *after* preaching, as was the custom amongst the Methodists, but that they gave him one *before* preaching as well. If this custom be common amongst the Independents, we need not wonder at the prevalence of intemperance amongst Independent ministers. A glass of wine before and a glass of wine after each sermon, would be six glasses a Sunday, where the minister preaches three times. Now this of itself is enough to intoxicate a man who is not thoroughly seasoned with drink. I never could drink a single glass without feeling its influence in my head.

While I resided in Sheffield, I more than once saw Montgomery the poet. I was never in company with him at his house, but I met him repeatedly at public meetings, and addressed meetings of which he was the chairman. He was a little man, and delicate and womanly in his appearance, as well as in his manner. He had no great power as a public speaker, though he generally spoke sensibly. His head was rather large in proportion to the size of his body, and yet not large enough to render him a man of great power. I should have been glad to have had a little intercourse with him, but I did not think myself of importance sufficient to deserve his notice: I felt as though I should be intruding to visit him. Besides, he lived with two elderly maiden ladies, and how I got the impression I cannot tell, but I *had* the impression, that neither Montgomery nor the ladies he lived with, took pleasure in visitors.

I think I stated that I had two or three times brief interviews with Ebenezer Elliot, the anti-corn-law poet. I had not however sufficient intimacy with him to enable me to form an opinion of his character. My impression was that he was a mild, a gentle, and an affectionate man, and that his spirit and behaviour in private might almost be imagined to form a contrast with the fiery and denunciatory energy of his rhymes. But nothing is more common, I believe, than for men of affectionate and gentle natures, to be stern and terrible in their public denunciations of fraud, injustice and cruelty. I think I have met with several instances in which the soft, the tender, the affectionate in private and social life, have been united with all that was strong in argument, with all that was stern in reprobation, with all that was terrible in denunciation, in public speeches and writings. But at the time I lived at Sheffield, I was not exactly qualified for forming a correct opinion of such men as Elliott and Montgomery. I was, for one thing, too exclusively a preacher, and, for another, too much of a Methodist. Theology was too much the region of my thoughts, and Methodism and Methodistical society too much the world in which I lived. I should be far better able to form an opinion of the character and talents of such persons now. But now I could have no expectation of being welcome to the private circle of Montgomery. If I was then too much of a Methodist to wander beyond the Methodistical fold, I should now be too little of an orthodox man to be endurable to the poet. How difficult it is for thinking men of the same age to get fairly and thoroughly acquainted with each other. What barriers there are to keep them apart, of which persons who know them only by their writings can form no conception.

Though I became a Teetotaler at Sheffield, and acted on the principle for nearly nine months, and though my experience of the benefits of Teetotalism made me anxious for the spread of Teetotalism among others, yet I never, that I recollect, once introduced the subject to my congregations in my sermons. I preached about temperance, but not in such a way as to make people properly understand what my peculiar opinions of temperance were. I saw people in my congregations that needed the teetotal principle as a means of personal salvation, and I also saw that the adoption of the principle of Teetotalism by professing Christians generally, could not fail to prove a blessing to mankind at large; yet I never once preached on the subject expressly, that I recollect. One reason was, no doubt, that the subject had not yet become sufficiently familiar to my mind. I had a great reluctance to speak on any subject in the pulpit, which had not become very familiar to my thoughts. Another reason would be that I had doubts as yet, as to whether Teetotalism were practicable in every case, and I was unwilling to speak on a subject which I could not enforce upon all. But another reason was, that there was a general understanding, an all-pervading feeling in the Connexion, that nothing should be uttered in the pulpit on moral subjects, but what was *general ;* that though evil might be assailed in the lump, no direct attack should be made on any *particular* vice; or at least, that no direct and special attack should be made on any such vice as was patronised or practised among the leading friends; that nothing should be said in the pulpit calculated to disturb the peace of the society, to offend the friends and supporters of the *cause,* to drive away seat-holders or contributors to the funds. A preacher would be allowed to speak against *injustice* in *general,* but not against *any particular kind* of injustice common amongst members of the societies, or persons in the congregations. We were allowed to speak against *intemperance* and in favour of *sobriety,* but not against *spirit drinking, wine drinking,* or *ale drinking,* or in favour of *Teetotalism.* This spirit which pervaded the leaders of the Connexion would allow us to recommend people to be sober, but would not allow us to recommend Teetotalism as the only or the most effectual means of *becoming* sober. This feeling pervades all religious societies, and rules all the priesthoods of the earth. It is a standing law in all denominations, not always *written*, but universally *understood*, that no preacher shall say anything in the pulpit calculated to give offence to the supporters of the cause, to the contributors to the funds, to the individuals who hold a respectable and influential position in society. It is understood, for instance, amongst all the denominations and priesthoods of this kingdom, that nothing shall be said in the pulpit against following *bad businesses*. It is known among the sects and the *priesthoods*, that there *are* bad businesses, and that those bad businesses are followed by members of their churches and congregations; but the law, the *common*, though perhaps *unwritten* law, requires, that nothing shall be *said* on the subject from the pulpit. It is known, for instance, that one member of the church is a publican or beer-shop-keeper, and that another is a dram-seller, or a keeper of spirit vaults; and it is also known that the publican, the beer-shop-keeper, and the spirit-seller are doing great mischief in society; that they are living by promoting vice and ruin; that they are raising fortunes by corrupting men's souls, by destroying their bodies, by extinguishing their domestic comforts, and by promoting and perpetuating every form of crime and wretchedness that torment and disorder society. All this, I say, is known; and it is also known, that public discourses against those bad businesses would put the men that follow them to shame, would be the likeliest means to bring them to abandon their bad ways, and live a life of harmlessness or usefulness: no matter; the preacher is not allowed to speak publicly on the subject, and public denunciation of those bad businesses on the part of the preacher would be followed with the loss of caste, the loss of confidence, and the loss of his place and salary. Hence the preachers are silent; or if not silent, they are soon expelled, and others are put in their places who will be more observant of the rules and proprieties of *religious* and *respectable* society.

Again; it is known that other members of the church live by fraud; that they make old clothes into new cloth, and sell the cloth for genuine wool-made cloth; that they even buy up woollen waste and rotten rags, and make them into cloth, and sell them for genuine wool-made cloth. No matter, those cheats and rogues pay their seat-rents; they subscribe their sixpence a week, and their shilling or guinea a quarter; they subscribe to the paternal, the beneficent and the contingent funds; to the Missionary Society, the chapel funds, the school funds; they entertain the preachers at their houses, spread a table of luxuries before them, bring them out wine and spirits and tobacco, lodge them for the night in their best beds, carry them home in their gigs or coaches, and show them respect next to worship; therefore no one is allowed to lift up his voice against them publicly. It is known in many churches that certain of their members are robbers; that they rob in trade; that they rob by making wicked plundering laws; that they rob the poor; that they support the vilest oppressions, and favour the most inhuman and unnatural legal enactments; that they appropriate to themselves vast sums of the public money without rendering the public in return any valuable services; that they act on the principle of taking the property of the labouring poor, and dividing it amongst themselves and their over-rich fellows, thus raising themselves by casting down a nation, and enriching themselves by starving surrounding millions. No matter; those thieves support the church; they honour the priesthood; they even vote the people's money in parliament for building churches; they make fresh bishops; they lend the power of the laws, and the power of the police and army, for the maintenance of the church's rights, or, in other words, for the perpetuation and enforcement of the people's wrongs; therefore no priest must hint at their misdoings. The homilies, the sermons, and the lectures of the priest, must all be so general, so vague, as to have no meaning, or a meaning so indefinite, that no one shall be in danger of applying what is said to himself, or even to his neighbour. In short, as we have said before, the priest must take care so to speak, as not to be thought, or as not to give any occasion to people for thinking, that he is reproving his hearers' vices, or inculcating virtues neglected by his flock. The priests may talk as much as they like about the wickedness of Sodom and Gomorrah, and the sins of the ancient Jews; about the treachery of Judas, the timidity of Peter, and the weakness and earthliness of the rest of Christ's disciples; he may talk about Hymeneus and Philetus, about ancient Felix and Agrippa, about Ahab and his false prophets; he may cry out against the sins of Jewish or Pagan idolaters; he may talk of the luxury of Belshazzar, of the pride of Nebuchadnezzar, of the oppressions of Solomon and Rehoboam; he may cry out against the corruptions of the ancient Scribes and Pharisees, and the corruptions of ancient priests and rulers: if he be a Methodist he may sometimes talk of the errors of Calvinism; if he be a Calvinist he may sometimes be allowed to hint at the errors of Arminianism; if he be a Protestant he may inveigh against the errors of Popery; if he be in England he may talk of the benighted millions of Ireland; if he be in Ireland, he may talk of the doleful state of China, Turkey, or Hindostan; and so he may go on, talking of anything that is far enough before or far enough behind; but of nothing just at hand, of nothing prevailing in his own congregation or church. He would give offence if he were to point out the correspondence between the rebelliousness of the ancient Jews, and the rebelliousness of modern professors of Christianity, and were to come to particulars in his comparisons. He would give offence if he were to show that the idolatry of the ancient Jews was a trifling matter, compared with the idolatry or mammonism of priests and professors of the present day. He would give offence if he were to apply the language of the ancient prophets, when denouncing the oppressions of their day, to the oppressions of unjust rulers of the present day. He would give offence if he were to show the people how many there are who, like Judas, betray their best benefactors, and the best benefactors of their race. In a word, he would give offence to leading friends, to respectable members, and to influential supporters, to respectable patrons, to liberal contributors, if he were to make use of truth in such a manner as to expose, rebuke, and denounce the iniquities of his own times, and the iniquities of his own hearers. The priest may talk as much as he likes about the priests and the rulers that took counsel against Jesus in ancient times, and against the Scribes and the Pharisees of those days, who joined a high profession of religion and great pretensions to sanctity, with the basest hypocrisy and the most outrageous and offensive villany: but if he were to talk in such a way as to give his hearers to understand who are the priests and the rulers of the present day that answer to the murderers of Christ, and who are the Scribes and Pharisees of the present day that answer in their character to the Scribes and Pharisees of old, he would be dragged from his pulpit; some of his hearers would leave him in the midst of his sermon, and others would cut the sermon itself short in the middle, and cast him out of the synagogue. Such is the law of the sects.

Under this law *I* was placed, and by this law I felt myself at one time bound. I never could avoid transgressing it altogether: I never passed a whole year in any circuit without transgressing it repeatedly; but as a general rule, I believed myself bound to regard it. When I ventured, out of regard to a higher law, to transgress this law, I was charged with indiscretion, and admonished of the danger to which I was exposing myself. I was told, at one time, by Mr. Allin, that of a hundred ministers who had been expelled from their places in a certain denomination in America, not five of them had been expelled for flagrant crimes, while more than ninety-five had been expelled for indiscretion. I had similar warnings from others. By my indiscretion in saying occasionally more than I was paid for saying, and making truth plainer than most people wished it to be made, and betraying my impatience with the prevalence of hypocrisy and villany in the church, and allowing my feelings of indignation at the sanction commonly given to iniquity by professors and preachers to escape me at times in expressions of rebuke and admonition, I frequently exposed myself to danger. I alienated from me many connexional friends, and subjected myself to many shy looks, and to much distrust and opposition.

I say I considered myself, at one time, bound by this iniquitous law. At that time I did not regard it as iniquitous; nor was I aware, in fact, of its prevalence and power. I was bound by it, influenced by it, ruled by it, without understanding its character, without being aware of its evil. I had got the idea, as most preachers have, that the first thing to be considered was the unity and prosperity of the church. I also laboured under the impression that all those evils which disgraced the church would give way of themselves by and bye, or that they all might be reformed, when the convenient season arrived, without giving offence, without causing disturbances, without incurring reproach or persecution. As the drunkard and the profligate fancy that they may one day reform without difficulty, so certain preachers and professors imagine that they may one day reform the church, and establish purity and righteousness in the midst thereof, without difficulty. Then again, young preachers fancy that they must not go far in attempting reforms, till they have gained more influence, till they have reached a higher position in the body. They are taught, and they are led to believe, that the elders of the church are the parties to decide what ought to be done; and many of them therefore content themselves with doing nothing for the present, but with purposes of doing something in the future. I am speaking now of the *best* class of preachers,—of those who become preachers for the sake of doing good,—of those who desire both to know and to do what is right themselves, and to promote the knowledge and the practice of what is right amongst others. *Many* preachers, perhaps five out of six, become preachers for selfish objects, and never think of doing good; but some few become preachers for *better* objects, and *do* think of doing good. But even those, when they become preachers in connection with the sects, and get mixed with the common run of priests, are imperceptibly enslaved, are stripped of their freedom and power, and disabled from doing anything in a large and effectual way for the reformation and salvation of the world. I found myself in this position. I was in chains; I was enslaved; I was almost disabled. I was not *content* in my slavery; I hugged my chains very awkwardly; I made many efforts, though fitful and irregular ones, to emancipate myself, and at length I *did* emancipate myself completely: but alas! for a long length of years I did little as I might have done, and little as I *should* have done, if my position had been one of true liberty.

I say I preached no sermons during the time that I lived at Sheffield on teetotalism, and I have stated the influences which prevented me from publicly speaking on that subject from the pulpit. But after I removed to Chester, my mind broke loose from its bands to some extent, and there I acted differently. As I have intimated already, I spoke repeatedly from the pulpit on the subject of teetotalism in the Chester circuit. I more than once delivered lectures on the subject in the principal chapel at Chester, and I *frequently* lectured on the subject in the *country* chapels. I lectured on the subject in the chapels at Hawarden, Wepre, Dublin, Greenfield, Bretton, Handbridge, Tarvin, Oscroft, Delamere, &c. I also referred to the subject repeatedly in my sermons. As I have intimated before, I gave offence by so doing at Chester, and exposed myself to rebuke and censure. But rebuke and censure had now less influence upon me; nay, the means which were used to prevent me from inculcating teetotalism from the pulpit, rather caused me to inculcate it more frequently and faithfully than I had done before.

While I was at Sheffield, I had occasional correspondence with J. S. Buckingham, Esq., who was at that time one of the Members of Parliament for Sheffield. It was in reply to a letter I received from him, accompanying a copy of the *Sun*, a London paper, that I wrote the following letter. It was on the refusal of his claims by the House of Commons.

My dear Sir,—

I received a copy of the *Sun*, and was much distressed with the fate of your Bill. We had prepared petitions, and they were numerously and respectably signed. Indeed there was a general and powerful influence excited in your favour, and the petitions would have been sent off to London before this, had we at all anticipated such an early decision of the House on the question. I was astonished at the hastiness, the injustice, and the inhumanity of the decision. But the evil is done. You are robbed and ruined, and those who should have been eager to help you, have wickedly taken away from you all hope of redress. I felt keenly when I read your letter, and I cannot refrain from tears, at times, when I think of your misfortunes and injuries. And there seems such a contrast between your merits and your portion; your character and your humiliation. A Briton, whose character and achievements illustrate and glorify that name; who has laid his country under many mighty obligations, is robbed and trampled on by a corrupt and powerful company, and unaided, unpitied, and insulted by his countrymen. Then shame on England; everlasting shame on the Parliament. Well; there is yet One to whom you may look, One who will not disappoint the soul that trusts in Him. His eye beholds the wrongs that are done on earth, and He always takes the side of the injured. His ear is never closed against the cries of the oppressed, nor is He ever regardless of their sorrows; and when he riseth to plead their cause, the pride of the tyrant and of the tyrant's helpers melteth away as the hoar frost of the morning before the rising sun. He gives comfort to His afflicted ones, and raiseth the downcast to honour and happiness.

I feel satisfied, that in pointing you to Heaven for redress, I shall not be considered as adding mockery to your affliction. It strikes me, that in your past sorrows, you must have had frequent recourse to Heaven for help and consolation, or you would never have been able to bear up under your trials. I believe I am only speaking in accordance with your own feelings, when I say, in the beautiful, affecting, and truly philosophical language of an ancient, 'Be anxious for nothing, but by prayer and supplication with thanksgiving let your requests be made known unto God, and the peace of God which passeth understanding shall keep your heart and mind through Christ Jesus.' I cannot refrain from quoting the words of other ancient worthies, who, in their day, had experience of wrong and disappointment. 'Like as a father pitieth his children, so the Lord pitieth them that fear Him.' 'And we know that all things work together for good to them that love God.' 'The Lord reigneth, and though darkness and clouds are round about Him, yet righteousness and truth are the habitation of His throne.' The cries of the poor, and of those that have none to help them, enter His ears, and He is the friend and helper of all such. And I doubt not but that application to that best, that truest, that mightiest of all friends in your behalf, will be successful. If you obtain not that which you seek after, you will, if faithful to duty, obtain that which will prove more valuable. 'To the upright there ariseth light in darkness.' To the upright evil is turned into good, cursing into blessing, sorrow into joy.. The very troubles which he is called to endure are rendered subservient to his improvement and welfare. 'The righteous cry, and the Lord heareth him, and delivereth him out of all his troubles;' or if He does not deliver him *out* of all his troubles, He supports and comforts him in the midst of them, and renders them a greater blessing than ease and prosperity would prove.

I hope you will be able to bring yourself to acquiesce in the will of God, and to learn, in whatsoever state you are, to be content. God does not always redress the wrongs of His people by returning to them what their foes take away; but to them that patiently wait His pleasure, He does that which in truth is far better. He does not always bless us in the way in which we *desire*, but He blesses us in that way which is *best*. He does not consult our *wishes* always, but He always consults our *wants*. He does not minister to our present pleasure in all things, but He always consults our real welfare. He will do for us that which is best, though not that which is most agreeable. He will give us that which we shall find most valuable in the end, though it may not be that which we shall most highly prize at present.

I have had some experience of sorrow, and I have proved the truth of what I now write. For a time I stood erect and unhumbled under trials; but it was foolish. Such conduct is unsuitable to man when chastened by God. I saw my error at length. I yielded, I acknowledged my error, and welcomed my sorrows, and said, 'It is the Lord, let Him do what seemeth Him good.' I did not neglect the dictates of prudence, or the duties of my situation. I did what I could, consistent with duty, to help or relieve myself; but I placed myself at the disposal of Heaven when I had done, and said, 'Father, if it be possible, let this cup pass from me; nevertheless not as I will, but as thou wilt:' and my mind was relieved. I said within myself, 'I will henceforth be careful to please my heavenly Father, and to serve my fellowmen, and I will be careful for nothing further. I will labour to accomplish the end for which I was placed upon earth, and I will leave all other things with God.' And God has enabled me, thus far, to keep my vow. I meet with many troubles still, yet I enjoy life. I am poor, but I am content. I am in difficulties at times, but I am not anxious. I bow to the storm which I cannot prevent or control, and seek refuge beneath the shadow of the rock that is nigh. The best that have gone before me have suffered, and why should not I? Their sufferings have ended in joy, and why should not mine? Their character was perfected by suffering, and I trust that mine will be the same. The wisest and the best one that ever lived had not where to lay his head. The most single-minded Reformer that ever grappled with evil, the truest philanthropist that ever toiled for our race, was not only doomed to poverty, but to reproach, to persecution, and to death itself. And those who share his spirit, and tread in his steps, must expect to share his lot. Reformers cannot pass their life untroubled, nor can they always meet with redress for their wrongs, or with protection from their persecutors. The man who devotes himself to the war against evil, must make up his mind to be a sacrifice. If we espouse the cause of Christ, we must prepare to bear his fate. If we make him our exemplar in virtue, we must expect to have him, to some extent, for our exemplar in suffering. If we wish to resemble him in worth and glory, we must be content to resemble him in suffering and reproach. We must seek our joy in the consciousness of having done our duty, and served our fellow-creatures; and in the hopes of future recompense in heaven. And this is enough. The consciousness of having helped forward the regeneration of the world; the consciousness of having contributed to the destruction of evil, and to the triumph of truth and righteousness; the consciousness of having served God by blessing his creatures, and of having sown a harvest of bliss which we are justified in expecting to reap in the eternal future, should be enough to content and cheer us amidst all our troubles.

I feel willing, myself, to bear my share of the sorrows of Christ, if I may contribute my share towards the accomplishment of that great and glorious work in which he lived and died. I feel willing to part with the outward, that I may enjoy the inward; to sacrifice pleasure, that I may secure profit; and to forego the present, in the anticipation of the future. In a word, I am willing that God should appoint me my portion, both in this life and in the life to come; content to know that His will is always best.

Wishing you success in all your efforts to promote the interests of freedom, and righteousness, and truth, and hoping that you may be able, notwithstanding all your trials, to enjoy the bliss of life and the hopes of immortality,

I am, your's very respectfully
and affectionately,
JOSEPH BARKER.

I have since met Mr. Buckingham on the temperance platform; but whether he remembered me as his Sheffield correspondent or not, I do not know.

While I was at Sheffield, a person in the neighbourhood was prosecuted for church-rates. He defended the cause against the priests and their men, and got himself into difficulties. He then applied to a number of friends in the neighbourhood for help; but it is easiest for people to obtain help before they get into difficulties. The person referred to found it difficult, when he had incurred expense on his own responsibility, to get others to share the expense with him. He got up a public meeting in the Town Hall and invited me to attend it. I did attend it, and there I delivered my first address on political subjects. A dispute arose at the meeting as to whether it should act with a view to church-rates generally, or to the particular case of the individual who had called the meeting. Several that were disposed to labour for the abolition of church-rates generally, were not disposed to take part in the business of the individual who had involved himself in difficulty by refusing to pay the rates levied upon him. How the matter ended I do not remember; but I recollect that sometime afterwards a public meeting on the subject of church-rates was held in the Music Hall, and that I was invited to speak on the occasion, and that there I delivered a more lengthy address on the subject.

While I was at Sheffield I was invited to attend a meeting of a Sabbath Observance Society. At that time I regarded the first day Sabbath as a Christian institution, and was prepared to take a part in labouring for the objects of the society; but what became of the society, I have no recollection. I never heard anything of its operations, nor was I ever invited, that I remember, to a second meeting. It is astonishing what lots of societies are formed, and how little is accomplished by many of them. A public-meeting is got up; a committee is formed; the committee meet once or twice, and pass a few resolutions; but unless the object of the meeting be sectarian, or unless there be some funds to handle, it is seldom that anything further is done. Most of the associations with which I then came in contact, were got up by preachers, or were entrusted to their management; and I do not recollect a single case in which they accomplished anything considerable. The BIBLE Society is still carried on, but the work is done in general by hired agents. And the TRACT Society goes forward; but the work in that society is also done by hired agents. Here and there a few individual priests may be found who take part in getting up public-meetings, and in many places where public-meetings are once got up, priests may be found who are not only willing to address them, but who will quarrel with their brethren to obtain an opportunity of addressing them; but as for regular, persevering, vigorous efforts amongst the priests to improve the funds and increase the usefulness of public associations, you shall look for them in vain; I remember no such efforts.

I had two colleagues or superintendents while in Chester circuit. The first was James Wilson, who was superintendent the first year; the second was James Ousey, who was superintendent the second year. James Wilson was quite a different character from James Ousey. He was cheerful, and hearty, and friendly. He was tolerant and liberal, intelligent and benevolent. He was no teetotaler; but he had no disposition to oppose teetotalism; or if he did oppose it on any occasion, he did it in an open, manly, creditable, good-tempered way. But, in truth, his occasional remarks on the subject of teetotalism could hardly be called opposition. They were the remarks of a generous, open-hearted, kind individual, who, though not easily converted to teetotalism himself, was rather pleased than otherwise to see others converted. He would frequently talk with me on the subject; but never in a nasty, malignant, or intolerant manner. He would sometimes talk on the subject with others, but never in such a manner as to give much encouragement to the drunkard, or much annoyance to the abstainer. He heard me speak on the subject of teetotalism at the first public meeting that I addressed in Chester. He spoke with me afterwards on the subject of my speech, either asking a question with respect to some part of it, or proposing an objection to something I had said; but all in a friendly way. There was nothing mean, ill-natured, or discreditable in his manner. But, in truth, James Wilson was altogether a superior man. He was a lump of cheerfulness, intelligence, and love. He loved all mankind; he wished all men well. He was a man of peace; he would quarrel with no one if he could help it, nor would he let others quarrel amongst themselves if he could hinder them. I have seldom met with a man in whose company I felt more at home than in his. He had a way of his own, whenever he heard a pleasing story, or received any kind of agreeable intelligence, or heard any one express a pleasing expectation, of saying, that is comfortable; or that was comfortable; or that will be comfortable. Of all the words in the dictionary, he used the word comfortable the oftenest. And the use of that word was not accidental, it was the natural result of the kind and comfortable disposition of his own soul. He was himself a comfortable man, and he took delight in seeing others comfortable; and he liked to hear that people *had* been comfortable; and he liked to believe that people *would* be comfortable; and he liked to look upon every thing that happened on the comfortable side, and to believe, that however painful it was, it would have a comfortable issue. He liked to be comfortable himself, and he liked to see every body comfortable about him. His looks, and his words, and his ways, and the manner in which he spoke his words, and the way in which he did all that he did, had something in it particularly calculated to make people comfortable. He spoke the word comfortable itself in a more pleasing and comfortable way than most people. He uttered it in such a manner, that the very sound of the word had a tendency to make those comfortable that heard it.

He was very fond of books, and had a good rich library, and took great pleasure in his library. There was no man in the Connexion that had so large and so rich a collection of books as he had. And many of his books were exceedingly rare. But his rare books were not peculiar for their rarity alone; they were generally peculiar for their goodness as well as their rarity. It was quite a treat to me to look at his library, and a still greater treat to have the privilege of reading some of the works that it contained. I am sorry I cannot give a list of a number of his books, and an account of their contents and character; but among the rest he had a volume by Baxter that I had never seen before; a metrical version of all the Psalms, with a collection of other poetical pieces by Baxter. This metrical version of the Psalms was, in my judgment, superior to any I have seen, not even excepting the version of Watts. Watts spiritualises many of the Psalms, and passes off from David to Christ; thus giving to the words of the Poet of Israel, a meaning which the poet himself never contemplated. Baxter's translations, if I recollect rightly, are clear of this error, expressing the meaning of the Psalmist himself alone. Baxter's metrical version of the Psalms had this peculiarity also, that nearly every Psalm, if *not* every Psalm, could be sung in two different metres, by putting in or leaving out in each line a word of two syllables, a word that was not essential to the sense, and yet no obscuration of the sense. Mr. Wilson had another work called, 'HAKEWELL ON PROVIDENCE, OR A DECLARATION OF THE POWER AND PROVIDENCE OF GOD IN THE GOVERNMENT OF THE WORLD; CONSISTING IN AN EXAMINATION AND CENSURE OF THE COMMON ERROR TOUCHING NATURE'S PERPETUAL AND UNIVERSAL DECAY; DIVIDED INTO SIX BOOKS.' The work was a small thick folio. The object of the work was to show that the former days were not better than the present; that things had not, from the beginning, been perpetually waxing worse; that the human race itself had not degenerated; that arts and sciences had not declined; that religion and manners had not grown worse; that men were now as healthy, as strong, and as tall as they ever were; that they were as wise and as good and as happy as they ever were; that in divinity, philosophy, and nature, things had been *progressing* through past ages, rather than retrograding; that neither in the sun, the moon, and stars, nor in the earth and its mountains, the rivers and plains, nor in trees or vegetables, or fruits or flowers, nor in animals, nor in man, was there any universal or general degeneracy. And cleverly did the writer handle his subject. But no one can imagine *how* cleverly, unless he had seen the work for himself. The amount of useful philosophical and historical matter that the book contained, was immense. The tendency of the work was certainly to give men cheering views of God and Providence, and to promote exactly that feeling which pervaded so thoroughly the soul of Mr. Wilson, and which he so frequently expressed by the sweet word COMFORTABLE.

It appears to have been the custom of many in Hakewell's time, to extol the ancient Romans, and to represent them as superior in all things to the moderns. This error he combats at great length. He treats of the religion of the Romans, and exposes their beastly and barbarous worship. He exposes the cruelty of the Romans towards the Jews, the Christians, other nations, and towards each other. He speaks of their excessive covetousness, and of their unjust methods of acquiring wealth. He speaks at length of Roman luxury, incontinence, and drunkenness; of their excessive gluttony; of their extravagant luxury in building, in dressing, in ornaments; of their extreme arrogance and boasting, together with their gross and base flattery, especially of their Emperors. He examines into the accounts touching the justice, prudence, and fortitude of the ancient Romans, comparing those Romans in all things with the English of his own times. And thus he goes on. But it would take me a day to give a just or a full account of the contents of that remarkable volume. Mr. Wilson also had beautiful copies of rare editions of ancient works, especially the moral and philosophical writings of the ancient Greeks and Romans. He had some strange old collections of anecdotes, proverbs, and wise sayings. But alas! it is too late for me now to give a just or worthy account of this man's library. It was a rich and singularly interesting collection of books, especially for a Methodist preacher.

And, as I said, James Wilson took great delight in his library, and made good use of it. He read his good books carefully; he understood them well, and prized their contents highly. He carried his library in his soul. No man, I believe, with whom I ever was acquainted, had a more thorough knowledge of his books, than poor James Wilson. He differed as much from most people in the thoroughness of his acquaintance with his library, as his library itself differed from the libraries of most Methodist preachers.

And he was quite as willing that his library should be useful to other people as to himself. He had nothing exclusive or niggardly about him. True, he would have felt uncomfortable at the idea of losing any of his books, but not at the thought of lending them to people who were likely to feel interested in them, or who were disposed to read them and get good from them, and then return them. I never asked him for a book without receiving it, and I often received from him books without asking for them. He soon saw my taste. He soon discovered that I took pleasure in reading, and he soon made it manifest that he took pleasure in ministering to my pleasure in this particular. Whenever he put his hand upon a book in his library that he thought I should like to read, he would instantly put it under his arm, put on his hat, take up his stick, and trudge along to our house; and I could tell well enough as he came in, that he thought he had got something extra for me. He would walk along the passage and enter the room with the most exquisitely good natured smile on his countenance that a good old man could wear, and then, in his kind and humourous way, would give me to understand, that he had got something for me; and if he found that he had just met my taste, that he had brought me a book that I never had' seen before, and especially a book that I had wished to see, he would gently shrug up his shoulders, smiling, and say, 'Now that is comfortable; I thought you would like that; that is comfortable.'

He was no teetotaler, as I have said; but he once met with a thick old volume on drunkenness; a volume full of wit and wisdom, abounding in argument and raillery; and he instantly marched off with it under his arm to show me it. 'Have not I got something for you now?' said he, 'what will you give me for this?' And with other such playful and kind expressions, endeavouring to excite my curiosity beyond its usual bounds, would he give me the book, smiling as if the whole fulness of his good, kind soul beamed forth from his countenance at once.

I say he was a liberal man; and so he was. His liberality was in proportion to his intelligence and benevolence. I could speak with him on any subject. I could express before him any sentiment, however heterodox; and he never was the man to complain; he never was the man to take advantage of my freedom and confidence. If I uttered a secret in his hearing, it was as safe with him as with the grave. If I acted indiscreetly in his judgment, in any matter, it was all the same. He might gently admonish me, or humourously reprove me, or affectionately, without anything bordering on arrogance, presumption, or insolence, or any assumption of superiority whatever, give me a word of counsel, but never farther. A father could not be kinder towards his child, than he was towards me. The closest friend on earth could not be more affectionate, or faithful, or truehearted, than he was.

But though he had all the kindness of a father, he affected nothing of a father's authority. I never met with his equal among preachers before, and I have never met with his equal among preachers since. And he was a good, clever preacher: not unusually powerful; not a man to be unusually popular; but a good, plain, rich and clever preacher. He always talked sense. I never remember to have heard him utter a foolish sentence, or an unintelligible word, either in a sermon or in a public address.

And his prayers were as good as his sermons. Both his prayers and his sermons were like strings of pearls. His style was sententious, but never abrupt or obscure. It was rich, but not affected. It was a treat to hear him. I never could bear to hear a man talk long and say nothing. Nothing could be much more vexatious to me in a public speaker, than to hear him turn out big sentences without meaning; and bawl forth huge masses of words without point, or fitness, or power. And nothing could be much more agreeable, nothing could be much more comfortable, than to hear a man preach, whose words were always full of meaning; whose tones were natural; and whose natural tones were those of affection and piety; and who, for thirty, or forty, or fifty minutes together, would pour forth rich streams of light, and love, and joy. And this was the case, to a great extent, with Mr. Wilson.

And his conduct to me, was not much better than his conduct to other people. He liked me better than many, I believe; but he was kind, and good, and generous, and gentle towards all.

And he carried out the principle of lending, hoping for nothing again, in its literal meaning. There was a man lived in Chester, a supernumerary preacher, the very opposite to Wilson, in almost all respects. He was a bad, a crabbed, a sour, a malignant, a passionate, a proud, an insolent, an exclusive, intolerant, dishonest, intemperate, and persecuting man; that would lie, and steal, and cheat, and drink, and guzzle, and gormondise, and borrow without a thought of returning what he borrowed, and run into debt without the slightest intention of paying; and swindle, and embezzle, without the least apparent remorse or misgiving. His name was Chapman. Though I was thought patient and mild by many, I never could have much to do with Chapman, without being dreadfully tempted to speak unadvisedly or harshly with my tongue. It was a difficult matter to keep my tongue within bounds, when obliged to come in close contact with this man. Yet Mr. Wilson seemed never to be put out of the way with him. To-day he would borrow Wilson's walking-stick, and never return it; to-morrow he would borrow his umbrella, and never mention it after. By and by he would borrow his cloak; and never make mention of it after. Next week he would meet Wilson's class, take up the pennies and shillings, and put them in his pocket; but Mr. Wilson never mentioned it. Chapman was like a bottomless pit, that devoured all that was cast into it, and restored nothing. Wilson could see his pride; but his own humility was such, that the pride of another seemed to give him no uneasiness: or if it gave him uneasiness, excited no passion, or called forth no signs or expressions of resentment. He could see his dishonesty; but even when Chapman had robbed him of the cloak that should cover his shoulders, he still had another and a larger cloak of charity, to throw over Chapman in return. I used to speak strongly of Chapman, and I used to speak strongly *to* Chapman: I *felt* strongly. I was disgusted with him. I was indignant that such a wicked, worthless man, should still be recognised as a preacher. And Wilson could see how uneasy I felt in his presence, and how grieved I was at his ways; and he would sometimes smile in a sort of arch and significant way, as much as to say, 'Ay, my good lad, you have got a strange kind of subject to deal with:' but he always contrived in some way to put the damper on my indignation, or to lift up the safety valve, so as to let it escape in some gentle, some harmless, or some tolerable way. Of all the men in the world that ever pretended to be Christians, or put themselves forward as preachers of the Gospel, I never knew one poor wretched creature more blameable, or more pitiable, and, whether blameable or pitiable, more unfit to stand forward as an example or teacher of Christianity, than this same Chapman: yet Wilson could bear with him apparently without any difficulty. I have borne many things which would have made some people explode almost with wrath; but Wilson could bear things which would have almost made me explode; or which, if they had not made me explode, would have made it necessary for me to guard myself with two-fold, or three-fold care.

This Chapman had quarrelled with the people in every circuit in which he had travelled. He had broken up some circuits, and shattered several others. He had also quarrelled with every young preacher with whom he had been stationed, or else, which was worse, had so abused and frightened the poor creatures, that they had not the courage to oppose him, to rebuke him, or to complain of him.

Then again, in every circuit in which he had travelled, he had got into debt, especially for porter, ale and spirits; and with all his creditors he had had quarrels; and in every case, so far as I could learn, had carried the quarrel to a law-suit; and then, when the law and authorities went against him, succumbed, and engaged to pay expenses. If he went on a horse or in a gig, he would quarrel with the toll-gate keepers. If he had to put up at an Inn, he would quarrel with the ostler and the Inn-keeper. If he had to walk, he would quarrel with the children in the streets; and he had become so notorious for his quarrelsomeness in Chester, that the wilder and more mischievous kind of children made a regular practice of teasing him as he went along. So vexed would he be at this, that he would smite the ground with his stick, stamp with his feet, and look so wild and horrible, and be so enraged, that his whole body would tremble and shake from head to foot; and expressions which no man of decency would use, would come from his lips. On one occasion he went to the magistrates to complain of the children. But he preferred his complaint in such a way, that the magistrates could do nothing to help him. He then began to quarrel with the magistrates.

He was, besides, a greedy, gluttonous eater, and a greedy, immoderate drinker. When he used to dine at the quarterly meeting, where he got his dinner free, he would act in the most disgraceful way. He seemed afraid of eating anything but flesh meat, lest something less valuable should fill its place within him; and when a pint of ale came near him, he would guzzle it all at a draught, and guzzle as many other pints as he could get within his reach. Yet he was an advocate of the Temperance Society. He *hated* TEETOTALISM; but was loud in his praises of temperance. On some occasion the advocates of the Moderation System had paid him a compliment, and this had delighted him to such an extent, that he seemed to imagine himself the great representative and unparalleled advocate of the Moderation Scheme; yet the reason he was not drunk daily, was simply his inability to obtain sufficient drink. I have seen him drink spirits and water almost immediately after breakfast, and drink *enough* too to make a man drunk.

His pride was unbounded. He seemed to imagine, when he was himself a preacher in regular standing, that he had a right to oppress and to torture any young preacher. The first time I met with him was at Halifax. He was then stationed at Todmorden, and had come over to Halifax to assist at a Missionary Meeting. At this very time, the first time I saw him, I saw him drink spirits and water after breakfast in the morning. We had to go about five or six miles into the country, to attend a Missionary Meeting that day. I was the young preacher in that circuit, though I was married. Among the very first words that I heard him speak, were words to the effect, 'that the young preachers did not know themselves now; that they had quite forgotten their places; that when *he* was a young preacher, things were different; young men knew their places then, and understood their duty; and there were men in those days who *made* them know their places, and who made them attend to their duty. Age was then venerable, and the word of a superintendent preacher was good for something: but things were not so now. Young preachers were spoiled; they came out without either knowledge, or talents, or good manners. A set of silly people, that had no more sense, would praise them, and then their heads were turned, and there was no doing anything with them. But if *I* had them in hand, I'd let them see.' All this, I suppose, was intended for me; though at first I was too dull to perceive it. We had not walked far, before Chapman took me in hand in a practical way, to teach me a lesson. He had got a great cloak on his arm, and he said, ' Here, take that, young man:' so I took it, and carried it. I had a coat and some other things of my own to carry, and I was, besides, not very well. It was a wearisome work for me to carry his cloak as well as my own great coat, while he walked insolently and proudly by the side of another. However, I did carry it. I bore his insolence patiently; but not without thinking and feeling, and not without forming my opinion respecting him. But I had no intention of describing this man, especially in the present place. I only introduced him for the purpose of exhibiting more clearly and more fully the excellent character and Christian worth of my colleague and superintendent, James Wilson.

James Wilson was doomed to live in the same town with

this man. He was doomed to have him as a constant visitor. He was doomed to have him also as his assistant leader in the class. He was doomed to sit with him in the leaders' meetings, the local preachers' meetings, and the quarterly meetings. He was doomed to witness all his follies, all his extravagances, all his weaknesses, all his vices. He was doomed to be a witness of his acts of deceit, and fraud, and dishonesty, and to hear his outbursts of passion, and see his wretched and unseemly exhibitions of intemperance, selfishness, and rage, in his conduct towards his neighbours, his customers, and the like. And yet, though brought into such close quarters with this man, though placed in circumstances so trying, I never once knew Wilson lose his temper. I never once knew him utter an angry or an unkind word; I never saw upon his countenance an unkind look; I never heard him, either in private or in public, speak hardly or harshly of him. He would tell me at times how he borrowed his stick, his umbrella, his cloak, or his books: how he embezzled the money at the class; how he got into his debt in other ways, and forgot it, or purposely and studiously took care never to mention it; but even this was not done in unkindness to Chapman. His object in speaking of these things, was more to convince me that he had more reason to complain than I, and that if *he* could put up with such annoyances, I also might put up with them; 'And then you know,' he would say, 'that will be comfortable.'

END OF VOLUME ONE.

WORTLEY NEAR LEEDS: PRINTED BY JOSEPH BARKER.

CHEAP BOOKS AND TRACTS,

PUBLISHED

By JOSEPH BARKER, Wortley, near Leeds.

AND MAY BE HAD OF HIS AGENTS.

Also of W. BRITTAIN, 34, Paternoster Row, London, and other Booksellers.

---

* *A liberal allowance to the trade, or to persons taking large quantities,*

N. B. You may have tracts, &c., set up and printed at the Barker Steam Press on the following terms: 1000 copies, 12 pages each, 12 mo. demy, 1*l*. 15*s*.: 2000 do., 2*l*. 15*s*.: 3000 do., 3*l*. 10*s*.: 4000 do., 4*l*. 10*s*: 5000 do., 5*l*. 5*s*. Tracts of other sizes in proportion. Smaller type charged extra for the first thousand.

Channing's (Dr.) complete Works, New Edition,

in six volumes, 12 mo., about 300 pages each, stitched, 1s. per volume; Cloth bds., 1s. 4d. per volume. The complete Works in half-calf, bound in three volumes, 10s. 6d. Any volume may be had separately.

"Never, in my judgment, since man was placed upon the earth, has any one written with more of the spirit of truth and love, than W. Ellery Channing. His words are remarkable for fitness and beauty, his thoughts are the effulgence of the eternal light, and his feelings are the fulness of the heavenly life. It is impossible that his works should be read without profit. It is impossible that they should be universally diffused, without effecting a beneficent revolution amongst every class, and in every institution of society. I feel exceedingly thankful, that I have been enabled to publish this cheap Edition of those works, and thus to place them in the hands of so many of my poorer brethren."—EDITOR.

The Doctrine of Original Sin, by Dr. John Taylor.

pp. 232. 1s. 4d. Cloth bds.

Serious Call to a Devout and Holy Life, by

W. Law. With notes, Appendix, &c,, by J. Barker. pp. 280. 1s. 4d. Cloth bds.

The Atonement a display of Love, not of Wrath;

by Noah Worcester. pp. 142. 1s.

"An excellent work."

Norton's (Andrews) Statement of Reasons for

not believing the Doctrines of Trinitarians concerning the nature of God, and the person of Christ. pp. 266. 1s. 4d. Cloth bds.

" Societies or Individuals wishing to circulate this useful work extensively, may be supplied with copies, at the rate of 25*l*. per 1000 in sheets.

Interesting Memoirs and Documents relating to

American Slavery, and the glorious struggle now making for Complete Emancipation. pp. 288. 1s. Cloth bds.

"This is the first volume of the 'Barker Library,' respecting which see the separate prospectuses. The Price of the volumes to Subscribers 9d, bds.

The Life of William Penn, the Celebrated
Quaker and Founder of Pennsylvania. By Joseph Barker. Price 1s. The second volume of the 'Barker Library.'

A Popular Introduction to Astronomy. By W.
Jevons, Esq., with many Engravings on Wood, Price 1s. The third volume of the 'Barker Library.'

Narrative of the Life of Frederick Douglass, for-
merly an American Slave. Written by himself. Price 1s. 6d.

Memoir of Mrs. Jane Mawson, of Newcastle-
upon-Tyne, Compiled from her Diary and Correspondence, showing the progressive influence of truth upon the mind of a sincere inquirer. Price 1s.

The Garland, or Poetry for Childhood and Youth,
In stiff paper covers, Price 4d. Cloth ditto, 6d.

Anecdotes, in two volumes, stiff covers. Price
6d. each.

Authentic Report of the PUBLIC DISCUSSION,
between JOSEPH BARKER and WILLIAM COOKE, in the Lecture Room, NEWCASTLE-UPON-TYNE, on August 19th, 20th, 21st, 22nd, 26th, 27th, 28th, and Sept. 2nd, 3rd, and 4th, 1845, with an APPENDIX. pp. 620. 2s. 6d. Cloth bds.
"This Discussion was on the question, What is a Christian? and branched out into such subjects as the Atonement, the Trinity, Natural Depravity, Eternal Torments, &c. Many persons have renounced the prevailing doctrines on those subjects, after reading this faithful and interesting report."

Christianity Triumphant, by J. BARKER.
pp 448. 12 mo., 2s. Cloth bds.
"This work contains an enlarged View of the tendency of the Religion of Christ, showing that it is every way calculated to remedy the evils of a disordered and miserable world, and to make men throughout all Lands, all that is good, and great, and happy."

Barker's Tracts and Sermon's, in ten volumes,
1s. 4d. each. Cloth bds.
"These volumes contain the full series of Tracts published by J. Barker."

Finney's Lectures to Professing Christians,
2s. Cloth bds.

The New Testament Doctrine of the Atonement,
in six Tracts, by J. BARKER, bound together in Cloth, 1s.

Truth and Reform Against the World, in Seven
Letters to W. Cooke, in reply to his attacks on J. Barker. 1s. Cloth bds.

The Character and Tendency of Christianity,
By J. Barker. 4d stitched, or, with the Tracts on True Religion, Grace and the means of Grace, and the Christian Character, 1s. Cloth bds.

Dr. Priestley on the Miraculous Conception, 3d.

www.ingramcontent.com/pod-product-compliance
Lightning Source LLC
Chambersburg PA
CBHW062125160426
43191CB00013B/2200